IREX II - IQCE

Iris Quality Calibration and Evaluation

Performance of Iris Image Quality Assessment Algorithms

NIST Interagency Report 7820

E. Tabassi, P. Grother, and W. Salamon

Information Access Division

National Institute of Standards and Technology

September 30, 2011

ACKNOWLEDGMENTS

The authors would like to thank the Department of Homeland Security's Science and Technology Directorate for supporting this work. We extend our thanks to the U.S. Department of Defense, and Prof. Stephanie Schuckers of Clarkson University for providing iris imagery to the project. The authors are immensely grateful to Rick Lazarick and James Matey for many good discussions, technical advice, and their careful review of the document. Also, special thanks to Liz Lennon for editing the document.

Finally, thanks go to IQCE participants for their contributions toward the ISO/IEC 29794-6 standard and the development of the IQCE test specification.[1]

DISCLAIMER

Specific hardware and software products identified in this report were used in order to perform the evaluations described in this document. In no case does identification of any commercial product, trade name, or vendor imply recommendation or endorsement by the National Institute of Standards and Technology, nor does it imply that the products and equipment identified are necessarily the best available for the purpose.

---

[1]The formal CON-OPS and API specification is available at http://biometrics.nist.gov/cs_links/iris/irexII/IQCE_conops_API_v44_26apr10.pdf.

| A2a=NEUROTECHNOLOGY-a | B3=CROSSMATCH | C4s=CAMBRIDGE-s | D3=AWARE | E2a=IRITECH-a | G1=IRISID-1 | I1=KYNEN | Hz1=L1-z1 |
| A2f=NEUROTECHNOLOGY-f | C4x=CAMBRIDGE-x | C4f=CAMBRIDGE-f | F1=MORPHO | E2f=IRITECH-f | G2=IRISID-2 | Hx=L1-x | Hz2=L1-z2 |

Contents

| A2a=NEUROTECHNOLOGY-a | B3=CROSSMATCH | C4s=CAMBRIDGE-s | D3=AWARE | E2a=IRITECH-a | G1=IRISID-1 | I1=KYNEN | Hz1=L1-z1 |
| A2f=NEUROTECHNOLOGY-f | C4x=CAMBRIDGE-x | C4f=CAMBRIDGE-f | F1=MORPHO | E2f=IRITECH-f | G2=IRISID-2 | Hx=L1-x | Hz2=L1-z2 |

| A2a=NEUROTECHNOLOGY-a | B3=CROSSMATCH | C4s=CAMBRIDGE-s | D3=AWARE | E2a=IRITECH-a | G1=IRISID-1 | I1=KYNEN | Hz1=L1-z1 |
| A2f=NEUROTECHNOLOGY-f | C4x=CAMBRIDGE-x | C4f=CAMBRIDGE-f | F1=MORPHO | E2f=IRITECH-f | G2=IRISID-2 | Hx=L1-x | Hz2=L1-z2 |

EXECUTIVE SUMMARY

Iris is rapidly gaining acceptance and support as a viable biometric. United States Visitor and Immigrant Status Indicator Technology (US-VISIT), Personal Identity Verification (PIV) and Unique Identification Authority of India (UID) programs are either using or considering iris as their secondary or primary biometric for verification. While there are several academic publications addressing the problem of iris image quality, NIST Iris Quality Calibration and Evaluation (IQCE) is the first public challenge in iris image quality aimed at identifying iris image quality components that are algorithm- or camera-agnostic.

IQCE is the second IREX activity. The Iris Exchange (IREX) program was initiated by NIST in late 2007 to support interoperable exchange of iris imagery in high performance biometric applications. The first activity in the program, the IREX I evaluation, was conducted in cooperation with the iris recognition industry to develop and test standard image formats, and to demonstrate that iris recognition algorithms can maintain their accuracy and interoperability with compact images.

This evaluation supports homeland security, counter-terrorism, and border control applications by enhancing reliability and accuracy of iris recognition, and significantly improves requirement planning and system design.

Automatically and consistently determining the quality of a given biometric sample for identification and/or verification is a problem with far-reaching ramifications. If one can detect low-quality biometric samples, the information can be used to initiate the acquisition of new data and improve system performance. The same quality measure can be used to selectively improve an operational biometric database by replacing low-quality biometric samples with high-quality samples of the same biometric. Weights or schemes for multimodal biometric fusion can be selected to allow biometric sample quality to influence and direct the fusion process. All of these applications require that the quality of the biometric sample be determined prior to identification or verification. Most of these applications also require that the quality of the biometric sample be computed in real time during data acquisition and/or comparison. Current state-of-the-art iris recognition systems perform at reasonably low error rates. However, as with all biometrics, the performance degrades substantially as the quality of the input samples drops. Although only a small fraction of input data are of poor-quality, the bulk of recognition errors can be attributed to poor quality samples. Poor-quality samples decrease the likelihood of a correct verification and/or identification, while extremely poor-quality samples might be impossible to verify and/or identify. If quality can be improved, either by sensor design, by user interface design, or by standards compliance, better performance can be realized. For those aspects of quality that cannot be designed in, an ability to analyze the quality of a live sample is needed.

Quality assessment is useful primarily in initiating the reacquisition from a user, but also for the real-time selection of the best sample, the selective invocation of different processing methods, or fusion. Accordingly, biometric quality measurement algorithms are increasingly deployed in operational systems. US-VISIT, PIV, the European Visa program (EU VIS), and India's UID each mandate the measurement and reporting of quality scores of captured images. With the increase in deployment of quality algorithms, the need to standardize an interoperable way to store and exchange biometric quality scores and methods for evaluating the effectiveness of quality algorithms increases.

IQCE is motivated by this need. It aims to define and quantify iris image properties that are influential on performance of iris recognition. The findings of IQCE provides quantitative support to the development of ISO/IEC 29794 Biometric sample quality - Part 6: Iris image.

Nine iris recognition vendors participated; they submitted 14 iris quality assessment algorithms (IQAA) to IQCE. The

4

IQCE participants are identified on the bottom of each page. In addition, iris technology providers were invited to submit iris recognition algorithms (comparators) that compare two iris images and produce a dissimilarity score for each pair of images. IQCE examined the effectiveness of the IQAAs in their ability to predict the recognition performance of submitted comparators, both the native (IQAA and comparator from the same organization) and non-native (IQAA and comparator from two different organizations). Furthermore, IQCE evaluated the IQAAs on their computational efficiency (i.e., computation speed) and reports on the robustness (i.e., (ability to successfully process images) of the implementations.

The performance of the IQAAs varies among the datasets. Interestingly, the IQAAs which are the best predictor of recognition performance are also the fastest (i.e., the shortest computation time). Additionally, with no failure to compute a quality score, they are the most robust.

The primary results of IQCE are listed below.

▷ IQCE is the first large scale evaluation of iris image quality assessment algorithms.

IQCE evaluated the ability of 14 image quality assessment algorithms in predicting the performance of iris recognition algorithms, their computation speed, and their robustness.

In doing so, IQCE devised metrics and developed procedures for evaluation and visualization of the core algorithmic capability of implementations that measure quality of biometric samples. See Section 5.

▷ Quality Matters.

High-quality images give few recognition errors.

Rejection of 10% lowest quality images reduced FNMR from 0.1 to 0.07. (IQAA C4x – Dataset QFIRE I5 and IQAA E2a – Dataset ICE2006)

The baseline recognition error rates vary greatly across test datasets. The difference in the false non-match rate between the highest-quality dataset (OPS) and the lowest-quality dataset (QFIRE I05) can be as high as two orders of magnitude. Similarly, within images of a dataset, the difference in FNMR of the images with the highest and the lowest quality can be as large as two orders of magnitude.

If iris image quality can be improved, either by better sensor design, or better capture process (user interface, environment condition, etc.), better performance can be realized.

▷ What are the uses of quality scores?

Quality measurement plays a vital role in improving biometric system accuracy and efficiency during the capture process (as a control-loop variable select an acceptable image or to initiate reacquisition), in database maintenance (sample update), in enterprise-wide quality assurance surveying, and in invocation of quality-directed processing of samples. Neglecting quality measurement will adversely impact accuracy and efficiency of biometric recognition systems (e.g., verification and identification of individuals).

▷ Scalar vs. Vector: One quality score representing overall quality of an image, or a set of quality scores representing different aspects of iris image quality?

A set of measurements that constitute a quality vector will clearly convey more information than just a summary scalar value. However, two outstanding issues remain. First is that the vector in itself is not immediately useful

| A2a=NEUROTECHNOLOGY-a | B3=CROSSMATCH | C4s=CAMBRIDGE-s | D3=AWARE | E2a=IRITECH-a | G1=IRISID-1 | I1=KYNEN | Hz1=L1-z1 |
| A2f=NEUROTECHNOLOGY-f | C4x=CAMBRIDGE-x | C4f=CAMBRIDGE-f | F1=MORPHO | E2f=IRITECH-f | G2=IRISID-2 | Hx=L1-x | Hz2=L1-z2 |

when a decision has to be made to e.g., accept the captured image or prompt for re-capture. Another example is to decide, among the captured images, which one to use. These usages of quality score require a single quality number indicative of the match-ability of the image.

The second issue is that the quality vectors are less interoperable than scalar values if the specific components of the vectors and their computation method are not standardized.

That said, a set of measurements of different aspects of quality, makes quality scores "actionable". They could be used to specifically direct reacquisition attempts (e.g., camera settings), provide feedback to the subject (e.g., look into the camera or step forward) or direct enhancement of image (e.g., contrast adjustment).

IQCE evaluated the predictive power of scalar quality as well as specific quality components.

▷ Predictive power of scalar quality: Is the technology mature?

IQCE evaluated scalar quality scores of 14 implementations from nine organization, which covers almost all the major players in iris recognition technology industry and research community.

Several IQAAs demonstrated core algorithmic capability to predict recognition performance of iris recognition algorithms, and at least one implementation demonstrated operational readiness with having a zero failure to compute rate.

▷ Comparative analysis of the IQAAs' ability to predict the match-ability of iris images: Which IQQQs' scalar quality performed better?

Implementations from Cambridge University are the most effective in predicting recognition performance of their own native iris recognition algorithm as well as others. Furthermore, these three algorithms never failed to compute a quality score even for the most challenging images.

The second tier of performance belongs to IQAAs Hx, E2a, F1, and A2a.

The least effective in predicting performance are IQAAs D3 and I1. Their SCALAR QUALITY scores correlate very poorly with the observed recognition errors. See Section 8.

▷ Interoperability of IQAA and iris recognition algorithms: Do IQAAs perform better for their native iris recognition algorithm?

IQCE evaluated whether an IQAA is capable of generalizing across all (or a class of) comparators.

It is a common contention that the efficacy of a quality algorithm is necessarily tied to a particular comparator. This one-comparator case is useful in a limited fashion: when the deployed comparator is known, fixed and not subject to change. For all other cases, an IQAA that can be generalized to non-native recognition algorithms is preferred.

Generality to multiple recognition algorithms can be thought of as an interoperability issue: can implementation A's quality measure be used with implementation B's recognition algorithm? Such a capability will exist to the extent that pathological samples (such as droopy eyes) or impairments caused by poor capture condition or processing (such as lack of SHARPNESS) do present problems to both A and B's recognition algorithms. Generality to multiple recognition algorithms avoids vendor lock-in and reduces the cost of incremental technology update due to change in recognition algorithm provider.

Behavior and performance of IQAAs are generally similar across the comparators except for IQAAs B3, and G1. That is, most of the IQAAs are recognition algorithm agnostic and can be used regardless of the deployed comparator.

| A2a=NEUROTECHNOLOGY-a | B3=CROSSMATCH | C4s=CAMBRIDGE-s | D3=AWARE | E2a=IRITECH-a | G1=IRISID-1 | I1=KYNEN | Hz1=L1-z1 |
| A2f=NEUROTECHNOLOGY-f | C4x=CAMBRIDGE-x | C4f=CAMBRIDGE-f | F1=MORPHO | E2f=IRITECH-f | G2=IRISID-2 | Hx=L1-x | Hz2=L1-z2 |

IQAA B3 is the best predictor of its native iris recognition algorithm, but it is not effective in predicting recognition performance of other algorithms. The same is true for IQAA G1; its performance drops for non-native iris recognition algorithms, but not as severely as B3.

▷ Predictive power of quality components: Which of the examined iris image properties influence the recognition performance?

USABLE IRIS AREA has the greatest effect on recognition performance followed by IRIS PUPIL CONTRAST , PUPIL SHAPE , IRIS SCLERA CONTRAST , GAZE ANGLE and SHARPNESS .

IQCE results for MOTION BLUR and SIGNAL TO NOISE RATIO are inconclusive.

A high level summary of the effect of each iris image property studied by IQCE follows the Executive Summary. The high level summary is sorted based on the importance of the iris covariates. Additionally, results are listed Table 1 and sorted based on predictive power.

The accuracy of IQAAs depend on the quality components they assess and the dataset used. Some perform better on certain quality components or certain datasets, but perform poorly others.

Generally IQAAs performed better on ICE2006 dataset, which is not surprising given that the ICE2006 dataset has been publicly available for several years, and so has been studied by the research community extensively.

▷ Evaluation of IQAAs' robustness: Failure-to-compute and no-attempt-to-compute rates

IQAAs with high failure-to-compute or no-attempt-to-compute-quality rates are not operationally feasible.

The most robust IQAAs are C4x, C4f, C4s, F1 and A2a. They generated a quality score for every image.

IQAAs I1, D3 and B3 had the highest rates of failures.

Unless otherwise stated, the results presented in this document are for cases where image quality computation *did not* fail. That is IQCE metrics did not include a penalty for cases that an IQAA did not generate a quality score, and evaluated IQAAs based on the goodness of the quality scores that they were able to generate. The caveat is that this decision might make an IQAA with high failure-to-compute or no-attempt-to-compute a quality score to seem to be more effective than a *robust* IQAA which has a zero failure-to-compute rate.

▷ Evaluation of IQAAs' efficiency: How fast are they?

Across IQAAs quality computation time varies by two order of magnitudes. The three submissions from Cambridge University (IQAA C4x, C4s, and C4f) are the fastest implementations, with an average 30 millisecond per image across all four datasets.

The difference between the "slow but accurate" and "fast" submissions of two participants is substantial. A2a is an order of magnitude slower than A2f.

Quality computation time across datasets varies, but the order of IQAAs stays the same.

▷ Evaluation of the proprietary quality scores

Some IQAAs generated proprietary quality scores. IQCE evaluated the proprietary quality scores, and results will be published in a follow-up document.

▷ Data used in IQCE

The IQCE study employed data from three collections of iris images. Two of the collections, ICE2006 and OPS, are the same datasets used in IREXI. The ICE2006 dataset contains low-quality images, due to relaxed quality

| A2a=NEUROTECHNOLOGY-a | B3=CROSSMATCH | C4s=CAMBRIDGE-s | D3=AWARE | E2a=IRITECH-a | G1=IRISID-1 | I1=KYNEN | Hz1=L1-z1 |
| A2f=NEUROTECHNOLOGY-f | C4x=CAMBRIDGE-x | C4f=CAMBRIDGE-f | F1=MORPHO | E2f=IRITECH-f | G2=IRISID-2 | Hx=L1-x | Hz2=L1-z2 |

controls at the time of capture; therefore ICE2006 images vary greatly in quality. However, no ground truth on the source or cause of low quality was available to the authors. QFIRE is a subset of the dedicated collection from Clarkson University. Its acquisition protocol was designed to assure inclusion of impaired images, which makes QFIRE images more suitable for quality evaluations. Specifically, QFIRE A5 consists of a wide range of images with off-axis gaze angle, and QFIRE I5 consists of images captured under varying levels of illumination intensity and intentional defocus blur.

See Section 4.

▷ Remark about IQAAs C4x and C4s

Performance of IQAAs C4x and C4s are almost identical and very similar to C4f. Any statement in this document regarding IQAA C4x is applicable to IQAAs C4s and C4f and vice versa.

| A2a=NEUROTECHNOLOGY-a | B3=CROSSMATCH | C4s=CAMBRIDGE-s | D3=AWARE | E2a=IRITECH-a | G1=IRISID-1 | I1=KYNEN | Hz1=L1-z1 |
| A2f=NEUROTECHNOLOGY-f | C4x=CAMBRIDGE-x | C4f=CAMBRIDGE-f | F1=MORPHO | E2f=IRITECH-f | G2=IRISID-2 | Hx=L1-x | Hz2=L1-z2 |

RECOMMENDATION FOR DEVELOPMENT OF ISO/IEC 29794-6

▷ Given the lack of implementation support for HEAD ROTATION and MAGNIFICATION. IQCE recommends exclusion of these two from ISO/IEC 29794-6.

▷ IQCE recommends exclusion of IRIS SHAPE. Its high correlation with other quality components suggests that IRIS SHAPE is not statistically independent from other quality components, and its effect on performance has been already accounted for by other quality components.

▷ SIGNAL TO NOISE RATIO is a capture device characteristic. Methodology and metrics for measurement of sensor noise is needed.

RECOMMENDATION FOR FUTURE RESEARCH

▷ Camera specification and certification

Iris recognition is a multistep process starting with image acquisition. Therefore the first step to improve iris image quality is to improve the image acquisition device.

Capture device characteristics such as sensor noise or spatial sampling rate, or Modulation Transfer Function (MTF) requirements directly affects quality and match-ability of iris images produced by the device.

There is a need for further effort in developing methods for iris image acquisition device evaluation.

The authors are available to discuss and brief this report.

| A2a=NEUROTECHNOLOGY-a | B3=CROSSMATCH | C4s=CAMBRIDGE-s | D3=AWARE | E2a=IRITECH-a | G1=IRISID-1 | I1=KYNEN | Hz1=L1-z1 |
| A2f=NEUROTECHNOLOGY-f | C4x=CAMBRIDGE-x | C4f=CAMBRIDGE-f | F1=MORPHO | E2f=IRITECH-f | G2=IRISID-2 | Hx=L1-x | Hz2=L1-z2 |

0 No.	1 Section number	2 Quality Component	3 Does it affect FNMR?	4 Signif effect on genuine distribution?	5 Signif effect on impostor distribution?	6 Does sameness matters?	7 # of submissions	8 Performance 1st Best IQAA (s) / 2nd Best IQAA (s)	9 FNMR worst 15% Q / best 15% Q	10 ICE2006 FNMR baseline after 3% reject
1	8	SCALAR QUALITY	YES	YES	YES	No	14	C4x / Hx, E2a, F1, A2a	0.0546 / 0.0046	0.100 / 0.0892
2	9.4	USABLE IRIS AREA	YES	YES	YES	YES	12	C4x, Hx	0.0473 / 0.0071	0.100 / 0.09011
3	9.6	IRIS PUPIL CONTRAST	YES	YES	YES	YES	13	C4s / Hx, E2a	0.0418 / 0.0043	0.100 / 0.09085
4	9.8	PUPIL SHAPE	YES	YES	yes	No	9	C4x, E2a, Hx	0.0341 / 0.0062	0.100 / 0.0922
5	9.5	IRIS SCLERA CONTRAST	YES	YES	yes	YES	13	C4x, E2a	0.0427 / 0.0047	0.100 / 0.0940
6	9.13	GAZE ANGLE	YES	YES	No	YES	8	C4x / E2a	0.0331 / 0.0099	0.100 / 0.0941
7	9.10	SHARPNESS	YES	YES	YES	No	13	C4x, F1	0.0238 / 0.0064	0.100 / 0.0980
8	9.3	DILATION	yes	yes	YES	YES	14	Similar	0.0157 / 0.0039	0.100 / 0.0967
9	9.14	INTERLACE	yes	yes	yes	No	9	E2a, A2a, D3	0.0222 / 0.0048	0.100 / 0.0954
10	9.1	GRAY SCALE SPREAD	yes	yes	yes	Algorithm dependent	10	Similar	0.0211 / 0.0052	0.100 / 0.100
11	9.7	IRIS SHAPE	Inconclusive	Algorithm dependent	No	yes	9	Similar	0.0231 / 0.0107	0.100 / 0.0998
12	9.2	IRIS SIZE	yes	yes	yes	YES	9	C4x / E2a, A2a	0.0269 / 0.0169	0.100 / 0.0976
13	9.11	MOTION BLUR	Inconclusive	Inconclusive	Inconclusive	Inconclusive	3	None	0.0111 / 0.0079	0.100 / 0.0971
14	9.12	SIGNAL TO NOISE RATIO	Inconclusive	Inconclusive	Inconclusive	Inconclusive	9	None	0.0140 / 0.0055	0.100 / 0.0999
15	9.9	MARGIN	yes	Algorithm dependent	No	No	5	None	0.0111 / 0.0100	0.100 / 0.0990

Table 1: Summary of IQCE IQAA performance. The table summarizes the finding of this document.
Column 1 lists the Section of this document that contains the results for the specified quality components.
Column 2 lists the image property that the IQAAs attempt to assess.
Column 3 indicates whether the specified quality component affects FNMR.
YES means significant and large effect, and **yes** means significant but small effect.
Columns 4 and 5 summarizes the result of the Tukey Honest Significant Difference test and shows whether the quality component has a significant effect on the genuine (3th column) or the impostor (4th column) distributions.
YES means significant and large effect, and **yes** means significant but small effect.
Column 6 summarizes the results of the heatmaps, and answers the question whether "sameness" matters, i.e., whether image pairs with similar quality values give lower FNMR than others.
Column 7 shows the number of implementations evaluated. A small number may suggest that the assessment of the quality component is a technical challenge.
Column 8 lists the IQAAs who performed the best.
Column 9 shows the observed FNMR (at threshold that gives FMR = 0.0001) for the ICE2006 worst quality images (images whose quality scores are in the lowest 15 percentile) on the top, and its best quality images (quality scores in the upper 15 percentile) on the bottom. Quality scores are computed by the best IQAA (identified in the column 8) and its native iris recognition algorithm. For the quality components that a best performer was not identified, results for E2a is reported except for IRIS SHAPE where C4x's result is reported and MARGIN where A2a results are reported.
Column 10 shows the baseline FNMR on the top and the FNMR after rejecting the comparisons with the lowest *three percent* quality on the bottom of each cell. Quality scores are computed by the best IQAA (identified in the column 8) and its native iris recognition algorithm. For the quality components that a best performer was not identified (GRAY SCALE SPREAD , DILATION , MOTION BLUR , SIGNAL TO NOISE RATIO), results for E2a is reported except for IRIS SHAPE where C4x's result is reported.

A2a=NEUROTECHNOLOGY-a	B3=CROSSMATCH	C4s=CAMBRIDGE-s	D3=AWARE
A2f=NEUROTECHNOLOGY-f	C4x=CAMBRIDGE-x	C4f=CAMBRIDGE-f	F1=MORPHO

E2a=IRITECH-a	G1=IRISID-1	I1=KYNEN	Hz1=L1-z1
E2f=IRITECH-f	G2=IRISID-2	Hx=L1-x	Hz2=L1-z2

TECHNICAL SUMMARY

This section summarizes the findings for each of the quality components examined by IQCE .

The list is sorted based on the importance of the components, the one with the largest effect on recognition performance appears first.

The list is followed by Table 2 that aims to summarize likely causes of impairments and possible ways to mitigate.

▷ USABLE IRIS AREA

USABLE IRIS AREA is defined as the percentage of iris that is not occluded by eyelash, eyelid, specular reflections, ambient specular reflections (e.g., reflected sunlight, eye-wear reflections, reflections from nearby facial features such as nose, or glare and reflection from the scene). Occlusion reduces the amount of information available for comparison and can complicate and degrade iris segmentation accuracy if it occurs at the limbic or pupillary boundaries.

When the cause of occlusion is not intrinsic (i.e., anatomical), USABLE IRIS AREA can be improved by better design of imaging system (e.g., controlling the specular reflection) or improving the capture process (e.g., controlling reflections from the scene) or correcting subject behavior by, for example, prompting not to squint. Iris image acquisition systems should have illuminators placed in a way that prevents or at least minimizes occlusions of parts of the iris that are caused by reflections of the illuminators on the iris itself, on eyeglasses, the subject's nose, etc. The best practice guidance is to take glasses off at the time of capture. Examples of low USABLE IRIS AREA due to poor subject character are droopy eyelids or an iris affected by some medical condition.

Among all quality components, USABLE IRIS AREA has the greatest influence on performance. The difference between FNMR of images with the lowest USABLE IRIS AREA and the highest USABLE IRIS AREA can be as large as two orders of magnitude (IQAA E2a and G1 – Dataset ICE2006). The effect on FMR is greater for some comparators; Hz1 gives higher FMR on highly occluded images, where comparator A2a FMR is more stable.

Implementations from all IQCE participants except one organization measured USABLE IRIS AREA . This large support suggests that USABLE IRIS AREA can be measured universally, however, the wide range of the IQAAS' performance implies that reliable measurement of USABLE IRIS AREA is a challenge and requires dedicated image processing including a good segmentation of iris texture.

Overall, IQAAs Hx and C4s USABLE IRIS AREA scores are the best predictor of the match-ability of an iris image for their native iris recognition algorithm as well as other comparators. See Section 9.4.

▷ IRIS PUPIL CONTRAST

IRIS PUPIL CONTRAST is a measure of the image characteristics at the boundary between the iris region and the pupil. There is usually a lower contrast between iris and pupil than iris and sclera, making pupillary boundary detection the more difficult task.

The intrinsic IRIS PUPIL CONTRAST varies among human irises when images are captured with NIR illumination. Certain medical conditions such as cataracts or interocular lenses may impact IRIS PUPIL CONTRAST . It is also affected by capture device characteristics.

The IQCE results show that IRIS PUPIL CONTRAST has a significant effect on FNMR and FMR. The difference between FNMR of images with the lowest and the highest IRIS PUPIL CONTRAST can be as large as two orders of magnitude

11

(IQAA C4x – Dataset ICE2006).

FNMR increases slightly as the difference between the IRIS PUPIL CONTRAST scores of the two images being compared increases.

Among the IQAAs, C4x performs the best and it predicts recognition performance of its native iris recognition algorithm as well as other non-native ones. IQAAs Hx and E2a are the second best performers. See Section 9.6.

▷ PUPIL SHAPE

PUPIL SHAPE is a measure of regularity in pupil-iris boundary. Given that the iris portion just around the pupil has high information content, the accurate detection of iris-pupil boundary is of the utmost importance. PUPIL SHAPE is not circular, and not even elliptical. The non-regular shape complicates iris segmentation.

The non-circularity could be either natural anatomical variation (subject character) or due to non-frontal gaze (subject behavior) or both. Certain medical conditions will induce highly non-circular pupils. PUPIL SHAPE is mostly a characteristic of the subject than of the capture device or capture environment. As such, iris recognition technologies have to adapt to the population characteristic.

PUPIL SHAPE significantly affects the genuine score distributions. Images with poor PUPIL SHAPE inflate FNMR. Images with the worst PUPIL SHAPE scores result in up two orders of magnitude higher FNMR than the images with the best PUPIL SHAPE scores (IQAA C4x – Dataset QFIRE I5, IQAA C4x, and Hx – Dataset QFIRE A5 and IQAAs E2a, Hx and A2a – Dataset ICE2006). FNMR is not affected by the difference in PUPIL SHAPE scores of the two images being compared.

The effect on FMR is small.

IQAA C4x, E2a and Hx perform better than other IQAAS.
See Section 9.8.

▷ IRIS SCLERA CONTRAST

IRIS SCLERA CONTRAST is a measure of the image characteristics at the boundary between the iris region and the sclera. The source of variation in IRIS SCLERA CONTRAST can be extrinsic (e.g., illumination wavelength and other capture device characteristics), or intrinsic, (i.e., subjects character such as eye disease, albinism, shadow of eyelash on iris, etc.). IRIS SCLERA CONTRAST can be improved by better acquisition system and capture process design.

IRIS SCLERA CONTRAST greatly influences performance of iris recognition algorithms. Images with low IRIS SCLERA CONTRAST give high FNMR. The difference in FNMR can be up to two orders of magnitude (IQAA C4x – Dataset QFIRE I5 and ICE2006).

The effect on FMR is small, but significant.

Comparisons of images with similar IRIS SCLERA CONTRAST scores give lower FNMR than when the images' IRIS SCLERA CONTRAST scores differ from each other. The change in FNMR is the largest for IQAA Hx.

IQAA C4s, C4x and E2a IRIS SCLERA CONTRAST scores performed the best. See Section 9.5.

▷ GAZE ANGLE

GAZE ANGLE is the deviation of the optical axis of the subject's iris from the optical axis of the camera. This occurs when the subject does not look directly into the camera – either because the gaze is averted or the head is rotated or tilted. Off-axis images are a well known challenge for iris recognition systems.

| A2a=NEUROTECHNOLOGY-a | B3=CROSSMATCH | C4s=CAMBRIDGE-s | D3=AWARE | E2a=IRITECH-a | G1=IRISID-1 | I1=KYNEN | Hz1=L1-z1 |
| A2f=NEUROTECHNOLOGY-f | C4x=CAMBRIDGE-x | C4f=CAMBRIDGE-f | F1=MORPHO | E2f=IRITECH-f | G2=IRISID-2 | Hx=L1-x | Hz2=L1-z2 |

A better user interface can correct GAZE ANGLE by guiding subjects through the process (e.g., visual or audio feedback on where to look).

GAZE ANGLE significantly affects FNMR. Images with the worst GAZE ANGLE scores result in up to an order of magnitude higher FNMR than the images with the best GAZE ANGLE scores.

FNMR increases as the difference between the GAZE ANGLE scores of the two images being compared increases.

Overall, among the eight submissions that generate GAZE ANGLE scores, IQAA C4x performs the best, with almost perfect performance for its native iris recognition algorithm.

Rejection of QFIRE A5 images with the worst IQAA Hx's GAZE ANGLE scores improves comparator Hz1's FNMR, but it is not effective for other comparators. QFIRE A5 dataset contains intentionally large gaze angles.

IQAA E2a is the best performer on ICE 2006 images, but its performance drops on QFIRE A5 images.

See Section 9.13.

▷ SHARPNESS

SHARPNESS, defined as the absence of defocus blur, can result from many sources, but in general, defocus occurs when the object is outside the depth of field of the camera. The further an object is from the focal plane the higher the degree of defocus. Depth of field is affected by aperture size, the smaller the aperture size the greater the depth of field.

SHARPNESS can be improved by better image acquisition optical design and better user interface to guide subject for optimal position relative to the camera.

SHARPNESS affects FNMR and FMR. The difference in FNMR of images with the highest and the lowest SHARPNESS score is as large as two order of magnitudes (IQAAs F1, C4x, A2a, and E2a – Dataset QFIRE I5 and C4x – Dataset ICE 2006).

Images with low SHARPNESS inflate FMR .

The difference between SHARPNESS scores of the two images being compared does not affect the FNMR.

IQAA C4x and F1 are most effective in their assessment of SHARPNESS, for their own native iris recognition algorithm as well as others.
See Section 9.10.

▷ DILATION

DILATION is defined as the ratio of the pupil radius to iris radius. Different IQAAs and different comparators behave differently in response to DILATION , and there are discernible trends that indicate that sometimes "sameness matters", and often the performance is poorer when extreme values of DILATION are present.

There is no clear cut determination of any IQAA being superior to the others in terms of their ability to predict the observed FNMR, but further study using a dataset with a wider (and perhaps controlled) range of DILATION may be more revealing.
See Section 9.3.

▷ INTERLACE

All contemporary iris acquisition devices use progressive scan rather than interlace, but interlace artifact remains an important issue for legacy data captured by older cameras. Interlace can reduce the effective vertical resolution by a factor of two.

| A2a=NEUROTECHNOLOGY-a | B3=CROSSMATCH | C4s=CAMBRIDGE-s | D3=AWARE | E2a=IRITECH-a | G1=IRISID-1 | I1=KYNEN | Hz1=L1-z1 |
| A2f=NEUROTECHNOLOGY-f | C4x=CAMBRIDGE-x | C4f=CAMBRIDGE-f | F1=MORPHO | E2f=IRITECH-f | G2=IRISID-2 | Hx=L1-x | Hz2=L1-z2 |

The difference in mean pairwise INTERLACE score of ICE2006 images involved in successful verification attempts is significantly larger than the mean pairwise score of the images resulting in false rejection. In other words, INTERLACE significantly affects genuine comparison scores. However, it affects FNMR less than the other image impairments.

The difference between the INTERLACE scores of the two images being compared does not affect FNMR.
See Section 9.14.

▷ GRAY SCALE SPREAD

An image with a high GRAY SCALE SPREAD (good quality) is a properly exposed image, with a wide, well distributed spread of intensity values. An underexposed image would have too few high intensity (too many blackish) pixels, and, conversely, an overexposed image would have too few low intensity (too many white-ish) pixels. Saturation or poor illumination can cause lack of well-spread intensity values. Therefore better performance can be achieved for iris acquisition systems capable of producing images with high contrast and large dynamic range.

Performance of the 10 IQAAs that measured GRAY SCALE SPREAD are comparable, where an order of magnitude difference is observed between FNMR of images with the highest GRAY SCALE SPREAD quality and the ones with the lowest quality.

For some comparators, FNMR degrades as the difference in GRAY SCALE SPREAD scores of the two images being compared increases.
See Section 9.1.

▷ IRIS SHAPE

IRIS SHAPE is defined as the shape of iris-sclera boundary. The shape of an iris is very often not a circle or even an ellipse. The non-circularity could be either intrinsic (i.e., subject character) due to natural anatomical variation or be caused by subject behavior such as non-frontal gaze. Other than some medical condition and surgical procedure that can affect it, the IRIS SHAPE , is believed to be stable over the period of a human life.

IQCE evaluated IRIS SHAPE scores of six SDKs. For some IQAAs , their IRIS SHAPE scores correlate highly with other quality components, e.g. the IRIS SHAPE scores of IQAA D3 are highly correlated with its USABLE IRIS AREA scores. This high correlation suggests that IRIS SHAPE is not statistically independent of other quality components, and its effect on performance is accounted for by other quality components. Rejection of up to 10% of the lowest pairwise IRIS SHAPE scores, improves FNMR by no more than 0.01 from its baseline value of 0.1.

For these reasons, IQCE recommends exclusion of IRIS SHAPE as a quality component.
See Section 9.7.

▷ IRIS SIZE

IRIS SIZE is defined as the number of pixels across the iris radius, when the iris boundary is modeled by a circle. Irises too small or too large increase the likelihood of FNMR and FMR.

IRIS SIZE is determined by the spatial sampling rate (e.g. line-pairs/radian) of the image acquisition device and the distance between the subject and the acquisition device.

Down sampling ICE2006 images by a factor of two did not affect FNMR or FMR, suggesting that an iris radius of [58-62] pixels is sufficient for recognition (iris radius of the ICE2006 images has a mean of 120 and an inter-quartile range of [116-124]).

Better FNMR is achieved when the IRIS SIZE of two images being compared are similar.

IQAA C4x's IRIS SIZE scores are good predictor of performance, followed by IQAAs E2a and A2a.
See Section 9.2.

▷ MOTION BLUR

MOTION BLUR is defined as the blur cause by motion of the camera or the iris, or both.

None of the MOTION BLUR scores generated by any of the three IQCE submissions were effective in prediction of performance. The number of distinct MOTION BLUR scores generated by either of the three IQAAs were quite small.

The few number of submissions implies that measurement of MOTION BLUR is not universal. Furthermore, the inability to compute distinct scores for the IQCE images suggests that either the imagery used does not represent a full range of MOTION BLUR impairment or computation of MOTION BLUR scores is a technical challenge not solved yet.

As such, IQCE results of effect of MOTION BLUR on performance are inconclusive. Further studies using images with a wide range of MOTION BLUR may be revealing.

IQCE recommends exclusion of MOTION BLUR from the ISO/IEC 29794-6 as a normative requirement. The impairment caused by MOTION BLUR is similar to defocus blur, therefore measuring SHARPNESS could detect and flag poor quality images due to MOTION BLUR .
See Section 9.11.

▷ SIGNAL TO NOISE RATIO

Measuring SIGNAL TO NOISE RATIO from an image is impossible if the noise model is not known. The major source of noise in an iris image is believed to be sensor noise, which can be measured or modeled by imaging targets.

Nine IQCE submissions generate SIGNAL TO NOISE RATIO scores, but none of them were effective in predicting recognition performance. Their performance on QFIRE I5 images was worse than on the ICE2006 images, which given that QFIRE I5, by design, represents a wider range of SIGNAL TO NOISE RATIO quality, suggests that the computed SIGNAL TO NOISE RATIO scores are not an accurate measurement of actual signal to noise ratio within the image.

The recommendation for the development of ISO/IEC 29794-6 is to consider SIGNAL TO NOISE RATIO as a capture device quality component instead of an image quality component, where sensor noise should be estimated by imaging dedicated test target(s).
See Section 9.12.

| A2a=NEUROTECHNOLOGY-a | B3=CROSSMATCH | C4s=CAMBRIDGE-s | D3=AWARE | E2a=IRITECH-a | G1=IRISID-1 | I1=KYNEN | Hz1=L1-z1 |
| A2f=NEUROTECHNOLOGY-f | C4x=CAMBRIDGE-x | C4f=CAMBRIDGE-f | F1=MORPHO | E2f=IRITECH-f | G2=IRISID-2 | Hx=L1-x | Hz2=L1-z2 |

No.	Section Number	Quality Component	Impairment or its source	What to fix?
1	8	scalar quality		
2	9.1	gray level spread	Illumination, Saturation	Device, Environment
3	9.2	iris size	Resolution, Distance to camera	Device MTF, Behavior
4	9.3	Dilation	Ambient light, Intrinsic	Environment, Behavior
5	9.4	usable iris	Occlusion (reflections, eye-wear. etc.)	Device, Character or Environment
6	9.5	iris-sclera contrast	Intrinsic Illumination	Device, Character or Environment
7	9.6	iris-pupil contrast	Intrinsic Illumination	Device, Character or Environment
8	9.7	iris shape	Disease, Off-axis gaze	Character, Behavior
9	9.8	pupil shape	Disease, Off-axis gaze	Character, Behavior
10	9.9	margin	Improper cropping Subject-device alignment	Capture practice, Image processing
11	9.10	sharpness	Defocus, Compression	Device, Processing
12	9.11	motion blur	Distortion due to motion	Capture practice, Behavior
13	9.12	signal to noise ratio	Imaging device parameters	Device
14	9.13	gaze angle	Optical axis of camera and eye not lined up	Behavior, Capture practice
15	9.14	interlace	Loss of vertical resolution	Device

Table 2: Possible causes of quality degradation and likely mitigations.
Column 1 is the Section of the document containing the result for the specified quality component.
Column 2 is the image property that the IQAAs attempt to assess.
Column 3 lists the possible impairment and its likely source(s).
Column 4 points to what could be improved to fix the specific quality issue.

CAVEATS

As with all biometric evaluations, the results of this test must be carefully interpreted before any conclusions can be made. Users should factor the following into policy, planning and operational decisions.

1. IQCE did not address evaluation or standardization of cameras, interfaces, and complete systems. It does not establish operational requirements, nor does it consider transmission protocols, and security issues such as algorithm vulnerabilities. These issues, must be addressed operationally, and may impact design trade-offs.

2. As with all other evaluations, results of IQCE is reflective of the properties of the images used. While care was taken to develop evaluation corpora that are representative of *all* possible iris image defects, given the difficulty in acquiring and collecting images suitable for the evaluation, some impairments might be under represented.

3. The results presented in this document are for cases where image quality computation *did not* fail. That is IQCE metrics did not include a penalty for cases that an IQAA failed to generate a quality score. As such, IQCE evaluated the IQAAs based on the goodness of the quality scores that they were able to generate. The caveat is this decision might make an IQAA with high failure-to-compute or no-attempt-to-compute a quality score (basically ignoring "difficult" cases) to seem to be more effective than a *robust* IQAA which computes has a zero failure-to-compute rate.

4. The absolute error rates quoted herein were measured by using the provided implementations on three large fixed corpora of operational and non-operational iris images. As with all offline biometric tests, the relevance of the results to operational reality must be considered in light of the fact that post-capture samples are used. Error rates observed in real-world applications are almost always strongly dependent on acquisition related factors. Generically these include:

   ▷ The degree to which the design compels, induces, or incentivizes the user to use the camera in a mode intended by its designers;

   ▷ Cooperativeness of the user population (an uncooperative subject may try to evade acquisition and be very hard to image, a non-cooperative user may similarly not look at, or properly present to, the camera);

   ▷ Environment (e.g., low ambient light levels may impede detection);

   ▷ The number of verification attempts allowed (typically more attempts lead to lower false rejection, and higher false acceptance);

   ▷ Demographics (e.g., children and older adult populations may not present as quickly or as easily); and

   ▷ Habituation (users who regularly interact with system often yield lower rejection rates).

5. The sensor and the enrollment policy affect error rates. For example, iris cameras almost always compute quantitative quality criteria in an auto-capture loop either in the camera's firmware, or sometimes in a client-side application, or both. This may produce some failure-to-enroll occurrences, but will improve downstream matching error rates.

6. With respect to iris recognition specifically, the accuracy and speed of operational transactions will generally depend on a number of factors, including the following:

   ▷ The template generation and matching algorithms are strongly influential on error rates;

| A2a=NEUROTECHNOLOGY-a | B3=CROSSMATCH | C4s=CAMBRIDGE-s | D3=AWARE | E2a=IRITECH-a | G1=IRISID-1 | I1=KYNEN | Hz1=L1-z1 |
| A2f=NEUROTECHNOLOGY-f | C4x=CAMBRIDGE-x | C4f=CAMBRIDGE-f | F1=MORPHO | E2f=IRITECH-f | G2=IRISID-2 | Hx=L1-x | Hz2=L1-z2 |

▷ The number of eyes imaged;

▷ The number of images available for matching;

▷ The quality of the enrollment procedure particularly whether a verification was done at time of original enrollment; and

▷ The communications channel and interface.

| A2a=NEUROTECHNOLOGY-a | B3=CROSSMATCH | C4s=CAMBRIDGE-s | D3=AWARE | E2a=IRITECH-a | G1=IRISID-1 | I1=KYNEN | Hz1=L1-z1 |
| A2f=NEUROTECHNOLOGY-f | C4x=CAMBRIDGE-x | C4f=CAMBRIDGE-f | F1=MORPHO | E2f=IRITECH-f | G2=IRISID-2 | Hx=L1-x | Hz2=L1-z2 |

TERMS AND DEFINITIONS

No.	Term	Definition
Organizations		
1	DHS	U. S. Department of Homeland Security
2	DoD	U. S. Department of Defense
3	ISO	International Organization for Standardization
4	IEC	International Electrotechnical Commission
5	NIST	National Institute of Standards and Technology
6	SC 37	ISO/IEC JTC 1 Subcommittee responsible for development of biometrics standards
Programs		
7	IREX	Iris Exchange - NIST's umbrella program for supporting iris interoperability
8	IQCE	Iris Quality and Calibration Evaluation - NIST's second activity under IREX
9	MINEX	Minutiae Exchange - NIST's umbrella program supporting fingerprint minutia interoperability
Standards		
10	ISO/IEC 29794-6:201X	International iris image quality standard, the focus of this report, under development
11	ISO/IEC 19794-6:2011	International iris image data format standard, completed in 2011
Data elements		
12	Proprietary template	Usually unpublished feature representation of matchable iris data - comparable only with a template from the same vendor and product line
13	Enrollment template	Synonym for reference template
14	Reference template	Template, logically from the enrollment or first-encounter sample
15	Verification template	Template generated from a subsequent sample of a subject or from an un-enrolled, unknown, or impostor sample
Function and process terms		
16	SDK	Software Development Kit
17	API	Application Programming Interface
18	IQAA	Image Quality Assessment Algorithm
19	Comparator	A comparator is logically a function that compares two proprietary templates and produces a dissimilarity score. Physically it compares two proprietary templates.
20	Generator	Software function that accepts an image and produces a proprietary template
21	Native mode	Comparison by SDK X and quality scores by IQAA X
22	Interoperable mode	Comparison by SDK X and quality scores by IQAA Y different than X
23	Genuine	Comparison of data from the same person
24	Impostor	Comparison of data from different individuals
25	Verification	One-to-one comparison
26	Authentication	Synonym for verification
27	Localization	Image processing operations to locate the iris and pupil boundaries
28	Segmentation	Synonym for localization
Metrics		
29	FAR	False accept rate (i.e., transactional outcome)
30	FRR	False reject rate (i.e., transactional outcome)
31	FMR	False match rate (i.e., 1:1 single sample comparison outcome)
32	FNMR	False non-match rate (i.e., 1:1 single sample comparison outcome)
33	DET	Detection Error Trade-off characteristic

Table 3: Glossary of IQCE -related terms

TIME LINE OF IRIS STANDARDIZATION

Table 4 lists the key dates in the evolution of IREX and IQCE. The Table includes items related to the standards.

No.	Period	Event
1	July, 2009	ISO/IEC 29794-6 - Iris Image Quality New Work Item is approved.
2	October, 2009	Announcement of IQCE.
3	February, 2010	IQCE concept of operation (con-ops) is finalized. SDK submission period began.
4	February – October, 2010	Rounds of testing (interim reports were delivered to the participants).
5	October, 2010	IQCE SDK submission period ended.
6	March, 2011	Generation of quality scores and comparison scores completed.
7	July, 2011	ISO/IEC 19794-6 - Biometric data format - Part 6: Iris Image is completed.
8	September, 2011	Publication of final report

Table 4: IQCE chronology and related events.

A2a=NEUROTECHNOLOGY-a	B3=CROSSMATCH	C4s=CAMBRIDGE-s	D3=AWARE	E2a=IRITECH-a	G1=IRISID-1	I1=KYNEN	Hz1=L1-z1
A2f=NEUROTECHNOLOGY-f		C4x=CAMBRIDGE-x	C4f=CAMBRIDGE-f	F1=MORPHO	E2f=IRITECH-f	G2=IRISID-2	Hx=L1-x	Hz2=L1-z2

1   Introduction

1.1   Motivation

Automatically and consistently determining the quality of a given biometric sample for identification and/or verification is a problem with far-reaching ramifications. If one can detect low-quality biometric samples, the information can be used to initiate the acquisition of new data and improve system performance. The same quality measure can be used to selectively improve an operational biometric database by replacing low-quality biometric samples with high-quality samples of the same biometric. Weights or schemes for multimodal biometric fusion can be selected to allow biometric sample quality to influence and direct the fusion process. All of these applications require that the quality of the biometric sample be determined prior to identification or verification. Most of these applications also require that the quality of the biometric sample be computed in real time during data acquisition and/or comparison.

Current state-of-the-art iris recognition systems perform at reasonably low error rates. However, as with all biometrics, the performance degrades substantially as the quality of the input samples drops. Although only a small fraction of input data are of poor-quality, the bulk of recognition errors can be attributed to poor quality samples. Poor-quality samples decrease the likelihood of a correct verification and/or identification, while extremely poor-quality samples might be impossible to verify and/or identify. If quality can be improved, either by sensor design, by user interface design, or by standards compliance, better performance can be realized. For those aspects of quality that cannot be designed in, an ability to analyze the quality of a single live sample is needed. Note that an initial computation of comparison scores is not possible because there is no other instance of the same biometrics with which to be compared.

Quality assessment is useful primarily in initiating the reacquisition from a user, but also for the real-time selection of the best sample, the selective invocation of different processing methods, or fusion. Accordingly, biometric quality measurement algorithms are increasingly deployed in operational systems [16, 12]. US-VISIT, PIV, EU VIS, and India's UID each mandate the measurement and reporting of quality scores of captured images. With the increase in deployment of quality algorithms, the need increases to standardize an interoperable way to store and exchange biometric quality scores and methods for evaluating the effectiveness of quality algorithms.

IQCE is motivated by this need. It aims to define and quantify iris image properties that are influential on performance of iris recognition. Iris recognition is rapidly gaining acceptance and support as a viable biometric. US-VISIT, PIV and India's UID are either using or considering iris as their secondary or primary biometric for verification. While there are several academic publications on iris image quality, IQCE is the first public challenge in iris image quality aimed at identifying iris image quality components that are algorithm- or camera-agnostic.

1.2   Purpose and scope

IQCE is motivated by a need to quantitatively define iris image quality and seeks to identify image properties that are influential on recognition accuracy. The IQCE activity supports a new formal standard addressing iris quality. The standard, ISO/IEC 29794-6 Biometric sample quality–Part 6:Iris image, was initiated by the Working Group 3 of the ISO SC 37 committee in July 2009. The standard will define a vector of quality components each of which is a quantitative measure of a subject-specific or image-specific covariate. The current working draft (SC 37 N 4649) defines 19 image acquisition or subject covariates and 16 metrics for assessing the utility of an iris image. The primary output of this evaluation is a refined list of image quality components for that Standard and for more general use. For example, quality components IRIS SHAPE , MAGNIFICATION and HEAD ROTATION are recommended to be excluded from the iris image quality standard. The secondary outcome is establishment of tolerance bounds for some of the quality components such as IRIS SIZE.

2 Prior and related work

2.1 Relation to other NIST activities

NIST's iris interoperability program, IREX, was initiated to support an expanded marketplace of iris recognition applications in identity management deployments. IREX I was conducted to give quantitative support to the recently completed ISO/IEC 19794-6 standard which regulates cross-party interchange of iris imagery. IREX II gives quantitative support to the currently under development ISO/IEC 29794-6 standard which will regulate iris quality definition and computation.

IREX I evaluation was conducted in cooperation with the iris recognition industry to demonstrate that standardized image formats can be interoperable and compact. This is required for federated applications in which iris data is exchanged between inter-operating systems, passed across bandwidth-limited networks, or stored on identity credentials. The IREX I quantified the core algorithmic capability of nineteen iris recognition implementations from ten organizations. It studied the effect of iris image compression on error rates, confirming the findings of previous studies that increasing compression gives graduated increases in false rejection. While IREX I showed that iris images captured in the near infrared are viable biometrics for verification and identification, it also confirmed findings in related studies [22, 8, 18, 25] that similar to other biometrics, its performance drops when comparing images captured from imperfect sources (e.g., subject blinking) or under imperfect conditions (e.g., out of focus). Three IREX I participants reported scalar overall iris image quality scores on the standard range of [0-100]. The IREX I study examined the predictive power of iris image quality scores, and reported that two of the quality algorithms generated quality scores correlated with image-specific error rates.

The IREX activities are distinct from NIST's prior Iris Challenge Evaluations (ICE) and Multiple Biometric Grand Challenge (MBGC) activities, which had more basic research-goals.

2.2 Literature survey

A list of academic papers on iris image quality is compiled at http://www.nist.gov/itl/iad/ig/iris_image_qual_reading.cfm.

3 Participation

NIST invited commercial providers, universities, and non-profit research laboratories and consultancies with capabilities in producing iris quality score, either overall scalar quality or specific aspects of quality (e.g., sharpness), to participate. Furthermore, organizations who implemented biometric verification software using iris images were invited to participate in IQCE . The comparison scores generated by such submissions were used to quantify the goodness of quality scores.

| A2a=NEUROTECHNOLOGY-a | B3=CROSSMATCH | C4s=CAMBRIDGE-s | D3=AWARE | E2a=IRITECH-a | G1=IRISID-1 | I1=KYNEN | Hz1=L1-z1 |
| A2f=NEUROTECHNOLOGY-f | C4x=CAMBRIDGE-x | C4f=CAMBRIDGE-f | F1=MORPHO | E2f=IRITECH-f | G2=IRISID-2 | Hx=L1-x | Hz2=L1-z2 |

Subsequently, NIST received fourteen IQAAs from nine organizations. All fourteen IQAAs computed scalar quality, and a subset of quality components as identified in IQCE API and test plan. Table 5 shows quality metrics computed by different IQAAs. IQAAs A2f, C4x, D3, F1, Hx, and I1 are standalone IQAAs, where the remaining IQAAs performed quality assessment as part of template generation. IQAAs E2a, E2f and D3 implemented the largest number of the quality components. There was no support for quality components MAGNIFICATION and HEAD-ROTATION. Ignoring these two quality components, only E2a and E2f implemented all the quality components. Ignoring MOTION BLUR in addition to the two previously mentioned quality components, IQAA D3, supported all the other quality components.

Additionally, six out of the nine participants submitted iris verification implementations (comparators). Four of the six submitted two implementations for evaluation. As such, IQCE received the following ten iris verification SDKs from six organizations: A2A, B3, C4F, C4S, E2A, E2F, G1, G2, HZ1 and HZ2. Comparison scores of these submissions were used to quantify the predictive power of quality components generated by submitted IQAAs.

To keep the number of graphs somehow manageable, results for only one submission per organization are included in this document. Where there was multiple submissions from an organization, the IQAA with the better performance was chosen. These are referred to as the "primary" submissions. Results for the submissions that are not included here are posted at http://www.nist.gov/itl/iad/ig/irexii_report_extra.cfm.

The detection error trade-off (DET) curves of Figure 1 show the accuracy of the IQCE comparators. Table 6 summarizes the role and functionality of IQCE submissions.

No.	Q Component	IQAA submissions													
1	scalar quality	A2a	A2f	B3	C4x	C4s	C4f	D3	E2a	E2f	F1	G1	G2	Hx	I1
2	gray level spread	A2a	A2f					D3	E2a	E2f	F1	G1	G2	Hx	I1
3	iris size	A2a	A2f		C4x	C4s	C4f	D3	E2a	E2f					I1
4	pupil_iris ratio	A2a	A2f	B3	C4x	C4s	C4f	D3	E2a	E2f	F1	G1	G2	Hx	I1
5	usable iris			B3	C4x	C4s	C4f	D3	E2a	E2f	F1	G1	G2	Hx	I1
6	iris-sclera contrast	A2a	A2f		C4x	C4s	C4f	D3	E2a	E2f	F1	G1	G2	Hx	I1
7	iris-pupil contrast	A2a	A2f		C4x	C4s	C4f	D3	E2a	E2f	F1	G1	G2	Hx	I1
8	iris shape	A2a			C4x	C4s	C4f	D3	E2a	E2f				Hx	I1
9	pupil shape		A2f		C4x	C4s	C4f	D3	E2a	E2f	F1			Hx	
10	margin	A2a	A2f					D3	E2a	E2f					
11	sharpness	A2a	A2f	B3	C4x	C4s	C4f	D3	E2a	E2f	F1	G1	G2	Hx	
12	motion blur								E2a	E2f					
13	signal to noise ratio	A2a	A2f					D3	E2a	E2f	F1	G1	G2		I1
14	magnification														
15	head rotation														
16	gaze angle				C4x	C4s	C4f	D3	E2a	E2f				Hx	I1
17	interlace	A2a	A2f		C4x	C4s	C4f	D3	E2a	E2f				Hx	

Table 5: IQCE IQAA submissions' support for specific quality component measurement

Functionality	A2a	A2f	B3	C4x	C4s	C4f	D3	E2a	E2f	F1	G1	G2	Hx	Hz1	Hz2	I1
comparison algorithm	✓		✓		✓	✓		✓	✓		✓	✓		✓	✓	
quality at template generation	✓		✓		✓	✓		✓	✓		✓	✓				
stand alone quality		✓		✓			✓			✓			✓			✓

Table 6: Functionality of IQCE submissions. The first character is the supplier code. The numeral is the index number for the submission by supplier N. The last character (if present) specifies the Class of participation ("x", "z") or the type as specified by the supplier ("a"=accurate, "f"=fast, "s"=slow). Class X submissions (the last character = "x") perform quality computation. Class Z submissions perform comparison.

A2a=NEUROTECHNOLOGY-a	B3=CROSSMATCH	C4s=CAMBRIDGE-s	D3=AWARE	E2a=IRITECH-a	G1=IRISID-1	I1=KYNEN	Hz1=L1-z1
A2f=NEUROTECHNOLOGY-f	C4x=CAMBRIDGE-x	C4f=CAMBRIDGE-f	F1=MORPHO	E2f=IRITECH-f	G2=IRISID-2	Hx=L1-x	Hz2=L1-z2

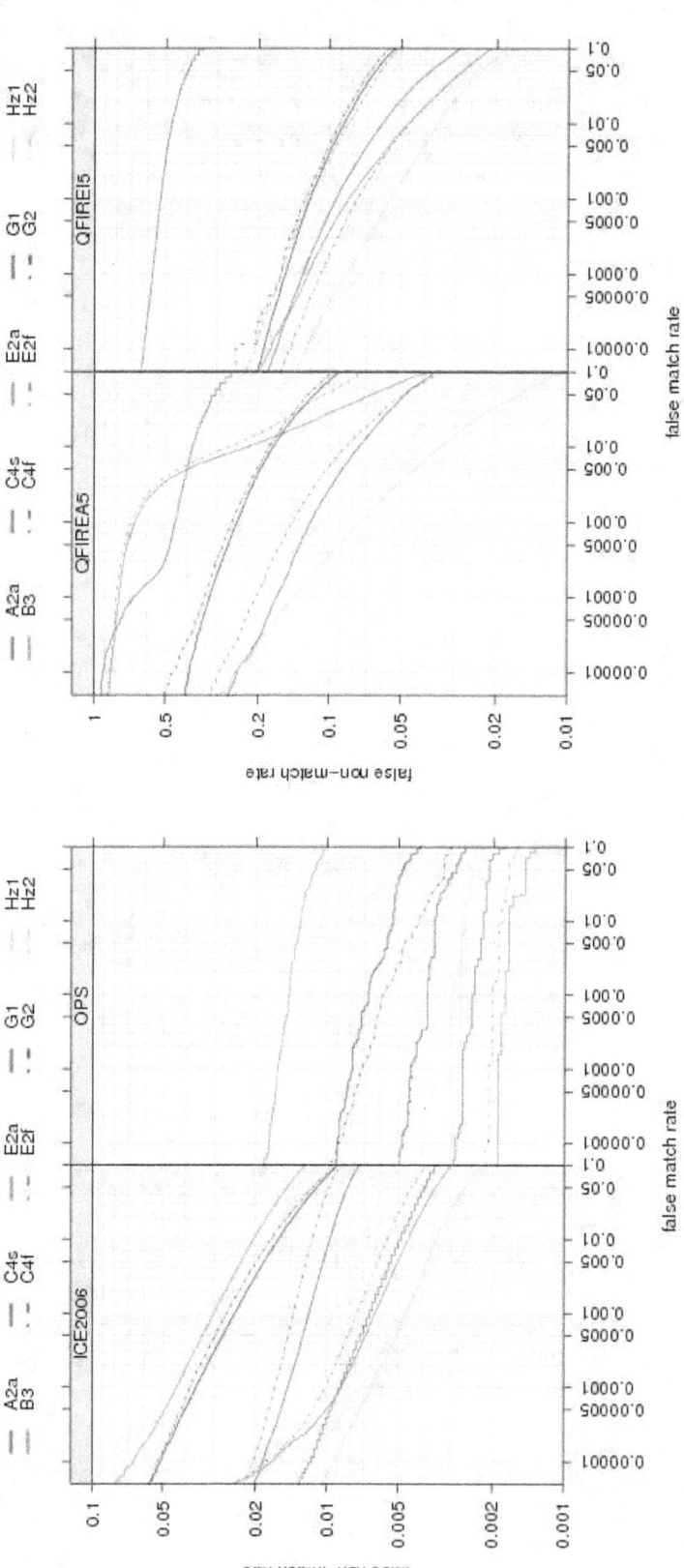

Figure 1: Detection Error Trade-off for IQCE comparators. The plots show baseline recognition error rates vary greatly across the datasets. The observed FNMR on the highest-quality dataset OPS is approximately two order of magnitude smaller than the lowest-quality dataset QFIRE A5 . Also, note that the y-axis scale are different between the left and right DET plots.

| A2a=NEUROTECHNOLOGY-a | B3=CROSSMATCH | C4s=CAMBRIDGE-s | D3=AWARE | E2a=IRITECH-a | G1=IRISID-1 | I1=KYNEN | Hz1=L1-z1 |
| A2f=NEUROTECHNOLOGY-f | C4x=CAMBRIDGE-x | C4f=CAMBRIDGE-f | F1=MORPHO | E2f=IRITECH-f | G2=IRISID-2 | Hx=L1-x | Hz2=L1-z2 |

4   Datasets

Performance evaluation of IQAAs is meaningful only if the test data contains low-quality images. The ideal case is to have some "ground truth" on the types of defect and their prevalence. For example gaze is non-frontal, and gaze angle is 30 degrees to the right, or that the iris is occluded by 19%. However, measuring or obtaining such "ground truth" information is nearly impossible and very labor intensive.

Use of synthetic data is one way of making images with specific controlled defects, at least for some specific impairments. Starting with a pristine image, some pixels in the iris can be masked, or the image can be blurred, or noise can be added. As a result, for each original image, a set of impaired images are constructed, where the type and exact amount of the impairment are known. The iris community objected to IQCE using synthetic images, arguing that the world is too complex to be synthesized. They reasoned that the synthetically impaired images would not be a fair representation of the real-world low-quality images. This method fails to capture the interaction of several simultaneous defects in an image, as is the case in real-world non-laboratory data.

Another way of obtaining such "ground truth" information is to collect images with controlled specific defects. Dedicated data collection can be conducted where capture device settings, or environment conditions, or subjects' behavior are varied by design. This approach has the advantage of producing real-world (or real-sensed) images. In addition, to some extent, it allows for designing the type and amount of impairments. However, it has its own shortcomings: a) precise control of acquisition is challenging, so inevitably ground truth will be noisy. For example, capturing an iris image with gaze angle exactly 30 degrees to the left is cumbersome; b) keeping the confounding variables, i.e., subject/acquisition parameters, uniform is unattainable. For example, having uniform usable iris area when capturing images with different gaze angle is difficult because the subject will blink or the fraction of the iris that is occluded by reflection will change.

Considering all the above, the IQCE study employed data from three collections of iris images. Two of the collections, ICE2006 and OPS , are the same datasets used in IREXI. The OPS dataset is an operational set, and is included in IQCE specifically to construe IQAAs performance on operational images. However, because of the procedure used to select OPS images by the agency that sent it to NIST (details below), OPS images are "easy to match". Only a very small fraction of images are causing failures. Consequently, OPS is not the appropriate dataset for evaluation of IQAAs . Nevertheless, knowing the performance of IQAAs on iris images collected under operational condition is valuable information. The ICE2006 dataset contains low-quality images, due to its data collection protocol. Minimal quality-based filtering was allowed at the time of capture; therefore ICE2006 images vary greatly in quality. However, no ground truth on source or cause of low quality was available to the authors. The third data source, QFIRE, is a subset of the dedicated collection done by Clarkson University. As explained below, the acquisition design assures inclusion of impaired images , which makes QFIRE images attractive for IQCE .

The IQCE test datasets are summarized in Table 7. The following subsections describe the IQCE datasets. The descriptions of the ICE2006 and OPS are copied from the IREXI report (copied text are in smaller font and blue color).

4.1   The OPS dataset

The operational dataset consists of two captures of the left and right irises of 8160 individuals. This gives a total of 32640 distinct images. The images were collected using the PIER 2.3 camera from Securimetrics. The files were extracted from

| A2a=NEUROTECHNOLOGY-a | B3=CROSSMATCH | C4s=CAMBRIDGE-s | D3=AWARE | E2a=IRITECH-a | G1=IRISID-1 | I1=KYNEN | Hz1=L1-z1 |
| A2f=NEUROTECHNOLOGY-f | C4x=CAMBRIDGE-x | C4f=CAMBRIDGE-f | F1=MORPHO | E2f=IRITECH-f | G2=IRISID-2 | Hx=L1-x | Hz2=L1-z2 |

Dataset ID	Origin	Number of subjects	Number of images	Camera Citation
OPS	An operational set	8160	32640	Pier 2.3[2]
ICE	Extract of Notre Dame 2005-2006 ICE images	193	56871	LG IrisAccess 2200[3]
QFIREI05	Extract of Clarkson University QFIRE images	136	14165	Dalsa [10]
QFIREA05	Extract of Clarkson University QFIRE images	135	4365	Dalsa [10]

Table 7: Summary of the IQCE datasets.

a large multimodal dataset, according to a fixed criterion. This was applied by the provider of the data. The authors did not have any role in the selection process. The selection criteria were such that a person was included in the IREX partition if the following logical expression was TRUE.

$$\text{RULE 1} \quad \textbf{and} \quad (\text{RULE 2} \quad \textbf{or} \quad \text{RULE 3} \quad \textbf{or} \quad (\text{RULE 4} \quad \textbf{and} \quad \text{RULE 5}))$$

Where

RULE 1   the subject's ten-print fingerprints were matched by an operational AFIS system[4] at some threshold

RULE 2   the subject's pair of left eyes matched with iris recognition algorithm X at a score below threshold τ_1

RULE 3   the subject's pair of right eyes matched with iris recognition algorithm X at a score below threshold τ_1

RULE 4   the subject's pair of left eyes matched with iris recognition algorithm X at a score below threshold τ_2

RULE 5   the subject's pair of right eyes matched with iris recognition algorithm X at a score below threshold τ_2

It is known that $\tau_2 > \tau_1$. The provider of the OPS dataset stated that using X with the τ_1 and τ_2 threshold produced "zero FMR" in $O(10^{10})$ comparisons. The authors assume that

▷ this applied to person-pairings, i.e., a second (L,R) pair was bound to a first (L,R) pair with zero false pairings;

▷ ground truth was defined by the AFIS implementation; and

▷ single images may still come from different persons because of RULES 2 and 3.

While the known use of an iris recognition algorithm in the construction of a test dataset is not best practice, it is allowed by the ISO/IEC 19795 standards provided the practice is disclosed.

The application of the X algorithm to the selection process means that recognition accuracy reported on OPS dataset, is likely to be high - more specifically, that the iris left and right eye *pairs* are matchable (at some threshold). Thus we anticipate that any L-R fusion procedure should give error rates of zero for iris recognition algorithms of similar capability to X. Critically, however, this does not hold for single *images*, and non-zero matching error rates should be expected and are, in fact, observed. Given these factors, the authors used the dataset because:

▷ The images are likely to be more representative of **enrollment** samples in which care had been taken to produce a pristine and matchable image.

▷ The population size, at 8160, is a factor of 34 larger than the ICE2006 or QFIRE datasets, and while this is invaluable to capture the natural variation between persons in order to better characterize false match performance, it remains too small to support robust quantitative estimation of false match performance in national-scale 1:N applications.

A2a=NEUROTECHNOLOGY-a	B3=CROSSMATCH	C4s=CAMBRIDGE-s	D3=AWARE	E2a=IRITECH-a	G1=IRISID-1	I1=KYNEN	Hz1=L1-z1
A2f=NEUROTECHNOLOGY-f	C4x=CAMBRIDGE-x	C4f=CAMBRIDGE-f	F1=MORPHO	E2f=IRITECH-f	G2=IRISID-2	Hx=L1-x	Hz2=L1-z2

▷ It is representative of the geometric and photometric properties of contemporary mainstream identity management applications.

▷ The ICE2006 dataset has its own detracting properties (see Section 4.2).

▷ Images from the ICE2006 dataset have been disseminated publicly and thus IQCE providers perhaps anticipated and tuned to that dataset. These disadvantages motivated use of the OPS dataset.

4.2   The ICE2006 dataset

This set of data was provided to the authors by the MBGC program[9]. A representative disjoint set of images had been released under the ICE 05 development program. The ICE2006 corpus used in IREX (both IREX I and IREX II) consists of left and right iris images collected from a university population over six semesters running from 2004 to 2006. The images are formally described[19] thus:

> The ICE 2006 images were acquired using an LG EOU 2200 iris scanner. The LG EOU 2200 is a complete acquisition system and has automatic image quality control checks. By agreement between U. of Notre Dame and Iridian, a modified version of the acquisition software was provided. The modified software allowed all images from the sensor to be saved under certain conditions, as explained below.

> The iris images are 48x640 in resolution, see Figure 2 [suppressed]. For most "good" iris images, the diameter of the iris in the image exceeds 200 pixels. The images are stored with 8 bits of intensity, but every third intensity level is unused. This is the result of a contrast stretching automatically applied within the LG EOU 2200 system. In our acquisitions, the subject was seated in front of the system. The system provides 32 recorded voice prompts to aid the subject to position their eye at the appropriate distance from the sensor. The system takes images in "shots" of three, with each image corresponding to illumination of one of the three infrared (IR) light emitting diodes (LED)s used to illuminate the iris.

> For a given subject at a given iris acquisition session, two "shots" of three images each are taken for each eye, for a total of 12 images. The system provides a feedback sound when an acceptable shot of images is taken. An acceptable shot has one or more images that pass the LG EOU 2200's built-in quality checks, but all three images are saved. If none of the three images pass the built-in quality checks, then none of the three images are saved. At least one third of the iris images do pass the Iridian quality control checks, and up to two thirds do not pass.

> A manual quality control step at Notre Dame was performed to remove images in which, for example, the eye was not visible at all due to the subject having turned their head.

The use of these images proved controversial in the ICE 2006 evaluation because the suppression of the camera's quality control apparatus caused operationally non-representative images (e.g., eyes closed, non-axial gaze, blur) to be present in the dataset. The presence of degraded images adversely affected iris recognition accuracy, and while larger error rates give better statistical significance to FNMR estimates, the test results have less relevance to operational reality.

The authors found ICE2006 images useful for comparative analysis of IQAAs. Its range and diversity of image impairments makes it suitable for investigating the causes of failure and viability of algorithms on the core iris feature extraction and matching problem.

4.3 The QFIRE dataset

Below is an excerpt from [10]:

QFIRE is a multi-biometric database which include iris and face quality images for varying distances and a range of quality. The experimental setup has been designed for acquiring images for the second phase of DHS/NSF Dynamic Decisional Fusion Face/Iris Database grant. QFIRE images are collected over five distances: baseline, 5, 7, 11, 15, and 25 feet. Subjects were asked to walk through a "portal" at 7 and 15 feet to introduce motion blur. To produce non-uniformity in the dataset, variability in the data was introduced through six factors (resolution, ambient (or external) illumination, out-of-focus blur, multiple faces, gaze/pose angles, motion blur). Additionally, an occlusion factor was introduced for iris images. For each factor, the data acquisition equipment (Dalsa and Canon cameras) was controlled to achieve high, medium, and low quality iris and face images.

Over 175 subjects are included with at least two visits each. The dataset also includes soft biometrics such as height and weight, for subjects of different age groups, ethnicity and gender with variable number of sessions/subject.

Equipment List

- Dalsa 4M30 infrared camera, Dalsa Corporation
- Tamron AF 70-300mm 1:4.5-5.6 LD DI lens B+W 66mm 092 IR filter (removes 680 nm and below) Set at 230 mm / f4.5 for 5/7/11 feet
- Sigma APO 300-800mm F5.6 EX DG HSM lens, Sigma Corporation of America B+W 46mm 092 IR filter (removes 680 nm and below) Kenko Extension tubes (16mm+20mm+36mm) Set at 630 mm / f5.6 for 15/25 feet
- Exposure time: 7500 s for 5/7/11 feet, 30000 s for 15/25 feet, motion blur: 5000 s

Illumination intensity We seek to achieve varying levels of illumination through fixed illumination plus varying levels of lights (based on LED arrays) positioned two feet from subject. There is a total of 8 LED-based lights which can be independently turned on/off.

- Lighting: LED-based portal (830 nm with angle of 30 degrees, 5 Watts each)
- High lighting/contrast: 8 LED-based (5, 7, 11 feet)
- Medium lighting/contrast: 6 LED-based (5, 7, 11 feet)
- Low lighting/contrast: 4 LED-based (5, 7, 11 feet)

Out of focus blur A 6 sec. video sequence of a subject will be taken with gradual change of the focus by changing the focus ring on the camera. This will ensure that the true in-focus image and the images with different amount of blur are captured. For each setup, the camera will be focused and turned until it is (just) completely out of focus. Once the camera is recording, the collector will change focus until the image is in focus and then go beyond focus point to completely out of focus again.

Off-Angle Gaze angles will be achieved through markings on a movable stand. Different gaze positions are achieved with head fixed straight forward.

- Five positions for 30 degrees gaze variation (approximate drop off point for performance in commercial systems based on Iris06 from Authenti-Corp6 report)
- First position is neutral gaze (straight ahead).
- XY plane (parallel with the floor at eye level) 30 degree (right), and 30 degrees (left).
- YZ plane (slice body symmetrically) 30 degree (up), 30 degree (down).

The IQCE used two subsets of the QFIRE collection. QFIRE A5 is a subset of the off-angle experiment. QFIRE I5 is a subset of the out-of-focus/blur experiment, which also included varying levels of illumination intensity. Thus, the QFIRE A5 contains images with various gaze angle, but are in focus. All QFIRE A5 images were captured with eight LEDs on. The QFIRE I5 contains images with various illumination intensity (number of LEDs 4, 6, or 8) and different focus settings. Images were captured from subjects standing five feet from the camera. NIST prepared ISO/IEC 19794-6 KIND CROPPED for both sets, meaning that the iris is centered in QFIRE A5 and QFIRE I5 images and margins are set to $0.6R$ horizontally and $0.2R$ vertically according to specifications in ISO/IEC 19794-6. All the images were manually inspected for correct eye labeling.

While we know the QFIRE A5 contains many images with non-frontal gaze, we do not know the "ground truth" on how non-frontal they are. Similarly, for QFIRE I5 images, we do not know the "ground truth" on sharpness per image, but we do know the number of LEDs used for each image.

Example images of QFIRE A5 and QFIRE I5 with specific defect are in Figure 2. As is shown, the range of defects in QFIRE A5 and QFIRE I5 images is somewhat broader than the categories of angles and focus. Some have poor contrast, some have significant occlusion, and some have specularities (e.g., due to glasses).

5 Metrics

This section documents methods for the quantitative evaluation of systems that produce quality scores that can be either a scalar summary of a biometric sample's quality or a measurement of a specific aspect of quality (quality component). The quality measurement algorithm is regarded as a black box that takes an input iris image and outputs a scalar quality along with a vector of quality components. Evaluations are done by quantifying the association between quality scores and the observed matching results.

Mostly nonparametric descriptive analysis is performed.

5.1 Notation

Consider a dataset D containing two samples, $d_i^{(1)}$ and $d_i^{(2)}$, collected from each of $i = 1, \ldots, N$ individuals. Without loss of generality, the first sample can be regarded as an enrollment image, and the second as a user sample collected later for verification or identification purposes. Suppose a quality algorithm Q is run on the i-th enrollment sample to produce a

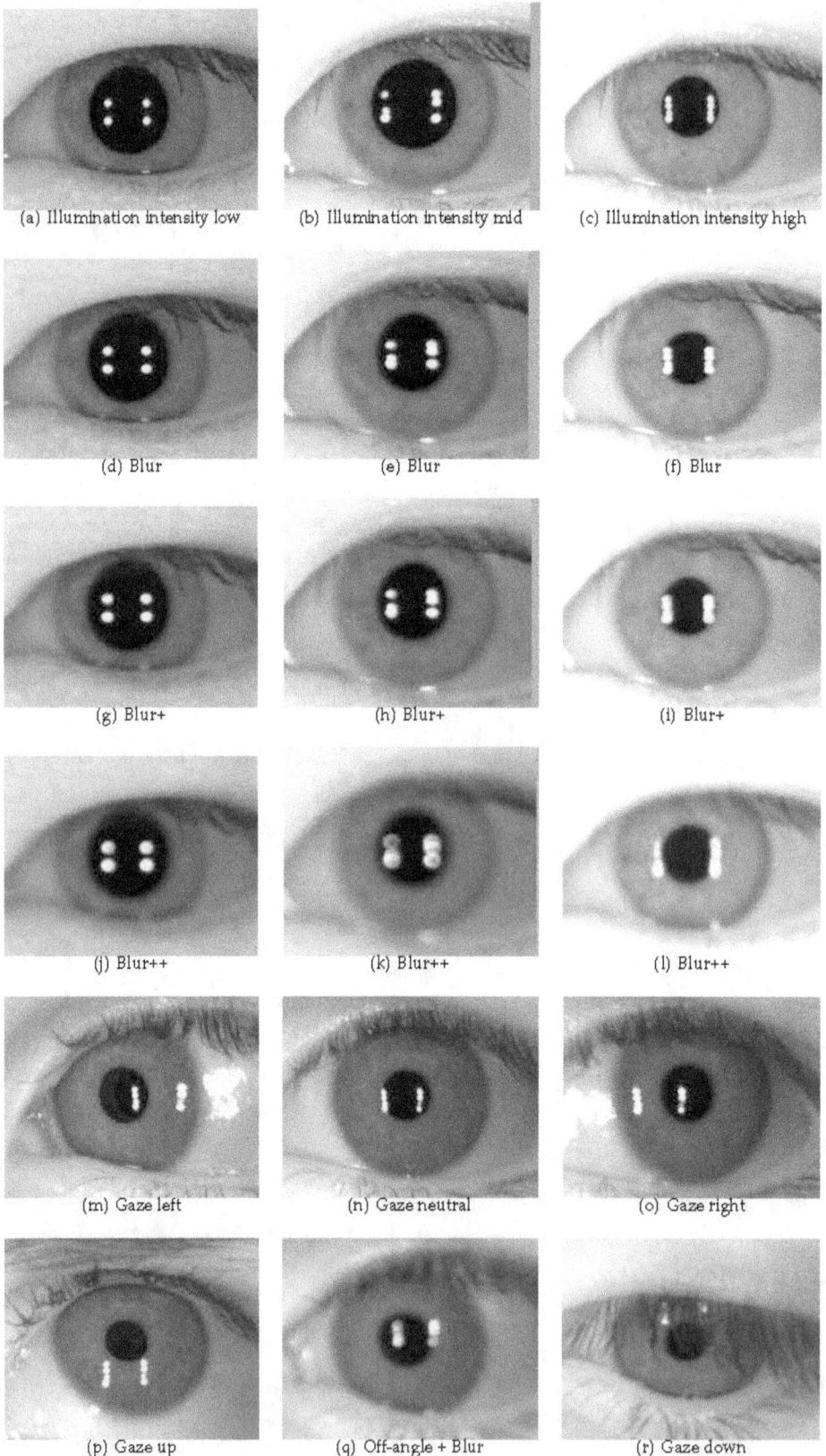

Figure 2: Example images

quality value:

$$q_i^{(1)} = Q(d_i^{(1)}) \tag{1}$$

and likewise for the authentication (or verification) sample:

$$q_i^{(2)} = Q(d_i^{(2)}) \tag{2}$$

Per the definition of biometric quality, quality values q_i should be a monotonic increasing function of performance, where high-quality samples give low-dissimilarity scores when involved in genuine comparisons.

For quality components for which the monotonic increasing assumption is not valid, such as DILATION (which is the ratio of pupil radius to iris radius), the quality score is transformed as below, *only* for the Error vs Reject analysis.

$$T(q_i) = 1.0 - \frac{|q_i - \text{mean}(q_i)|}{\text{max}(q_i) - \text{min}(q_i)} \tag{3}$$

where $\text{max}(q_i)$ and $\text{min}(q_i)$ are the maximum and minimum values and $\text{mean}(q_i)$ is the mean computed over all the quality scores. Equation 3 transform gives images with raw score values closer to the mean high quality scores, indicating good quality. Likewise, images with raw score closer to the extreme values (too large or too small) are assigned low quality scores, indicating poor quality.

5.2   Combining two samples' quality values

Biometric matching involves at least two samples and the challenge is then to relate performance (which involves two samples) to quality values $q^{(1)}$ and $q^{(2)}$. We simplify the analysis by combining the two qualities according to:

$$q_i = M(q_i^{(1)}, q_i^{(2)}) \tag{4}$$

It is usually the case that operationally an IQAA can be used to assess whether an enrollment sample is of high quality. The enrollment sample will be compared later with a sample that typically is of less controlled quality. $M(x, y) = \min(x, y)$ captures the concept that the worse of two samples drives the similarity score. Some other relevant pair-wise combination functions for M includes (but certainly not limited to) the arithmetic and geometric means, $M(x, y) = (x + y)/2$ and $M(x, y) = \sqrt{xy}$ (see [11]), and the difference function $M(x, y) = |x - y|$. We note that whatever M is used, it should be well-defined for allowed values of x and y (e.g., positive values for the geometric mean).

Throughout this report, we have used either geometric mean or the minimum of the two samples being compared to estimate their pairwise quality.

5.3   Biometric error rates

If s denotes a matcher dissimilarity score obtained by comparing two samples from the same person, and $M(\tau)$ is the number of such scores above threshold, τ:

$$M(\tau) = \sum_{s \in \mathcal{G}} H(s - \tau) \tag{5}$$

| A2a=NEUROTECHNOLOGY-a | B3=CROSSMATCH | C4s=CAMBRIDGE-s | D3=AWARE | E2a=IRITECH-a | G1=IRISID-1 | I1=KYNEN | Hz1=L1-z1 |
| A2f=NEUROTECHNOLOGY-f | C4x=CAMBRIDGE-x | C4f=CAMBRIDGE-f | F1=MORPHO | E2f=IRITECH-f | G2=IRISID-2 | Hx=L1-x | Hz2=L1-z2 |

where $\mathcal{G}$ denotes the set of all genuine comparison scores. $H(x)$ is the step function defined here as:

$$H(x) = \begin{cases} 0 & x \le 0 \\ 1 & x > 0 \end{cases} \tag{6}$$

The inequality placement is unconventional (for the Heaviside step function) and is used so that scores equal to the threshold correspond to acceptance.

FNMR is then the fraction of genuine comparisons for which the score is above the operating threshold:

$$\text{FNMR}(\tau) = \frac{M(\tau)}{M(-\infty)} \tag{7}$$

where $M(-\infty)$ is just the number of genuine comparisons considered. Likewise, when s denotes a score obtained by comparing samples from different persons, and $N(\tau)$ is the number of such scores below threshold, τ,

$$N(\tau) = \sum_{s \in \mathcal{I}} 1 - H(s - \tau) \tag{8}$$

where $\mathcal{I}$ denotes the set of all impostor scores.

FMR is then the fraction of impostor comparisons resulting in a score less than or equal to the operating threshold:

$$\text{FMR}(\tau) = \frac{N(\tau)}{N(\infty)} \tag{9}$$

where $N(\infty)$ is the number of impostor comparisons conducted.

In 1:N negative identification applications (e.g., watchlist, duplicate detection), FMR measures the rate at which a search sample is incorrectly associated with an enrolled sample. In 1:1 positive authentication applications, FMR is regarded as a measure of security, i.e., the fraction of illegitimate matching attempts that result in success. In any case, these error rates must be understood as being *matching* error rates, not *transactional* rates. The ISO/IEC SC 37 Working Group 5 has established different terms for these rates: FMR and FNMR refer to comparisons of single samples, while FAR and FRR apply to the outcome of a human-system transaction in which a user might, for example, make multiple attempts with multiple eye presentations.

5.4   Image-specific error rates

To examine performance variation among different images, we define the following image-specific error rates

  ▷ **Image false match rate**, iFMR - the proportion of comparisons for which an image produces false matches (i.e., non-match comparisons at or below the operating threshold).

  ▷ **Image false non-match rate**, iFNMR - the proportion of comparisons for which an image produces a false non-match (i.e., genuine comparisons above the operating threshold).

Specifically, if we define s_{kl}^{ij} to be the comparison score of the k-th image of subject i with the l-th image of subject j, then the set of impostor scores of the k-th image of subject i is

$$\mathcal{I}(i,k) = \{\, s_{kl}^{ij} \,,\; i \neq j \,,\; j = 1 \ldots J \,,\; l = 1 \ldots N_j \} \tag{10}$$

for comparison against all N_j images of all J persons in an enrolled set. The image false match rate is then defined as

$$\text{iFMR}\,(\tau, i, k) = \frac{\sum_{s \in \mathcal{I}(i,k)} 1 - H(s - \tau)}{\sum_{s \in \mathcal{I}(i,k)} 1} \tag{11}$$

where $H(s)$ is the step function of equation 6. If the threshold is set to τ in the conventional manner (i.e., over some large cross comparison set) to give a global FMR of f, then the general case is that iFMR $\neq f$.

For the image false non-match rate, we use the set of (not identically the same image) genuine scores of the k-th image of subject i ($k \neq i$)

$$\mathcal{G}(i,k) = \{\, s_{kl}^{ii}, l = 1 \ldots N_i, k \neq l \,\} \tag{12}$$

to compute:

$$\text{iFNMR}\,(\tau, i, k) = \frac{\sum_{s \in \mathcal{G}(i,k)} H(s - \tau)}{\sum_{s \in \mathcal{G}(i,k)} 1} \tag{13}$$

where $H(x)$ is again the step function of equation 6.

Unless otherwise stated, iFMR and iFNMR are computed for each comparison algorithm by substituting the comparison scores of the algorithm in equations 11 and 13 above, using the following datasets: ICE 2006, QFIRE A5, and QFIRE I5. The threshold can be set to any value. Here it is set over all impostor comparisons of each dataset to achieve FMR = 0.0001.

5.5   Treatment of failure to process an image

5.5.1   Failure to compute quality scores

IQCE API had defined several return values to distinguish between an SDK's voluntary refusal to process an image or its involuntary failure to do so. Some of the SDKs crashed on certain QFIRE I5 or QFIRE A5 images. All cases of failure to compute quality scores (i.e., voluntarily or software crash) are excluded from main analyses, but their frequencies are reported in section 6. Therefore, unless otherwise stated, the graphs and tables in this report are generated using only images whose quality computations were successful.

5.5.2   Failure to compute comparison scores

We observed no instances where template generation succeeded for an image pair, but comparison of the templates failed. All failure to compute comparison scores were due to the failure to generate templates. Failure to generate templates also causes failure to compute quality scores. All such cases have been excluded from analyses.

A2a=NEUROTECHNOLOGY-a	B3=CROSSMATCH	C4s=CAMBRIDGE-s	D3=AWARE	E2a=IRITECH-a	G1=IRISID-1	I1=KYNEN	Hz1=L1-z1
A2f=NEUROTECHNOLOGY-f	C4x=CAMBRIDGE-x	C4f=CAMBRIDGE-f	F1=MORPHO	E2f=IRITECH-f	G2=IRISID-2	Hx=L1-x	Hz2=L1-z2

5.6   Data analysis and visualization techniques

This section describes the data analysis and visualization techniques employed. The following sections discuss observations and conclusions drawn by applying these techniques to scalar quality and quality vector components.

5.6.1   Relationship between quality scores and genuine scores

Scatter plots are one of the simplest and most useful data exploratory tools to visualize the relationship between two quantitative variables. We can use scatter plots to explore the relationship between genuine comparison scores and quality scores. However, due to over plotting of data points in our large dataset, trends can be obscured in dense clouds of points. To avoid this problem, for each plot, we grouped the data into ten equal count bins by abscissas (x-coordinates) and then plotted a box and whisker diagram at the abscissa value for each of the bins. The result is ten box plots arranged along the x-axis; this enables efficient comparisons of the mean, median, spread and outliers as a function of the x coordinate.

If quality is an indicator of performance, lower dissimilarity scores will be achieved for high-quality images of the same eye. In other words, the proper behavior is to have low-quality scores for high genuine score bins. Recall that the lower the genuine comparison scores, the higher the likelihood that the images belong to the same eye.

An example is shown in Figure 3. Each cell shows boxplots of pairwise quality scores vs. bins of genuine comparison scores for four datasets. Quality scores are generated by the IQAA identified at the top of the cell. Comparison scores are generated by comparator C4s.

These graphs aim to determine if high image quality scores results in low genuine comparison scores. An IQAA is not effective if the quality scores increase or stay constant as the genuine comparison scores increase. Additionally, one can look for a particular order for the boxes corresponding to different datasets. As explained in section 4, the OPS images are better quality than the ICE2006. The QFIRE A5 and QFIRE I5 are of much lower quality than the other two datasets.

Section 8 shows the relationship between genuine scores and the scalar quality of IQAAs for different datasets and different comparators. Similar results for other quality components are shown in section 9.

The procedure to produce figures like Figure 3 is as follows:

▷ For each IQCE comparator,

▷ For each IQAA , and for each dataset,

1. Divide the genuine comparison scores into ten equal count bins. The end-point of each bin is computed such that roughly the same number of observations fall in each bin. Therefore, the first bin contains image pairs that result in the lowest 10% of the genuine comparison scores. Similarly, image pairs with genuine comparison scores in the upper 10 percentile form the last (10th) bin. Successive bins overlap by 5%. That is, the upper 5% of the data in one bin, also belongs to the next one (as the lowest 5% of the next bin).

2. For each IQAA , compute pairwise quality scores. We used geometric mean, i.e. $\sqrt{q_1 * q_2}$.

3. Compute the mean of the pairwise quality scores as the summary statistics of each bin's quality scores.

4. Bootstrap each bin's pairwise quality scores.

5. Plot box and whiskers of the bootstrapped mean of each bin's pairwise quality scores.

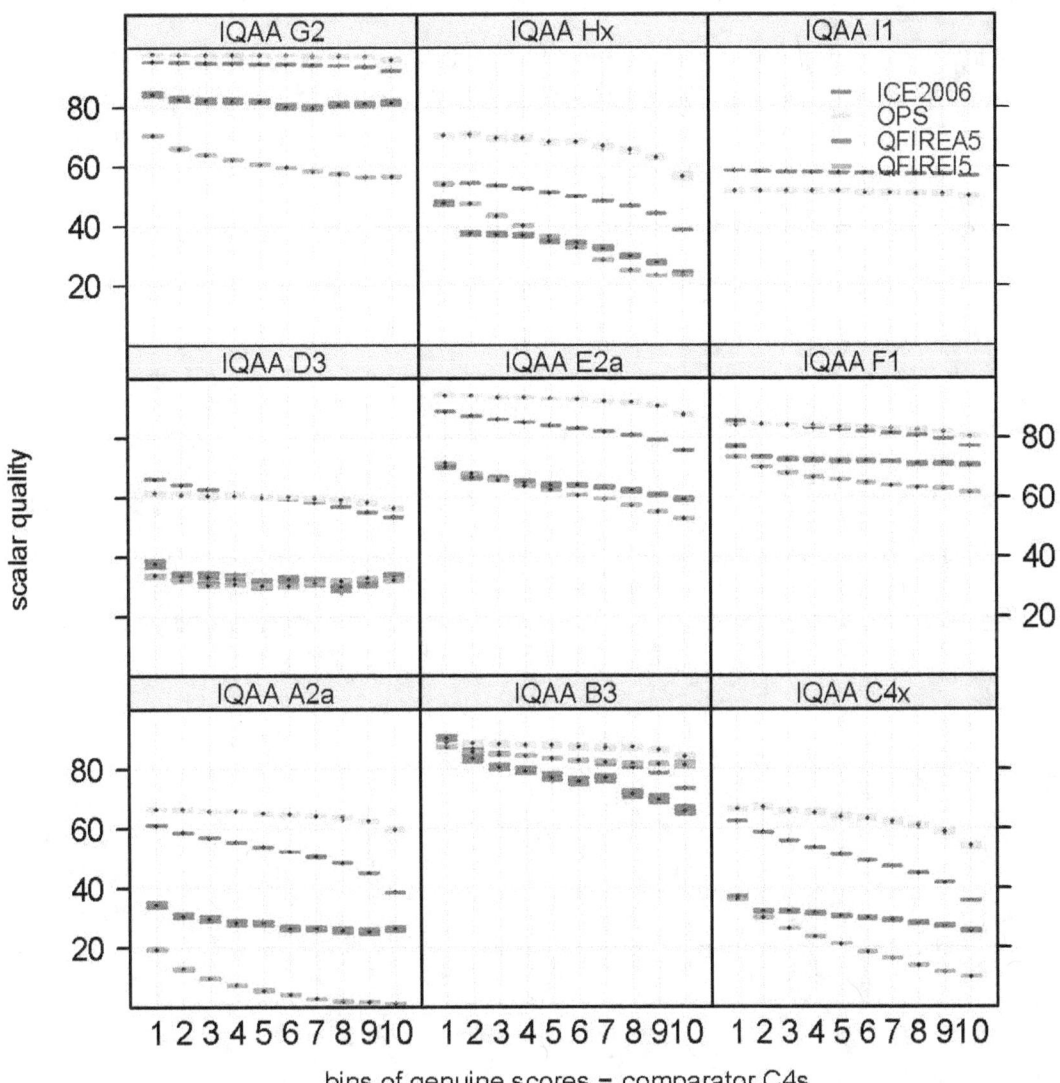

Figure 3: Pairwise SCALAR QUALITY scores vs genuine comparison scores generated by comparator C4s. Each cell shows quality scores computed by a different IQAA for four datasets, in different colors. Genuine comparison scores are divided equally into ten groups. Groups overlap by 5 percent, meaning 5% of the data in one bin also belongs to the next. The Bootstrapped average pairwise quality for each group is shown in a box and whisker plot. Pairwise quality is computed as geometric mean of the quality of the two samples being compared. The proper behavior is to have high quality scores for low genuine score bins. (High genuine comparison scores lead to false rejection.) No change or increase in quality scores for high genuine scores indicate that the IQAA is not effective. Among the four datasets OPS has the best quality, followed by ICE2006. QFIRE A5 and QFIRE I5 are of much lower quality than OPS and ICE2006. Therefore, we expect an ordering of the boxes in each cell, from top to bottom, to be quality scores of OPS dataset (yellow boxes), then ICE2006 dataset (purple boxes), followed by QFIRE I5 (pink) and finally QFIRE A5 (green boxes).

5.6.2 Relationship between quality scores and impostor scores

To examine the relationship between quality scores and impostor scores, we follow the same procedure explained in 5.6.1 by replacing the genuine scores with the impostor scores. An example is shown in Figure 4.

When examining these graphs, one should look for either no change or an improvement in quality as the impostor comparison score increases. Lower-quality scores for smaller impostor scores suggest that low-quality images contribute to the false match rate. As shown in sections 8 and 9, different comparators exhibit different relationships between impostor scores and quality scores of their own or other IQAA.

The same rank ordering of the datasets described in section 5.6.1 is expected.

| A2a=NEUROTECHNOLOGY-a | B3=CROSSMATCH | C4s=CAMBRIDGE-s | D3=AWARE | E2a=IRITECH-a | G1=IRISID-1 | I1=KYNEN | Hz1=L1-z1 |
| A2f=NEUROTECHNOLOGY-f | C4x=CAMBRIDGE-x | C4f=CAMBRIDGE-f | F1=MORPHO | E2f=IRITECH-f | G2=IRISID-2 | Hx=L1-x | Hz2=L1-z2 |

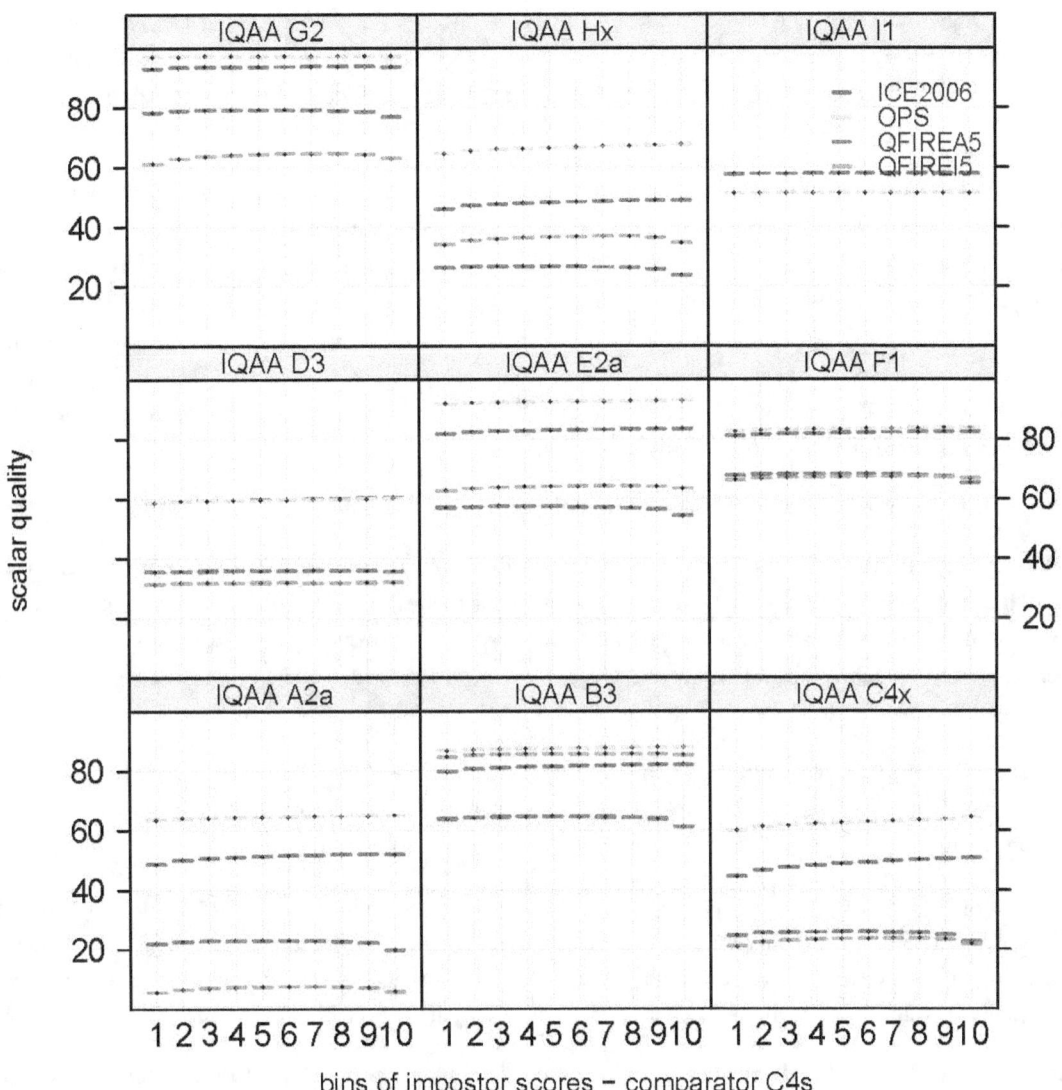

Figure 4: Pairwise SCALAR QUALITY scores vs impostor comparison scores generated by comparator C4s. Each cell shows quality scores computed by a different IQAA for four datasets, in different colors. Impostor comparison scores are divided equally into ten groups. Groups overlap by 5 percent, meaning 5% of the data in one bin also belongs to the next. The bootstrapped average pairwise quality for each group is shown in a box and whisker plot. Pairwise quality is computed as geometric mean of the quality of the two samples being compared. Among the four datasets OPS has the best quality, followed by ICE2006. QFIRE A5 and QFIRE I5 are of much lower quality than OPS and ICE2006. Therefore, we expect an ordering of the boxes in each cell, from top to bottom, as quality scores of OPS dataset (yellow boxes), then ICE2006 dataset (purple boxes), followed by QFIRE I5 (pink) and finally QFIRE A5 (green boxes).

A2a=NEUROTECHNOLOGY-a	B3=CROSSMATCH	C4s=CAMBRIDGE-s	D3=AWARE	E2a=IRITECH-a	G1=IRISID-1	I1=KYNEN	Hz1=L1-z1
A2f=NEUROTECHNOLOGY-f	C4x=CAMBRIDGE-x	C4f=CAMBRIDGE-f	F1=MORPHO	E2f=IRITECH-f	G2=IRISID-2	Hx=L1-x	Hz2=L1-z2

5.6.3 Ranked DET

DET characteristic curves are the primary performance metric for offline testing of biometric recognition algorithms [17], [3]. Each point on a DET curve exhibits the false match (equation 9) and false non-match rates (equation 7) associated with a certain threshold value. The DET curve spans the whole range of possible threshold values, which is normally the range of the comparison scores. An IQAA is useful if it can at least give an ordered indication of an eventual performance. For example, for L distinct quality levels, there should notionally be L DET characteristics that do not cross.

Using the geometric mean of the two samples ($\sqrt{q_1 * q_2}$) as their pairwise quality, we divide each comparator's comparison scores into three groups based on the pairwise quality of the images being compared. The set of the lowest quality contains comparison scores with pairwise qualities in the lowest 15 percentile. Comparisons with pairwise quality in the middle 70 percent comprise the second or medium quality set. Finally, comparison scores of images whose pairwise quality are in the highest 15 percentile make up the third or best quality set. Three DET characteristic curves, one for each set above, are generated, as shown in Figure 5. Each cell in Figure 5 shows three DET curves where quality scores of the identified IQAA are used to partition the comparison scores generated by comparator Hz1. To reveal the dependence of FNMR and FMR on quality at a fixed threshold, τ, the DET curves of each cell are connected at false non-match and false match rates that are observed at the "same threshold" values.

Comparator Hz1 was chosen because it gives the best performance among all comparators.

An IQAA is effective if the DET curves are separated, with the DET curve corresponding to the lowest quality images appearing at the top (i.e., higher FNMR), and the DET curve of highest quality images at the bottom (i.e., lower FNMR). The proper behavior is to observe lower FNMR and FMR as quality improves. Overlapping DET curves indicate poor IQAA performance. A higher separation among these three curves indicates a more effective IQAA. For example, in Figure 5, IQAA C4x provides the best separation while IQAA D3 fails to predict performance of comparator Hz1.

DET curves of the OPS images are not separated. This is because the OPS images are "easy to match" (see section 4.1). The observed false match and false non-matches are probably due to reasons other than geometric or photometric property of the images.

The ranking and the separation of the DET curves, as explained above, will reveal the effect of quality on FNMR. Effect of quality on FMR is demonstrated by the lines connecting the DET curves (the brown lines of Figure 5). Assuming the correct ranking, a positive slope is expected meaning high-quality images produce low FMR. A negative slope means that high-quality images produce higher FMR than the low-quality images, which is not desired.

Another observation to make is which IQAA is the best predictor of the comparator whose comparison score was used to generate the graph, in case of Figure 5, comparator Hz1. It is rightly assumed that an IQAA would be the best predictor of its mated comparator, but it is not always the case. As we can see in Figure 5, IQAA C4s or F1 provide a better separation of DET curves than Hx, which is Hz1's mated IQAA.

One point to consider when examining ranked DET curves for the OPS images: Because of the way images in the OPS dataset were selected, it consists of *matchable* images. The small percentage of images which cause biometric recognition errors, might not be problematic in quality. So it is difficult for IQAAs to detect and quantify image impairments to a fine degree. As a result, the DET curves of low, mid, high quality OPS images show less separation than the other datasets.

Results and discussion for different datasets and different comparators can be found in sections 8.3 and 9.

| A2a=NEUROTECHNOLOGY-a | B3=CROSSMATCH | C4s=CAMBRIDGE-s | D3=AWARE | E2a=IRITECH-a | G1=IRISID-1 | I1=KYNEN | Hz1=L1-z1 |
| A2f=NEUROTECHNOLOGY-f | C4x=CAMBRIDGE-x | C4f=CAMBRIDGE-f | F1=MORPHO | E2f=IRITECH-f | G2=IRISID-2 | Hx=L1-x | Hz2=L1-z2 |

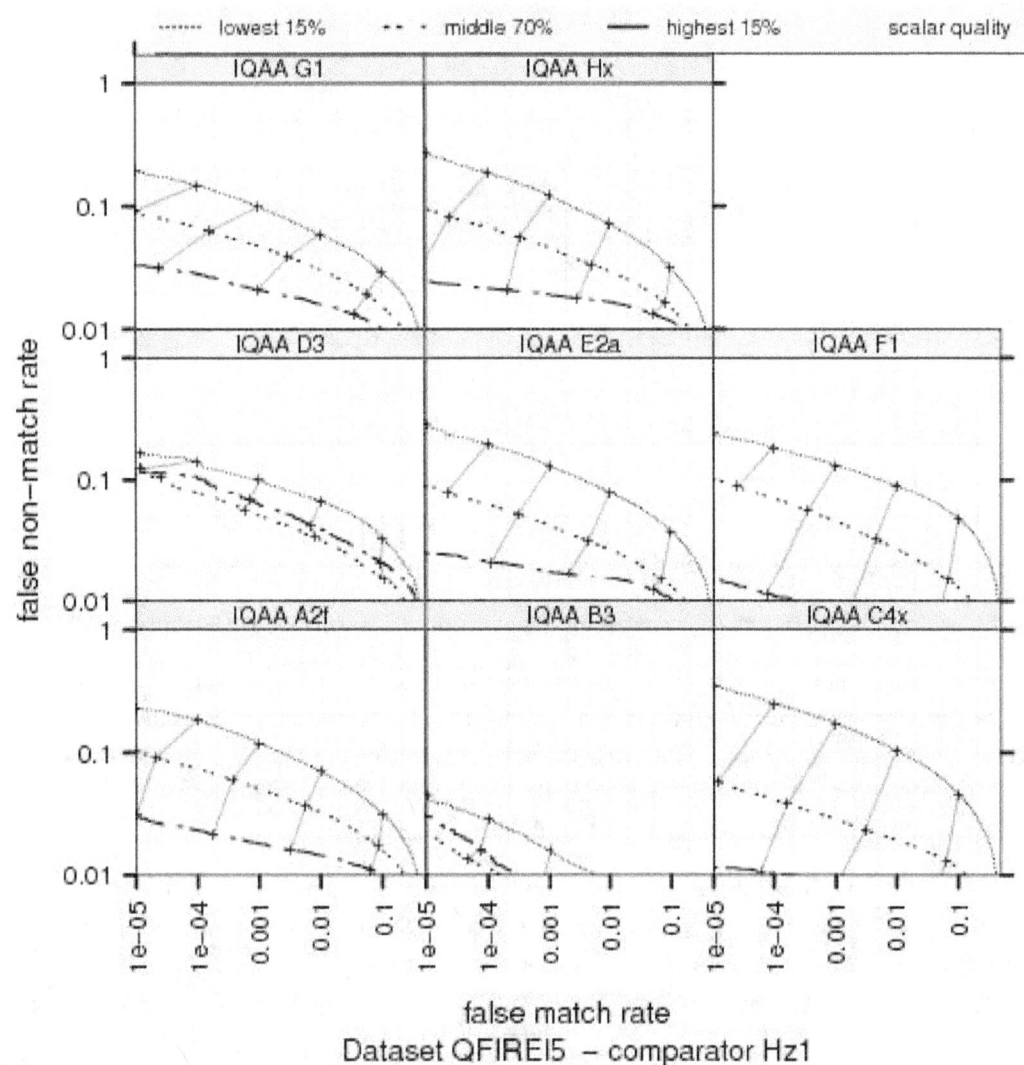

Figure 5: Ranked DET curves for comparator Hz1 and Datasets QFIRE I5. The set of all comparisons are partitioned into three groups based on the pair-wise SCALAR QUALITY scores of the images being compared. The lowest quality set contains comparisons with pairwise quality in the lowest 15 percentile. The highest quality set contains comparisons with pairwise quality in the highest 15 percentile. The rest of the comparisons, namely the middle 70%, make up the third set. The DETs are connected at the same score threshold values (brown lines). Lower FNMR and FMR rates are expected for higher quality images. That means well separated curves in each cell, with the DET curve corresponding to the lowest quality appearing above, and the DET curve of highest quality below all the other curves. Assuming the correct ranking of the DETs, the lines connecting the DET curves have a positive slope if FMR is improved with quality. Note that the DET curves are computed for images that the quality computation succeeded. That is why IQAA B3 shows lower error rates, there were approximately 65K less genuine scores making up its DET curves.

5.6.4 Error vs. reject curve

One metric for comparative evaluation of IQAAs is the error versus reject curves. The goal is to demonstrate how efficiently rejection of low-quality samples results in improved performance. This models the operational case in which quality is maintained by reacquisition after a low-quality sample is detected. Consider that a pair of samples (from the same subject) with qualities $q_i^{(1)}$ and $q_i^{(2)}$ are compared to produce a genuine score, and this is repeated for N such pairs.

| A2a=NEUROTECHNOLOGY-a | B3=CROSSMATCH | C4s=CAMBRIDGE-S | D3=AWARE | E2a=DERMALOG-a | G1=IRISID-1 | I1=KYNEN | Hz1=L1-z1 |
| A2f=NEUROTECHNOLOGY-f | C4n=CAMBRIDGE-N | C4f=CAMBRIDGE-f | F1=MORPHO | E2f=DERMALOG-f | G2=IRISID-2 | Hx=L1-x | Hz2=L1-z2 |

We introduce thresholds u and v that define levels of acceptable quality and define the set of low-quality entries as

$$R(u,v) = \left\{ j \,:\, q_j^{(1)} < u, \quad q_j^{(2)} < v \right\} \tag{14}$$

We compute FNMR as the fraction of genuine scores above threshold computed for the samples *not* in this set

$$\text{FNMR}(\tau) = \frac{M_\psi(\tau)}{M_\psi(-\infty)} \tag{15}$$

$$M_\psi(\tau, u, v) = \sum_{s \in \mathcal{G} \cap R^C} H(s - \tau) \tag{16}$$

where R^C is the complement of R.

If the quality values are perfectly correlated with the genuine comparison scores, setting threshold τ to give an overall FNMR of x and then rejecting x percent with the lowest qualities should result in FNMR of zero after recomputing FNMR.

Figure 6 shows an example of error vs. reject curve for QFIRE I5 images and SHARPNESS scores.

Each cell shows error vs reject curves generated using comparison scores of the comparator identified at the top of the cell and the quality scores of the different IQAAs in different colors. We set the value of τ to give a false non-match rate of ten percent. u and v are varied to show the dependence of FNMR on quality. Pairwise quality is computed using the minimum quality of the two images being compared. Behavior of a perfect IQAA is displayed by the gray dotted line where the rejection of the lowest 10% quality would result in an FNMR of zero.

For an effective IQAA, FNMR should decrease quickly with the fraction of comparisons rejected. An almost flat curve (as in the case with IQAA E2f) suggests that the quality algorithm is not effective in predicting the performance. In each cell, the IQAA closest to the gray dotted line is the best predictor of performance for the cell's comparator. Figure 6 is useful in determining if an IQAA is generalizable to other comparators than its mated one. SHARPNESS scores generated by IQAA C4s is generalizable to all other comparators: it is the best predictor of performance for comparators E2a, G2, C4s, and Hz1, and the second best performer for comparator B3 after its mated IQAA .

The most operationally relevant part of the error vs. reject curves is usually on the left side where a small fraction, x, of low-quality rejections would be tolerable from the perspective of forcing a second enrollment attempt. We set $x = 0.1$, because rejection of more than 10% is not operationally feasible. We note that for ICE2006, QFIRE I5, and QFIRE A5 databases used here, the appropriate fraction is probably larger than 10% because, in the case of ICE2006 dataset, the camera's own quality measurement apparatus was suppressed and QFIRE datasets, by design, contains low quality images (see section 4).

Most of the curves trend in the correct direction (FNMR improves as more low-quality samples are rejected). However, even after rejection of 10%, the FNMR value has fallen by no more than about half of its starting point.

The results of this analysis for SCALAR QUALITY and quality components are discussed in sections 8.4 and 9.

A2a=NEUROTECHNOLOGY-a	B3=CROSSMATCH	C4s=CAMBRIDGE-s	D3=AWARE	E2a=IRITECH-a	G1=IRISID-1	I1=KYNEN	Hz1=L1-z1
A2f=NEUROTECHNOLOGY-f	C4x=CAMBRIDGE-x	C4f=CAMBRIDGE-f	F1=MORPHO	E2f=IRITECH-f	G2=IRISID-2	Hx=L1-x	Hz2=L1-z2

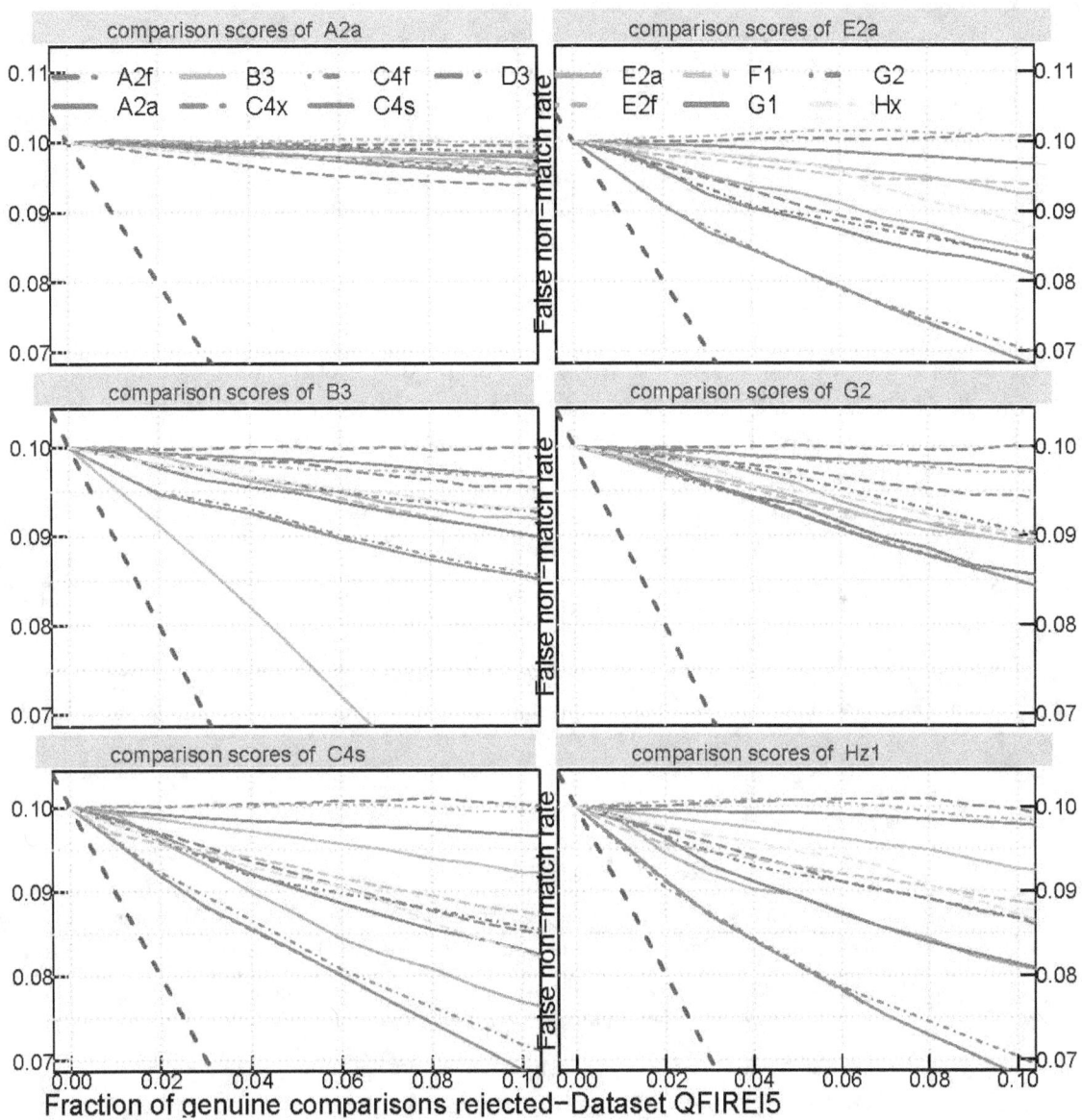

Figure 6: FNMR vs reject curves for SHARPNESS scores on datasets QFIRE I5. The threshold is set to give an initial FNMR = 0.1. The gray dotted line shows the ideal case where the rejection of the ten percent lowest quality results in zero FNMR. IQAAs D3, E2a, A2a, or A2f SHARPNESS scores are not effective. IQAA C4s SHARPNESS scores is a good predictor of performance of all comparators, and performs better than the mated IQAA for comparators Hz1, G2, or E2a. IQAA B3 peforms well only for its native recognition algorithm. Also, recall that B3 has a high failure-to-compute-quality on QFIRE I5 dataset.

5.6.5 Tukey mean difference

Assuming poor quality is the primary reason for false matches or false non-matches, low-quality scores are expected from the images that are falsely rejected or falsely accepted. We perform Tukey Honost Significant Difference (HSD) to test if the difference in mean of quality scores are significant. Table 9 in Section 8 shows the 95% confidence interval for the difference in mean of quality scores for images that are correctly matched (successful verification attempt) and those that are falsely rejected (failed verification attempt) for all combinations of IQAA and comparators. If the interval contains zero, the difference is not significant, and therefore quality scores are not predictive of performance. Furthermore, for IQAAs with monotinically increasing quality scores, the difference should be a positive number (e.g., higher score indicating better quality). Negative intervals suggest that images involved in failed verifications have higher-quality values than those involved in successful verification. Such an outcome contradicts the monotonically increasing in performance assumption.

The procedure that generates Table 9 follows:

▷ For each dataset,

▷ For each IQCE comparator, and each IQAA,

1. Compute the pairwise quality (geometric mean) for all genuine comparisons.

2. Compute the mean of pairwise quality for image pairs involved in successful verification attempts, i.e., $s \leq \tau$ where s is a genuine score and τ is the threshold which we set to give FMR = 0.001.

3. Compute the mean of pairwise quality for image pairs involved in failed verification attempts, i.e., $s > \tau$ where s is a genuine score and τ is the threshold which we set to give FMR = 0.001.

4. Perform Tukey HSD to test if the mean of the above two sets are significantly different.

Similarly, the Tukey HSD test is applied to the pairwise quality of image pairs that are correctly rejected and those that result in false matches. Specifically,

▷ For each dataset,

▷ For each IQCE comparator, and each IQAA,

1. Compute the pairwise quality (geometric mean) for all impostor comparisons.

2. Compute the mean of pairwise quality for image pairs involved in successful verification attempts, i.e., $s > \tau$ where s is a impostor score and τ is the threshold which we set to give FMR = 0.001.

3. Compute the mean of pairwise quality for image pairs involved in failed verification attempts, i.e., $s \leq \tau$ where s is an impostor score and τ is the threshold which we set to give FMR = 0.001.

4. Perform the Tukey HSD to test if the mean of the above two sets are significantly different.

Results for SCALAR QUALITY are shown in Section 8, Tables 9 and 10 and in Section 9 for other quality components. Each cell of Table 10 contains 95% confidence intervals of difference in mean of pairwise quality for the two groups: a) image pairs involved in impostor comparisons that generate comparison scores larger than the threshold (i.e., correctly rejected), and b) those that generate comparison scores less than or equal to the threshold (i.e., falsely matched). The quality scores are generated by the algorithm identified by the column and the comparison scores by the algorithm identified by the row. Likewise, each cell of Table 9 contains 95% confidence intervals of difference in mean of pairwise quality for images involved in successful verification (i.e., genuine score less than or equal the threshold) and those falsely rejected (i.e., genuine score larger than the threshold).

A2a=NEUROTECHNOLOGY-a	B3=CROSSMATCH	C4s=CAMBRIDGE-s	D3=AWARE	E2a=IRITECH-a	G1=IRISID-1	I1=KYNEN	Hz1=L1-z1
A2f=NEUROTECHNOLOGY-f	C4x=CAMBRIDGE-x	C4f=CAMBRIDGE-f	F1=MORPHO	E2f=IRITECH-f	G2=IRISID-2	Hx=L1-x	Hz2=L1-z2

5.6.6 Heatmaps: Investigating the effect of quality variation between the two images involved in a comparison on performance

All the evaluation methods discussed so far explain the relationship between either comparison scores or biometric error rates (FNMR and FMR) to the *pairwise* quality of the two images being compared. While there are many valid technical reasons and operational relevance to justify combining the quality scores of the images, pairwise quality fails to exhibit the effect of variation between the quality of the two images being compared on performance. To examine dependence of FNMR on similarity (or lack of) quality scores of the two images being compared, we use heatmaps (i.e., surface plots) to visualize the three variables $(qv, qe, N(\text{FNMR}))$, where

$$N(\text{FN\"MR}) = 1 - \exp(1 - \frac{\text{FN\"MR}}{\text{FNMR}_0}) \tag{17}$$

FNMR_0 is the nominal FNMR which is the false non-match rate computed over all the images at a given threshold. The normalized FNMR, FN\"MR , is the false non-match rate realized for the samples with enrollment and verification quality scores in the ranges defined by qe and qv respectively, at the same comparison score threshold as FNMR_0, in this case at FMR = 0.001.

The result for IQAA F1's SHARPNESS score on QFIRE I5 images is shown in Figure 7.

Below is the procedure to generate Figure 7 and similar figures in this document.

▷ For each IQAA , and each comparator

1. Set threshold τ such that FMR = 0.001 over all the images. Compute FNMR_0 at threshold τ. Note that τ and FNMR_0 are different for different comparators.

2. Divide the set of verification quality scores, q_{verif}, into ten equal count bins using its quantiles as bin boundaries. Call these ten bins $qv_1, ..., qv_{10}$.

3. Divide the set of enrollment quality scores, q_{enrol}, into ten equal count bins using its quantiles as bin boundaries. Call these ten bins $qe_1, ..., qe_{10}$. The two steps above make a rectangular grid defined by q_{verif} and q_{enrol} values.

4. Compute $N(\text{FNMR})$ (Equation 17) for the set of enrolled images that have quality in the qe_j bin and verification images with quality in the qv_i bin. Conceptually, the $N(\text{FNMR})$ values form a matrix where the q_{verif} and q_{enrol} represent rows and columns of that matrix, with the corresponding $N(\text{FNMR})$ as its z value.

5. Plot a surface (or heatmap) plot for the $(qv, qe, N(\text{FNMR}))$s.

Each cell in Figure 7 shows dependence of FNMR of different comparators on IQAA F1's SHARPNESS scores. The x-axis shows the intervals of enrollment image quality score. The y-axis represents intervals for verification image quality scores. The normalized FNMR observed for enrollment images whose quality scores are in the ith quantile and verification images with their quality scores in the jth quantile is illustrated by color and its intensity.

The color key on the right shows the $\frac{\text{FN\"MR}}{\text{FNMR}_0}$:

- Improvements in FNMR , $(\frac{\text{FN\"MR}}{\text{FNMR}_0} < 1)$, are shown in shades of yellow/green, where darker means a bigger improvement.

- Degradations in FNMR , $(\frac{\text{FN\"MR}}{\text{FNMR}_0} > 1)$, are shown in shades of blue, where darker indicates more severe degradation.

| A2a=NEUROTECHNOLOGY-a | B3=CROSSMATCH | C4s=CAMBRIDGE-s | D3=AWARE | E2a=IRITECH-a | G1=IRISID-1 | I1=KYNEN | Hz1=L1-z1 |
| A2f=NEUROTECHNOLOGY-f | C4x=CAMBRIDGE-x | C4f=CAMBRIDGE-f | F1=MORPHO | E2f=IRITECH-f | G2=IRISID-2 | Hx=L1-x | Hz2=L1-z2 |

- No change in FNMR ($\frac{FNMR}{FNMR_0} = 1$) is shown in white.

Images with IQAA F1's SHARPNESS scores less than 11 increase FNMR. Images with IQAA F1's SHARPNESS scores larger than 70 decrease FNMR.

The lowest FNMR should be achieved if both images have high SHARPNESS scores (top right corner of each cell). Highest FNMR should occur when either enrolled or verification image has a very low SHARPNESS score (left edge and lower edge).

Interestingly, FNMR improves if both images have very low SHARPNESS scores (bottom left corner of each cell).

Another possible (and acceptable) outcome is when images with similar quality scores produce low FNMR, and FNMR increases as the difference in the quality scores gets larger. An example is Figure 32(b). This characteristic or trend is referred to as "sameness" in this report.

Figure 7 allows for the assessment of how well an IQAA can predict performance of non-native iris recognition algorithms. For example, in the case of Figure 7, since the behavior is the same across all comparators, we conclude that IQAA F1 SHARPNESS measure could be used to assess matchability of images for its native iris recognition algorithm as well as other comparators.

6 Evaluation of IQAAs robustness

IQAAs with high failure-to-compute or no-attempt-to-compute-quality rate are not operationally feasible.

Table 8 shows the number of images that fail to produce a quality vector per IQAA and dataset. Except for SDKs G1 and G2, all failures were due to involuntary failure to extract features (i.e., the SDKs' return values = 6 per IQCE con-ops). SDKs G1 and G2 return values were 2 or 4 for images that no quality vector was generated. Return values 2 or 4 indicate voluntary refusal to generate a template or process the image.

Unless otherwise stated, the results presented in this document are for cases where image quality computation **did not fail**. That is IQCE metrics did not consider a penalty for cases that an IQAA did not generate a quality score, and evaluated IQAAs based on the goodness of the quality scores that they were able to generate. The caveat is this decision might make an IQAA with high failure-to-compute or no-attempt-to-compute a quality score to seem to be more effective than a *robust* IQAA which computes has a zero failure-to-compute rate.

7 Evaluation of IQAAs computation speed

The box and whisker plots of Figure 8 show the times needed to generate the quality vectors. The plots include data for the various datasets and all IQAAs.

For each of the box and whisker plots, the green dot inside the box shows the median computation time. The box contains the middle 50% of the data, and the whiskers are drawn at the 1.5 times the inter-quartile range of the data which is roughly 2 standard deviations. The inter-quartile range is the difference between the first and third quartile. Points more than 1.5 times the inter-quartile range above the third quartile and points more than 1.5 times the inter-

| A2a=NEUROTECHNOLOGY-a | B3=CROSSMATCH | C4s=CAMBRIDGE-s | D3=AWARE | E2a=IRITECH-a | G1=IRISID-1 | I1=KYNEN | Hz1=L1-z1 |
| A2f=NEUROTECHNOLOGY-f | C4x=CAMBRIDGE-x | C4f=CAMBRIDGE-f | F1=MORPHO | E2f=IRITECH-f | G2=IRISID-2 | Hx=L1-x | Hz2=L1-z2 |

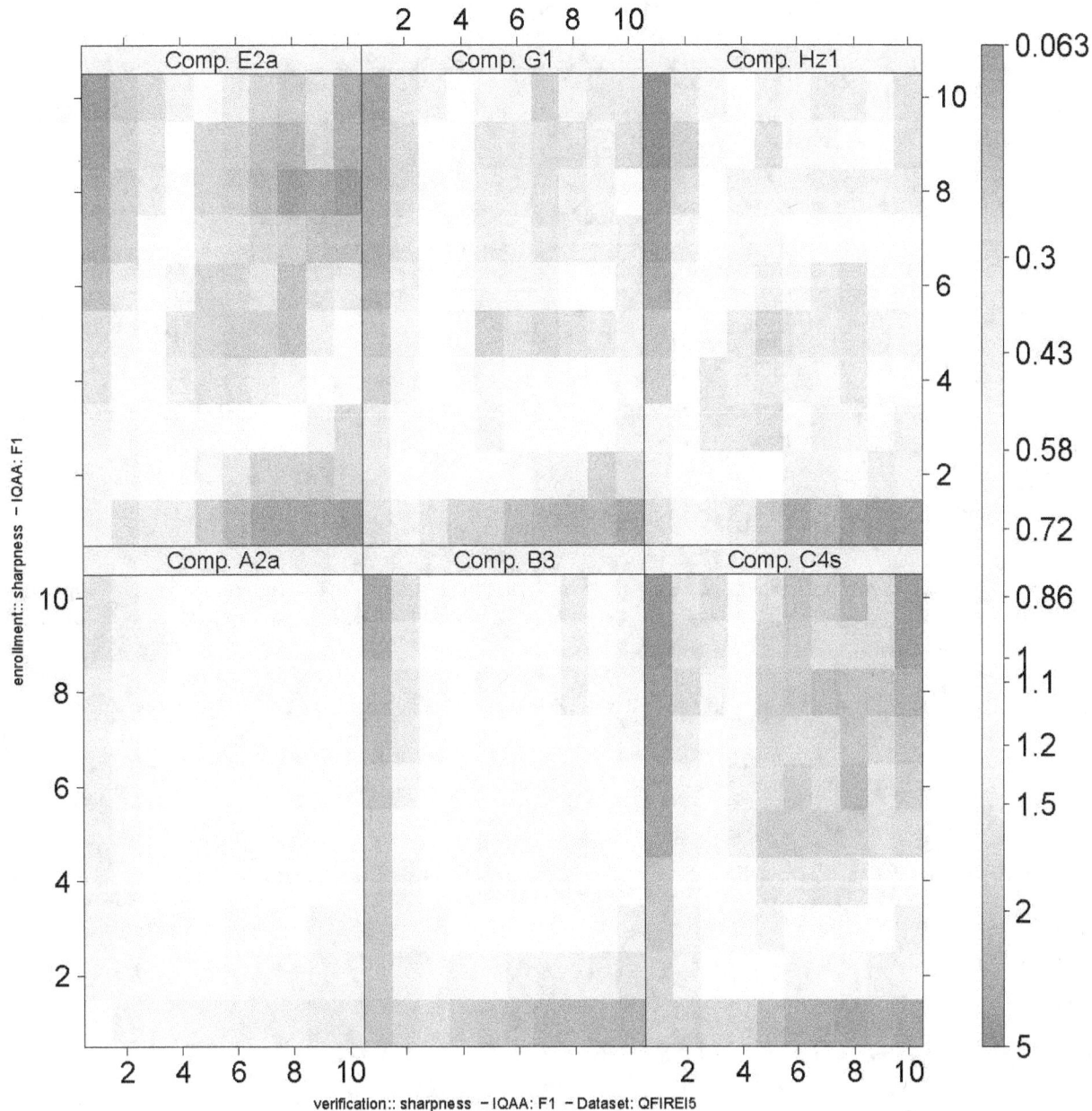

Figure 7: FNMR vs (q_{verif}, q_{enrol}). The y-axis represents quality of the enrollment samples. Quality of verification samples are on the x-axis. The color in each cell represents the identified comparator's $\frac{FNMR}{FNMR_0}$ on QFIRE I5 images with the given pair of the IQAA F1's SHARPNESS scores. $FNMR_0$ is the nominal FNMR which is the false non-match rate computed over all the images at the same comparison score threshold, in this case at FMR = 0.001. Yellow/Green color represent an improvement in FNMR. Blue color represent a degradation of FNMR. White color means no change in FNMR.

quartile range below the first quartile are defined as outliers and are plotted individually shown as the green points outside the whiskers.

Dataset	ICE2006	OPS	QFIREA5	QFIREI5
# images	56871	32640	4365	14165
# gen. comp	4121195	16320	24908	238390
IQAA				
A2a	20	5	525	3712
A2f	0	0	0	0
B3	168	255	28	2541
C4f	0	0	0	0
C4s	0	0	0	0
C4x	0	0	0	0
D3	113	928	2195	8224
E2a	4	0	0	1
E2f	7	0	3	23
F1	0	0	0	0
G1	392	22	75	177
G2	248	28	23	121
Hx	0	2	0	4
I1	0	0	-	-

Table 8: IQAA Robustnss: Number of images failed by each IQAA per datasets. Number of images in each test datasets is reported in the second row under dataset name.

The notable results on computational efficiency are as follows:

▷ Across IQAAs quality computation time varies by two orders of magnitude. The three submissions from Cambridge University (IQAA C4x, C4s, and C4f) are the fastest implementations, with an average 30 milliseconds per image across all four datasets.

▷ IQAA I1 is the slowest on ICE2006 and OPS datasets. Results for I1 is not available on QFIRE datasets since it failed on all the images.

▷ The difference between the "slow but accurate" and "fast" submissions of two participants is substantial. A2a is an order of magnitude slower than A2f.

▷ Quality computation time across datasets varies, but the order of IQAAs stays the same.

A2a=NEUROTECHNOLOGY-a	B3=CROSSMATCH	C4s=CAMBRIDGE-s	D3=AWARE	E2a=IRITECH-a	G1=IRISID-1	I1=KYNEN	Hz1=L1-z1
A2f=NEUROTECHNOLOGY-f	C4x=CAMBRIDGE-x	C4f=CAMBRIDGE-f	F1=MORPHO	E2f=IRITECH-f	G2=IRISID-2	Hx=L1-x	Hz2=L1-z2

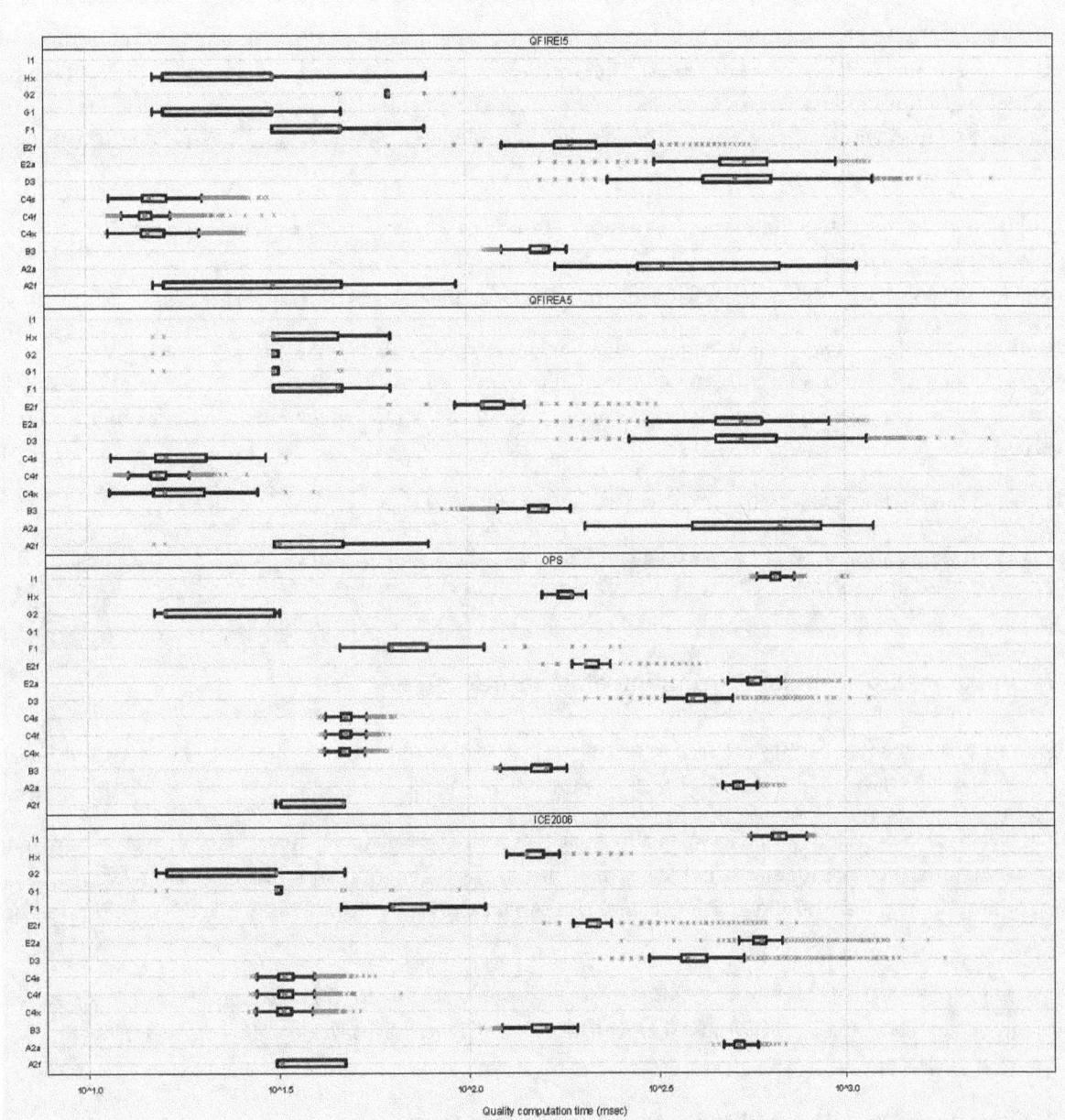

Figure 8: Box and whisker plots of the IQAAs computation time. The green dot inside the box shows the median computation time. The box contains the middle 50% of the data, and the whiskers are drawn at the 1.5 times the inter-quartile range of the data which is roughly 2 standard deviations. The inter-quartile range is the difference between the first and third quartile. Points more than 1.5 times the inter-quartile range above the third quartile and points more than 1.5 times the inter-quartile range below the first quartile are defined as outliers and are plotted individually shown as the green points outside the whiskers. Across IQAAs quality computation time varies by two orders of magnitude. The three submissions from Cambridge University (IQAA C4x, C4s, and C4f) are the fastest implementations, with an average 30 milliseconds per image across all four datasets. Quality computation time across datasets varies, but the order of IQAAs stays the same.

8 Predictive power of scalar quality

Biometric sample quality assessment algorithms are intended to produce quality scores that predict performance metrics such as false match or false non-match rates. Thus, quality scores should reflect the sensitivities and failure modes of matching algorithms. The term quality should not be solely attributable to the acquisition settings of the sample, such as image resolution, dimensions in pixels, or gray-scale/color bit depth. However, such factors may affect sample utility and could contribute to the overall quality score.

IQCE API required all IQAA submissions to produce a SCALAR QUALITY score for each input image. The SCALAR QUALITY scores shall be in the range of 0–100, plus 255 to handle the special case, where scores have not been computed. These values are in accordance with ISO/IEC 29794 Biometric sample quality – Part 1: Framework [2].

The design intent for an IQAA is to compute a scalar image quality score for which observed FNMR of high-quality images shall be smaller than for images with low-quality scores. An iris image with quality score of zero should be an unusable iris image. Quality score of 100 is the highest iris quality value, where lowest recognition error (or none) is expected.

The distribution of the SCALAR QUALITY scores is shown in Figure 9.

We evaluate the SCALAR QUALITY scores on their ability to predict the performance of IQCE comparators. The following subsections present the results.

8.1 Relationship with the distribution of genuine scores

Figure 10 shows the relationship between SCALAR QUALITY scores and genuine comparison scores for different IQAA and comparators. The procedure to generate this Figure is explained in Section 5.6.1.

All IQAAs trend in the right direction; low-quality images produce high genuine scores. Some display a sharper decrease in quality for high genuine (dissimilarity) scores than others. The best performer is IQAA C4x followed by IQAA Hx and A2a. Both are generalizable as the similar behavior is observed across all comparators, while this is not the case for IQAA B3.

IQAA A2a SCALAR QUALITY scores of QFIRE A5 images increase slightly for high genuine scores. This means some of the high-quality images can produce false non-matches. IQAA A2a performs well on ICE2006 and QFIRE I5 .

8.2 Relationship with the distribution of impostor scores

Figure 11 shows the relationship between SCALAR QUALITY quality scores and impostor scores. Mostly, quality scores do not change with impostor scores. Some IQAA like C4x exhibits an increase in quality for some comparators' high impostor scores. This can be interpreted as high-quality images contain sufficient information so that an impostor comparison results in a high dissimilarity score.

| A2a=NEUROTECHNOLOGY-a | B3=CROSSMATCH | C4s=CAMBRIDGE-s | D3=AWARE | E2a=IRITECH-a | G1=IRISID-1 | I1=KYNEN | Hz1=L1-z1 |
| A2f=NEUROTECHNOLOGY-f | C4x=CAMBRIDGE-x | C4f=CAMBRIDGE-f | F1=MORPHO | E2f=IRITECH-f | G2=IRISID-2 | Hx=L1-x | Hz2=L1-z2 |

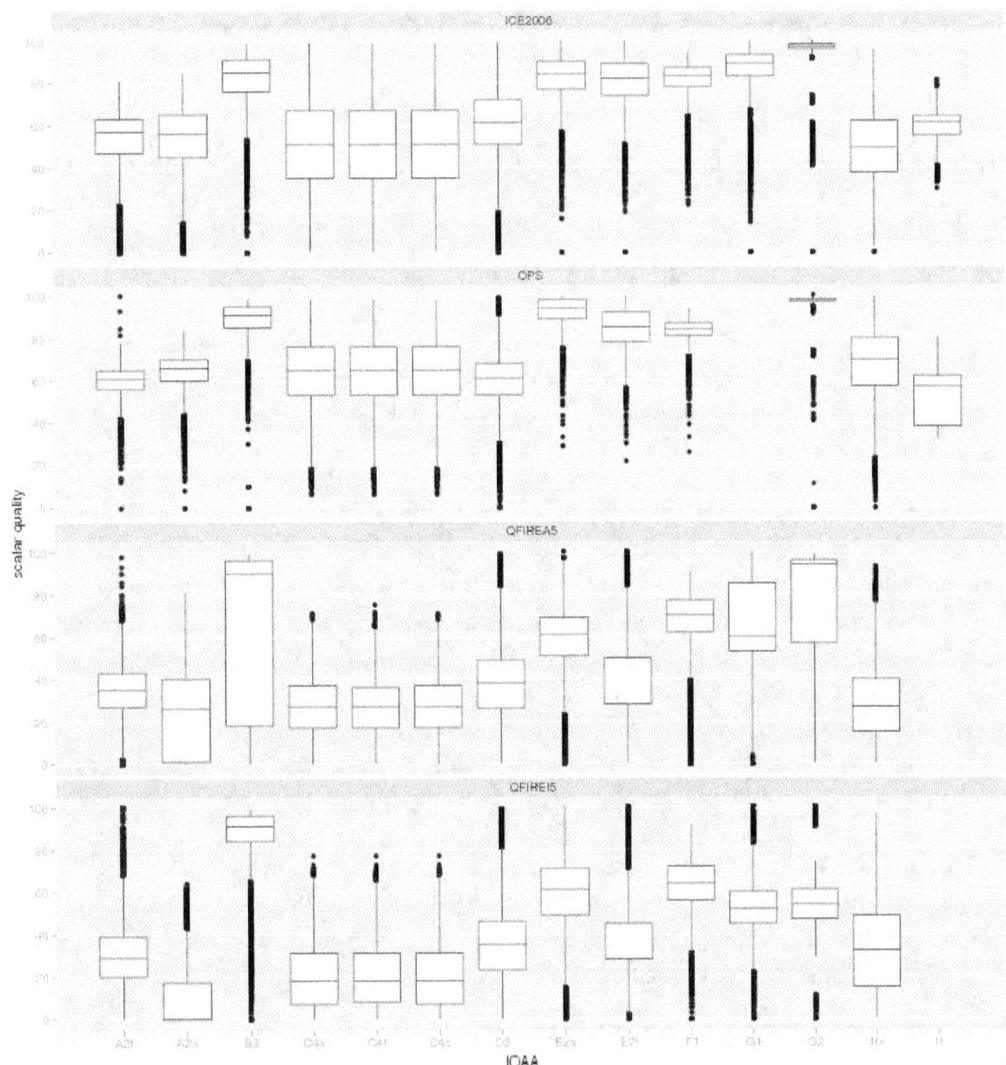

Figure 9: Box and whisker plots of SCALAR QUALITY scores across all IQAAs and for each dataset.

8.3   Ranked DET : Do low-quality images produce high FNMR or FMR?

DET curves for images with low, medium, and high SCALAR QUALITY quality scores are shown in Figure 12. See Section 5.6.3 for details on how Figure 12 is generated.

IQAA A2a, F1 and Hx give the best performance ranking, followed by IQAA C4x. IQAA C4x SCALAR QUALITY scores give a reasonable performance ranking for all comparators and all datasets except ICE2006. Its highest-quality images produce a higher FNMR than its medium quality. This is apparent by crossing of the DET curves in Figure 12(a). IQAA B3, G1, and E2a suffer from the same problem on the ICE2006 datase: high FNMR is observed for the highest quality images. Their FMRs trend in the right direction though, low FMR is observed for high-quality images. Also, note the flatness of the DET curves for these four IQAAs highest-quality images.

A2a=NEUROTECHNOLOGY-a	B3=CROSSMATCH	C4s=CAMBRIDGE-s	D3=AWARE	E2a=IRITECH-a	G1=IRISID-1	I1=KYNEN	Hz1=L1-z1
A2f=NEUROTECHNOLOGY-f	C4x=CAMBRIDGE-x	C4f=CAMBRIDGE-f	F1=MORPHO	E2f=IRITECH-f	G2=IRISID-2	Hx=L1-x	Hz2=L1-z2

IQAA D3 does not provide performance ranking for QFIRE I5 or QFIRE A5 images. IQAA I1 gives the worst performance ranking.

8.4   Effect of quality on FNMR : How quickly FNMR improves when poor quality samples are rejected?

The performance of IQAAs depends on the dataset, as shown in Figures 13 and 14.

For ICE2006 images, IQAAs E2a, Hx and F1 are generally the best performers. E2a slightly outperforms the other two, and performs close to the ideal case (gray dotted line) for its native recognition algorithm. IQAA A2a and B3 are good predictor of performance for their native recognition algoithms, but not for other comparators. The least effective IQAAs are G1, G2, and D3.

For OPS images, IQAAs performance are about the same. In the best case, 10% rejection reduces FNMR by only two percentage point (from 0.1 to 0.08). Recall that the procedure for selection of OPS images made them the "easiest to match" compared to the other three datasets used here. This is evident from the DET curves of Figure 3, where the OPS dataset has the lowest error rates. Being "easiest to match" implies that OPS images are mostly good quality, and the biometric errors are not necessarily due to image quality impairments. Nevertheless, IQAAs E2a, Hx, F1 and C4 are generally the better performers on the OPS dataset. In this group, E2a and Hz slightly outperform the rest. They are a better predictor of performance even for other IQAAs' native recognition algorithms. IQAA B3 is the best predictor of its native recognition algorithm. IQAA I1, D3 and G2 are the least effective quality assessment algorithms for the OPS images.

On QFIRE I5 images, IQAA C4x, C4s, and C4f are the best performers for all comparators, except B3. IQAA B3 is the best predictor of performance of its native recognition algorithm (B3), followed by IQAAs C4x, C4s, and C4f. IQAAs D3, A2a, and E2f are least-effective. Comparator A2a accuracy drops for QFIRE I5 images. As a result, its error vs. reject curves of QFIRE I5 images are incomprehensible for all IQAAS.

On QFIRE A5 images, except for comparator B3, IQAAs C4s and C4x are the best performers, even better than the other comparators' native IQAA. For comparator B3, E2f outperforms the other IQAAs including B3 which is the second best performer. For comparator G2, performance of C4x, C4s, C4f, B3, and Hx are comparable. IQAA D3, A2a are not effective for any comparators.

Reduction in FNMR after rejection of low-quality images is not significant for any IQAA. The best result is for IQAA Hx and comparator C4s, that after rejecting 10% of the lowest quality images, FNMR decreases to 0.08 from its original value of 0.1. Comparator A2a accuracy drops for QFIRE A5 images. Consequently, the error vs. reject curves are not meaningful.

8.5   Test of significance :: Do the images involved in successful verification attempts have significantly higher quality scores than those involved in failed verification attempts?

The results of the Tukey HSD tests of significance for the difference in SCALAR QUALITY scores are shown in Tables 9 and 10. The procedure to generate these tables is explained in Section 5.6.5.

| A2a=NEUROTECHNOLOGY-a | B3=CROSSMATCH | C4s=CAMBRIDGE-s | D3=AWARE | E2a=IRITECH-a | G1=IRISID-1 | I1=KYNEN | Hz1=L1-z1 |
| A2f=NEUROTECHNOLOGY-f | C4x=CAMBRIDGE-x | C4f=CAMBRIDGE-f | F1=MORPHO | E2f=IRITECH-f | G2=IRISID-2 | Hx=L1-x | Hz2=L1-z2 |

Table 9 shows the 95% confidence interval for difference in mean of pairwise quality for images verified correctly (i.e., the genuine score equal or less than threshold) and those rejected falsely (i.e., the genuine score larger than threshold). Few IQAAs failed the test of significance for the OPS images particularly comparators E2a and Hz1. As mentioned before, because of the way images in the OPS dataset were selected, it consists of *matchable* images. The very small percentage of images that cause biometric recognition errors (particularly for the more accurate comparators E2a, A2a and Hz1), makes it difficult for IQAAs to detect and quantify image impairments to a fine degree.

IQAA D3 does not produce significantly higher SCALAR QUALITY scores for QFIRE A5 images that are correctly verified by comparators C4s or Hz1. All other IQAAs give significantly higher SCALAR QUALITY scores to images involved in successful verification than those producing false rejects.

Table 10 shows the 95% confidence interval of difference in mean of pairwise quality for images correctly rejected (i.e., the impostor score equal or greater than threshold) and those falsely matched (i.e., the impostor score less than threshold). IQAA D3 fails the test of significance for at least two comparators on QFIRE A5 and QFIRE I5 images.

8.6 Effect of variation between the two samples: does sameness matter?

Figures 15-17 show the change in FNMR for arious quantiles of SCALAR QUALITY scores of dataset ICE2006, QFIRE A5, and QFIRE I5. The OPS dataset is ignored because the lack of images with sufficient impairments makes its surface plots incomprehensible.

Section 5.6.6 discusses the procedure that generates these figures. The x-axis shows the intervals of enrollment image quality score. The y-axis shows intervals for verification image quality scores. The $\frac{FNMR}{FNMR_0}$ observed for enrollment images whose quality are in the ith quantile and verification images with their quality in the jth quantiles is illustrated by the color. Improvements in FNMR, $(\frac{FNMR}{FNMR_0} < 1)$, are shown in shades of yellow/green, where darker means a bigger improvement. Degradations in FNMR, $(\frac{FNMR}{FNMR_0} > 1)$, are shown in shades of blue, where darker indicates more severe degradation. No change in FNMR $(\frac{FNMR}{FNMR_0} = 1)$ is shown in white. The color key on the right shows the $\frac{FNMR}{FNMR_0}$.

$FNMR_0$ is the nominal FNMR which is the false non-match rate computed over all the images at the same comparison score threshold, in this case at FMR = 0.001.

On ICE2006 images (Figure 15), IQAAs mostly trend in the right direction. High FNMR is observed, if either the enrolled sample or the verification sample is of low quality. This is shown by a dark blue color at the left most and bottom portion of each cell. FNMR decreases as the quality of either image improves.

Using IQAAs B3 or D3, comparator's B3 FNMR increases when the quality of the images being compared are very different.

IQAAs A2a, Hx, E2a, C4x, F1 and B3 illustrate higher discrimination of quality for ICE2006 images.

The IQAAs ' ability to differentiate "hard to match" from "easy to match" images drops when dealing with QFIRE A5 or QFIRE I5 images. The best performer is IQAA Hx with comparator C4s, followed by E2a and F1 for comparator Hz1. IQAA C4x is a reasonable predictor of performance for all comparators. IQAA B3 is a good predictor of its native recognition algorithm, but not for any other comparators. IQAA D3 is not effective in predicting performance of any comparators.

51

A2a=NEUROTECHNOLOGY-a	B3=CROSSMATCH	C4s=CAMBRIDGE-s	D3=AWARE	E2a=IRITECH-a	G1=IRISID-1	I1=KYNEN	Hz1=L1-z1
A2f=NEUROTECHNOLOGY-f	C4x=CAMBRIDGE-x	C4f=CAMBRIDGE-f	F1=MORPHO	E2f=IRITECH-f	G2=IRISID-2	Hx=L1-x	Hz2=L1-z2

8.7   Observations and conclusions

Overall, IQAA C4x SCALAR QUALITY scores are the best predictor of performance. It performs reasonably well for all datasets and comparators. It handles challenging images of QFIRE A5 and QFIRE I5 better than any other IQAA . With no failure to compute quality score, IQAA C4x is the most robust algorithm.

IQAAs Hx, E2a F1 and A2a perform reasonably well. IQAA B3 is the best predictor of its native recognition algorithm, but it is not generalizable to other comparators. Same is true for IQAA G1, its performance drops for non-native recognition algorithms, but not as severely as B3. The least effective IQAAs are D3 and I1.

A2a=NEUROTECHNOLOGY-a	B3=CROSSMATCH	C4s=CAMBRIDGE-s	D3=AWARE	E2a=IRITECH-a	G1=IRISID-1	I1=KYNEN	Hz1=L1-z1
A2f=NEUROTECHNOLOGY-f		C4x=CAMBRIDGE-x	C4f=CAMBRIDGE-f	F1=MORPHO	E2f=IRITECH-f	G2=IRISID-2	Hx=L1-x	Hz2=L1-z2

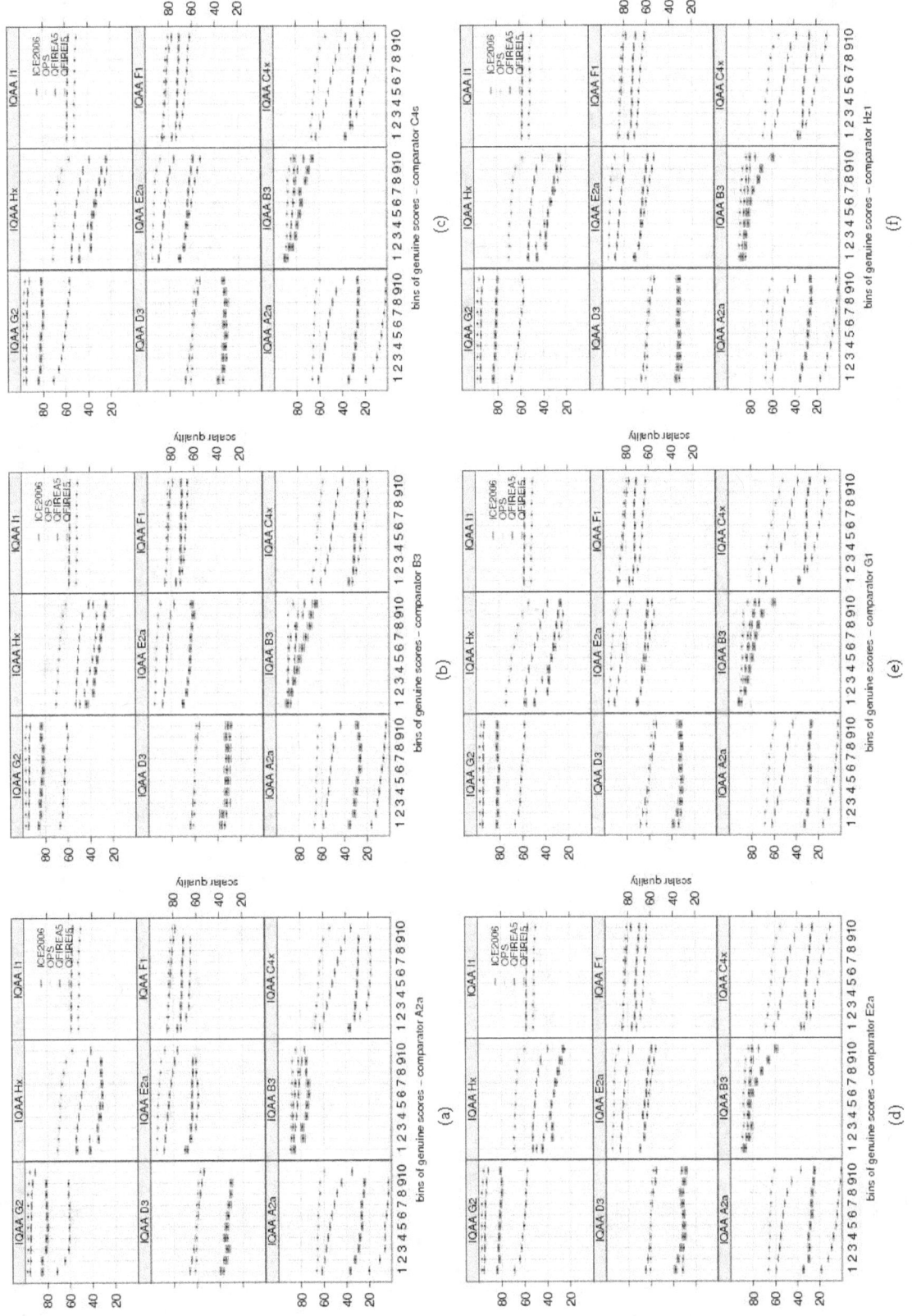

Figure 10: Pairwise SCALAR QUALITY scores vs. genuine score for the primary Class Z submissions of each participant. Each plot shows quality scores computed by a different IQAA. Genuine scores are divided equally into ten groups. Groups overlap by 5 percent, meaning 5% of the data in one bin also belongs to the next bin. The bootstrapped pairwise quality for each group is shown in a box and whisker plot. Pairwise quality is computed as geometric mean of the quality of the two samples being compared. All IQAAs show decrease in quality score as genuine comparison scores increases. IQAA C4s exhibits the highest change rate followed by IQAA Hx and then A2a.

| A2a=NEUROTECHNOLOGY-a | B3=CROSSMATCH | C4s=CAMBRIDGE-s | D3=AWARE | E2a=IRITECH-a | G1=IRISID-1 | I1=KYNEN | Hz1=L1-z1 |
| A2f=NEUROTECHNOLOGY-f | C4x=CAMBRIDGE-x | C4f=CAMBRIDGE-f | F1=MORPHO | E2f=IRITECH-f | G2=IRISID-2 | Hx=L1-x | Hz2=L1-z2 |

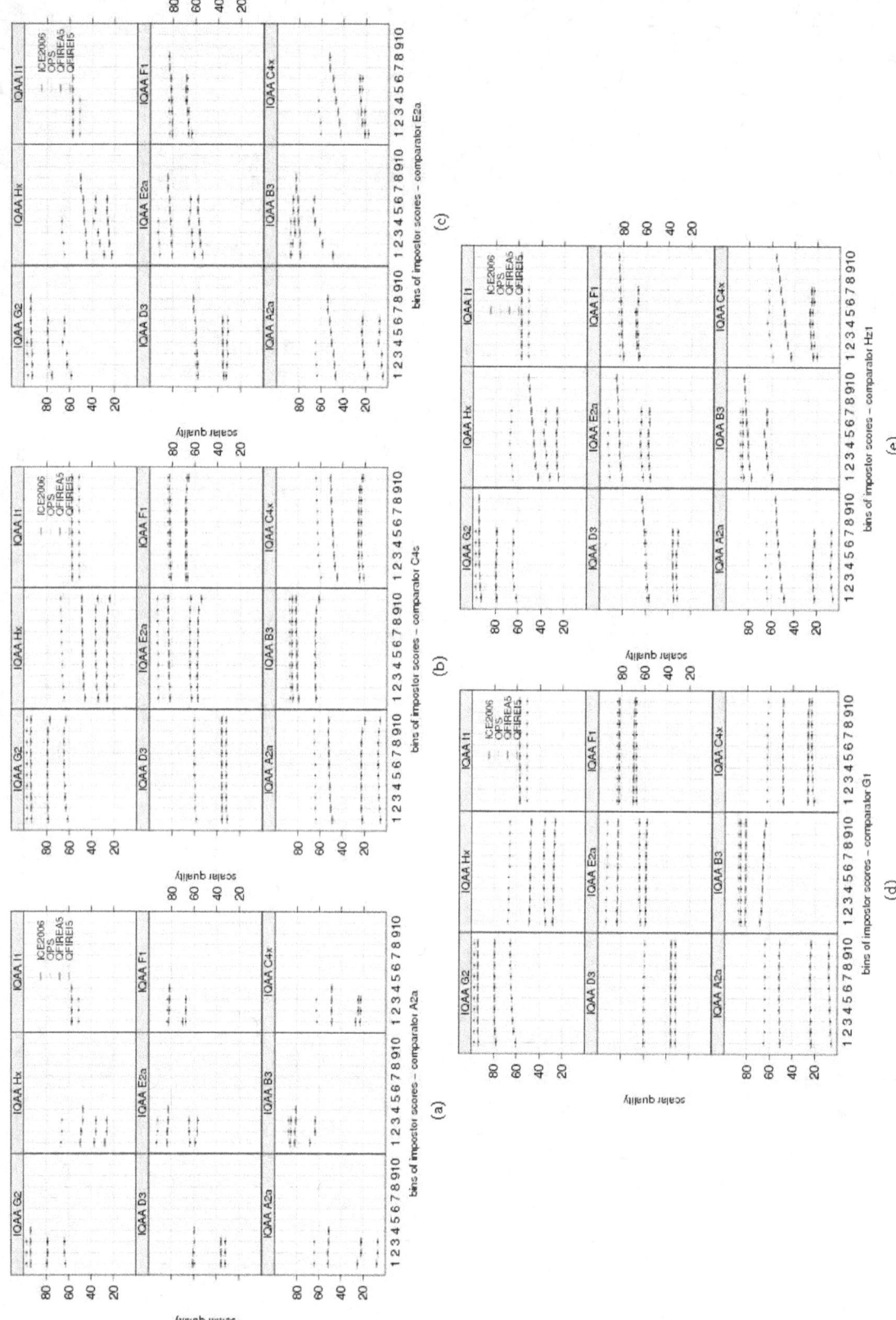

Figure 11: Pairwise SCALAR QUALITY scores vs. impostor scores for the primary Class Z submissions of each participant. Each plot shows quality scores computed by a different IQAA. Similar to plots of Figure 10, impostor scores are divided equally into ten groups, overlapping by 5 percent. The bootstrapped pairwise quality for each group is shown in a box and whisker plot. Pairwise quality is computed as geometric mean of the quality of the two samples being compared.

A2a=NEUROTECHNOLOGY-a	B3=CROSSMATCH	C4s=CAMBRIDGE-s	D3=AWARE	E2a=IRITECH-a	G1=IRISID-1	I1=KYNEN	Hz1=L1-z1
A2f=NEUROTECHNOLOGY-f	C4x=CAMBRIDGE-x	C4f=CAMBRIDGE-f	F1=MORPHO	E2f=IRITECH-f	G2=IRISID-2	Hx=L1-x	Hz2=L1-z2

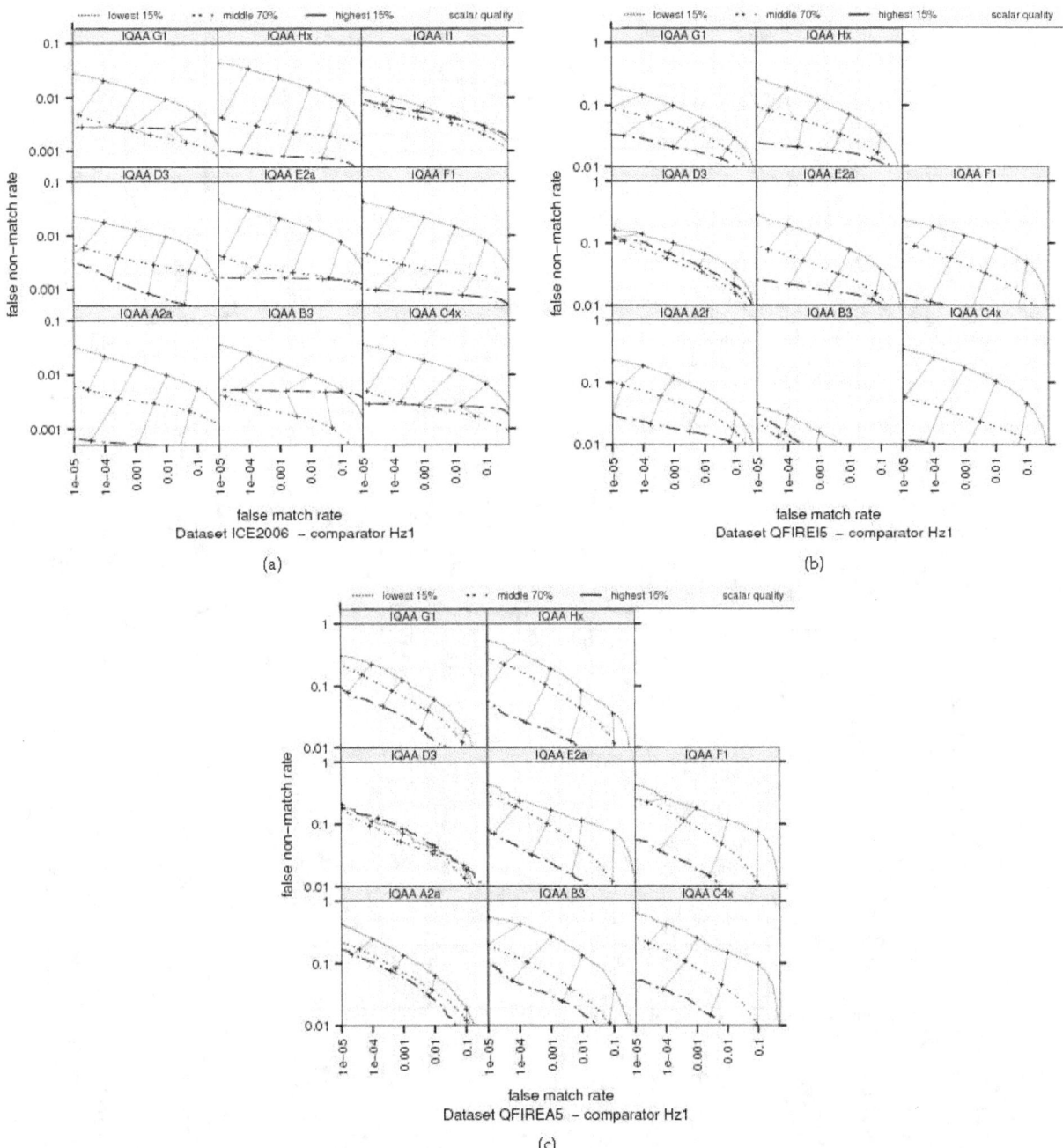

Figure 12: Ranked DET curves for comparator Hz1 and Datasets ICE2006, QFIRE A5, and QFIRE I5. The set of all comparisons are partitioned into three groups based on the pair-wise SCALAR QUALITY of the images being compared. The lowest quality set contains comparisons with pairwise quality in the lowest 15 percentile. The highest quality set contains comparisons with pairwise quality in the highest 15 percentile. The rest of the comparisons, namely the middle 70%, make up the third set. The DETs are connected at the same score threshold values (brown lines). Lower FNMR and FMR rates are expected for higher quality images.

A2a=NEUROTECHNOLOGY-a	B3=CROSSMATCH	C4s=CAMBRIDGE-s	D3=AWARE	E2a=IRITECH-a	G1=IRISID-1	I1=KYNEN	Hz1=L1-z1
A2f=NEUROTECHNOLOGY-f	C4x=CAMBRIDGE-x	C4f=CAMBRIDGE-f	F1=MORPHO	E2f=IRITECH-f	G2=IRISID-2	Hx=L1-x	Hz2=L1-z2

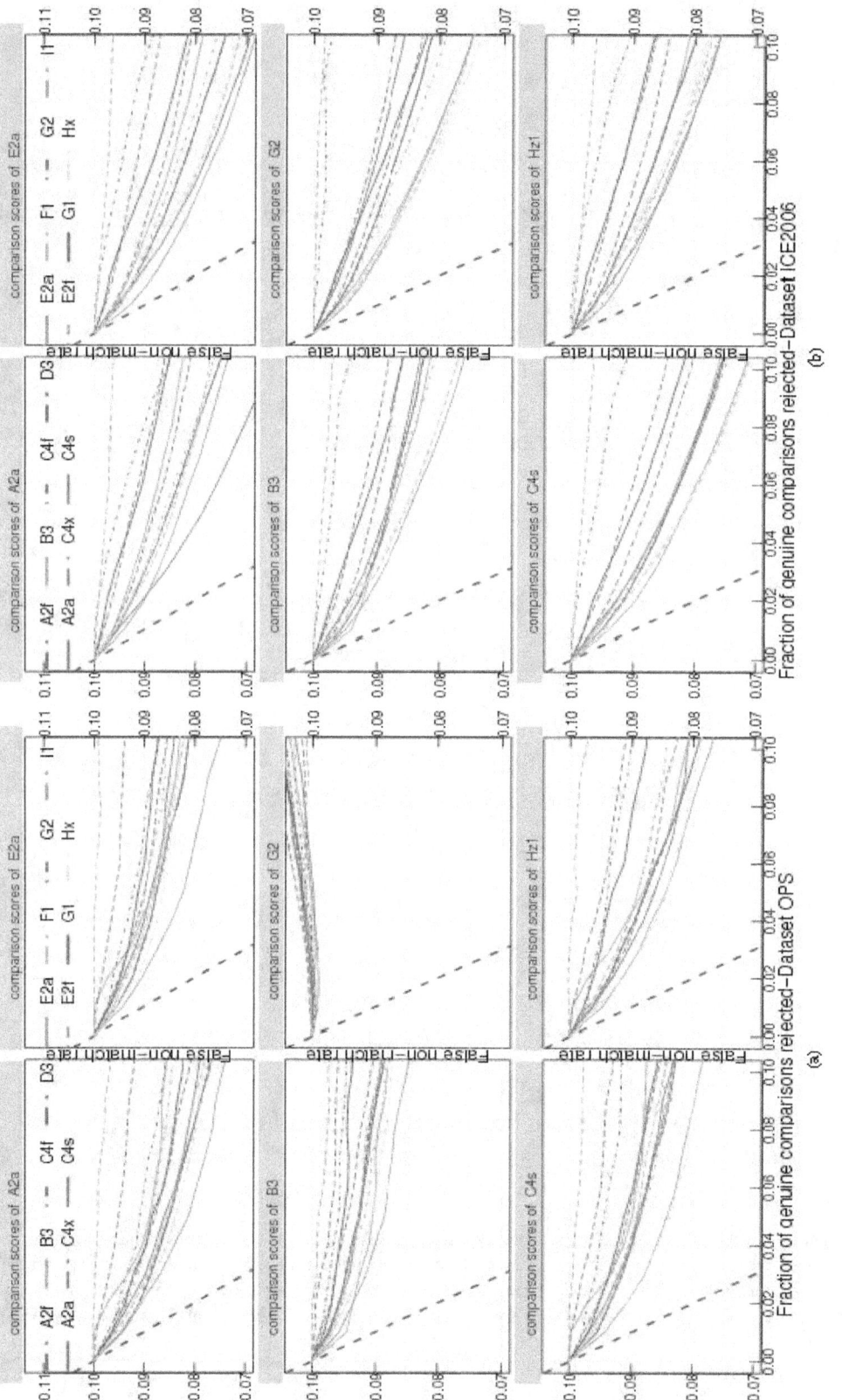

Figure 13: FNMR vs. reject curves for SCALAR QUALITY scores on datasets OPS and ICE2006. The threshold is set to give an initial FNMR = 0.1. The gray dotted line shows the ideal case where the rejection of the comparisons with the lowest ten percent quality results in zero FNMR. IQAA E2a is the best performer, followed by Hx and F1. IQAAs B3 and A2a perform better for their native recognition algorithms. The lowest performance is observed for IQAAs I1 and D3.

| A2a=NEUROTECHNOLOGY-a | B3=CROSSMATCH | C4s=CAMBRIDGE-s | D3=AWARE | E2a=IRITECH-a | G1=IRISID-1 | I1=KYNEN | Hz1=L1-z1 |
| A2f=NEUROTECHNOLOGY-f | C4x=CAMBRIDGE-x | C4f=CAMBRIDGE-f | F1=MORPHO | E2f=IRITECH-f | G2=IRISID-2 | Hx=L1-x | Hz2=L1-z2 |

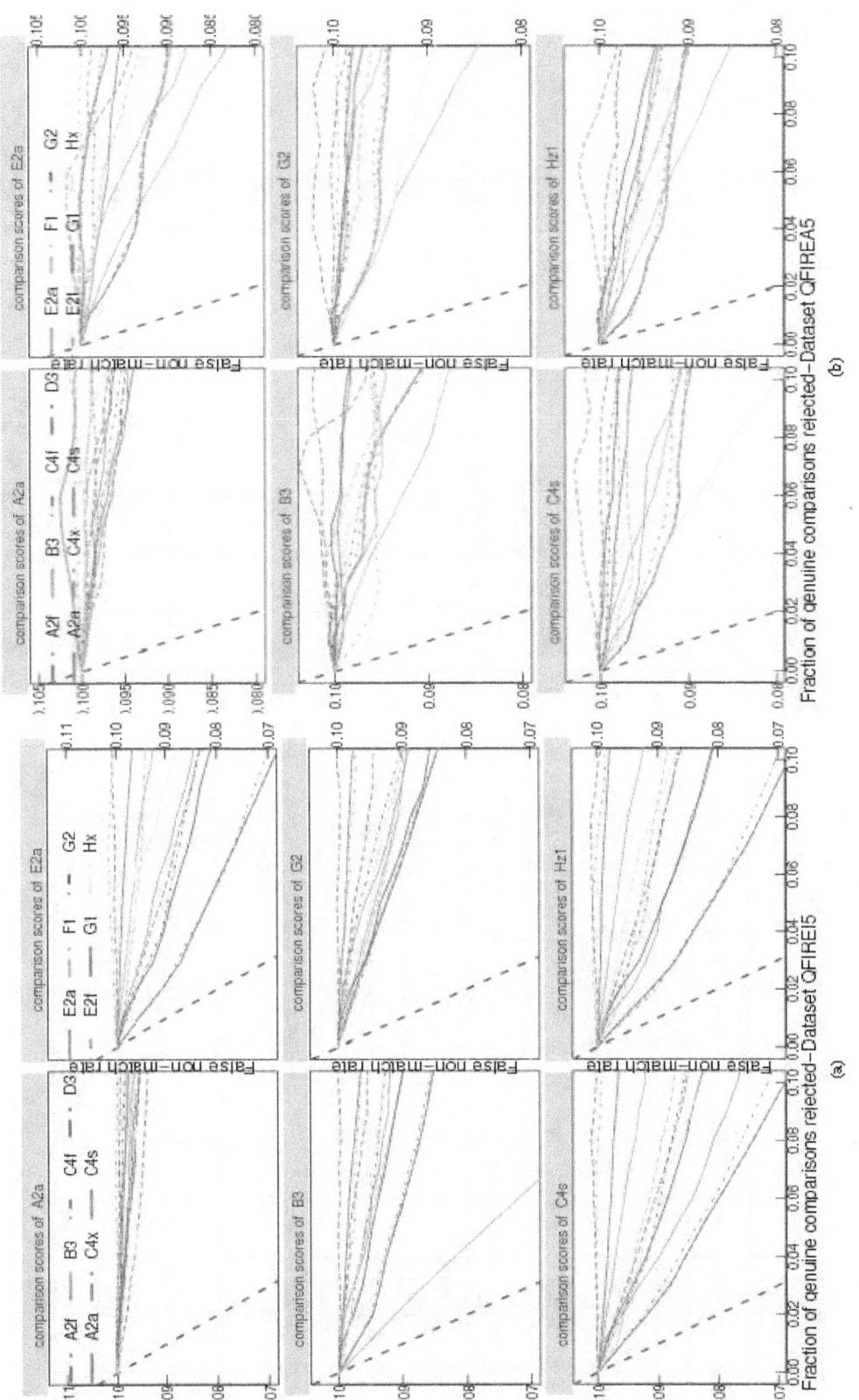

Figure 14: FNMR vs. reject curves for SCALAR QUALITY scores for QFIRE A5 and QFIRE I5 images. The threshold is set to give an initial FNMR = 0.1. The gray dotted line shows the ideal case when the rejection of the lowest ten percent quality results in zero FNMR. In general, the best performance is observed for IQAAs C4x, C4s and C4f. IQAA B3 is the best predictor of performance for its native recognition algorithm, but it is not generalizable. Comparator A2a accuracy drops for QFIRE A5 and QFIRE I5 images. This makes its error vs. reject curves of all IQAAs incomprehensible.

A2a=NEUROTECHNOLOGY-a   B3=CROSSMATCH   C4s=CAMBRIDGE-s   D3=AWARE   E2a=IRITECH-a   G1=IRISID-1   I1=KYNEN   Hz1=L1-z1
A2f=NEUROTECHNOLOGY-f   C4x=CAMBRIDGE-x   C4f=CAMBRIDGE-f   F1=MORPHO   E2f=IRITECH-f   G2=IRISID-2   Hx=L1-x   Hz2=L1-z2

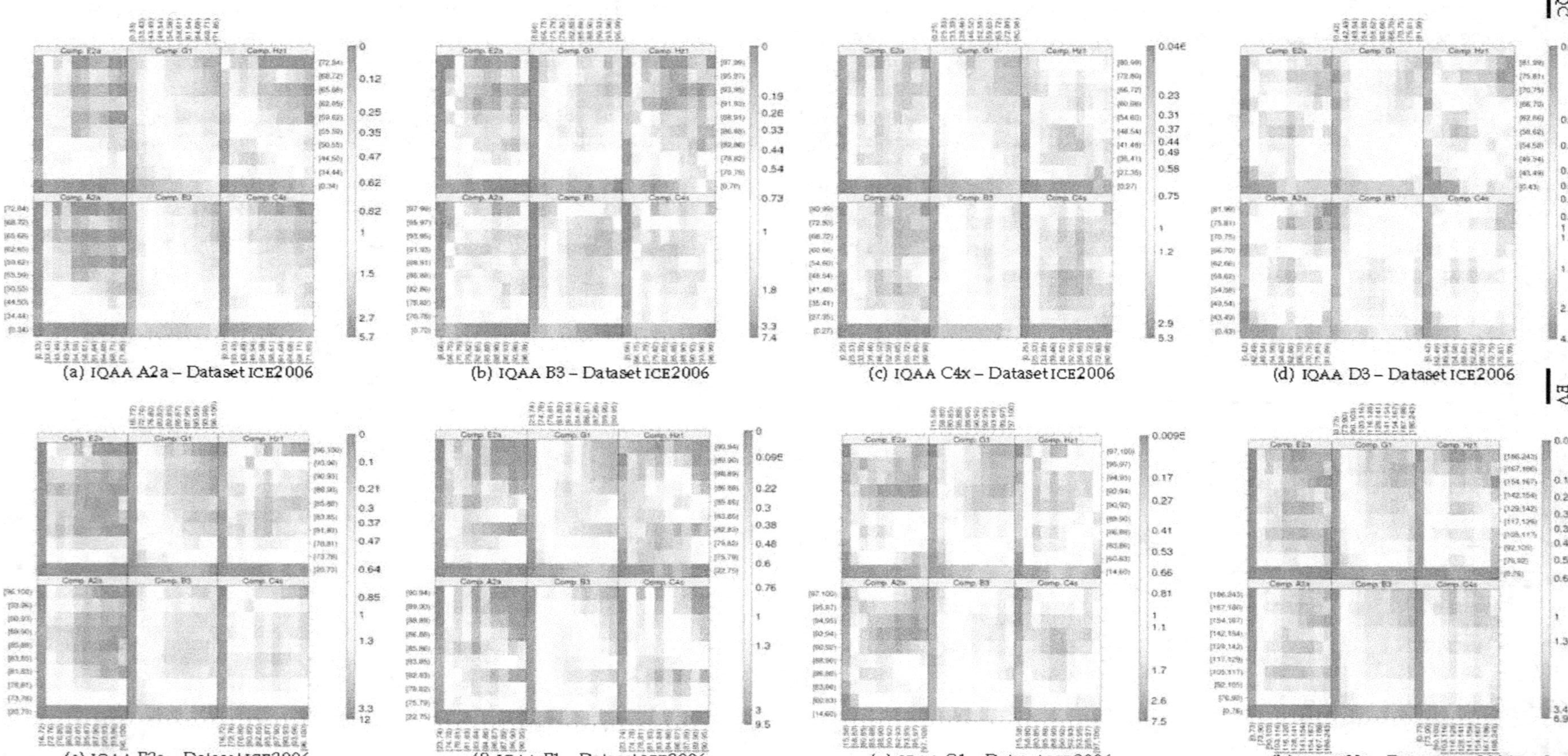

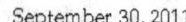

Figure 15: SCALAR QUALITY computed by primary IQAA submissions and FNMR for IQCE comparators for ICE2006 images. The y-axis represents enrollment samples' quality with verification samples' on the x-axis. The SCALAR QUALITY scores are quantized into 10 quantiles. The color scale plots $\frac{\text{FNMR}}{\text{FNMR}_0}$ for comparisons with verification and enrollment qualities ($q_{verification}, q_{enrollment}$). FNMR_0 is the nominal FNMR which is the false non-match rate computed over all the images at the same comparison score threshold, in this case at FMR = 0.001. Yellow/Green color represent an improvement in FNMR. Blue color represent a degradation of FNMR. White color means no change in FNMR.

(a) IQAA A2a – Dataset ICE2006
(b) IQAA B3 – Dataset ICE2006
(c) IQAA C4x – Dataset ICE2006
(d) IQAA D3 – Dataset ICE2006
(e) IQAA E2a – Dataset ICE2006
(f) IQAA F1 – Dataset ICE2006
(g) IQAA G1 – Dataset ICE2006
(h) IQAA Hx – Dataset ICE2006

| A2a=NEUROTECHNOLOGY-a | B3=CROSSMATCH | C4s=CAMBRIDGE-s | D3=AWARE | E2a=IRITECH-a | G1=IRISID-1 | I1=KYNEN | Hz1=L1-z1 |
| A2f=NEUROTECHNOLOGY-f | | C4x=CAMBRIDGE-x | C4f=CAMBRIDGE-f | F1=MORPHO | E2f=IRITECH-f | G2=IRISID-2 | Hx=L1-x | Hz2=L1-z2 |

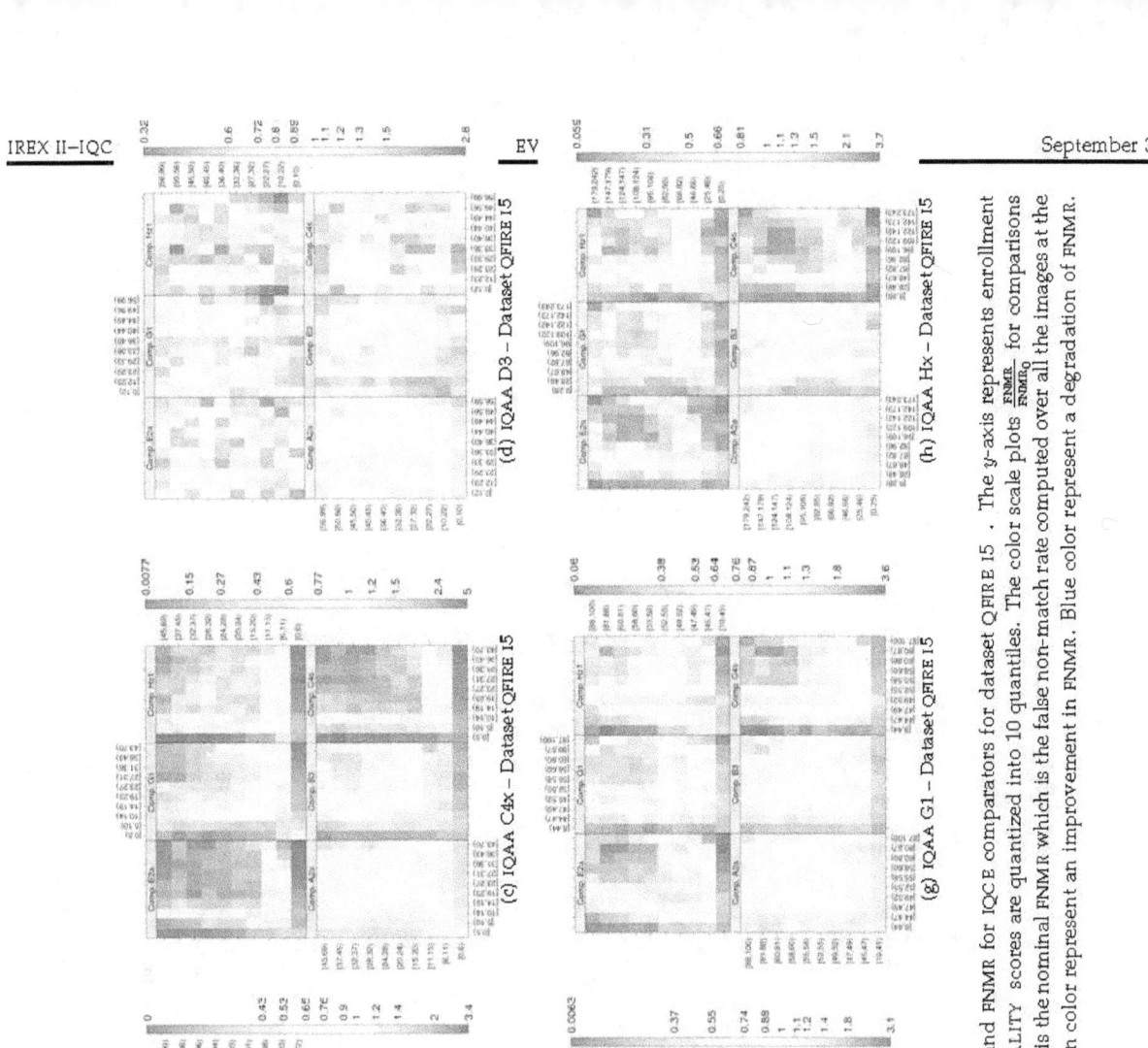

Figure 16: SCALAR QUALITY computed by primary IQAA submissions and FNMR for IQCE comparators for dataset QFIRE 15 . The y-axis represents enrollment samples' quality with verification samples' on the x-axis. The SCALAR QUALITY scores are quantized into 10 quantiles. The color scale plots $\frac{FNMR}{FNMR_0}$ for comparisons with verification and enrollment qualities ($q_{verification}, q_{enrollment}$). $FNMR_0$ is the nominal FNMR which is the false non-match rate computed over all the images at the same comparison score threshold, in this case at FMR = 0.001. Yellow/Green color represent an improvement in FNMR. Blue color represent a degradation of FNMR. White color means no change in FNMR.

A2a=NEUROTECHNOLOGY-a	B3=CROSSMATCH	C4s=CAMBRIDGE-s	D3=AWARE
A2f=NEUROTECHNOLOGY-f	C4x=CAMBRIDGE-x	C4f=CAMBRIDGE-f	F1=MORPHO

E2a=IRITECH-a	G1=IRISID-1	I1=KYNEN	Hz1=L1-z1
E2f=IRITECH-f	G2=IRISID-2	Hx=L1-x	Hz2=L1-z2

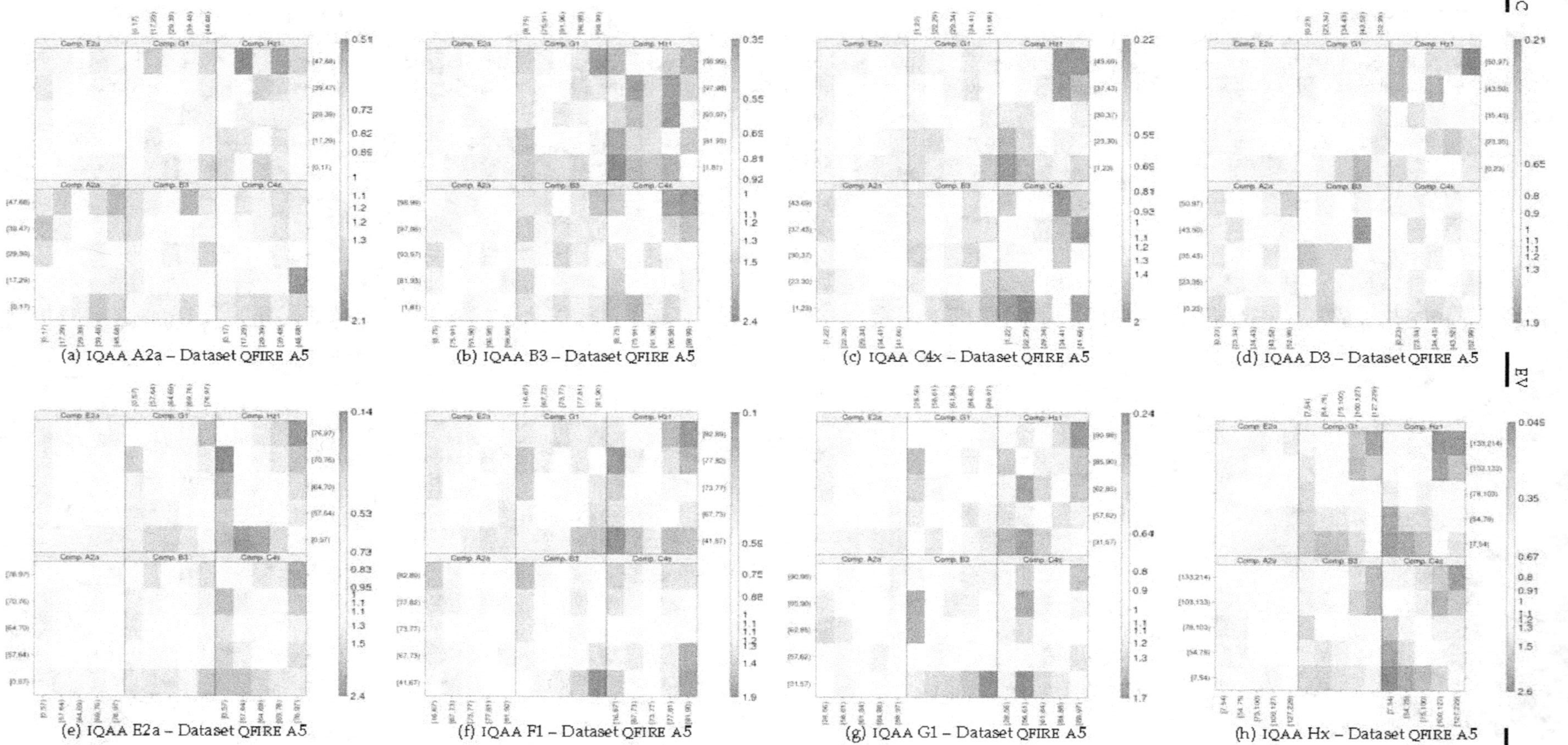

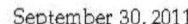

Figure 17: SCALAR QUALITY computed by primary IQAA submissions and FNMR for IQCE comparators for dataset QFIRE A5 . The y-axis represents enrollment samples' quality with verification samples' quality on the x-axis. The SCALAR QUALITY scores are quantized into 10 quantiles. The color scale plots $\frac{FNMR}{FNMR_0}$ for comparisons with verification and enrollment qualities ($q_{verification}$, $q_{enrollment}$). $FNMR_0$ is the nominal FNMR which is the false non-match rate computed over all the images at the same comparison score threshold, in this case at FMR $= 0.001$. Yellow/Green color represent an improvement in FNMR. Blue color represent a degradation of FNMR. White color means no change in FNMR.

(a) IQAA A2a – Dataset QFIRE A5
(b) IQAA B3 – Dataset QFIRE A5
(c) IQAA C4x – Dataset QFIRE A5
(d) IQAA D3 – Dataset QFIRE A5
(e) IQAA E2a – Dataset QFIRE A5
(f) IQAA F1 – Dataset QFIRE A5
(g) IQAA G1 – Dataset QFIRE A5
(h) IQAA Hx – Dataset QFIRE A5

| A2a=NEUROTECHNOLOGY-a | B3=CROSSMATCH | C4s=CAMBRIDGE-s | D3=AWARE | E2a=IRITECH-a | G1=IRISID-1 | I1=KYNEN | Hz1=L1-z1 |
| A2f=NEUROTECHNOLOGY-f | | C4x=CAMBRIDGE-x | | F1=MORPHO | E2f=IRITECH-f | G2=IRISID-2 | Hx=L1-x | Hz2=L1-z2 |

Dataset	comparator	IQAA A2a	IQAA B3	IQAA C4x	IQAA D3	IQAA E2a	IQAA F1	IQAA G1	IQAA Hx
ICE2006	A2a	(28.70,29.07)	(15.89,16.19)	(21.86,22.28)	(10.75,11.14)	(13.29,13.48)	(9.27,9.40)	(14.12,14.43)	(17.36,17.70)
ICE2006	B3	(12.84,13.01)	(14.78,14.91)	(13.00,13.20)	(5.32,5.49)	(7.87,7.96)	(5.72,5.78)	(7.95,8.09)	(13.68,13.83)
ICE2006	C4s	(20.72,21.00)	(14.71,14.93)	(21.41,21.72)	(8.97,9.24)	(9.94,10.08)	(7.61,7.71)	(11.39,11.63)	(15.06,15.30)
ICE2006	E2a	(23.27,23.65)	(21.30,21.60)	(21.29,21.72)	(10.95,11.33)	(14.31,14.51)	(10.57,10.71)	(13.61,13.95)	(20.00,20.34)
ICE2006	G2	(15.05,15.24)	(16.07,16.21)	(17.04,17.25)	(8.68,8.87)	(10.14,10.23)	(7.07,7.13)	(12.33,12.48)	(16.26,16.42)
ICE2006	Hz1	(13.50,13.97)	(10.42,10.77)	(11.72,12.23)	(9.09,9.51)	(8.86,9.09)	(6.43,6.59)	(6.79,7.17)	(12.30,12.70)
OPS	A2a	(7.15,11.21)	(8.57,16.78)	(2.90,11.31)	(1.75,8.61)	(4.32,7.97)	(2.60,5.22)	(1.79,6.39)	(6.67,15.08)
OPS	B3	(1.81,3.51)	(10.44,12.37)	(2.97,6.49)	(0.66,3.45)	(3.19,4.71)	(1.06,2.16)	(1.71,3.61)	(4.08,7.60)
OPS	C4s	(4.23,7.53)	(8.15,14.76)	(3.64,10.40)	(2.74,8.03)	(5.80,8.73)	(1.94,4.05)	(0.83,4.53)	(9.26,16.02)
OPS	E2a	(1.15,5.93)	(-3.46,6.22)	(-1.74,8.14)	(-3.75,4.08)	(2.42,6.72)	(0.22,3.31)	(-1.17,4.23)	(-0.14,9.75)
OPS	G2	(8.14,10.76)	(8.78,14.07)	(11.39,16.83)	(5.59,9.87)	(8.39,10.75)	(4.81,6.49)	(10.24,13.03)	(16.09,21.52)
OPS	Hz1	(3.04,6.87)	(1.25,9.02)	(-1.07,6.85)	(0.42,6.54)	(5.23,8.66)	(0.13,2.60)	(-0.80,3.52)	(4.39,12.29)
QFIREA5	A2a	(4.44,5.33)	(2.37,3.93)	(2.72,3.25)	(2.74,6.16)	(1.72,2.31)	(1.80,2.19)	(1.99,2.72)	(3.01,3.80)
QFIREA5	B3	(2.35,4.04)	(12.67,14.81)	(3.74,4.54)	(0.23,5.70)	(3.56,4.47)	(1.24,1.86)	(3.34,4.45)	(7.89,9.00)
QFIREA5	C4s	(1.23,2.76)	(11.39,13.48)	(4.88,5.59)	(-1.51,2.57)	(5.04,5.82)	(1.65,2.18)	(1.41,2.40)	(10.82,11.88)
QFIREA5	E2a	(4.22,5.33)	(9.39,10.80)	(3.33,3.83)	(2.71,5.55)	(3.62,4.16)	(2.35,2.71)	(3.15,3.83)	(5.99,6.72)
QFIREA5	G2	(1.97,3.15)	(13.64,15.13)	(3.49,4.03)	(0.41,3.84)	(4.07,4.65)	(1.55,1.94)	(2.28,3.02)	(8.67,9.45)
QFIREA5	Hz1	(1.50,3.36)	(19.78,22.32)	(4.51,5.41)	(-3.25,2.75)	(5.69,6.66)	(3.29,3.94)	(3.04,4.30)	(8.39,9.72)
QFIREI5	A2a	(6.58,6.84)	(3.59,4.10)	(7.46,7.71)	(3.12,4.55)	(3.21,3.49)	(3.33,3.50)	(3.80,4.05)	(8.31,8.69)
QFIREI5	B3	(6.06,6.69)	(17.35,17.73)	(6.40,6.65)	(3.83,5.64)	(2.50,2.75)	(2.83,3.00)	(3.55,3.81)	(4.22,4.62)
QFIREI5	C4s	(5.87,6.49)	(1.66,3.40)	(11.66,11.98)	(-3.40,-1.53)	(9.81,10.15)	(5.03,5.24)	(4.97,5.28)	(12.95,13.42)
QFIREI5	E2a	(6.26,6.93)	(3.14,4.95)	(11.32,11.65)	(-2.43,-0.39)	(6.73,7.09)	(3.26,3.48)	(4.43,4.76)	(11.36,11.86)
QFIREI5	G2	(5.34,5.90)	(6.10,6.95)	(8.71,8.99)	(-0.11,1.64)	(5.85,6.15)	(4.01,4.19)	(4.26,4.53)	(9.63,10.06)
QFIREI5	Hz1	(3.06,3.86)	(6.35,8.59)	(10.26,10.67)	(0.28,2.59)	(8.38,8.81)	(5.34,5.61)	(3.26,3.66)	(10.05,10.67)

Table 9: Tukey HSD difference in mean of SCALAR QUALITY scores. Each cell shows the 95% confidence level in difference in mean of pairwise quality for images verified correctly (i.e., the genuine score equal or less than threshold) and those rejected falsely (i.e., the genuine score larger than threshold). Quality scores were computed by the SDK identified by the column header and comparison scores were generated by the SDK identified by the row header. If the interval does not contain zero, the difference in mean is significant. Cells where difference in mean is not significant have pink background. For monotonically increasing quality components (all except DILATION, and depending on quality implementation GRAY SCALE SPREAD), the expected behavior is to have higher quality scores for the pair of enrollment and verification images that give genuine comparison scores less than threshold. The pairwise quality is computed as geometric mean of the quality of two samples being compared. Threshold is set to give false match rate of 0.001.

A2a=NEUROTECHNOLOGY-a   B3=CROSSMATCH   C4s=CAMBRIDGE-s   D3=AWARE   E2a=IRITECH-a   G1=IRISID-1   I1=KYNEN   Hz1=L1-z1
A2f=NEUROTECHNOLOGY-f   C4x=CAMBRIDGE-x   C4f=CAMBRIDGE-f   F1=MORPHO   E2f=IRITECH-f   G2=IRISID-2   Hx=L1-x   Hz2=L1-z2

Dataset	comparator	IQAA A2a	IQAA B3	IQAA C4x	IQAA D3	IQAA E2a	IQAA F1	IQAA G1	IQAA Hx
ICE2006	A2a	(1.61,2.50)	(-1.03,-0.33)	(3.03,3.96)	(-2.29,-1.52)	(-1.03,-0.60)	(-1.00,-0.70)	(-1.18,-0.35)	(-3.14,-2.39)
ICE2006	B3	(16.71,17.35)	(17.74,18.19)	(19.59,20.26)	(10.21,10.76)	(8.63,8.93)	(5.63,5.85)	(14.67,15.26)	(15.10,15.64)
ICE2006	C4s	(7.20,7.89)	(4.28,4.83)	(10.16,10.88)	(2.84,3.43)	(2.81,3.14)	(2.02,2.25)	(5.69,6.33)	(4.89,5.47)
ICE2006	E2a	(12.58,13.28)	(6.12,6.67)	(14.38,15.11)	(4.64,5.24)	(6.03,6.36)	(3.46,3.69)	(8.63,9.28)	(6.93,7.52)
ICE2006	G2	(2.00,2.72)	(-0.64,-0.08)	(1.12,1.87)	(-1.81,-1.19)	(-0.92,-0.58)	(-1.13,-0.91)	(-1.17,-0.56)	(-2.77,-2.17)
ICE2006	Hz1	(8.91,9.67)	(6.33,6.93)	(11.37,12.18)	(4.87,5.47)	(4.79,5.15)	(3.28,3.53)	(10.43,11.14)	(7.12,7.77)
OPS	A2a	(0.06,0.50)	(0.66,1.62)	(0.34,1.25)	(0.45,1.18)	(-0.59,-0.21)	(-0.10,0.18)	(-0.47,0.04)	(-2.15,-1.22)
OPS	B3	(3.26,3.61)	(4.86,5.28)	(9.16,9.90)	(3.22,3.81)	(2.87,3.18)	(2.24,2.46)	(4.63,5.04)	(8.55,9.31)
OPS	C4s	(2.09,2.45)	(1.96,2.75)	(6.66,7.41)	(2.12,2.73)	(1.58,1.89)	(1.71,1.94)	(2.97,3.39)	(4.77,5.53)
OPS	E2a	(1.07,1.44)	(-0.37,0.43)	(2.52,3.28)	(1.74,2.35)	(0.67,0.98)	(0.70,0.93)	(1.11,1.53)	(1.54,2.31)
OPS	G2	(-0.51,-0.15)	(0.62,1.41)	(-1.49,-0.74)	(-0.57,0.04)	(-0.82,-0.51)	(-0.60,-0.38)	(-0.96,-0.57)	(-2.16,-1.40)
OPS	Hz1	(2.13,2.49)	(1.90,2.69)	(6.99,7.74)	(2.25,2.85)	(2.06,2.36)	(1.79,2.02)	(3.29,3.70)	(4.32,5.08)
QFIREA5	A2a	(0.58,1.66)	(-1.30,1.00)	(1.64,2.34)	(1.18,4.33)	(2.06,3.02)	(2.99,3.62)	(-1.53,-0.46)	(3.09,3.92)
QFIREA5	C4s	(2.74,3.72)	(2.64,4.65)	(3.45,4.08)	(-0.82,2.20)	(2.00,2.87)	(2.39,2.97)	(2.29,3.19)	(1.70,2.46)
QFIREA5	E2a	(1.01,1.99)	(47.48,49.42)	(0.94,1.57)	(-0.38,6.04)	(-2.40,-1.53)	(3.05,3.62)	(1.80,2.65)	(1.34,2.09)
QFIREA5	G2	(3.77,4.78)	(-3.08,-1.02)	(1.53,2.17)	(-0.96,1.86)	(1.80,2.67)	(0.73,1.29)	(1.13,1.98)	(-0.19,0.59)
QFIREA5	Hz1	(3.90,4.88)	(22.09,24.11)	(5.80,6.43)	(-1.52,1.97)	(3.20,4.07)	(5.47,6.05)	(4.50,5.47)	(4.70,5.45)
QFIREI5	A2a	(-0.46,0.08)	(-0.87,-0.08)	(1.30,1.74)	(-5.21,-0.26)	(1.28,1.75)	(-0.50,-0.20)	(2.34,2.85)	(0.22,0.93)
QFIREI5	C4s	(4.36,4.83)	(2.81,3.49)	(6.85,7.23)	(-2.53,0.87)	(4.10,4.50)	(2.64,2.90)	(7.07,7.51)	(7.29,7.89)
QFIREI5	E2a	(5.61,6.08)	(-1.23,-0.55)	(10.79,11.18)	(-3.06,0.13)	(5.97,6.37)	(2.09,2.35)	(10.25,10.69)	(16.29,16.90)
QFIREI5	G2	(2.64,6.25)	(-1.47,3.65)	(5.07,7.99)	(-18.11,13.27)	(1.67,4.71)	(1.30,3.26)	(4.98,8.35)	(3.93,8.53)
QFIREI5	Hz1	(5.02,5.49)	(5.02,5.70)	(8.53,8.91)	(-4.32,-0.58)	(6.11,6.51)	(4.21,4.48)	(8.84,9.29)	(5.89,6.50)

Table 10: Tukey HSD mean difference in SCALAR QUALITY scores. Each cell shows the 95% confidence level in difference in mean of pairwise quality for images correctly rejected (i.e. the impostor score equal or greater than threshold) and those falsely matched (i.e. the impostor score less than threshold). Quality scores were computed by the SDK identified by the column header and comparison scores were generated by the SDK identified by the row header. If the interval does not contain zero, the difference in mean is significant. Cells where difference in mean is not significant are shaded in pink. For monotonic increasing quality components (all except DILATION, and depending on quality implementation GRAY SCALE SPREAD), the expected behavior is to have higher quality scores for the pair of (enrollment, verification) images that result in impostor comparison scores equal or greater than threshold. Pairwise quality is computed as geometric mean of the quality of two samples being compared. Threshold is set to give false match rate of 0.001.

A2a=NEUROTECHNOLOGY-a	B3=CROSSMATCH	C4s=CAMBRIDGE-s	D3=AWARE	E2a=IRITECH-a	G1=IRISID-1	I1=KYNEN	Hz1=L1-z1
A2f=NEUROTECHNOLOGY-f	C4x=CAMBRIDGE-x	C4f=CAMBRIDGE-f	F1=MORPHO	E2f=IRITECH-f	G2=IRISID-2	Hx=L1-x	Hz2=L1-z2

9   Predictive power of standard quality components

A set of measurements that constitute a quality vector will clearly convey more information than just a summary scalar value. However, two outstanding issues remain. First is that the vector in itself is not immediately useful when a decision has to be made to e.g., accept the captured image or prompt for re-capture. Another example is to decide, among the captured images, which one to use. These usages of quality score require a single quality number indicative of the match-ability of the image.

The second issue is that the quality vectors are less interoperable than scalar values if the specific components of the vectors are not standardized. This arises, in some part, because some biometric recognition algorithms are more sensitive to specific quality-related defects than others.

That said, a set of measurement of different aspects of quality, makes quality scores "actionable". They could be used to specifically direct reacquisition attempts (e.g., camera settings) or direct enhancement of image (e.g., contrast adjustment).

In order to identify iris image properties that are influential on recognition accuracy, and quantifying their effects, and in support of development of ISO/IEC 29794 Biometric sample quality Part 6: Iris image [2], IQCE invited submissions that compute the image quality components listed in the Table 4 of IQCE API (hereafter referred to quality components). The standard quality components were identified in consultation with industry and research community and are considered to potentially influence performance. The valid values deviates from that specified by ISO/IEC 29794 Biometric sample quality – Part 1: Framework [2]. The standard defines 0–100 as the valid range, and 254 and 255 to handle special cases of failure to compute quality and no attempt to compute quality, respectively. The reason was to allow for the reporting of actual measurement of the specified image property. This section gives quantitative results for the effect of each standard quality components.

Additionally, IQCE considered, allowed and encouraged vendor-defined quality components (hereafter referred to proprietary quality components). When reporting proprietary quality components, IQAAs could choose to disclose and document what image properties are being measured (gray box IQAA), or not disclose any information on its content (black box IQAA).

Computation of either standard or proprietary quality components were optional.

This section gives quantitative results for the effect of each of the standard quality components.

| A2a=NEUROTECHNOLOGY-a | B3=CROSSMATCH | C4s=CAMBRIDGE-s | D3=AWARE | E2a=IRITECH-a | G1=IRISID-1 | I1=KYNEN | Hz1=L1-z1 |
| A2f=NEUROTECHNOLOGY-f | C4x=CAMBRIDGE-x | C4f=CAMBRIDGE-f | F1=MORPHO | E2f=IRITECH-f | G2=IRISID-2 | Hx=L1-x | Hz2=L1-z2 |

9.1   Gray scale spread

An image with a high GRAY SCALE SPREAD (good quality) is a properly exposed image, with a wide, well distributed spread of intensity values. An underexposed image would have too few high intensity (too many blackish) pixels, and, conversely, an overexposed image would have too few low intensity (too many white-ish) pixels. Saturation or poor illumination can cause lack of well-spread intensity values. Therefore better performance can be achieved for iris acquisition systems capable of producing images with high contrast and large dynamic range. [1] specifies that a useful iris image should have a dynamic range of at least 256 grey levels, allocating at least 8-bits with a minimum of 7 bits of useful information. Saturation or poor illumination can cause lack of well-spread intensity values.

The following ten IQCE participants generate GRAY SCALE SPREAD score: A2a, A2f, D3, E2a, E2f, F1, G1, G2, Hx, and I1.

The distribution of their GRAY SCALE SPREAD scores is shown in Figure 18. In order to make the boxplots more readable, quality scores in [0–254] range were linearly scaled back to [0–100].

This section presents results on comparative analysis of their GRAY SCALE SPREAD scores.

Figure 19 shows a histogram of number of gray levels in QFIRE I5 images. The ICE2006 images, because of the contrast stretching automatically applied within the LG EOU 2200 system, every third intensity level is unused. Almost all of the ICE2006 images have 171 gray levels.

Whether the gray level is computed for the whole image or just the iris portion was not available to the authors.

RELATIONSHIP WITH THE DISTRIBUTION OF GENUINE SCORES

Figure 20 shows a small change in GRAY SCALE SPREAD scores for different quantiles of genuine scores. Images with high GRAY SCALE SPREAD scores result in a slightly higher genuine comparison scores. Only IQAA Hx GRAY SCALE SPREAD scores vary among the four datasets. GRAY SCALE SPREAD scores of other IQAAs are in the same range regardless of the difference in origin and acquisition settings of the data. There are several possible explanations. Either the IQCE datasets lack a wide range of gray level spread. Or there are confounding factors, for example, images with low GRAY SCALE SPREAD scores are also blurred.

RELATIONSHIP WITH THE DISTRIBUTION OF IMPOSTOR SCORES

GRAY SCALE SPREAD scores vs. quantiles of impostor scores are shown in Figure 21. No change is observed in GRAY SCALE SPREAD scores for different quantiles of impostor scores.

RANKED DET:: DO LOW-QUALITY IMAGES PRODUCE HIGH FNMR OR FMR?

DET curves of Figure 22 indicate that the performance of images with the highest or the lowest GRAY SCALE SPREAD are not dramatically different. This is probably due to lack of wide range of gray level spread in QFIRE I5 images - as shown in Figure 19.

EFFECT OF QUALITY ON FNMR :: HOW QUICKLY FNMR IMPROVES WHEN POOR QUALITY SAMPLES ARE REJECTED?

| A2a=NEUROTECHNOLOGY-a | B3=CROSSMATCH | C4s=CAMBRIDGE-s | D3=AWARE | E2a=IRITECH-a | G1=IRISID-1 | I1=KYNEN | Hz1=L1-z1 |
| A2f=NEUROTECHNOLOGY-f | C4x=CAMBRIDGE-x | C4f=CAMBRIDGE-f | F1=MORPHO | E2f=IRITECH-f | G2=IRISID-2 | Hx=L1-x | Hz2=L1-z2 |

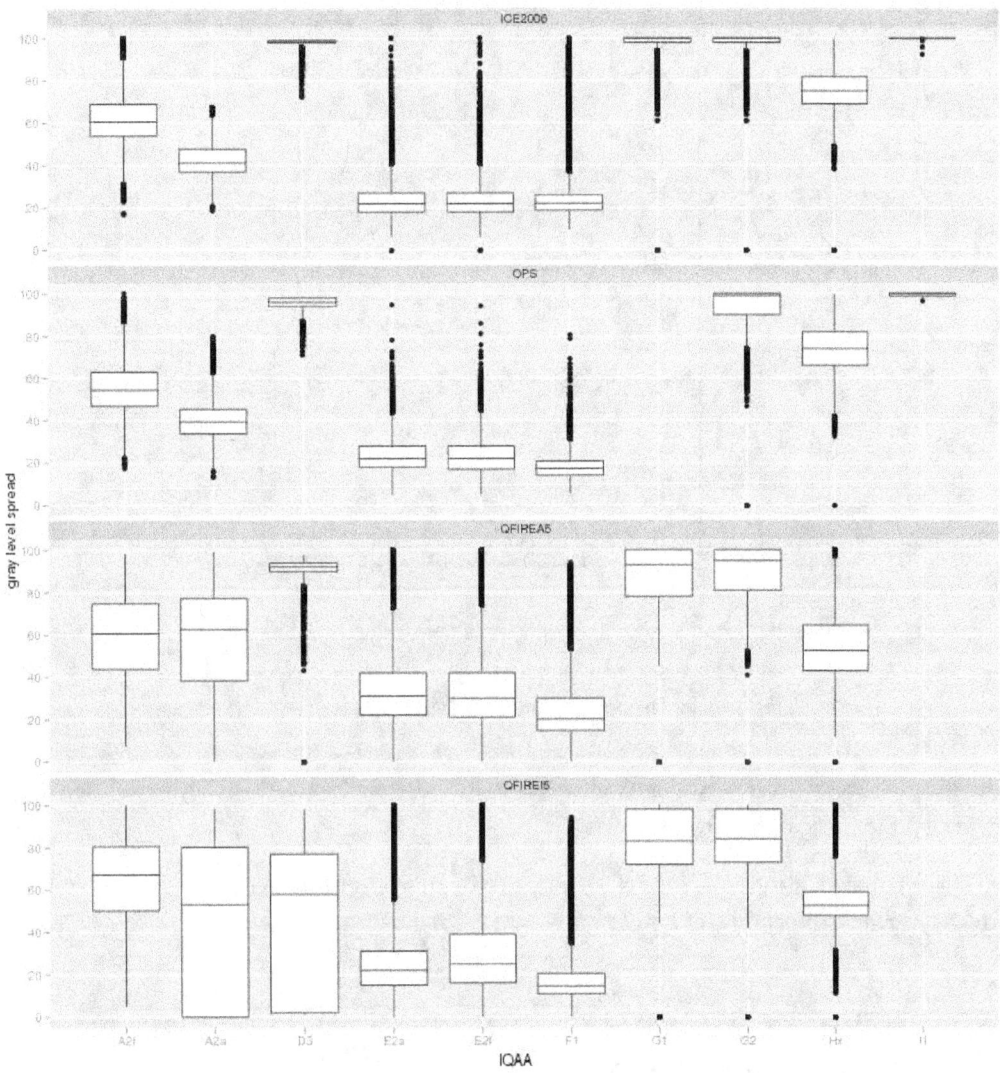

Figure 18: Box and whisker plots of the IQAAs that generate GRAY SCALE SPREAD scores.

The reject curves of Figure 23 are not encouraging. It implies all IQAAs GRAY SCALE SPREAD scores behave similarly and none is predictive of performance.

TEST OF SIGNIFICANCE :: DO THE IMAGES INVOLVED IN SUCCESSFUL VERIFICATION ATTEMPTS HAVE SIGNIFICANTLY HIGHER QUALITY SCORES THAN THOSE INVOLVED IN FAILED VERIFICATION ATTEMPTS?

Except for the OPS dataset, images involved in successful verification attempts have significantly different GRAY SCALE SPREAD scores than those with the result of false reject, as shown in Table 11. Note that significant difference does not necessarily mean a big difference.

Table 12 shows that for IQAAs A2f, E2a, E2f, and F1 lower GRAY SCALE SPREAD score indicates better performance. IQAAs

| A2a=NEUROTECHNOLOGY-a | B3=CROSSMATCH | C4s=CAMBRIDGE-s | D3=AWARE | E2a=IRITECH-a | G1=IRISID-1 | I1=KYNEN | Hz1=L1-z1 |
| A2f=NEUROTECHNOLOGY-f | C4x=CAMBRIDGE-x | C4f=CAMBRIDGE-f | F1=MORPHO | E2f=IRITECH-f | G2=IRISID-2 | Hx=L1-x | Hz2=L1-z2 |

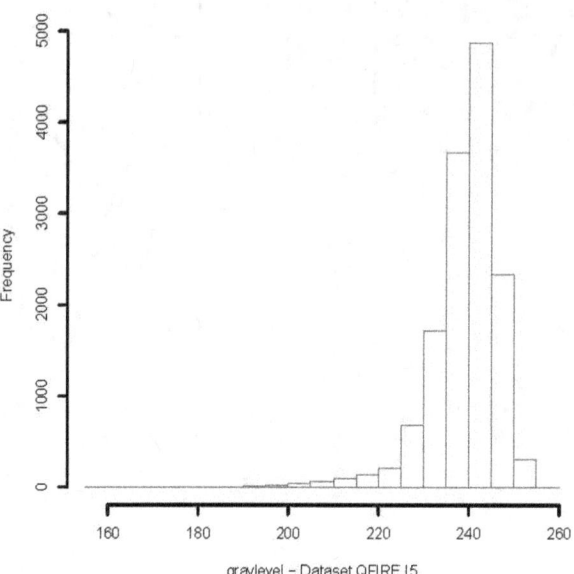

Figure 19: Histogram of number of gray levels in QFIRE I5 images.

G1, G2 and Hx give lower GRAY SCALE SPREAD scores to ICE2006 images that are falsely rejected, but higher scores to QFIRE A5 or QFIRE I5 images that are false rejected.

There is a small but significant difference between pairwise quality of ICE2006 images that are falsely matched and those correctly rejected. The difference is not significant for other datasets.

EFFECT OF VARIATION BETWEEN THE TWO SAMPLES:: DOES SAMENESS MATTER?

As illustrated in Figures 24 and 25, except for IQAA Hx, images with high GRAY SCALE SPREAD score inflate FNMR. Images with low IQAA Hx GRAY SCALE SPREAD scores are more likely to cause false non-match. The relationship between GRAY SCALE SPREAD scores and FNMR is more pronounced for ICE2006 images than QFIRE I5.

OBSERVATIONS AND CONCLUSIONS

The results presented suggest that GRAY SCALE SPREAD has a significant but small effect on performance. It should be noted that images used in this study might not have the diversity needed for revealing how greatly GRAY SCALE SPREAD affects performance.

Performance of the ten IQAAs that produce GRAY SCALE SPREAD scores are comparable. FNMR degrades as the difference in GRAY SCALE SPREAD scores of the two images being compared increases.

| A2a=NEUROTECHNOLOGY-a | B3=CROSSMATCH | C4s=CAMBRIDGE-s | D3=AWARE | E2a=IRITECH-a | G1=IRISID-1 | I1=KYNEN | Hz1=L1-z1 |
| A2f=NEUROTECHNOLOGY-f | C4x=CAMBRIDGE-x | C4f=CAMBRIDGE-f | F1=MORPHO | E2f=IRITECH-f | G2=IRISID-2 | Hx=L1-x | Hz2=L1-z2 |

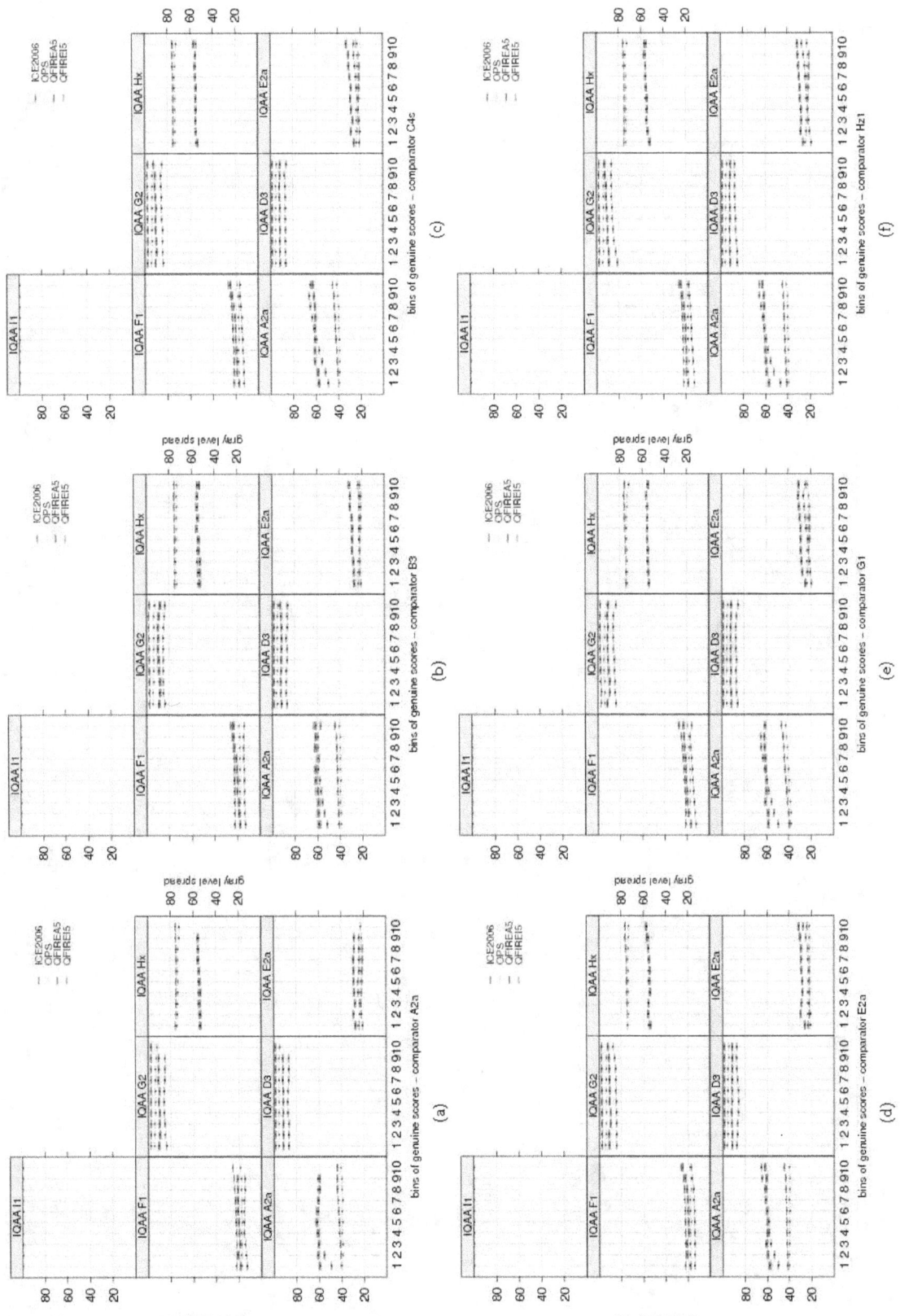

Figure 20: Pairwise GRAY SCALE SPREAD scores vs. genuine score for the primary Class Z submissions of each participant. Each plot shows quality scores computed by different IQAA. Genuine scores are divided equally into ten groups. Groups overlap by 5 percent, meaning 5% of the data in one bin also belongs to the next bin. The bootstrapped pairwise quality for each group is shown in a box and whisker plot. Pairwise quality is computed as geometric mean of the quality of the two samples being compared.

A2a=NEUROTECHNOLOGY-a	B3=CROSSMATCH	C4s=CAMBRIDGE-s	D3=AWARE	E2a=IRITECH-a	G1=IRISID-1	I1=KYNEN	Hz1=L1-z1
A2f=NEUROTECHNOLOGY-f	C4x=CAMBRIDGE-x	C4f=CAMBRIDGE-f	F1=MORPHO	E2f=IRITECH-f	G2=IRISID-2	Hx=L1-x	Hz2=L1-z2

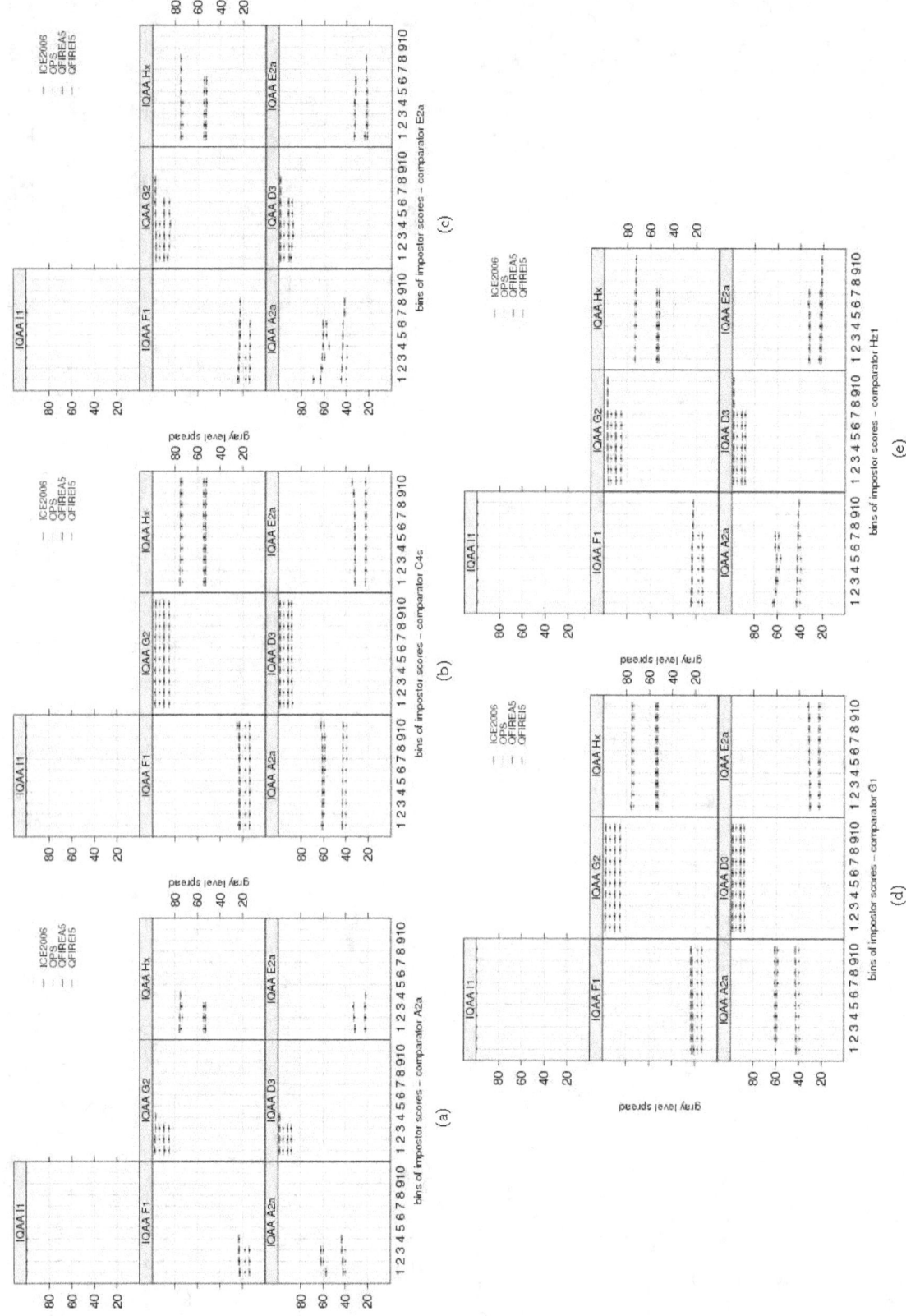

Figure 21: Pairwise GRAY SCALE SPREAD scores vs. impostor scores for the primary Class Z submissions of each participant. Each plot shows quality scores computed by different IQAA. Similar to plots of Figure 20, impostor scores are divided equally into ten groups, overlapping by 5 percent. The bootstrapped pairwise quality for each group is shown in a box and whisker plot. Pairwise quality is computed as geometric mean of the quality of the two samples being compared.

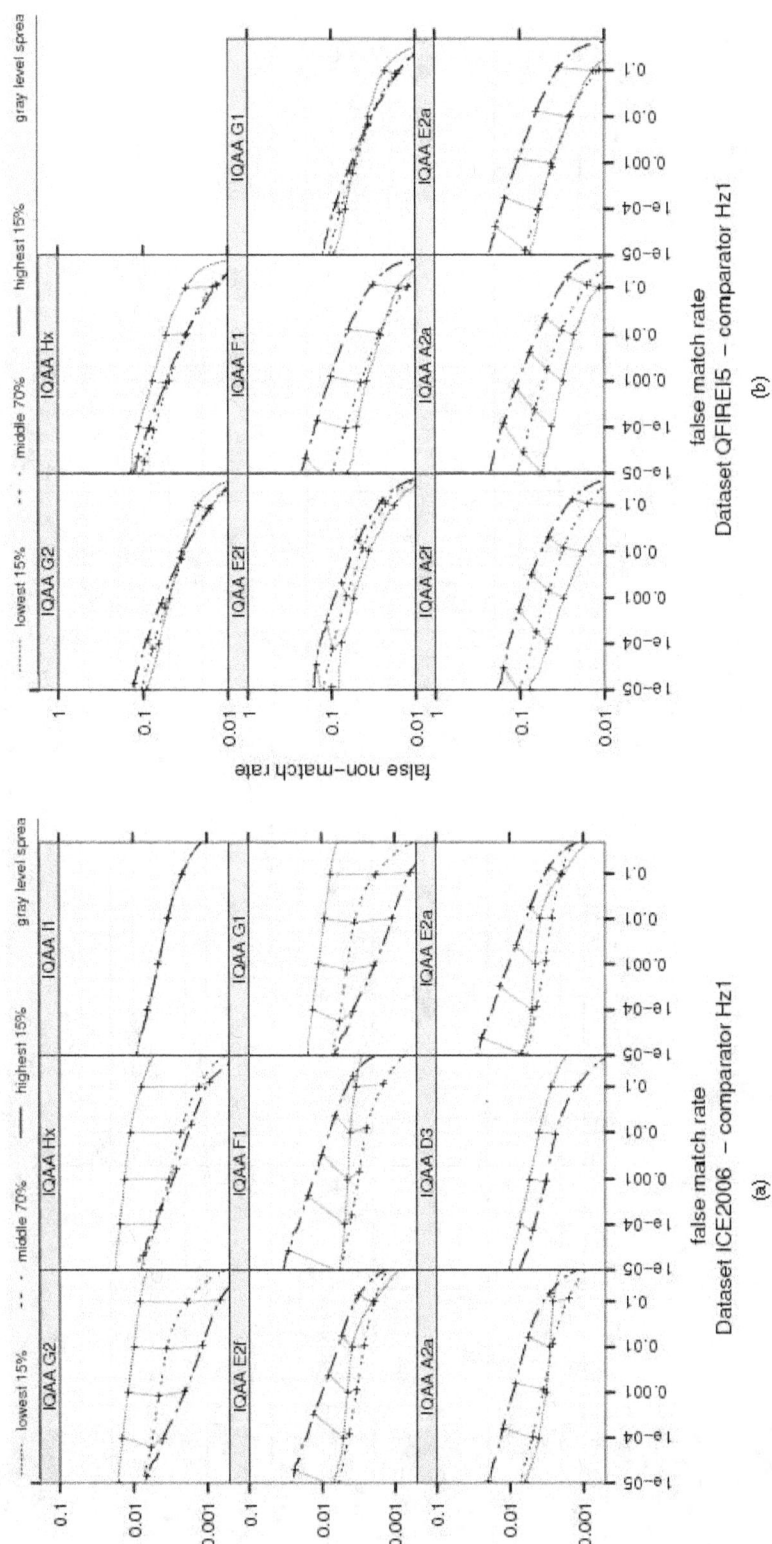

Figure 22: Ranked DET curves for comparator Hz1 and Datasets ICE2006 and QFIRE I5. The set of all comparisons are partitioned into three groups based on the pair-wise GRAY SCALE SPREAD quality of the images being compared. The lowest quality set contains comparisons with pairwise quality in the lowest 15 percentile. The highest quality set contains comparisons with pairwise quality in the highest 15 percentile. The rest of the comparisons, namely the middle 70%, make up the third set. The DETs are connected at the same score threshold values (brown lines). Lower FNMR and FMR rates are expected for higher quality images.

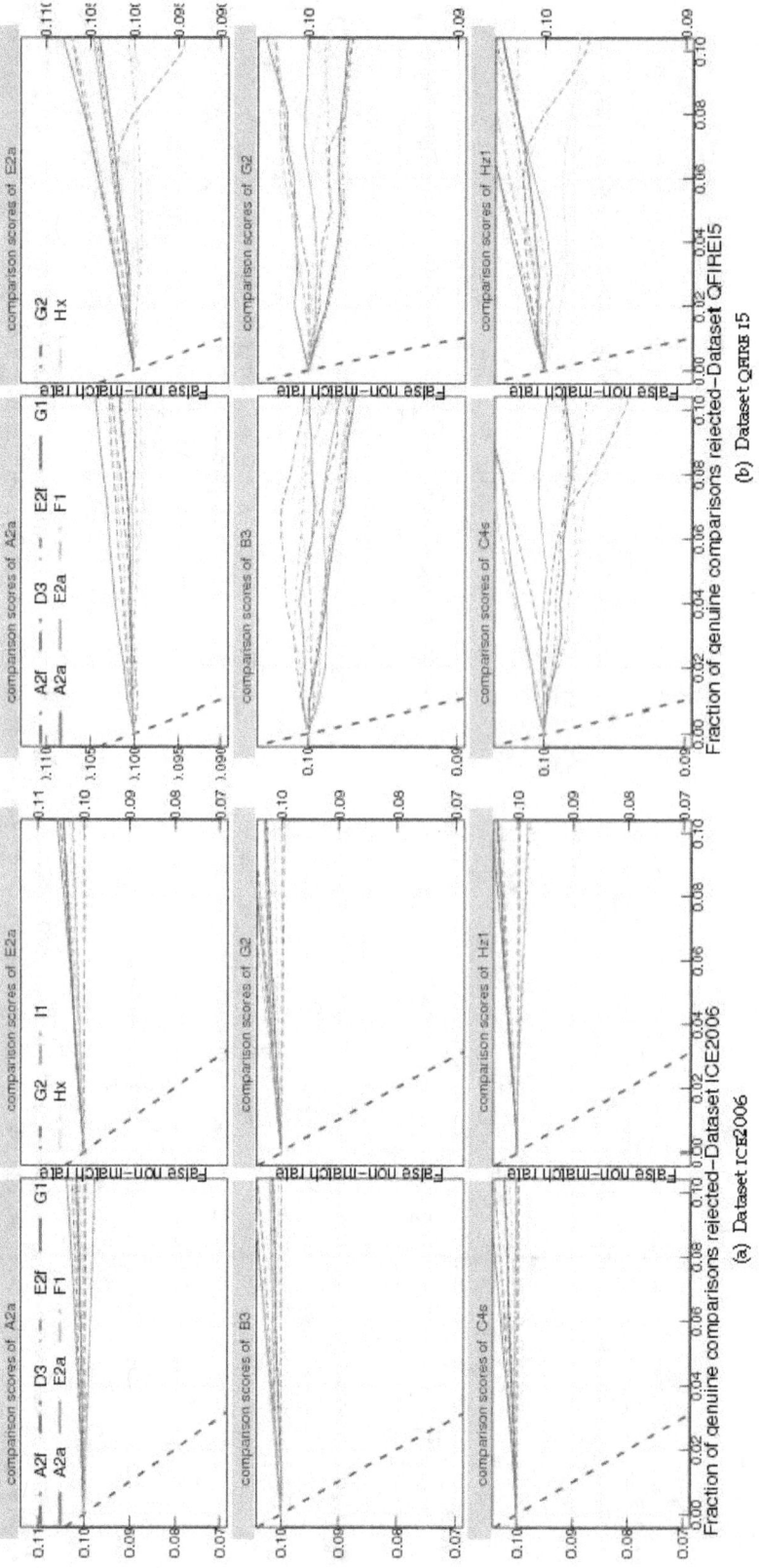

Figure 23: FNMR vs. reject curves for GRAY SCALE SPREAD scores on datasets ICE2006 and QFIRE I5. The threshold is set to give an initial FNMR = 0.1. The gray dotted line shows the ideal case where the rejection of the comparisons with the lowest ten percent quality results in zero FNMR.

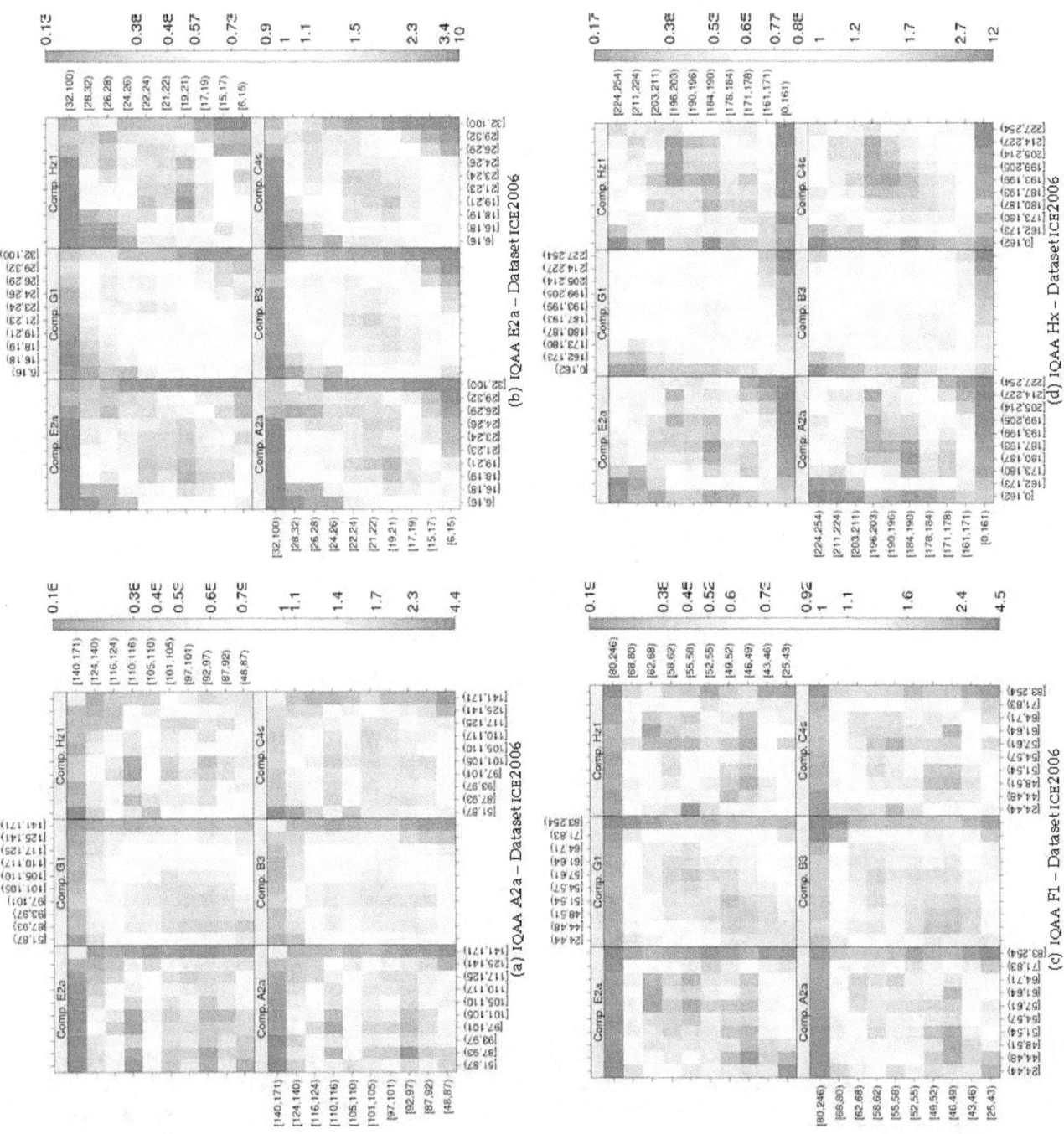

Figure 24: GRAY SCALE SPREAD computed by primary IQAA and FNMR for IQCE comparators for ICE2006 images. The y-axis represents enrollment samples' quality with verification samples' on the x-axis. The color scale plots $\frac{\text{FNMR}}{\text{FNMR}_0}$ for comparisons with verification and enrollment qualities $(q_{verification}, q_{enrollment})$. FNMR$_0$ is the nominal FNMR which is the false non-match rate computed over all the images at the same comparison score threshold, in this case at FMR = 0.001. Yellow/Green color represent an improvement in FNMR. Blue color represent a degradation of FNMR. White color means no change in FNMR.

71

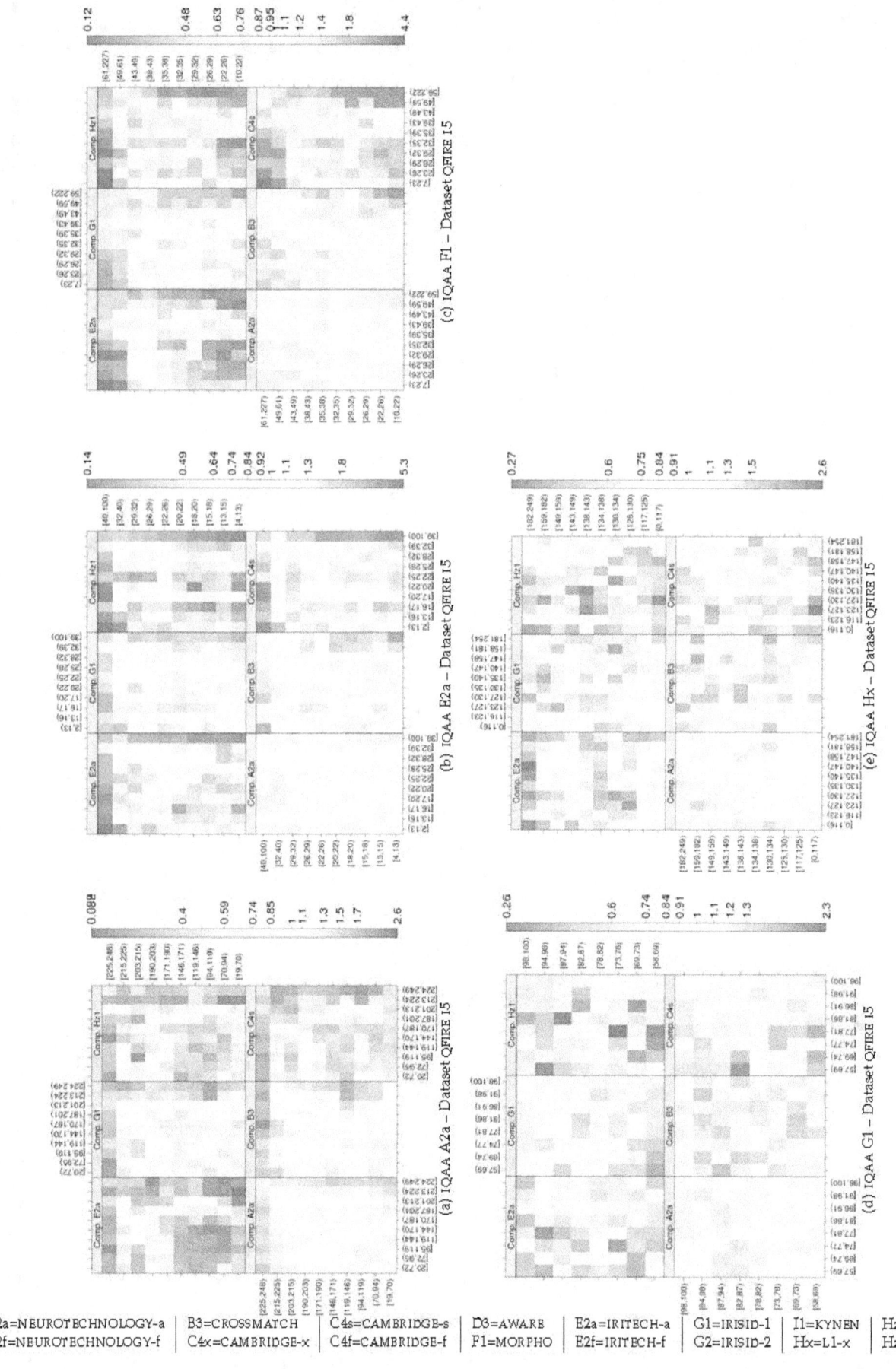

Figure 25: FNMR vs. (*q*verification, *q*enrollment). GRAY SCALE SPREAD computed by primary IQAA and FNMR for IQCE comparators for dataset QFIRE I5 . (see Figure 24 for more detail)

(a) IQAA A2a – Dataset QFIRE I5

(b) IQAA E2a – Dataset QFIRE I5

(c) IQAA F1 – Dataset QFIRE I5

(d) IQAA G1 – Dataset QFIRE I5

(e) IQAA Hx – Dataset QFIRE I5

| A2a=NEUROTECHNOLOGY-a | B3=CROSSMATCH | C4s=CAMBRIDGE-s | D3=AWARE | E2a=IRITECH-a | G1=IRISID-1 | I1=KYNEN | Hz1=L1-z1 |
| A2f=NEUROTECHNOLOGY-f | C4x=CAMBRIDGE-x | C4f=CAMBRIDGE-f | F1=MORPHO | E2f=IRITECH-f | G2=IRISID-2 | Hx=L1-x | Hz2=L1-z2 |

Dataset	comparator	IQAA A2f	IQAA E2a	IQAA E2f	IQAA F1	IQAA G1	IQAA G2	IQAA Hx
ICE2006	A2a	(-3.92,-3.69)	(-3.83,3.68)	(-3.59,-3.44)	(-4.99,-4.85)	(2.60,2.71)	(2.62,2.73)	(4.29,4.50)
ICE2006	B3	(-2.93,-2.83)	(-4.50,-4.43)	(-4.48,-4.41)	(-4.68,-4.62)	(1.28,1.32)	(1.30,1.35)	(0.67,0.76)
ICE2006	C4s	(-1.68,-1.51)	(-3.64,-3.53)	(-3.56,-3.45)	(-3.73,-3.62)	(3.58,3.66)	(3.59,3.66)	(4.56,4.72)
ICE2006	E2a	(-5.19,-4.95)	(-5.19,-5.04)	(-5.18,-5.03)	(-6.39,-6.25)	(2.41,2.53)	(2.25,2.36)	(4.28,4.50)
ICE2006	G2	(-6.70,-6.58)	(-2.91,-2.83)	(-2.83,-2.75)	(-7.61,-7.54)	(0.52,0.57)	(0.55,0.60)	(1.21,1.32)
ICE2006	Hz1	(-2.36,-2.09)	(-2.41,-2.24)	(-2.27,-2.11)	(-2.57,-2.40)	(2.96,3.09)	(2.98,3.10)	(4.46,4.70)
OPS	A2a	(-2.56,3.38)	(-1.61,2.54)	(-1.78,2.35)	(-3.34,-0.88)	(0.46,5.10)	(7.77,12.49)	(-2.56,3.12)
OPS	B3	(-0.15,2.25)	(-0.90,0.84)	(-0.94,0.80)	(-1.34,-0.31)	(1.97,3.88)	(1.91,3.84)	(0.01,2.38)
OPS	C4s	(-3.68,0.94)	(-2.96,0.38)	(-3.32,0.01)	(-4.11,-2.13)	(-1.67,2.06)	(-1.76,2.08)	(-1.73,2.83)
OPS	E2a	(-3.22,3.53)	(-1.55,3.32)	(-1.86,3.01)	(-2.67,0.22)	(-1.79,3.65)	(-1.91,3.69)	(-1.88,4.78)
OPS	G2	(-1.30,2.44)	(-0.85,1.85)	(-1.30,1.40)	(-2.68,-1.08)	(5.19,8.02)	(1.27,3.95)	(1.11,4.79)
OPS	Hz1	(-2.21,3.20)	(-1.60,2.30)	(-1.72,2.16)	(-3.12,-0.81)	(-1.13,3.25)	(0.80,5.29)	(-0.12,5.23)
QFIREA5	A2a	(-0.58,0.23)	(-0.48,0.09)	(-1.86,1.94)	(1.55,-1.01)	(-0.92,-0.37)	(-0.88,-0.35)	(-2.07,-1.39)
QFIREA5	B3	(0.18,1.43)	(-3.11,-2.32)	(-5.97,-1.59)	(-4.06,-3.22)	(-0.39,0.45)	(-0.53,0.28)	(-1.25,-0.21)
QFIREA5	C4s	(-1.23,-0.13)	(-4.33,-3.57)	(-5.41,-1.43)	(-5.07,-4.32)	(-2.33,-1.60)	(-2.40,-1.69)	(-2.22,-1.29)
QFIREA5	E2a	(-1.83,-1.08)	(-1.51,-0.97)	(-3.59,-0.69)	(-1.71,-1.19)	(-0.66,-0.15)	(-0.71,-0.22)	(-0.89,-0.24)
QFIREA5	G2	(-0.04,0.77)	(-2.74,-2.17)	(-3.19,-0.33)	(-3.76,-3.20)	(-1.34,-0.79)	(-1.36,-0.84)	(-1.63,-0.94)
QFIREA5	Hz1	(-1.53,-0.16)	(-3.18,-2.23)	(-1.23,3.36)	(-4.78,-3.84)	(-2.86,-1.95)	(-2.80,-1.92)	(-1.84,-0.68)
QFIREI5	A2a	(-4.15,-3.81)	(-1.02,-0.81)	(-2.35,-0.08)	(-0.80,-0.68)	(-0.26,-0.05)	(-0.31,-0.09)	(-0.16,0.02)
QFIREI5	B3	(-1.95,-1.58)	(-0.27,-0.08)	(-2.52,0.22)	(-0.26,-0.16)	(0.87,1.09)	(0.85,1.07)	(-0.67,-0.50)
QFIREI5	C4s	(-3.23,-2.79)	(-3.35,-3.09)	(-0.99,1.93)	(-2.22,-2.07)	(0.34,0.61)	(0.23,0.50)	(0.86,1.08)
QFIREI5	E2a	(-4.56,-4.10)	(-4.97,-4.70)	(-1.31,1.39)	(-2.73,-2.58)	(-2.44,-2.15)	(-2.54,-2.25)	(-2.08,-1.85)
QFIREI5	G2	(-2.24,-1.85)	(-2.55,-2.32)	(-6.54,-4.13)	(-1.92,-1.79)	(0.68,0.92)	(0.66,0.89)	(-0.53,-0.33)
QFIREI5	Hz1	(-5.12,-4.56)	(-4.86,-4.53)	(-2.75,0.30)	(-2.84,-2.66)	(-1.08,-0.73)	(-1.28,-0.93)	(0.65,0.94)

Table 11: Tukey HSD mean difference in GRAY SCALE SPREAD . Each cell shows the 95% confidence level in difference in mean of pairwise quality for images verified correctly (i.e., genuine score equal or less than threshold) and those rejected falsely (i.e., genuine score larger than threshold). Quality scores were computed by the SDK identified by the column header and comparison scores were generated by the SDK identified by the row header. If the interval does not contain zero, the difference in mean is significant. Cells where difference in mean is not significant have pink background. For monotonic quality components (all except DILATION , and depending on quality implementation GRAY SCALE SPREAD), the expected behavior is to have higher quality scores for pair of enrollment verification images that result in genuine comparison scores less than threshold. Pairwise quality is computed as geometric mean of the quality of two samples being compared. Threshold is set to give false match rate of 0.001.

Dataset	comparator	IQAA A2f	IQAA E2a	IQAA E2f	IQAA F1	IQAA G1	IQAA G2	IQAA Hx
ICE2006	A2a	(1.07,1.58)	(-0.57,-0.27)	(-0.52,-0.22)	(0.53,0.83)	(-1.36,-0.74)	(-1.20,-0.69)	(-1.61,-1.18)
ICE2006	B3	(-7.16,-6.79)	(-3.96,-3.74)	(-4.03,-3.81)	(-5.82,-5.59)	(3.38,3.82)	(2.42,2.78)	(-1.44,-1.14)
ICE2006	C4s	(-1.74,-1.34)	(-0.70,-0.47)	(-0.69,-0.45)	(-1.27,-1.03)	(0.27,0.75)	(0.22,0.62)	(-1.01,-0.68)
ICE2006	E2a	(-6.37,-5.97)	(0.11,0.35)	(0.17,0.41)	(-2.59,-2.35)	(1.75,2.23)	(1.61,2.01)	(0.18,0.52)
ICE2006	G2	(0.62,1.03)	(-0.41,-0.16)	(-0.33,-0.09)	(0.53,0.78)	(-0.75,-0.36)	(-0.26,-0.10)	(-0.92,-0.58)
ICE2006	Hz1	(-2.28,-1.83)	(-1.60,-1.34)	(-1.53,-1.27)	(-2.11,-1.84)	(4.89,5.42)	(3.09,3.53)	(-1.21,-0.86)
OPS	A2a	(-1.67,-1.03)	(-0.38,0.05)	(-0.33,0.09)	(-0.07,0.20)	(-1.14,-0.61)	(-1.10,-0.56)	(-1.44,-0.81)
OPS	B3	(-2.24,-1.72)	(-0.36,-0.02)	(-0.38,-0.03)	(-1.51,-1.29)	(-0.38,0.05)	(-0.09,0.35)	(-0.96,-0.45)
OPS	C4s	(-1.26,-0.73)	(0.12,0.46)	(0.15,0.49)	(-0.55,-0.33)	(-0.34,0.10)	(-0.35,0.11)	(-0.63,-0.11)
OPS	E2a	(-1.22,-0.68)	(-0.17,0.18)	(-0.14,0.22)	(-0.32,-0.09)	(-0.55,-0.10)	(-0.47,-0.01)	(-0.59,-0.06)
OPS	G2	(-0.49,0.04)	(-0.31,0.04)	(-0.29,0.06)	(-0.09,0.14)	(-0.91,-0.50)	(-0.91,-0.52)	(-1.16,-0.64)
OPS	Hz1	(-1.20,-0.68)	(0.23,0.57)	(0.24,0.59)	(-0.31,-0.09)	(0.01,0.45)	(0.16,0.61)	(-0.51,0.01)
QFIREA5	A2a	(-3.62,-2.67)	(-5.73,-4.93)	(-5.99,-1.28)	(-5.75,-5.07)	(0.41,1.15)	(0.42,1.06)	(1.16,1.93)
QFIREA5	C4s	(-1.95,-1.09)	(-1.78,-1.06)	(-4.17,-0.06)	(-1.37,-0.75)	(-0.04,0.59)	(-0.26,0.29)	(-0.64,0.06)
QFIREA5	E2a	(10.02,10.88)	(8.45,9.17)	(2.51,7.03)	(0.63,1.24)	(0.32,0.91)	(0.55,1.09)	(-0.75,-0.05)
QFIREA5	G2	(-0.79,0.10)	(-1.96,-1.23)	(-2.45,1.63)	(-1.60,-0.97)	(-1.00,-0.41)	(-1.01,-0.48)	(-0.19,0.51)
QFIREA5	Hz1	(-0.75,0.11)	(-0.78,-0.06)	(-3.03,1.38)	(-3.26,-2.64)	(-0.79,-0.11)	(-0.91,-0.33)	(-0.17,0.53)
QFIREI5	A2a	(-2.91,-2.21)	(0.07,0.39)	(-3.36,0.57)	(-0.14,0.04)	(-0.57,-0.18)	(-0.50,-0.11)	(0.29,0.59)
QFIREI5	C4s	(-6.62,-6.01)	(-1.14,-0.86)	(-2.59,0.73)	(-0.98,-0.82)	(-1.16,-0.82)	(-1.16,-0.83)	(0.27,0.53)
QFIREI5	E2a	(-13.39,-12.79)	(-6.81,-6.53)	(-9.17,-6.70)	(-3.12,-2.96)	(-5.50,-5.16)	(-5.55,-5.21)	(-2.95,-2.69)
QFIREI5	G2	(-8.74,-4.17)	(-1.34,0.76)	(-18.44,11.54)	(-0.74,0.43)	(-1.76,0.80)	(-1.88,0.63)	(-0.85,1.14)
QFIREI5	Hz1	(-7.48,-6.88)	(-1.88,-1.60)	(-4.28,-1.46)	(-0.94,-0.79)	(0.03,0.37)	(-0.07,0.26)	(-0.33,-0.07)

Table 12: Tukey HSD mean difference in GRAY SCALE SPREAD scores. Each cell shows the 95% confidence level in difference in mean of pairwise quality for images correctly rejected (i.e., the impostor score equal or greater than threshold) and those falsely matched (i.e., the impostor score less than threshold). Quality scores were computed by the SDK identified by the column header and comparison scores were generated by the SDK identified by the row header. If the interval does not contain zero, the difference in mean is significant. Cells where difference in mean is not significant are shaded in pink. For monotonic increasing quality components (all except DILATION, and depending on quality implementation GRAY SCALE SPREAD), the expected behavior is to have higher quality scores for the pair of (enrollment, verification) images that result in impostor comparison scores equal or greater than threshold. Pairwise quality is computed as geometric mean of the quality of two samples being compared. Threshold is set to give false match rate of 0.001.

A2a=NEUROTECHNOLOGY-a	B3=CROSSMATCH	C4s=CAMBRIDGE-s	D3=AWARE	E2a=IRITECH-a	G1=IRISID-1	I1=KYNEN	Hz1=L1-z1
A2f=NEUROTECHNOLOGY-f	C4x=CAMBRIDGE-x	C4f=CAMBRIDGE-f	F1=MORPHO	E2f=IRITECH-f	G2=IRISID-2	Hx=L1-x	Hz2=L1-z2

9.2 Iris size

IRIS SIZE is defined as the number of pixels across the iris radius, when the iris boundary is modeled by a circle. IRIS SIZE is determined by the spatial sampling rate of the image acquisition device and the distance between the subject and the acquisition device.

The IREXI showed that irises too big or too small cause recognition failure. Naturally IQCE specified IRIS SIZE as a covariate. The con-ops specified IRIS SIZE as the number of pixels across the iris radius, if iris is modeled by a circle.

The following nine participants computed iris size: A2a, A2f, C4x, C4s, C4f, D3, E2a, E2f, and I1.

The distribution of their IRIS SIZE scores is shown in Figure 26. In order to make the boxplots more readable, quality scores in [0–254] range were linearly scaled back to [0–100].

ICE2006 and QFIRE I5 are the more suited datasets to use for evaluation of IRIS SIZE. The off-axis gaze angle of QFIRE A5 could complicate measurement of IRIS SIZE. and result in noisy measurements of IRIS SIZE. Distribution of number of pixels across iris diameter for ICE2006 images is show in Figure 27.

RELATIONSHIP WITH THE DISTRIBUTION OF GENUINE SCORES

Figure 28 examines how genuine comparison scores vary with IRIS SIZE. IQAA C4x and E2a show higher IRIS SIZE scores for QFIRE A5 and QFIRE I5 images, but IQAA A2a shows smaller IRIS SIZE scores for these two datasets than OPS or ICE2006. The reason might be its high failure to process QFIRE A5 and QFIRE I5 images. Results shown here are only for images the IQAA were able to process and generate quality scores.

RELATIONSHIP WITH THE DISTRIBUTION OF IMPOSTOR SCORES

Figure 29 indicates that, at least for the range of IRIS SIZE in IQCE images, IRIS SIZE does not affect impostor scores.

RANKED DET:: DO LOW-QUALITY IMAGES PRODUCE HIGH FNMR OR FMR?

Comparison of the biometric performance of images with the highest 15%, the lowest 15% and the middle 70% is shown in Figure 30. Comparison scores of comparator HZ1 are used to generate these DET curves.

All IQAAs exhibit similar performance for the three partitions base on their IRIS SIZE scores. The best separation occurs for IQAAs C4x and E2a. Once again, note that the results are valid for the range and variation of the image covariate (in this caseIRIS SIZE) that exist in the test data. The effect of extreme values of IRIS SIZE on performance will not be observed if the test data does not contain such extreme values.

EFFECT OF QUALITY ON FNMR : HOW QUICKLY FNMR IMPROVES WHEN POOR QUALITY SAMPLES ARE REJECTED?

Figure 31 shows that FNMR improves slightly if ICE2006 images with the lowest IRIS SIZE scores are rejected. Performance of the IQAAs on the ICE2006 images are comparable, and all are generalizable, since their performance does not depend on the comparator.

| A2a=NEUROTECHNOLOGY-a | B3=CROSSMATCH | C4s=CAMBRIDGE-s | D3=AWARE | E2a=IRITECH-a | G1=IRISID-1 | I1=KYNEN | Hz1=L1-z1 |
| A2f=NEUROTECHNOLOGY-f | C4x=CAMBRIDGE-x | C4f=CAMBRIDGE-f | F1=MORPHO | E2f=IRITECH-f | G2=IRISID-2 | Hx=L1-x | Hz2=L1-z2 |

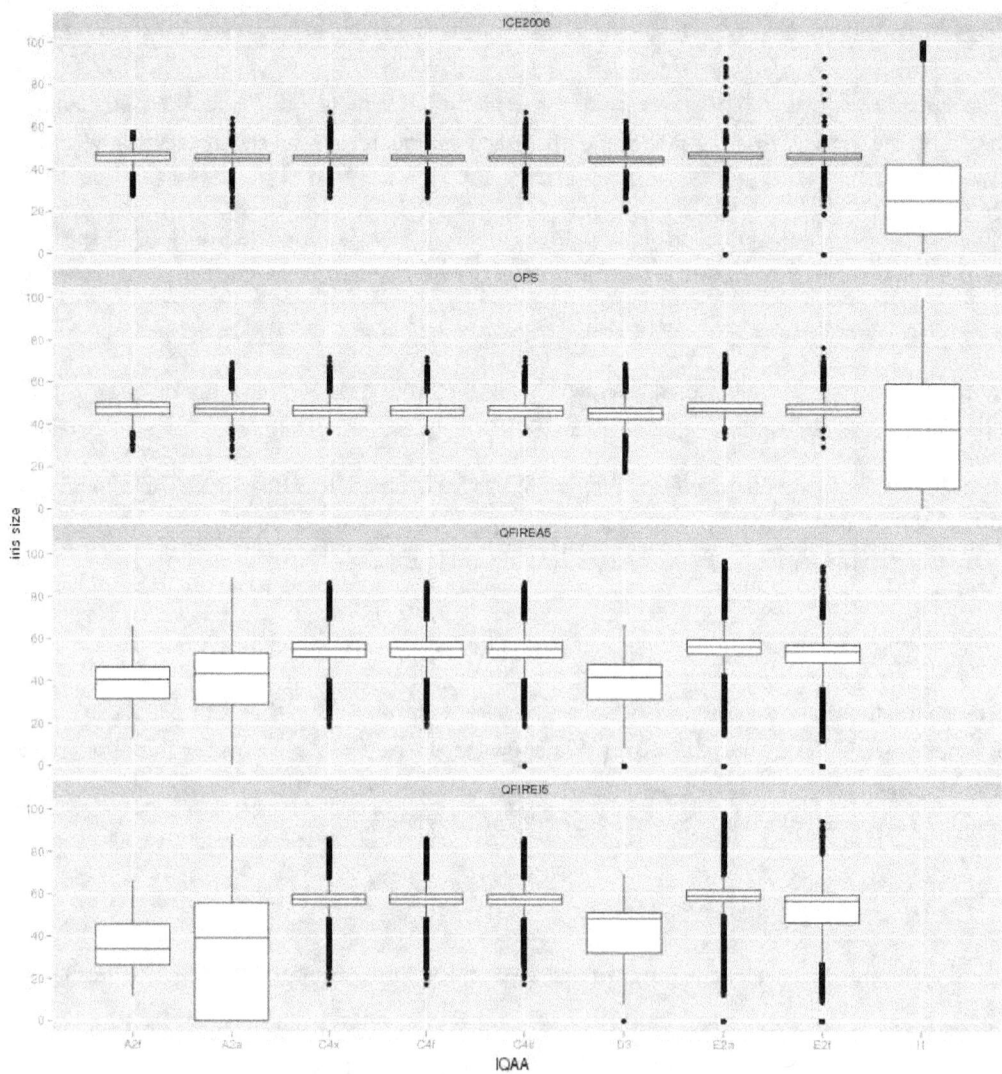

Figure 26: Box and whisker plots of the IQAAs that generate IRIS SIZE scores.

On QFIRE I5 images, A2a is the best predictor of performance for its mated comparator, but is not effective in prediction of performance of other comparators.

TEST OF SIGNIFICANCE :: DO THE IMAGES INVOLVED IN SUCCESSFUL VERIFICATION ATTEMPTS HAVE SIGNIFICANTLY HIGHER QUALITY SCORES THAN THOSE INVOLVED IN FAILED VERIFICATION ATTEMPTS?

The results of Tukey HSD in the mean of IRIS SIZE scores of images involved in successful verification attempts and those falsely rejected (or falsely accepted) are show in Table 13 (or Table 14). There is small but significant difference for ICE2006 and QFIRE images, but not for OPS images.

IQAA A2a Tukey HSD results suggest that its IRIS SIZE score is a monotonic decreasing function. Note that A2a was

76

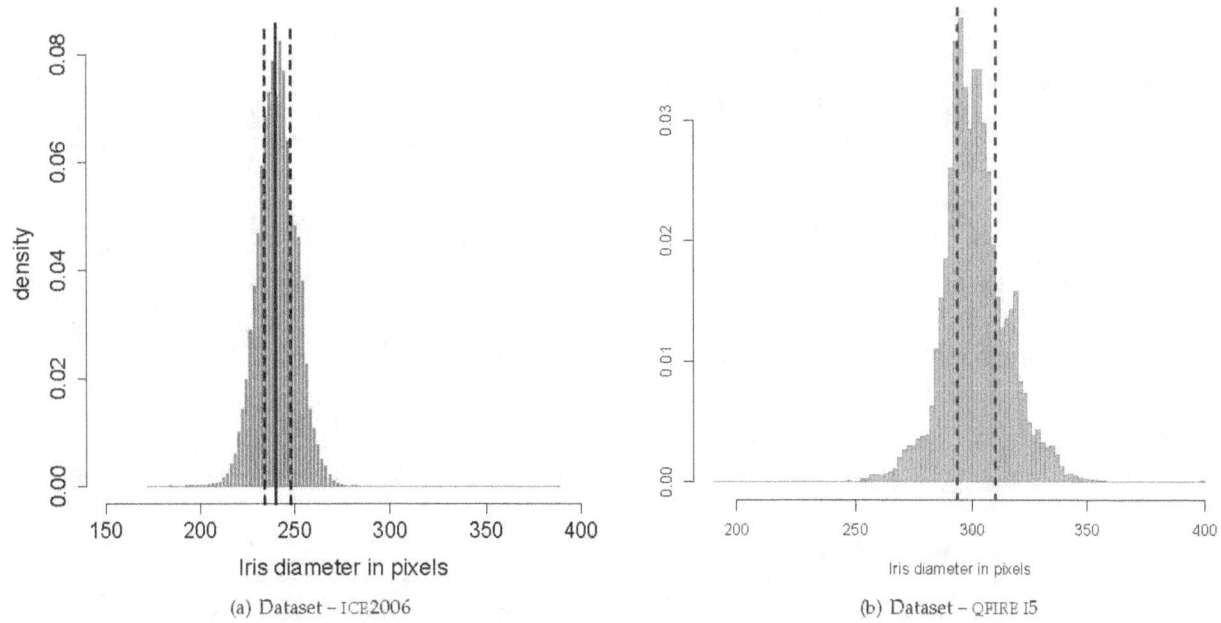

Figure 27: Histogram of the number of pixels across iris diameter.

unable to process many of the QFIRE I5 images; the results presented are for images for which A2a could generate a quality score and a template.

EFFECT OF VARIATION BETWEEN THE TWO SAMPLES:: DOES SAMENESS MATTER?

Figure 32 confirms findings of the above analysis. IQAA C4x IRIS SIZE scores are good predictor of performance, followed by IQAAs E2a and A2a. Furthermore, lower FNMR is observed when enrollment and verification images have similar IRIS SIZE scores, as is evident by darker blue colors at the bottom right and top left corners of the plots of Figure 32. IQAAs E2a and A2a are the second and third best performers. IQAAs I1 and D3 is the least effective, since the surface plots of Figure 32(e) are mostly light shades of blue or green color.

Only results for ICE2006 are presented here, since as mentioned above, QFIRE I5 images do not have the diversity of IRIS SIZE needed for meaningful analysis.

DEPENDENCE OF RECOGNITION PERFORMANCE ON SPATIAL SAMPLING RATE

To investigate the dependence of iris recognition on spatial resolution for a wider range of IRIS SIZE than exists in IQCE datasets, NIST generated synthetic images. To simulate iris images captured with a lower resolution iris camera, we down-sampled ICE2006 images by various factors. Performance of the degraded images were compared with their baseline (non-degraded) samples.

To mimic impairment caused by a lower resolution camera, we down-sampled images by factors 2, 4, 6, 8, and 10. Down

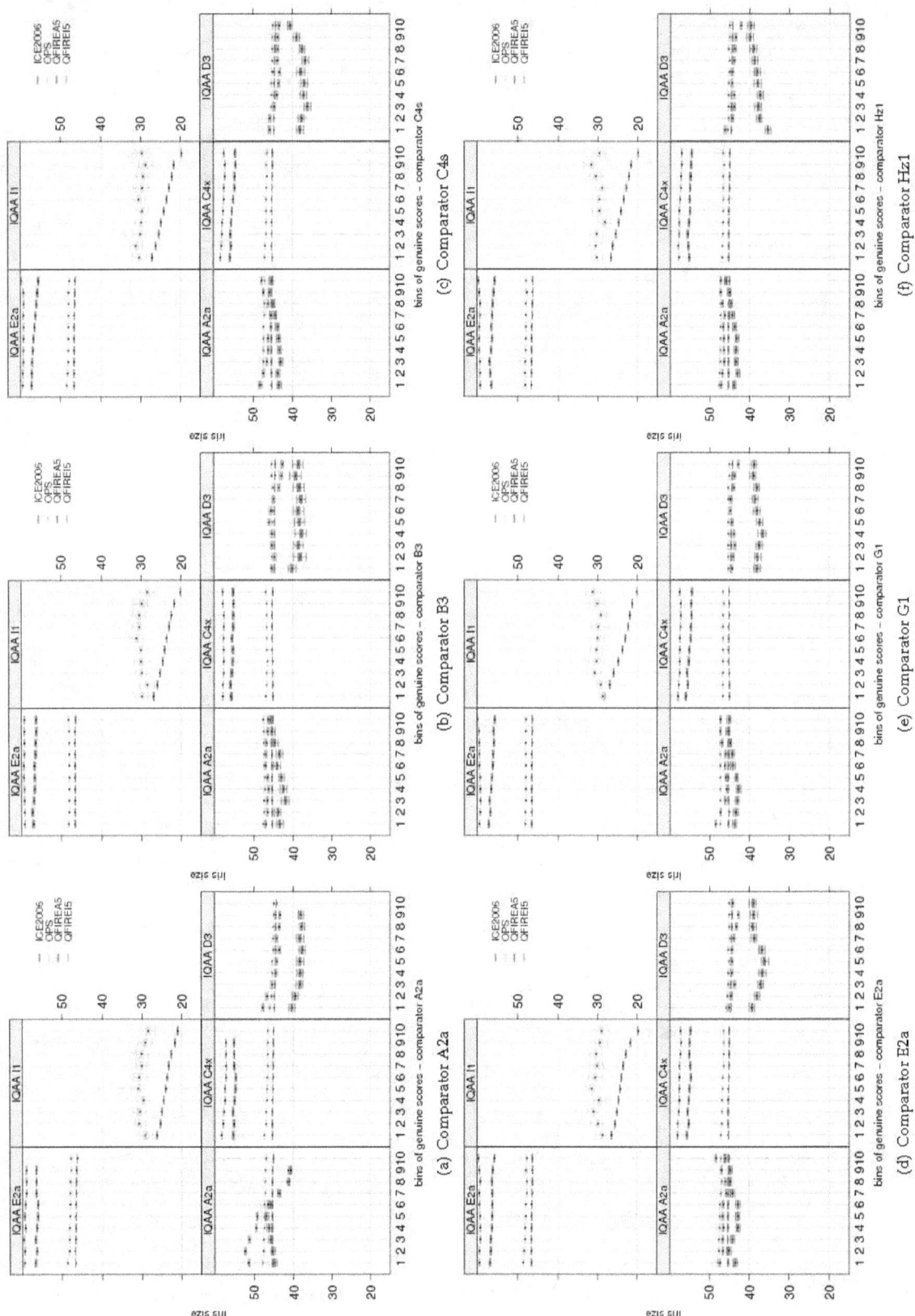

Figure 28: Pairwise IRIS SIZE scores vs. genuine score for the primary Class Z submissions of each participant. Each plot shows quality scores computed by different IQAA. Genuine scores are divided equally into ten groups. Groups overlap by 5 percent, meaning 5% of the data in one bin also belongs to the next bin. The bootstrapped pairwise quality for each group is shown in a box and whisker plot. Pairwise quality is computed as geometric mean of the quality of the two samples being compared.

| A2a=NEUROTECHNOLOGY-a | B3=CROSSMATCH | C4s=CAMBRIDGE-s | D3=AWARE | E2a=IRITECH-a | G1=IRISID-1 | I1=KYNEN | Hz1=L1-z1 |
| A2f=NEUROTECHNOLOGY-f | | C4x=CAMBRIDGE-x | C4f=CAMBRIDGE-f | F1=MORPHO | E2f=IRITECH-f | G2=IRISID-2 | Hx=L1-x | Hz2=L1-z2 |

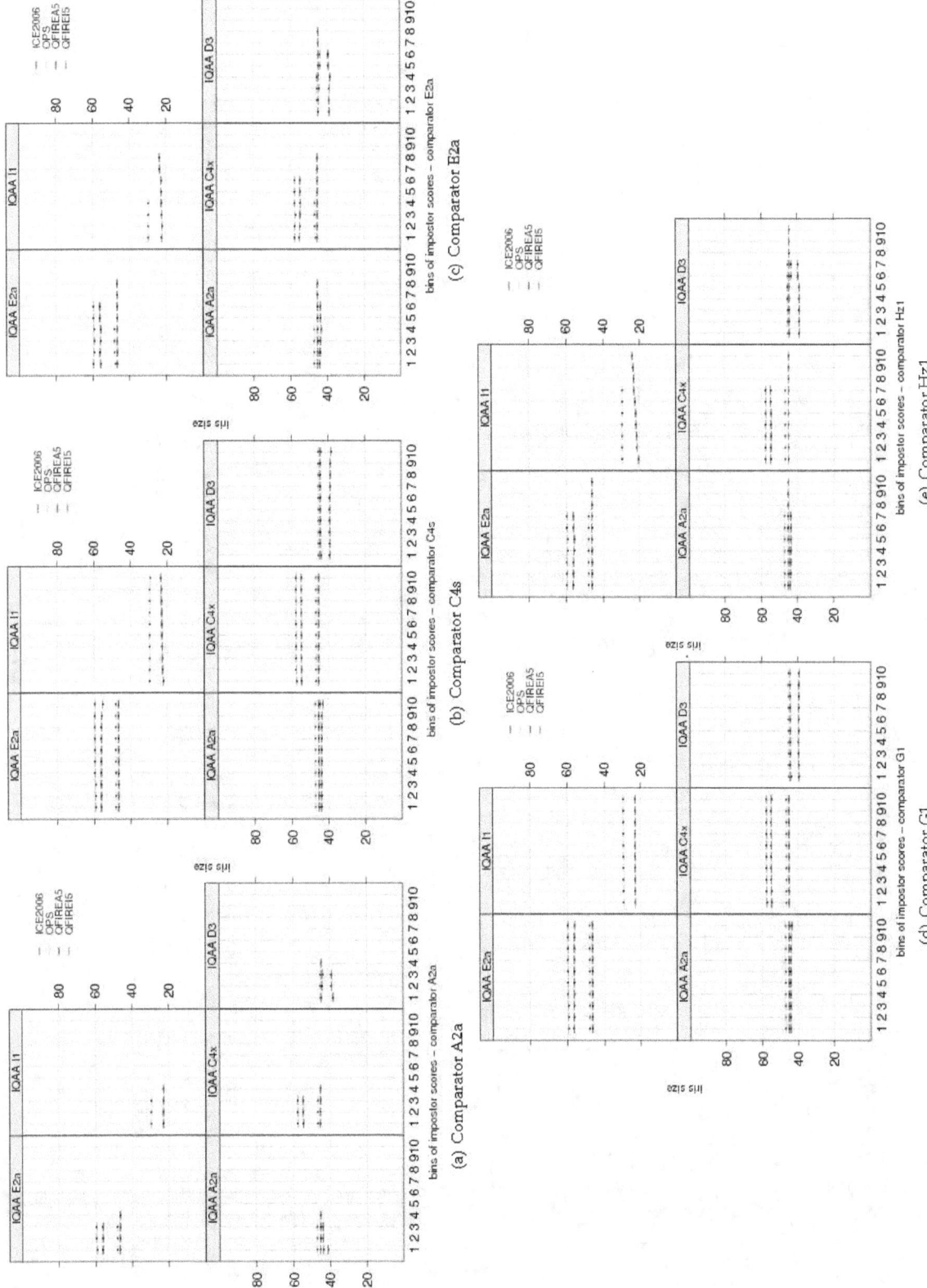

Figure 29: Pairwise IRIS SIZE scores vs. impostor scores for the primary Class Z submissions of each participants. Each plot shows quality scores computed by different IQAA. Similar to plots of Figure 28, impostor scores are divided equally into ten groups. Groups overlap by 5 percent. Bootstrapped pairwise quality for each group is shown in a box and whisker plot. Pairwise quality is computed as geometric mean of the quality of the two samples being compared. Impostor scores are not affected by IRIS SIZE scores.

| A2a=NEUROTECHNOLOGY-a | B3=CROSSMATCH | C4s=CAMBRIDGE-s | D3=AWARE | E2a=IRITECH-a | G1=IRISID-1 | I1=KYNEN | Hz1=L1-z1 |
| A2f=NEUROTECHNOLOGY-f | C4x=CAMBRIDGE-x | C4f=CAMBRIDGE-f | F1=MORPHO | E2f=IRITECH-f | G2=IRISID-2 | Hx=L1-x | Hz2=L1-z2 |

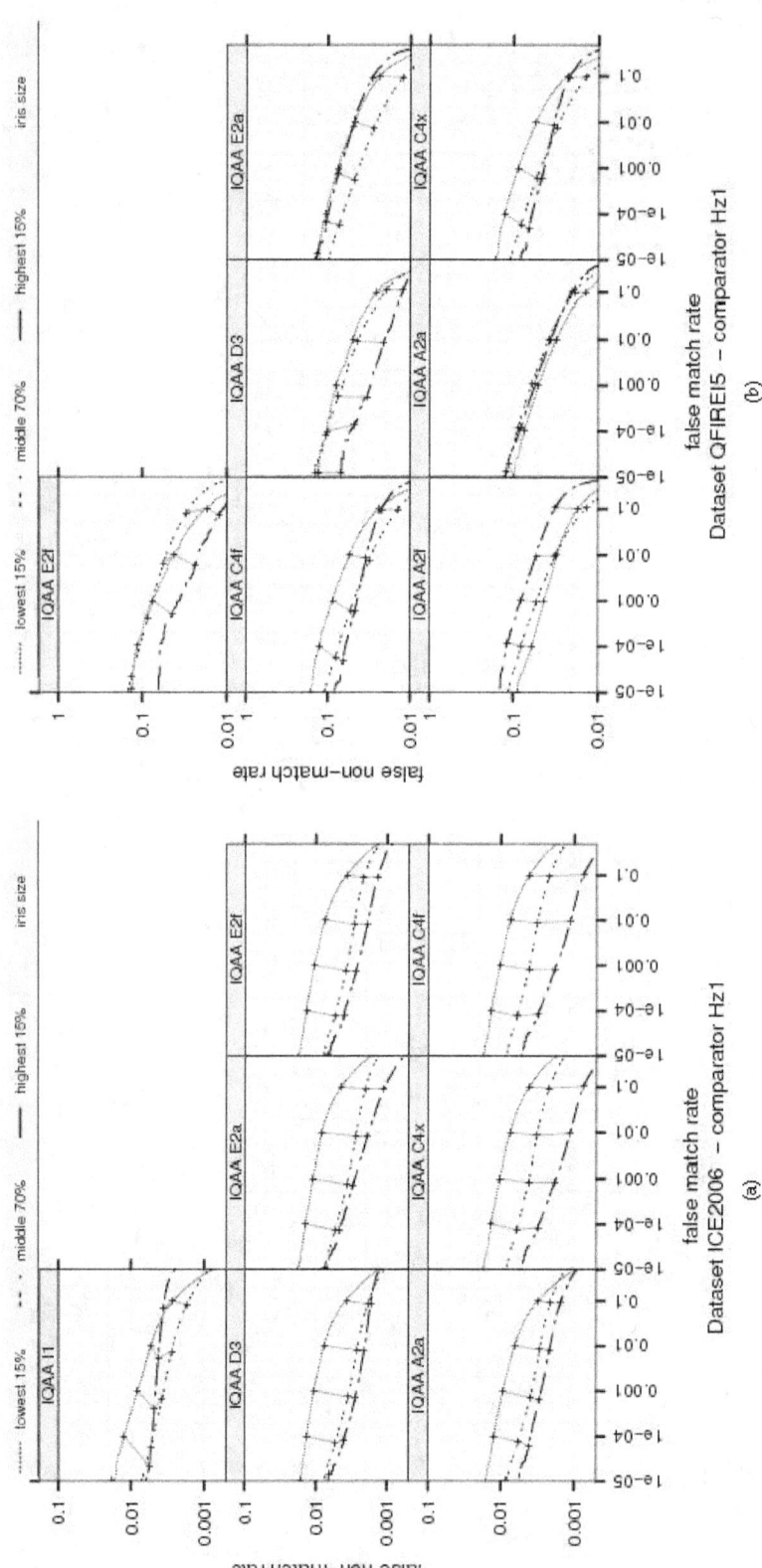

Figure 30: Ranked DET curves for comparator Hz1 and Datasets ICE2006 and QFIRE15. The set of all comparisons are partitioned into three groups based on the pair-wise IRIS SIZE quality of the images being compared. The lowest quality set contains comparisons with pairwise quality in the lowest 15 percentile. The highest quality set contains comparisons with pairwise quality in the highest 15 percentile. The rest of the comparisons, namely the middle 70%, make up the third set. The DETs are connected at the same score threshold values (brown lines). Lower FNMR and FMR rates are expected for higher quality images. The DET curves exhibit similar performance ranking is achieved for IQAAs C4x and E2a scores.

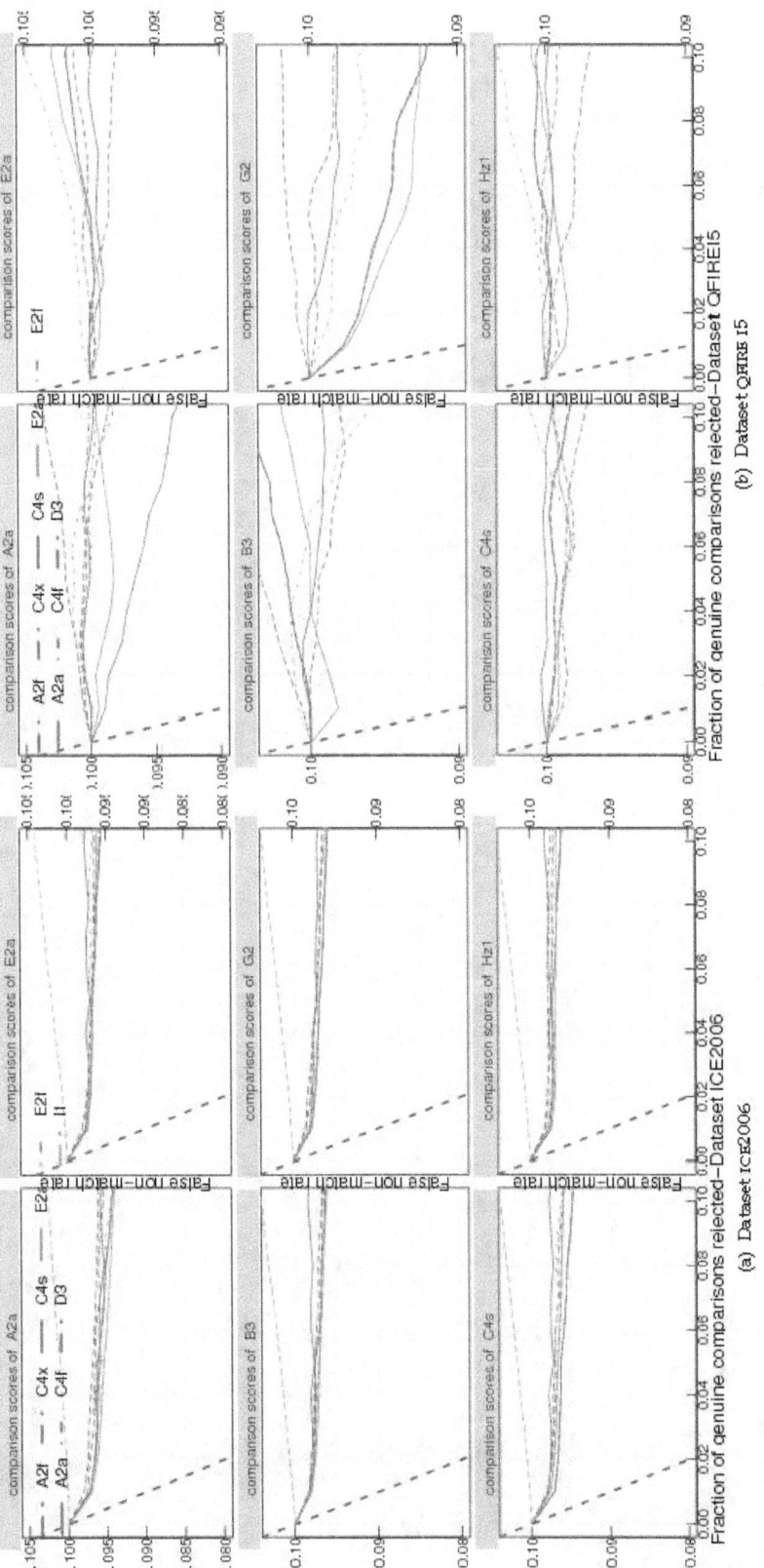

Figure 31: FNMR vs. reject curves for IRIS SIZE scores on datasets ICE2006 and QFIRE I5. The threshold is set to give an initial FNMR = 0.1. The gray dotted line shows the ideal case where the rejection of the comparisons with the lowest ten percent quality results in zero FNMR.

A2a=NEUROTECHNOLOGY-a   B3=CROSSMATCH   C4s=CAMBRIDGE-s   D3=AWARE   E2a=IRITECH-a   G1=IRISID-1   I1=KYNEN   Hz1=L1-z1
A2f=NEUROTECHNOLOGY-f   C4x=CAMBRIDGE-x   C4f=CAMBRIDGE-f   F1=MORPHO   E2f=IRITECH-f   G2=IRISID-2   Hx=L1-x   Hz2=L1-z2

Figure 32: FNMR vs. (𝑞𝑣𝑒𝑟𝑖𝑓𝑖𝑐𝑎𝑡𝑖𝑜𝑛, 𝑞𝑒𝑛𝑟𝑜𝑙𝑙𝑚𝑒𝑛𝑡). IRIS SIZE computed by primary IQAA submissions and FNMR for IQCE comparators for ICE2006 images. The y-axis represents enrollment samples with verification samples on the x-axis. The IRIS SIZE scores are quantized into 10 quantiles. The color scale plots $\frac{FNMR}{FNMR_0}$ for comparisons with verification and enrollment qualities (𝑞𝑣𝑒𝑟𝑖𝑓𝑖𝑐𝑎𝑡𝑖𝑜𝑛, 𝑞𝑒𝑛𝑟𝑜𝑙𝑙𝑚𝑒𝑛𝑡). $FNMR_0$ is the nominal FNMR which is the false non-match rate computed over all the images at the same comparison score threshold, in this case at FMR = 0.001. Yellow/Green color represent an improvement in FNMR. Blue color represent a degradation of FNMR. White color means no change in FNMR.

| A2a=NEUROTECHNOLOGY-a | B3=CROSSMATCH | C4s=CAMBRIDGE-s | D3=AWARE | E2a=IRITECH-a | G1=IRISID-1 | I1=KYNEN | Hz1=L1-z1 |
| A2f=NEUROTECHNOLOGY-f | C4x=CAMBRIDGE-x | C4f=CAMBRIDGE-f | F1=MORPHO | E2f=IRITECH-f | G2=IRISID-2 | Hx=L1-x | Hz2=L1-z2 |

sampling is effectively block-averaging $n * n$ pixel squares from an original $640 * 480$ image into one pixel. This reduces the actual number of pixels across the iris by a factor of n and produces a $(640/n) * (480/n)$ pixel image. This is repeated for $n = 2, 4, 6, 8, 10$ for all the images in our enrollment and verification sets. For $n = 2$, down-sampled images are $320 * 240$ and about 110 pixels across iris diameter. Similarly for $n = 4$, down-sampled images are $160 * 120$ and about 55 pixels across iris diameter. The down-sampled images which are not $640 * 480$ cannot be processed by the comparators; therefore we up-sampled images to their original $640 * 480$ size.

OpenCV cvResize [4] implementation was used to down-sample the images with interpolation method set to nearest-neighbor. Likewise, OpenCV cvResize was used to up-sample the images using bicubic Spline interpolation. Nearest neighbor is the simplest method for down-sampling which degrades an image more than bilinear or bicubic interpolations. Bicubic spline has been chosen for up-sampling, to minimize any additional and unwanted artifacts. Note that the information lost in down sampling will not be recovered regardless of the choice of up-sampling method.

Figure 33 shows a baseline image with its down-sampled versions. Image degradation increases as n increases, where severe impairment happens at $n = 6$ or more.

One question is how closely the impairment in our synthetic data models the impairment in the images captured with a capture device that produces iris images with the same iris diameter as our synthetic data. In a real-world scenario, spatial sampling rate is affected by several factors such as optical characteristic of the camera (e.g., MTF), focus, diffraction, subject-camera distance and their relative motion. In our study, all these factors stay almost constant, and only sensor pixel density varies. While our block averaging smooths the noise content, its effect on performance is smaller than the effect of loss of information due to down-sampling. An iris imaging device, with a certain pixel-density produces an iris image with P pixels across diameter, where P is proportional to the actual subject iris size (measured in millimeter) and is inversely proportional to the camera's pixel pitch (dots per inch). Our synthetic image degradation mimics the use of a sensor with similar optical properties but greater pixel pitch or larger subject-camera distance. We conclude that the variation in recognition performance for our synthetic data is a fair estimate of a real-world variation in recognition performance of irises with similar size.

To assess the effect of spatial sampling rate on performance, we computed detection error trade-off curves for the baseline and the degraded images (Figure 33).

One interesting point to observe is that for $n = 2$, false match rate improves slightly for all four algorithms, while false non-match rate suffers for all. This change is the smallest for comparator C4s and largest for E2a. At $n = 4$, false match rates are almost back to their corresponding baseline values. False non-match rates, however, have further degraded for all algorithms. At $n > 4$, both error rates (FNMR and FMR) are severely affected.

Thus, we conclude that irises suitable for recognition shall have at least 120 pixels across diameter (60 across radius).

Given that median iris diameter of our test data is 240 pixels with interquartile range of 234-248, images down-sampled by $n = 2$ have a median of 120 pixel across iris diameter and interquartile range of 116-124. This, over the range of average human irises (radius of 10.2 mm-13mm per [5]), corresponds to 10-12 pixels per millimeter.

OBSERVATIONS AND CONCLUSIONS

A small but significant effect on performance was observed for IQCE images. When segmentation is successful, large irises perform better than small irises. Better FNMR is achieved when the IRIS SIZE of two images being compared are similar.

| A2a=NEUROTECHNOLOGY-a | B3=CROSSMATCH | C4s=CAMBRIDGE-s | D3=AWARE | E2a=IRITECH-a | G1=IRISID-1 | I1=KYNEN | Hz1=L1-z1 |
| A2f=NEUROTECHNOLOGY-f | C4x=CAMBRIDGE-x | C4f=CAMBRIDGE-f | F1=MORPHO | E2f=IRITECH-f | G2=IRISID-2 | Hx=L1-x | Hz2=L1-z2 |

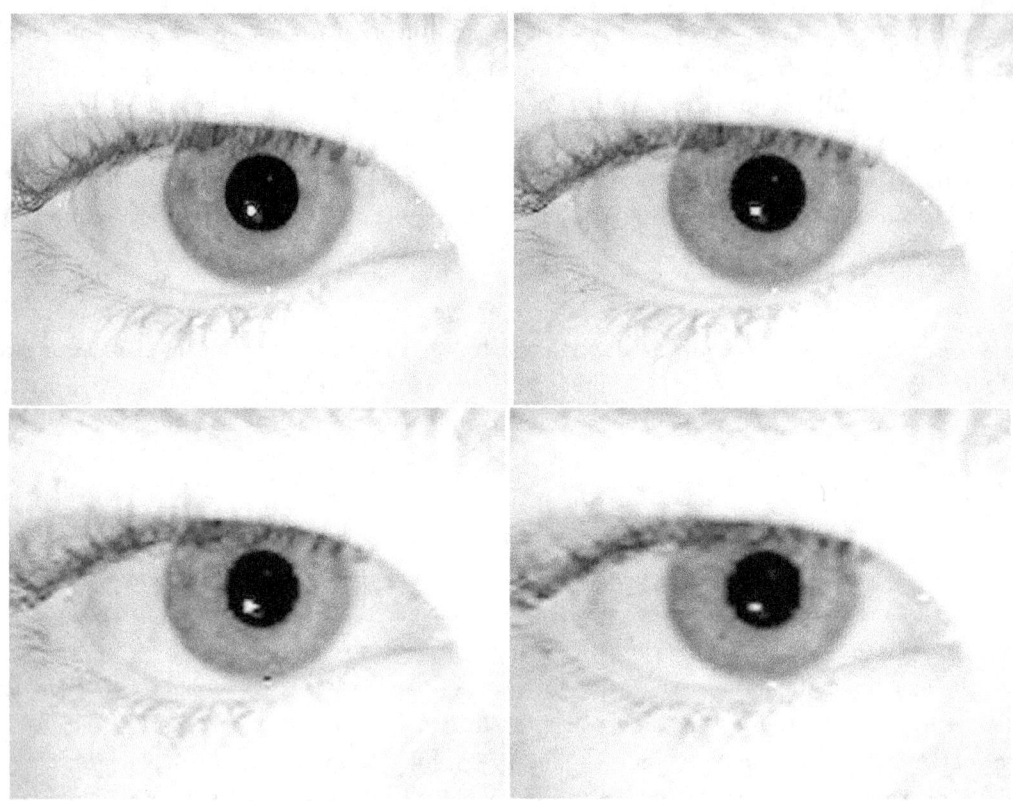

Figure 33: To simulate the effect of a low resolution iris camera, 71643 images of ICE2006 dataset are down-sampled by various factors and then up-sampled to their original sizes so that the iris recognition algorithms can process them. Down-sampling is basically a block average operation, where $n*n$ pixels are averaged to produce one pixel. Up sampling does not recover information lost by down sampling. We used bicubic spline for upsampling to avoid any other possible impairment or artifact. Counter clockwise from top left are the resultant images for $n = 2, 4, 6, 8$ and 10. For a baseline image of $640 * 480$ with 240 pixels across iris diameter, the top left ($n = 2$) is $240 * 320$ pixels with 120 pixels across iris, the top right ($n = 4$) is $120 * 160$ pixels with 60 pixels across iris, and so on. Note that iris texture detail is clear at $n = 2$, less clear at $n = 4$, and almost disappears at $n = 8$. OpenCV implementation cvResize were used to perform down-sample and up-sample operations. The interpolation method was set to CV_INTER_NN for down-sampling and CV_INTER_CUBIC for up sampling.

IQAA C4x IRIS SIZE scores are good predictor of performance, followed by IQAAs E2a and A2a.

Down sampling ICE2006 images with a factor of two, did not affect FNMR or FMR, suggesting iris radius of [58-62] pixels is sufficient for recognition (iris radius of the ICE2006 images has a mean of 120 and an inter-quartile range of [116-124]).

| A2a=NEUROTECHNOLOGY-a | B3=CROSSMATCH | C4s=CAMBRIDGE-s | D3=AWARE | E2a=IRITECH-a | G1=IRISID-1 | I1=KYNEN | Hz1=L1-z1 |
| A2f=NEUROTECHNOLOGY-f | C4x=CAMBRIDGE-x | C4f=CAMBRIDGE-f | F1=MORPHO | E2f=IRITECH-f | G2=IRISID-2 | Hx=L1-x | Hz2=L1-z2 |

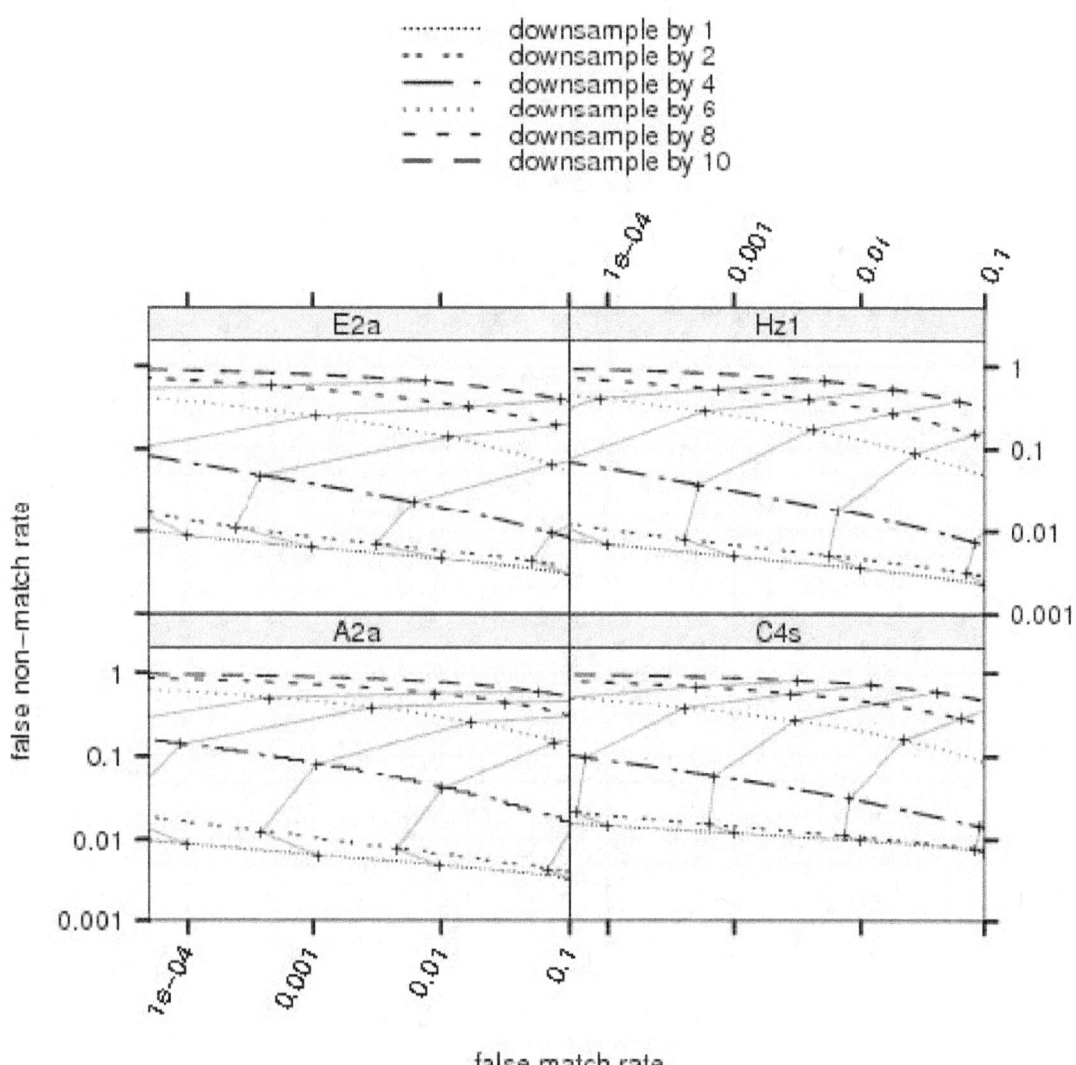

Figure 34: Each cell shows Detection Error Trade-Off (DET) curves for the baseline, and the synthetically degraded images for the iris recognition algorithm identified by the cell's label. The brown lines connects DETs at the same score threshold value. Note the severe increase in false match rate after down sampling by 6.

Dataset	comparator	IQAA A2f	IQAA C4x	IQAA E2a	IQAA E2f
ICE2006	A2a	(0.55,0.60)	(1.28,1.32)	(0.98,1.03)	(1.30,1.34)
ICE2006	B3	(0.34,0.37)	(0.41,0.43)	(0.39,0.41)	(0.41,0.43)
ICE2006	C4s	(0.38,0.42)	(0.38,0.42)	(0.72,0.75)	(0.85,0.88)
ICE2006	E2a	(0.80,0.86)	(1.68,1.72)	(1.41,1.46)	(1.50,1.54)
ICE2006	G2	(-0.06,-0.03)	(0.32,0.34)	(0.34,0.36)	(0.36,0.39)
ICE2006	Hz1	(0.70,0.77)	(0.97,1.02)	(0.78,0.83)	(0.97,1.02)
OPS	A2a	(-0.92,0.85)	(-2.60,-0.91)	(-2.08,-0.39)	(-2.27,-0.58)
OPS	B3	(-0.57,0.17)	(-0.72,-0.01)	(-0.74,-0.04)	(-0.73,-0.03)
OPS	C4s	(-0.77,0.65)	(-0.74,0.63)	(-0.70,0.66)	(-1.13,0.24)
OPS	E2a	(-1.68,0.41)	(-1.11,0.88)	(-0.93,1.05)	(-1.22,0.76)
OPS	G2	(0.29,1.86)	(-0.40,0.70)	(-0.38,0.72)	(-0.66,0.43)
OPS	Hz1	(-0.39,1.29)	(-0.43,1.17)	(0.12,1.72)	(-0.28,1.32)
QFIREA5	A2a	(0.15,0.56)	(-0.07,0.12)	(-0.14,0.05)	(-0.93,0.86)
QFIREA5	B3	(0.17,0.77)	(0.22,0.50)	(0.40,0.68)	(2.67,6.39)
QFIREA5	C4s	(-0.82,-0.25)	(0.60,0.86)	(0.99,1.25)	(2.09,4.27)
QFIREA5	E2a	(-0.60,-0.20)	(0.42,0.60)	(0.45,0.63)	(0.18,1.79)
QFIREA5	G2	(-0.45,-0.03)	(0.55,0.74)	(0.68,0.87)	(-0.04,1.39)
QFIREA5	Hz1	(-1.72,-1.02)	(0.44,0.76)	(0.67,0.99)	(-0.00,2.54)
QFIREI5	A2a	(0.19,0.35)	(0.52,0.57)	(0.37,0.45)	(0.39,1.71)
QFIREI5	B3	(1.60,1.76)	(-0.16,-0.11)	(-0.01,0.06)	(1.28,2.89)
QFIREI5	C4s	(-1.62,-1.43)	(0.25,0.32)	(-0.55,-0.45)	(-0.98,0.72)
QFIREI5	E2a	(-1.68,-1.47)	(0.26,0.33)	(-0.48,-0.39)	(-2.27,-0.70)
QFIREI5	G2	(0.02,0.19)	(0.08,0.14)	(-0.28,-0.20)	(1.96,3.41)
QFIREI5	Hz1	(-2.15,-1.90)	(0.35,0.43)	(-0.48,-0.36)	(-0.25,1.53)

Table 13: Tukey HSD mean difference in IRIS SIZE . Each cell shows the 95% confidence level in difference in mean of pairwise quality for images verified correctly (i.e., genuine score equal or less than threshold) and those rejected falsely (i.e., genuine score larger than threshold). Quality scores were computed by the SDK identified by the column header and comparison scores were generated by the SDK identified by the row header. If the interval does not contain zero, the difference in mean is significant. Cells where difference in mean is not significant have pink background. For monotonic quality components (all except DILATION , and depending on quality implementation GRAY SCALE SPREAD), the expected behavior is to have higher quality scores for pair of enrollment verification images that result in genuine comparison scores less than threshold. Pairwise quality is computed as geometric mean of the quality of two samples being compared. Threshold is set to give false match rate of 0.001.

A2a=NEUROTECHNOLOGY-a	B3=CROSSMATCH	C4s=CAMBRIDGE-s	D3=AWARE	E2a=IRITECH-a	G1=IRISID-1	I1=KYNEN	Hz1=L1-z1
A2f=NEUROTECHNOLOGY-f	C4x=CAMBRIDGE-x	C4f=CAMBRIDGE-f	F1=MORPHO	E2f=IRITECH-f	G2=IRISID-2	Hx=L1-x	Hz2=L1-z2

Dataset	comparator	A2f	IQAA C4x	IQAA E2a	IQAA E2f
ICE2006	A2a	(-0.62,-0.50)	(-0.53,-0.44)	(-0.53,-0.44)	(-0.54,-0.44)
ICE2006	B3	(-1.16,-1.07)	(-0.22,-0.16)	(-0.30,-0.24)	(-0.26,-0.19)
ICE2006	C4s	(-0.44,-0.35)	(-0.20,-0.13)	(-0.20,-0.12)	(-0.19,-0.12)
ICE2006	E2a	(-1.05,-0.95)	(-0.54,-0.47)	(-0.52,-0.45)	(-0.54,-0.47)
ICE2006	G2	(-0.30,-0.20)	(-0.26,-0.19)	(-0.31,-0.24)	(-0.32,-0.25)
ICE2006	Hz1	(-0.39,-0.29)	(-0.15,-0.07)	(-0.12,-0.04)	(-0.09,-0.02)
OPS	A2a	(-0.09,0.11)	(-0.01,0.18)	(0.02,0.21)	(0.04,0.23)
OPS	B3	(-0.06,0.10)	(0.06,0.21)	(0.08,0.23)	(0.10,0.26)
OPS	C4s	(0.04,0.21)	(0.07,0.23)	(0.10,0.26)	(0.11,0.27)
OPS	E2a	(0.32,0.49)	(0.39,0.55)	(0.42,0.58)	(0.42,0.58)
OPS	G2	(0.02,0.19)	(0.02,0.18)	(0.02,0.18)	(0.02,0.17)
OPS	Hz1	(0.11,0.28)	(0.16,0.32)	(0.18,0.34)	(0.19,0.35)
QFIREA5	A2a	(1.95,2.41)	(1.00,1.29)	(0.35,0.71)	(1.82,4.87)
QFIREA5	C4s	(0.16,0.58)	(0.15,0.41)	(-0.02,0.31)	(-0.34,2.33)
QFIREA5	E2a	(-4.64,-4.22)	(-1.56,-1.30)	(-1.36,-1.03)	(-6.44,-3.52)
QFIREA5	G2	(0.21,0.65)	(0.27,0.52)	(0.44,0.76)	(-0.95,1.71)
QFIREA5	Hz1	(-1.33,-0.91)	(-0.65,-0.39)	(-0.55,-0.22)	(-1.41,1.57)
QFIREI5	A2a	(0.43,0.74)	(0.28,0.37)	(0.46,0.59)	(0.38,3.18)
QFIREI5	C4s	(0.57,0.84)	(0.68,0.75)	(0.48,0.58)	(0.33,2.70)
QFIREI5	E2a	(-3.07,-2.80)	(-0.46,-0.39)	(-0.87,-0.76)	(-1.32,0.44)
QFIREI5	G2	(-0.93,1.13)	(0.07,0.62)	(-0.57,0.21)	(-4.67,17.26)
QFIREI5	Hz1	(0.62,0.89)	(0.34,0.41)	(0.40,0.51)	(1.56,3.57)

Table 14: Tukey HSD mean difference in IRIS SIZE scores. Each cell shows the 95% confidence level in difference in difference in mean of pairwise quality for images correctly rejected (i.e., the impostor score equal or greater than threshold) and those falsely matched (i.e., the impostor score less than threshold). Quality scores were computed by the SDK identified by the column header and comparison scores were generated by the SDK identified by the row header. If the interval does not contain zero, the difference in mean is significant. Cells where difference in mean is not significant are shaded in pink. For monotonic increasing quality components (all except DILATION, and depending on quality implementation GRAY SCALE SPREAD), the expected behavior is to have higher quality scores for the pair of (enrollment, verification) images that result in impostor comparison scores equal or greater than threshold. Pairwise quality is computed as geometric mean of the quality of two samples being compared. Threshold is set to give false match rate of 0.001.

87

A2a=NEUROTECHNOLOGY-a | B3=CROSSMATCH | C4s=CAMBRIDGE-s | D3=AWARE | E2a=IRITECH-a | G1=IRISID-1 | I1=KYNEN | Hz1=L1-z1
A2f=NEUROTECHNOLOGY-f | C4x=CAMBRIDGE-x | C4f=CAMBRIDGE-f | F1=MORPHO | E2f=IRITECH-f | G2=IRISID-2 | Hx=L1-x | Hz2=L1-z2

9.3   Dilation (Pupil_iris ratio)

IQCE con-ops defined DILATION as the ratio of pupil diameter to iris diameter. The distribution of the DILATION scores is shown in Figure 35. In order to make the boxplots more readable, quality scores in [0–254] range were linearly scaled back to [0–100].

Note the degree of agreement among the IQAAs ' measurement of DILATION seem to indicate that the IQAAs ' with similar range for DILATION are measuring the same image property, with E2a and E2f probably inverted. IQAA B3, Hx and I1 may be attempting to convert the center (e.g mean) of the actual measurement values (which is the ratio of pupil diameter to iris diameter) to a high quality score.

All fourteen IQAAs computed DILATION scores. High values of indicate a high degree of pupillary DILATION, and hence low USABLE IRIS AREA . Low values of DILATION indicate a constricted pupil that could complicate iris localization and adversely affect performance.

This section gives quantitative results for the effect of DILATION on performance.

RELATIONSHIP WITH THE DISTRIBUTION OF GENUINE SCORES

Figure 36 shows the dependency of genuine comparison scores on DILATION scores. The IQAAs behave differently. Their behavior is different across IQCE datasets, but the same across comparators.

ICE2006 images with high DILATION scores give high genuine comparison scores. This is true for all IQAAS, except for Hx scores which high genuine comparison scores are observed for images with low DILATION scores. High genuine comparison scores give false reject.

IQAA Hx gives the highest separation among datasets.

RELATIONSHIP WITH THE DISTRIBUTION OF IMPOSTOR SCORES

Figure 37 shows the dependency of impostor comparison scores on DILATION scores. Similar to genuine scores, the relationship of pairwise DILATION scores and impostor scores differs among datasets and IQAAs . Among datasets, the least change is observed for QFIRE A5 and then the OPS dataset. Among comparators, G1's impostor scores are least affected by variation in DILATION .

RANKED DET:: DO LOW-QUALITY IMAGES PRODUCE HIGH FNMR OR FMR?

The DET curves of Figure 38 compare the performance of images with the highest or lowest degree of DILATION with the images in the middle range.

The first observation is that the difference in performance is not substantial among the three partitions based on DILATION scores.

Secondly, in case of ICE2006, the DET curves cross. Images whose DILATION scores are in the middle 70 percentile of the distribution give the lowest FNMR (the lowest curve among the three). This result is expected and confirms other studies that irises highly dilated or highly constricted elevate FNMR. The lowest FMR and the flattest DET curve are observed

| A2a=NEUROTECHNOLOGY-a | B3=CROSSMATCH | C4s=CAMBRIDGE-s | D3=AWARE | E2a=IRITECH-a | G1=IRISID-1 | I1=KYNEN | Hz1=L1-z1 |
| A2f=NEUROTECHNOLOGY-f | C4x=CAMBRIDGE-x | C4f=CAMBRIDGE-f | F1=MORPHO | E2f=IRITECH-f | G2=IRISID-2 | Hx=L1-x | Hz2=L1-z2 |

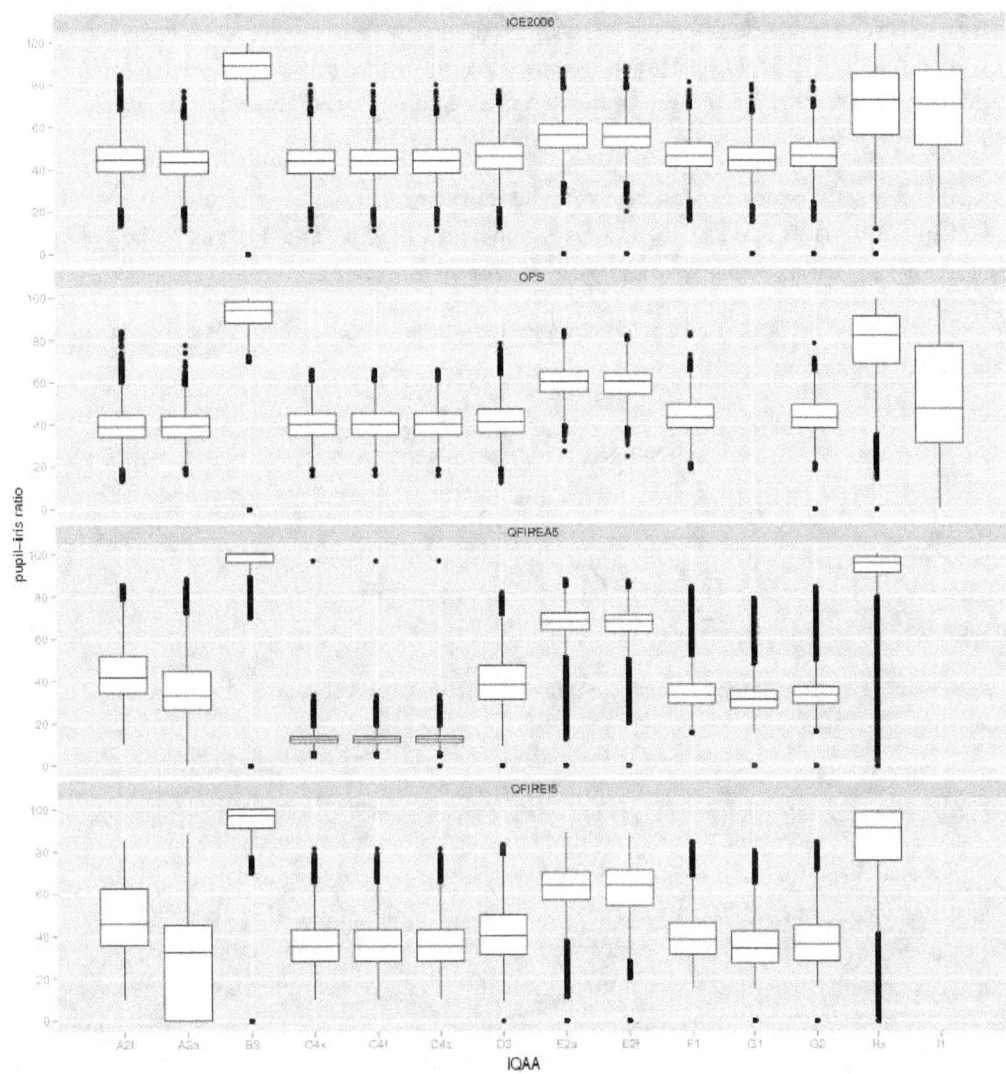

Figure 35: Box and whisker plots of the IQAAs that generate DILATION scores.

for the lowest pairwise DILATION scores of IQAA A2a, C4x, D3, F1, G1, and I1. IQAA B3, E2a, and Hx's highest DILATION scores give the lowest FMR and the flattest DET curve. The crossing of DET curves does not happen for QFIRE I5 images. There could be several explanations for that, but the authors suspect that other, more significant factors such as usable iris area or sharpness is probably the main reason.

EFFECT OF QUALITY ON FNMR : HOW QUICKLY FNMR IMPROVES WHEN POOR QUALITY SAMPLES ARE REJECTED?

IQCE asked for the actual measurement of the DILATION and defined it as the ratio of pupil diameter to iris diameter. As such, low and high DILATION scores would correspond to highly constricted and highly dilated pupils, which are undesirable trends. To this end, in generating the error vs. reject curves, DILATION scores are normalized per Equation 3 in Section 5. The result of this normalization is that images further away from the center of the DILATION distribution

A2a=NEUROTECHNOLOGY-a	B3=CROSSMATCH	C4s=CAMBRIDGE-s	D3=AWARE	E2a=IRITECH-a	G1=IRISID-1	I1=KYNEN	Hz1=L1-z1
A2f=NEUROTECHNOLOGY-f	C4x=CAMBRIDGE-x	C4f=CAMBRIDGE-f	F1=MORPHO	E2f=IRITECH-f	G2=IRISID-2	Hx=L1-x	Hz2=L1-z2

are given low normalized score (indicating poor quality) and images closer to the center are given high normalized score (indicating good quality). This normalization assumes that the center presents the "normal" DILATION values (good quality) and DILATION scores further away from the center represent highly dilated or constricted pupils, and therefore poor quality.

As mentioned before (with more discussions follow later in this section) IQAAs B3 and Hx seem to attempt to convert their assessment of DILATION into a quality scores where high values indicate high likelihood of match-ability, but this causes the IQCE normalization (Equation 3) not working for them.

Results are shown in Figure 39. Performance is comparable across all IQAAS. There is not clear cut determination of any IQAA being superior to the others.

TEST OF SIGNIFICANCE :: DO THE IMAGES INVOLVED IN SUCCESSFUL VERIFICATION ATTEMPTS HAVE SIGNIFICANTLY HIGHER QUALITY SCORES THAN THOSE INVOLVED IN FAILED VERIFICATION ATTEMPTS?

Ignoring dataset OPS, IQAAs C4x, G1 and Hx DILATION scores are significantly different between the images matched correctly and those result in false reject, however, the difference is small.

Table 16 shows that generally images which give false match have significantly different DILATION scores than those correctly rejected.

EFFECT OF VARIATION BETWEEN THE TWO SAMPLES:: DOES SAMENESS MATTER?

Figures 40 and 41 indicate that the performance of all IQCE comparators is affected by DILATION . Two trends are noticeable for many comparator – IQAA pairs: a) diagonal trend; the diagonal symmetry indicating Sameness, and b) centralization trend; the more green in the middle indicating middle values are better. Plots where the darker blue tends toward the upper left and lower right edges, with light shading in the upper right and lower left make the case that image pairs with similar DILATION give lower FNMR than dissimilar DILATION values. When the blue shading tends toward all 4 edges and the green cluster toward the middle, this indicates that performance is best when there is a "normal" level of DILATION. In these cases, when the darker green tends toward the middle-lower-left, this would indicate that the best performance is for constricted pupil (which gives higher USABLE IRIS AREA) but not extremely constricted and not highly dissimilar. See for example Figure 40, IQAA B3 mated, and Comparator Hz1 with IQAAs C4x, G1, F1. Also on Figure 40, IQAA A2a with its mated comparator (and some others as well) is an excellent example of "sameness matters", but this trend is not consistent across data sets or for all comparators.

From Figure 41, for IQAA Hx, note that for comparators C4s, Hz1, E2a and G1, the behavior of the heatmap is that expected for a monotonic quality measure (although inverted, with high scores yielding poor matching results). This supports the observation from Figure 35 that IQAA Hx appeared to be computing a quality factor in lieu of directly measuring the ratio itself.

Comparators B3 and G1 are the most affected by DILATION . Dissimilar values of DILATION increases Comparators G1's and B3's FNMR.

DILATION scores generated by IQAAs D3 is the least effective. Its surface plots have a low contrast, meaning most of the q_{enroll}, q_{verif} bins produce about the same FNMR. IQAA B3 is the best predictor of its mated comparator. IQAAs C4x, F1,

| A2a=NEUROTECHNOLOGY-a | B3=CROSSMATCH | C4s=CAMBRIDGE-s | D3=AWARE | E2a=IRITECH-a | G1=IRISID-1 | I1=KYNEN | Hz1=L1-z1 |
| A2f=NEUROTECHNOLOGY-f | C4x=CAMBRIDGE-x | C4f=CAMBRIDGE-f | F1=MORPHO | E2f=IRITECH-f | G2=IRISID-2 | Hx=L1-x | Hz2=L1-z2 |

G1, and Hx DILATION scores are generalizable. Images with their low (or high) DILATION score contribute to FNMR of any IQCE comparator.

OBSERVATIONS AND CONCLUSIONS

IREXI demonstrated that higher amounts of pupillary DILATION increase iFNMR and iFMR. It also demonstrated that the difference between the DILATION present in two iris images affects their comparison score. In particular, large disparities in DILATION elevate false rejection error rates, but do not change false match rates.

Different IQAAs and different comparators behave differently, and there are discernible trends that indicate that sometimes "sameness matters", and often the performance is poorer when extreme values of DILATION are present.

IQAAs E2f and E2a appear to be computing the inverse ratio. IQAAs B3 and Hx appear to be attempting to convert the DILATION score into a quality score.

There is not clear cut determination of any IQAA being superior to the others, but further study using datasets with a wider range of DILATION and perhaps consistently defined factors will be more revealing.

| A2a=NEUROTECHNOLOGY-a | B3=CROSSMATCH | C4s=CAMBRIDGE-s | D3=AWARE | E2a=IRITECH-a | G1=IRISID-1 | I1=KYNEN | Hz1=L1-z1 |
| A2f=NEUROTECHNOLOGY-f | C4x=CAMBRIDGE-x | C4f=CAMBRIDGE-f | F1=MORPHO | E2f=IRITECH-f | G2=IRISID-2 | Hx=L1-x | Hz2=L1-z2 |

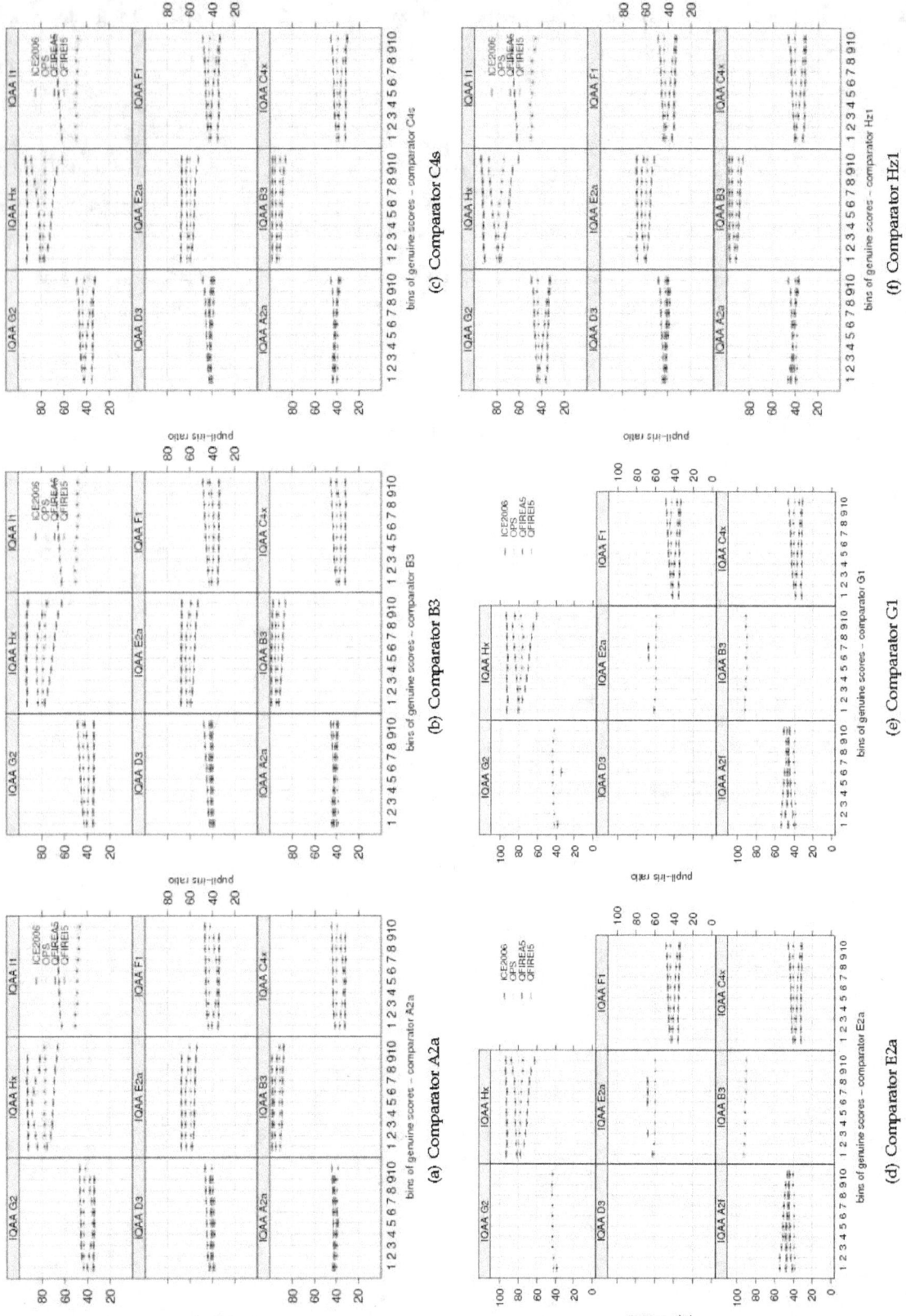

Figure 36: Pairwise DILATION scores *vs.* genuine score for the primary Class Z submissions of each participant. Each plot shows quality scores computed by different IQAA. Genuine scores are divided equally into ten groups. Groups overlap by 5 percent, meaning 5% of the data in one bin also belongs to the next bin. The bootstrapped pairwise quality for each group is shown in a box and whisker plot. Pairwise quality is computed as geometric mean of the quality of the two samples being compared.

A2a=NEUROTECHNOLOGY-a	B3=CROSSMATCH	C4s=CAMBRIDGE-s	D3=AWARE	E2a=IRITECH-a	G1=IRISID-1	I1=KYNEN	Hz1=L1-z1
A2f=NEUROTECHNOLOGY-f	C4x=CAMBRIDGE-x	C4f=CAMBRIDGE-f	F1=MORPHO	E2f=IRITECH-f	G2=IRISID-2	Hx=L1-x	Hz2=L1-z2

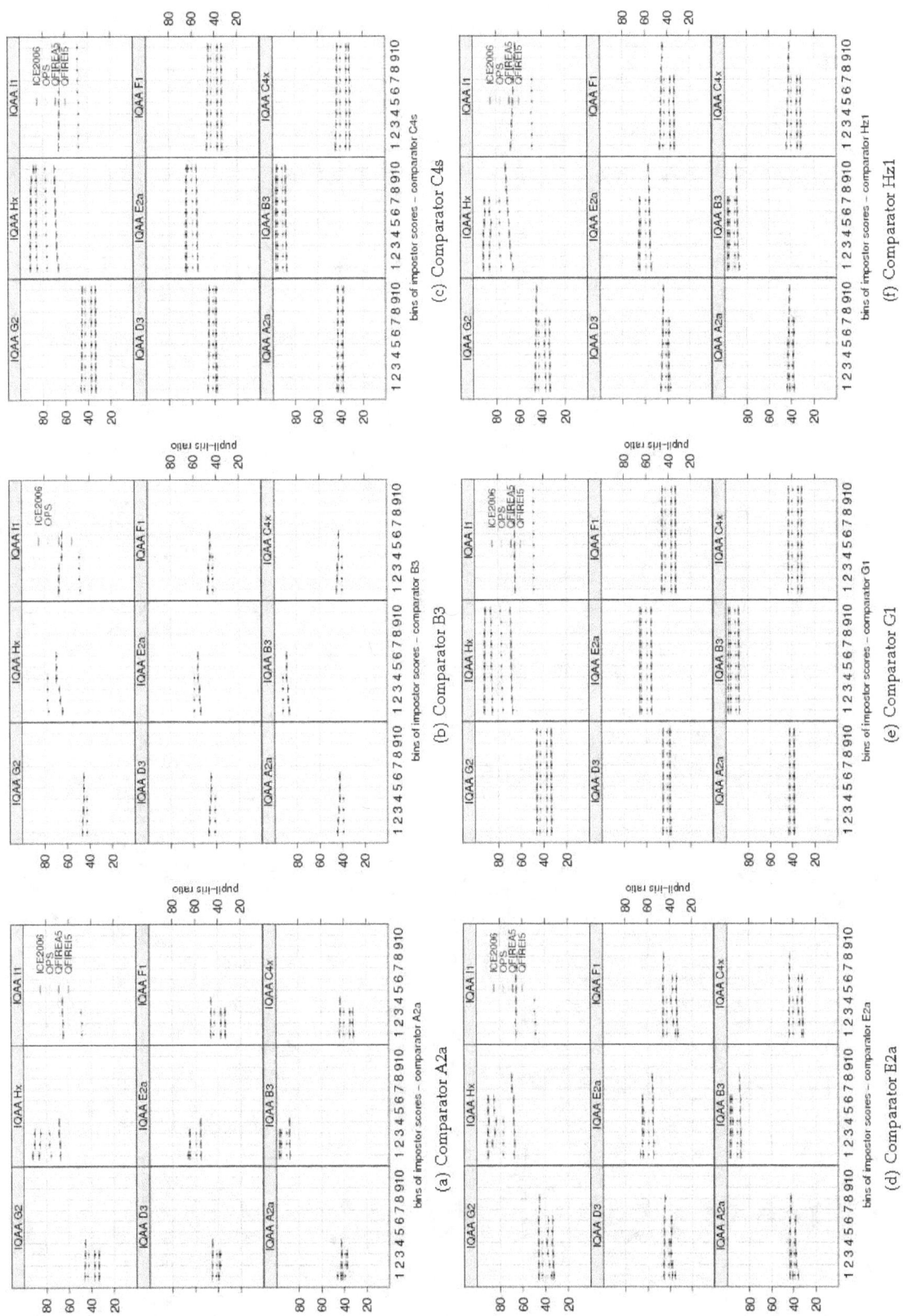

Figure 37: Pairwise DILATION scores vs. impostor scores for the primary Class Z submissions of each participant. Each plot shows quality scores computed by different IQAA. Similar to plots of figure 36, impostor scores are divided equally into ten groups, overlapping by 5 percent. The bootstrapped pairwise quality for each group is shown in a box and whisker plot. Pairwise quality is computed as geometric mean of the quality of the two samples being compared.

A2a=NEUROTECHNOLOGY-a   B3=CROSSMATCH   C4s=CAMBRIDGE-s   D3=AWARE   E2a=IRITECH-a   G1=IRISID-1   I1=KYNEN   Hz1=L1-z1
A2f=NEUROTECHNOLOGY-f   C4x=CAMBRIDGE-x   C4f=CAMBRIDGE-f   F1=MORPHO   E2f=IRITECH-f   G2=IRISID-2   Hx=L1-x   Hz2=L1-z2

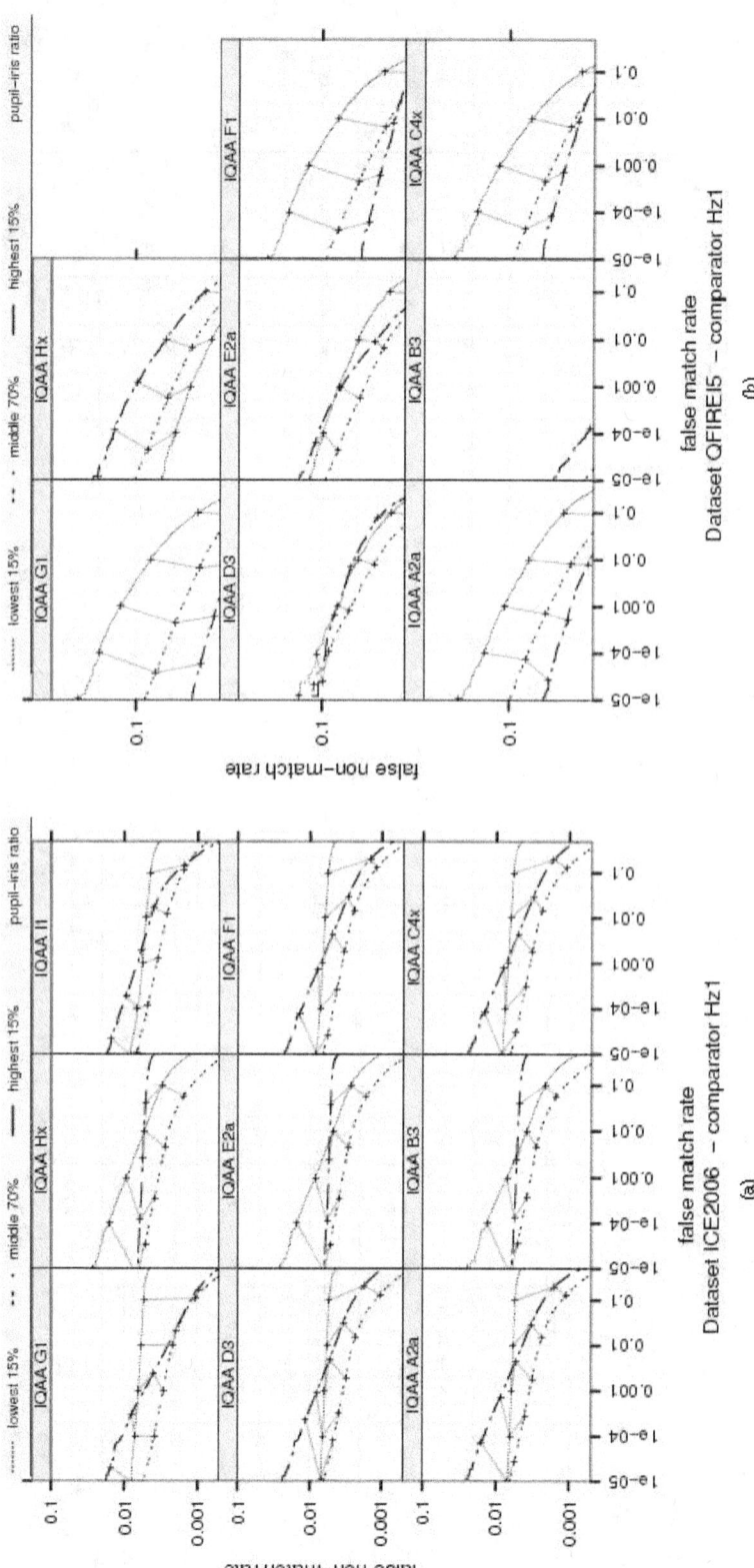

Figure 38: Ranked DET curves for comparator Hz1 and Datasets ICE2006 and QFIRE15 . The set of all comparisons are partitioned into three groups based on the pair-wise DILATION quality of the images being compared. The lowest quality set contains comparisons with pairwise quality in the lowest 15 percentile. The highest quality set contains comparisons with pairwise quality in the highest 15 percentile. The rest of the comparisons, namely the middle 70%, make up the third set. The DETs are connected at the same score threshold values (brown lines). Lower FNMR and FMR are expected for higher quality images.

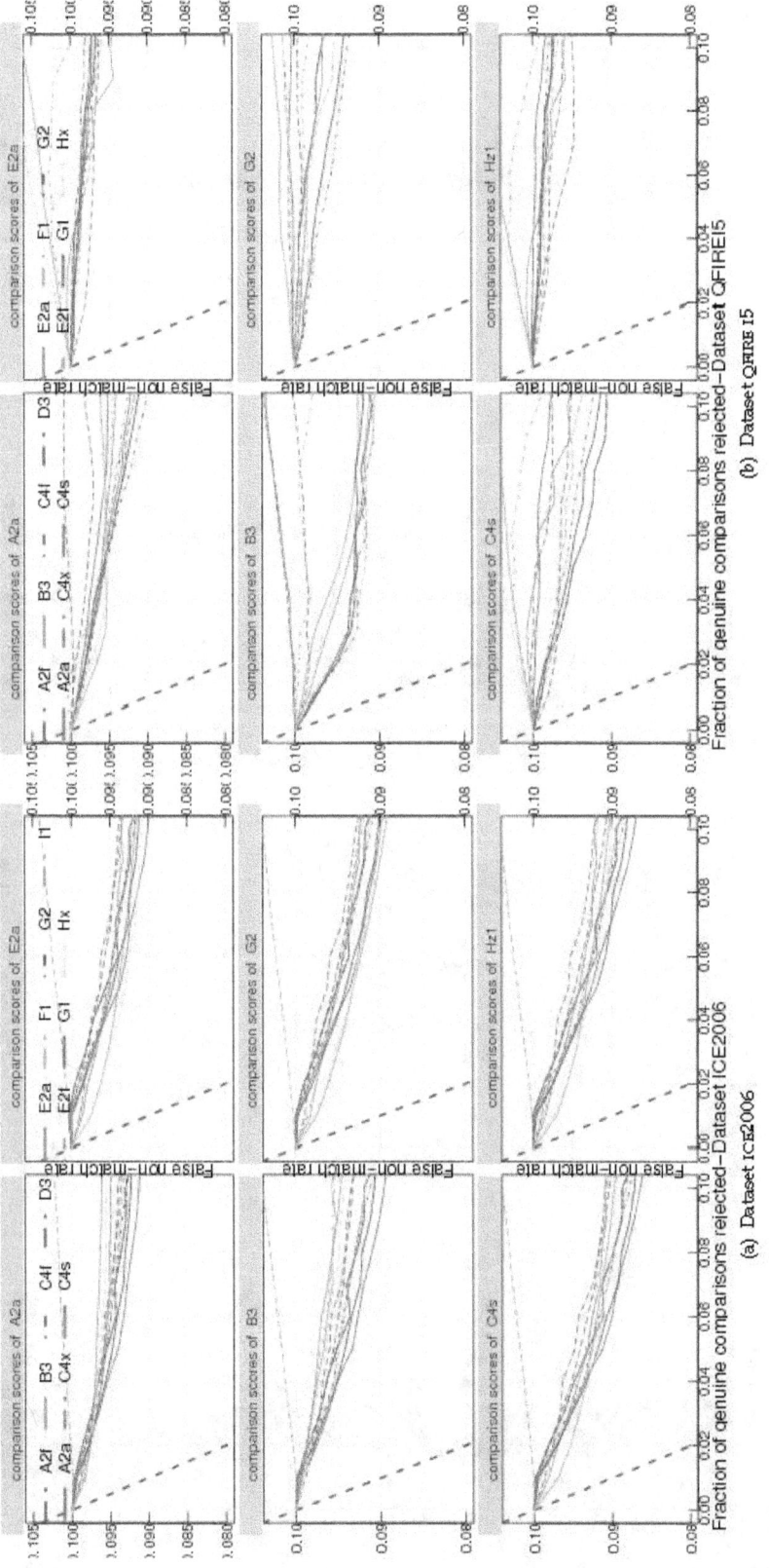

Figure 39: FNMR vs. reject curves for DILATION scores on datasets ICE2006 and QFIRE 15. The threshold is set to give an initial FNMR = 0.1. The gray dotted line shows the ideal case where the rejection of the comparisons with the lowest ten percent quality results in zero FNMR. IQAAs' DILATION scores are normalized according to Equation 3 in Section 5. The result of this normalization is that images further away from the center of the DILATION distribution are given low normalized score (indicating poor quality) and images closer to the center are given high normalized score (indicating good quality). This normalization does not work for IQAAs B3 and Hx and so the error vs. reject curve for these two IQAAs shall be ignored.

A2a=NEUROTECHNOLOGY-a	B3=CROSSMATCH	C4s=CAMBRIDGE-s	D3=AWARE	E2a=IRITECH-a	G1=IRISID-1	I1=KYNEN	Hz1=L1-z1
A2f=NEUROTECHNOLOGY-f	C4x=CAMBRIDGE-x	C4f=CAMBRIDGE-f	F1=MORPHO	E2f=IRITECH-f	G2=IRISID-2	Hx=L1-x	Hz2=L1-z2

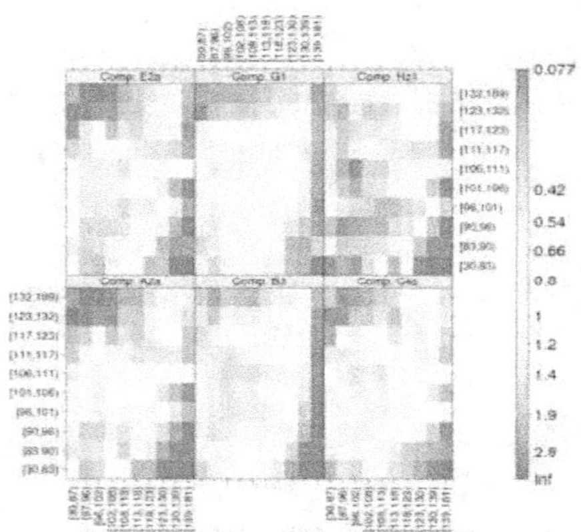

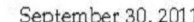

(a) IQAA A2a – Dataset ICE2006

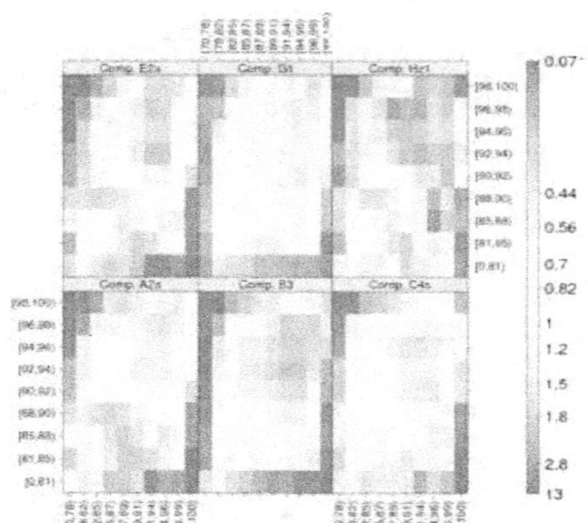

(b) IQAA B3 – Dataset ICE2006

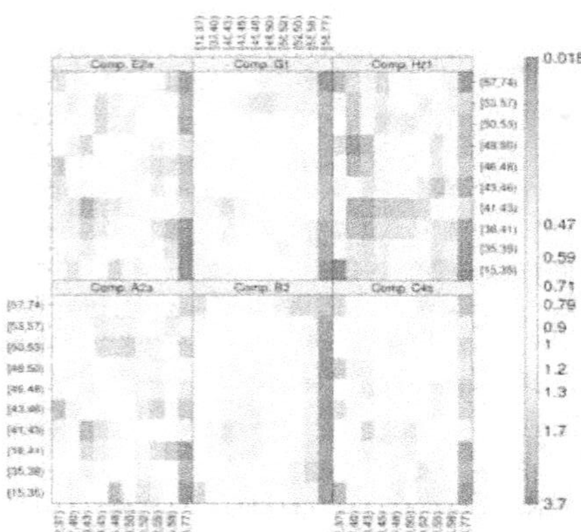

(c) IQAA D3 – Dataset ICE2006

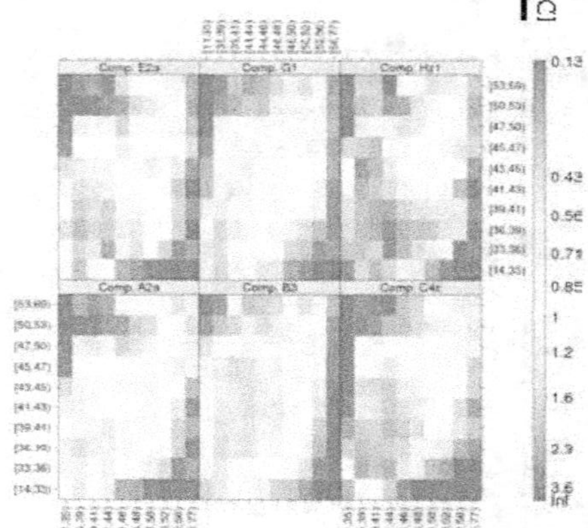

(d) IQAA C4x – Dataset ICE2006

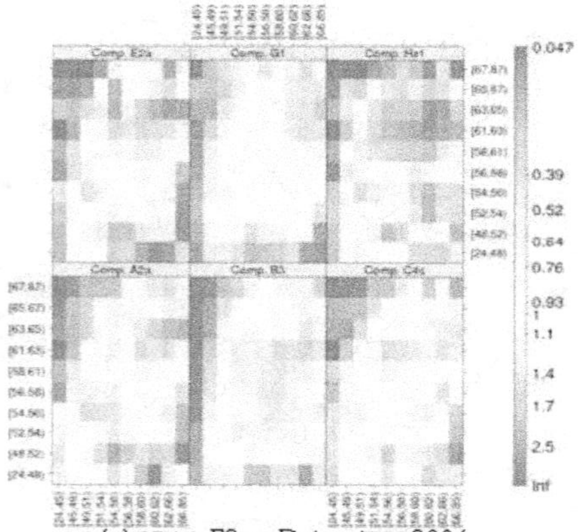

(e) IQAA E2a – Dataset ICE2006

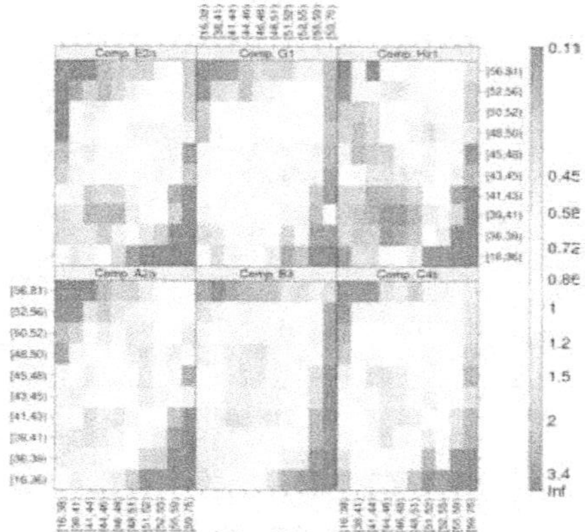

(f) IQAA F1 – Dataset ICE2006

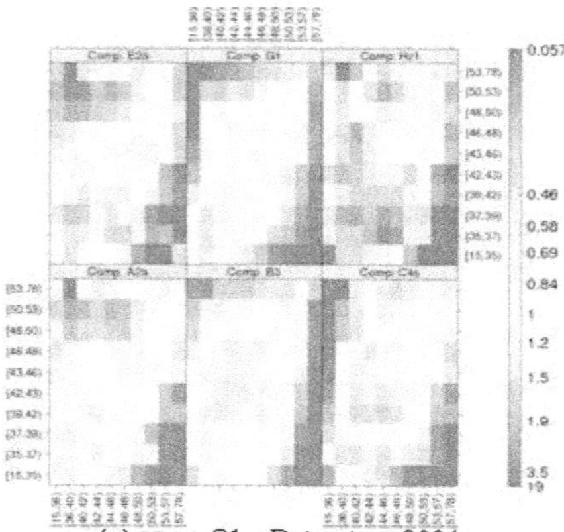

(g) IQAA G1 – Dataset ICE2006

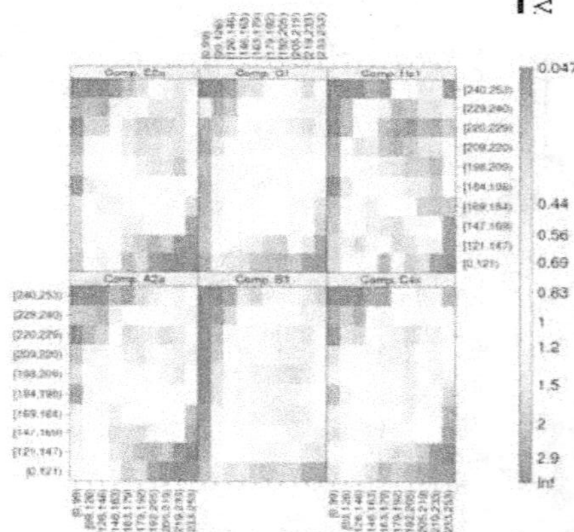

(h) IQAA Hx – Dataset ICE2006

Figure 40: DILATION computed by primary IQAA submissions and FNMR for IQCE comparators for ICE2006 images. The y-axis represents enrollment samples' quality with verification samples' on the x-axis. The DILATION scores are quantized into 10 quantiles. The color scale plots $\frac{FNMR}{FNMR_0}$ for comparisons with verification and enrollment qualities ($q_{verification}, q_{enrollment}$). FNMR$_0$ is the nominal FNMR which is the false non-match rate computed over all the images at the same comparison score threshold, in this case at FMR = 0.001. Yellow/Green color represent an improvement in FNMR. Blue color represent a degradation of FNMR. White color means no change in FNMR.

| A2a=NEUROTECHNOLOGY-a | B3=CROSSMATCH | C4s=CAMBRIDGE-s | D3=AWARE | E2a=IRITECH-a | G1=IRISID-1 | I1=KYNEN | Hz1=L1-z1 |
| A2f=NEUROTECHNOLOGY-f | C4x=CAMBRIDGE-x | C4f=CAMBRIDGE-f | F1=MORPHO | E2f=IRITECH-f | G2=IRISID-2 | Hx=L1-x | Hz2=L1-z2 |

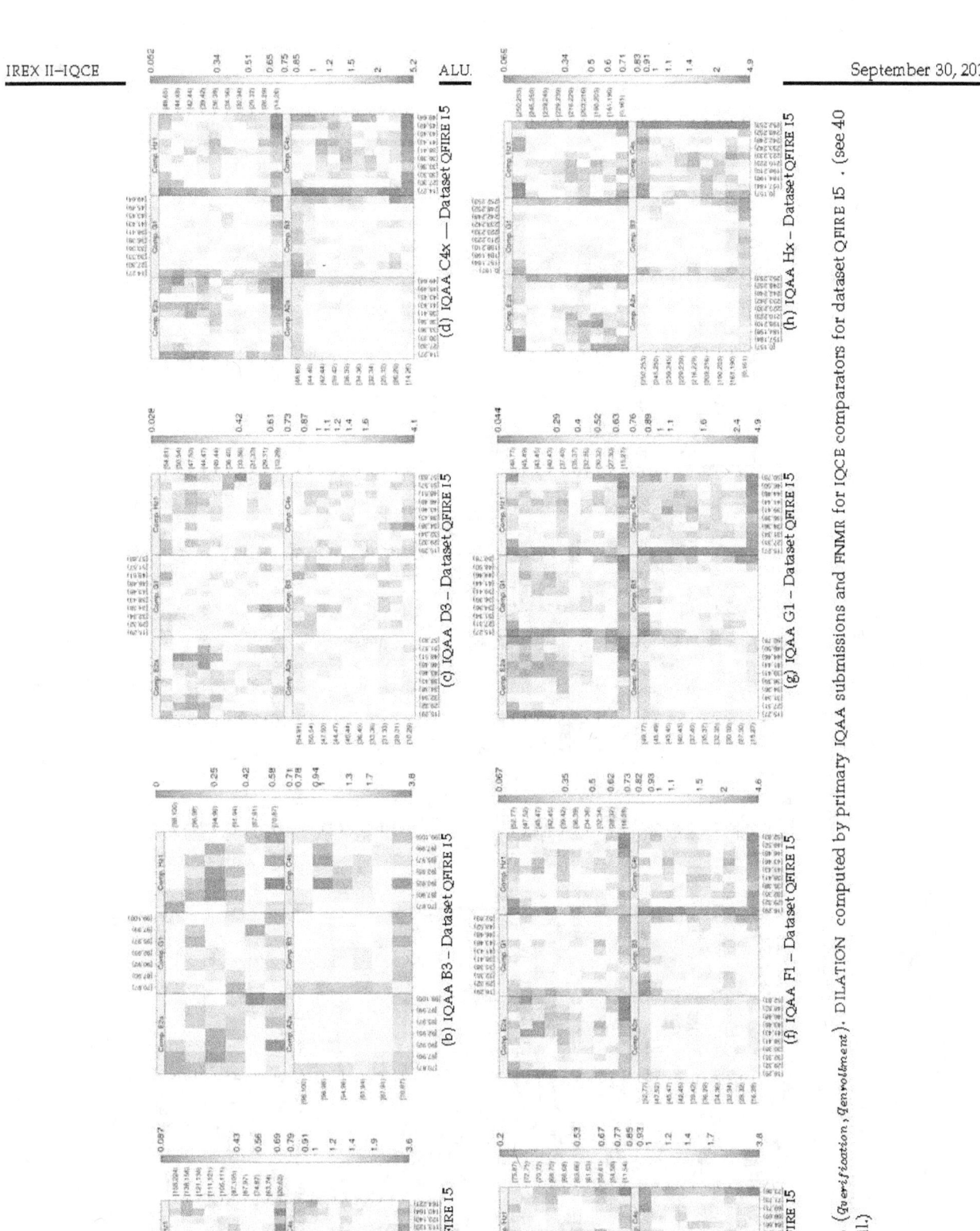

(a) IQAA A2a – Dataset QFIRE I5

(b) IQAA B3 – Dataset QFIRE I5

(c) IQAA D3 – Dataset QFIRE I5

(d) IQAA C4x – Dataset QFIRE I5

(e) IQAA E2a – Dataset QFIRE I5

(f) IQAA F1 – Dataset QFIRE I5

(g) IQAA G1 – Dataset QFIRE I5

(h) IQAA Hx – Dataset QFIRE I5

Figure 41: FNMR vs. $(q_{verification}, q_{enrollment})$. DILATION computed by primary IQAA submissions and FNMR for IQCE comparators for dataset QFIRE I5 . (see 40 caption for more detail.)

| A2a=NEUROTECHNOLOGY-a | B3=CROSSMATCH | C4s=CAMBRIDGE-s | D3=AWARE | E2a=IRITECH-a | G1=IRISID-1 | I1=KYNEN | Hz1=L1-z1 |
| A2f=NEUROTECHNOLOGY-f | | C4x=CAMBRIDGE-x | C4f=CAMBRIDGE-f | F1=MORPHO | E2f=IRITECH-f | G2=IRISID-2 | Hx=L1-x | Hz2=L1-z2 |

Dataset	comparator	IQAA A2a	IQAA B3	IQAA C4x	IQAA D3	IQAA E2a	IQAA F1	IQAA G1	IQAA Hx
ICE2006	A2a	(-1.72,-1.55)	(1.13,1.31)	(-0.69,-0.51)	(-1.80,-1.59)	(1.79,1.96)	(-0.73,-0.55)	(-0.39,-0.20)	(4.72,5.15)
ICE2006	B3	(-2.21,-2.13)	(2.19,2.27)	(-1.90,-1.81)	(-1.90,-1.81)	(2.58,2.66)	(-1.78,-1.69)	(-1.62,-1.54)	(7.83,8.02)
ICE2006	C4s	(-0.26,-0.13)	(0.64,0.77)	(1.51,1.64)	(-0.21,-0.06)	(0.59,0.71)	(0.21,0.34)	(2.09,2.24)	(3.07,3.38)
ICE2006	E2a	(-2.93,-2.75)	(2.56,2.74)	(-2.15,-1.97)	(-2.93,-2.72)	(3.13,3.31)	(-1.74,-1.56)	(-1.67,-1.47)	(8.93,9.36)
ICE2006	G2	(-3.81,-3.72)	(3.91,4.00)	(-3.42,-3.33)	(-3.77,-3.67)	(4.18,4.27)	(-2.53,-2.43)	(-3.12,-3.03)	(10.32,10.54)
ICE2006	Hz1	(-0.10,0.09)	(0.48,0.67)	(0.25,0.45)	(-0.58,-0.35)	(0.44,0.63)	(0.09,0.29)	(1.01,1.22)	(2.94,3.43)
OPS	A2a	(-3.96,-0.00)	(-4.41,12.26)	(-2.49,1.57)	(-4.16,0.50)	(-1.04,2.86)	(-3.01,1.20)	(-2.27,1.84)	(-3.25,5.96)
OPS	B3	(-2.76,-1.11)	(-0.15,1.31)	(-2.59,-0.90)	(-2.86,-0.97)	(1.00,2.62)	(-2.72,-0.97)	(-1.58,0.12)	(3.52,7.34)
OPS	C4s	(-2.94,0.26)	(0.77,7.11)	(-1.20,2.07)	(-3.13,0.48)	(-0.23,2.93)	(-2.07,1.32)	(-1.50,1.80)	(-1.95,5.45)
OPS	E2a	(-1.66,2.98)	(-6.17,3.08)	(-1.65,3.12)	(-1.01,4.32)	(-2.97,1.61)	(-1.50,3.45)	(-1.54,3.28)	(-5.85,4.96)
OPS	G2	(-1.11,1.47)	(0.44,5.50)	(0.05,2.68)	(-1.30,1.62)	(-1.46,1.09)	(-0.31,2.43)	(2.38,5.01)	(-4.04,1.94)
OPS	Hz1	(-2.49,1.25)	(-2.64,4.82)	(-1.91,1.93)	(-3.11,1.05)	(-0.71,3.02)	(-1.96,2.02)	(-1.65,2.23)	(-2.80,5.90)
QFIREA5	A2a	(-1.29,-0.68)	(-0.38,-0.20)	(0.03,0.29)	(-2.84,-0.70)	(-0.10,0.20)	(0.23,0.50)	(0.04,0.31)	(-0.67,-0.30)
QFIREA5	B3	(1.71,2.85)	(0.60,0.83)	(0.04,0.40)	(-0.60,2.85)	(0.18,0.63)	(0.42,0.81)	(0.52,0.88)	(0.01,0.55)
QFIREA5	C4s	(2.53,3.55)	(0.13,0.38)	(0.87,1.21)	(-1.11,1.57)	(-0.10,0.31)	(1.24,1.61)	(1.44,1.79)	(-1.04,-0.52)
QFIREA5	E2a	(0.99,1.75)	(-0.23,-0.06)	(0.56,0.80)	(-2.56,-0.68)	(-0.14,0.15)	(0.83,1.09)	(0.75,1.00)	(-0.95,-0.59)
QFIREA5	G2	(2.21,3.00)	(-0.19,-0.00)	(0.45,0.71)	(-1.82,0.45)	(-0.05,0.26)	(1.06,1.33)	(1.04,1.31)	(-0.79,-0.41)
QFIREA5	Hz1	(3.64,4.89)	(-0.41,-0.09)	(1.04,1.47)	(-2.85,1.09)	(-0.77,-0.26)	(1.50,1.95)	(1.59,2.04)	(-2.26,-1.62)
QFIREI5	A2a	(-0.30,-0.06)	(0.86,0.99)	(0.01,0.15)	(-0.86,-0.08)	(1.14,1.31)	(0.13,0.27)	(0.38,0.52)	(2.36,2.61)
QFIREI5	B3	(-0.45,0.04)	(1.74,1.85)	(-2.53,-2.39)	(-2.85,-1.79)	(2.68,2.83)	(-2.23,-2.08)	(-2.09,-1.95)	(5.71,5.99)
QFIREI5	C4s	(5.82,6.35)	(-1.06,-0.60)	(6.16,6.34)	(2.86,3.84)	(0.30,0.52)	(5.34,5.53)	(6.47,6.66)	(-5.74,-5.40)
QFIREI5	E2a	(6.98,7.54)	(0.08,0.57)	(4.01,4.20)	(1.67,2.75)	(0.68,0.90)	(4.63,4.83)	(4.77,4.97)	(-4.34,-3.97)
QFIREI5	G2	(2.52,3.01)	(0.05,0.28)	(1.73,1.89)	(0.03,0.97)	(0.79,0.98)	(2.09,2.26)	(3.40,3.57)	(-1.70,-1.39)
QFIREI5	Hz1	(5.16,5.84)	(-0.36,0.24)	(2.89,3.13)	(-0.60,0.62)	(1.65,1.93)	(3.70,3.95)	(4.19,4.43)	(-3.68,-3.24)

Table 15: Tukey HSD mean difference in DILATION . Each cell shows the 95% confidence level in difference in mean of pairwise quality for images verified correctly (i.e., genuine score equal or less than threshold) and those rejected falsely (i.e., genuine score larger than threshold). Quality scores were computed by the SDK identified by the column header and comparison scores were generated by the SDK identified by the row header. If the interval does not contain zero, the difference in mean is significant. Cells where difference in mean is not significant have pink background. For monotonic quality components (all except DILATION , and depending on quality implementation GRAY SCALE SPREAD), the expected behavior is to have higher quality scores for pair of enrollment verification images that result in genuine comparison scores less than threshold. Pairwise quality is computed as geometric mean of the quality of two samples being compared. Threshold is set to give false match rate of 0.001.

A2a=NEUROTECHNOLOGY-a	B3=CROSSMATCH	C4s=CAMBRIDGE-s	D3=AWARE	E2a=IRITECH-a	G1=IRISID-1	I1=KYNEN	Hz1=L1-z1
A2f=NEUROTECHNOLOGY-f	C4x=CAMBRIDGE-x	C4f=CAMBRIDGE-f	F1=MORPHO	E2f=IRITECH-f	G2=IRISID-2	Hx=L1-x	Hz2=L1-z2

Dataset	comparator	IQAA A2a	IQAA B3	IQAA C4x	IQAA D3	IQAA E2a	IQAA F1	IQAA G1	IQAA Hx
ICE2006	A2a	(-1.58,-1.25)	(0.86,1.34)	(-1.42,-1.08)	(-1.07,-0.66)	(0.94,1.27)	(-1.39,-1.04)	(-1.60,-1.18)	(2.71,3.59)
ICE2006	B3	(-3.71,-3.47)	(3.67,3.90)	(-3.94,-3.70)	(-4.15,-3.86)	(4.01,4.25)	(-3.87,-3.62)	(-1.74,-1.44)	(10.26,10.90)
ICE2006	C4s	(-2.00,-1.75)	(1.78,2.15)	(-2.01,-1.75)	(-2.12,-1.82)	(1.80,2.06)	(-1.98,-1.71)	(-1.51,-1.18)	(4.65,5.33)
ICE2006	E2a	(-1.44,-1.18)	(1.04,1.41)	(-1.46,-1.19)	(-1.67,-1.36)	(1.44,1.70)	(-1.20,-0.93)	(-0.19,0.14)	(3.48,4.17)
ICE2006	G2	(-1.18,-0.92)	(0.72,1.10)	(-1.14,-0.87)	(-0.90,-0.57)	(0.74,1.00)	(-1.06,-0.78)	(-1.19,-0.88)	(2.48,3.19)
ICE2006	Hz1	(-2.14,-1.86)	(2.26,2.66)	(-2.18,-1.89)	(-2.80,-2.49)	(2.10,2.38)	(-2.16,-1.86)	(0.53,0.89)	(5.41,6.16)
OPS	A2a	(-1.50,-1.12)	(1.29,2.21)	(-1.44,-1.04)	(-1.51,-1.06)	(1.07,1.45)	(-1.56,-1.15)	(-1.49,-1.09)	(2.50,3.44)
OPS	B3	(-1.55,-1.24)	(1.14,1.42)	(-1.54,-1.22)	(-1.85,-1.49)	(1.16,1.47)	(-1.68,-1.34)	(-1.49,-1.16)	(2.93,3.69)
OPS	C4s	(-0.85,-0.53)	(0.72,1.48)	(-0.87,-0.55)	(-1.06,-0.69)	(0.53,0.84)	(-0.95,-0.62)	(-0.88,-0.55)	(1.55,2.32)
OPS	E2a	(0.25,0.57)	(-0.70,0.07)	(0.27,0.60)	(0.13,0.50)	(-0.59,-0.28)	(0.23,0.57)	(0.17,0.51)	(-1.52,-0.73)
OPS	G2	(-1.26,-0.94)	(0.95,1.71)	(-1.30,-0.98)	(-1.31,-0.94)	(0.97,1.29)	(-1.37,-1.03)	(-1.29,-0.97)	(2.52,3.30)
OPS	Hz1	(-1.30,-0.99)	(0.96,1.72)	(-1.34,-1.01)	(-1.49,-1.12)	(0.96,1.27)	(-1.43,-1.09)	(-1.28,-0.95)	(2.59,3.36)
QFIREA5	A2a	(-7.78,-7.17)	(0.52,0.90)	(-0.91,-0.60)	(-3.88,-2.11)	(0.96,1.59)	(-1.19,-0.83)	(-0.37,0.02)	(3.07,4.03)
QFIREA5	C4s	(0.42,0.98)	(-0.10,0.23)	(-0.53,-0.25)	(-0.78,0.92)	(0.41,0.97)	(-0.05,0.28)	(-0.01,0.32)	(0.46,1.34)
QFIREA5	E2a	(5.56,6.11)	(-1.85,-1.52)	(1.67,1.95)	(1.94,5.53)	(-4.17,-3.64)	(1.90,2.22)	(1.55,1.86)	(-5.45,-4.57)
QFIREA5	G2	(0.59,1.16)	(-0.17,0.15)	(-0.35,-0.07)	(-0.57,1.00)	(0.58,1.12)	(-0.18,0.14)	(-0.29,0.02)	(1.38,2.18)
QFIREA5	Hz1	(2.68,3.24)	(-0.45,-0.12)	(0.37,0.65)	(-1.27,0.69)	(-0.10,0.45)	(0.41,0.73)	(0.76,1.11)	(1.15,2.02)
QFIREI5	A2a	(-11.45,-10.97)	(-0.67,-0.48)	(0.02,0.26)	(-0.54,2.50)	(-0.36,-0.07)	(0.07,0.33)	(0.04,0.30)	(-2.38,-1.87)
QFIREI5	C4s	(0.03,0.45)	(0.71,0.88)	(-0.64,-0.42)	(2.86,4.95)	(0.94,1.20)	(-0.43,-0.20)	(-0.29,-0.07)	(1.60,2.05)
QFIREI5	E2a	(5.37,5.79)	(-3.14,-2.98)	(5.63,5.84)	(5.46,7.41)	(-4.34,-4.08)	(6.00,6.23)	(6.26,6.48)	(-9.49,-9.04)
QFIREI5	G2	(-1.60,1.58)	(-0.16,1.09)	(-1.03,0.60)	(-5.18,13.64)	(0.51,2.41)	(-0.96,0.78)	(-0.73,0.97)	(-0.17,3.20)
QFIREI5	Hz1	(1.07,1.48)	(0.89,1.06)	(-1.16,-0.94)	(-0.12,2.18)	(1.73,1.98)	(-0.75,-0.52)	(-0.63,-0.41)	(2.37,2.82)

Table 16: Tukey HSD mean difference in DILATION scores. Each cell shows the 95% confidence level in difference in mean of pairwise quality for images correctly rejected (i.e., the impostor score equal or greater than threshold) and those falsely matched (i.e., the impostor score less than threshold). Quality scores were computed by the SDK identified by the row header. If the interval does not contain zero, the difference in mean is significant. Cells where difference in mean is not significant are shaded in pink. For monotonic increasing quality components (all except DILATION, and depending on quality implementation GRAY SCALE SPREAD), the expected behavior is to have higher quality scores for the pair of (enrollment, verification) images that result in impostor comparison scores equal or greater than threshold. Pairwise quality is computed as geometric mean of the quality of two samples being compared. Threshold is set to give false match rate of 0.001.

A2a=NEUROTECHNOLOGY-a   B3=CROSSMATCH   C4s=CAMBRIDGE-s   D3=AWARE   E2a=IRITECH-a   G1=IRISID-1   I1=KYNEN   Hz1=L1-z1
A2f=NEUROTECHNOLOGY-f   C4x=CAMBRIDGE-x   C4f=CAMBRIDGE-f   F1=MORPHO   E2f=IRITECH-f   G2=IRISID-2   Hx=L1-x   Hz2=L1-z2

9.4 Usable iris area

USABLE IRIS AREA is defined as the percentage of iris that is not occluded by eyelash, eyelid, or specular reflections, ambient specular reflections e.g., reflected sunlight, eye-wear reflections, reflections from nearby facial features such as nose, or glare and reflection from the scene.

It has been reported that iris occlusion by eyelash, eyelid, or reflections is problematic for segmentation or matching. [13] suggests that the percentage of apparent iris and texture energy are the most important quality factors. Daugman [7] assigns a mask to ignore bits of his iris code where the iris region is obscured by eyelids, contains any eyelash occlusions, specular reflections, boundary artifacts of hard contact lenses, or poor signal-to-noise ratio. Occlusion can be caused by specular reflections from dedicated illumination sources, ambient illumination sources, or reflections from glasses or the subject's nose. A good iris acquisition devices would control specular reflections from dedicated illuminators to minimize the overlap with the iris tissue portion of the image.

In addition, eyelids and eyelashes can occlude the iris. Eyelids often occlude the upper and lower part of iris. Eyelashes can occlude part of iris. Eyelid or eyelash occlusions are caused by either subject behavior, for example, subject is blinking or squinting or it can be part of subject character due to genetic factors or medical conditions such as droopy eyelids. When the cause of occlusion is not intrinsic (i.e., anatomical), USABLE IRIS AREA can be improved by better design of imaging system (controlling the specular reflection) or improving the capture process (e.g., controlling reflections from the scene) or correcting subject behavior by, for example, prompting not to squint. Iris image acquisition systems should have illuminators placed in a way that prevents or at least minimizes occlusions of parts of the iris that are caused by reflections of the illuminators on the iris itself, on eyeglasses, the subject's nose, etc. The best practice guidance is to take glasses off at the time of capture.

If occlusion occurs at the limbic or pupillary boundaries, it not only reduces the amount of usable iris (and hence the information available for matching) but can also decrease the iris segmentation accuracy, which will increase recognition error.

Measuring the USABLE IRIS AREA of an image will require full segmentation to determine iris area (in pixels) as well as full detection of all non-iris pixels such as eyelashes because their strong contrast and energy content will introduce error/noise.

Twelve IQAAs (B3, C4f, C4s, C4x, D3, E2a, E2f, F1, G1, G2, Hx, and I1) provided USABLE IRIS AREA scores. [2] and IQCE API defined USABLE IRIS AREA as the percentage of iris potion of the image that is not occluded by eyelash, eyelid, or reflections such as specular reflections, ambient specular reflections (e.g., reflected sunlight), eye-wear reflections, or reflections from nearby facial features such as nose.

The distribution of the USABLE IRIS AREA scores is shown in Figure 42. In order to make the boxplots more readable, quality scores in [0–254] range were linearly scaled back to [0–100].

Results on effect of USABLE IRIS AREA on prformance is presented below.

RELATIONSHIP WITH THE DISTRIBUTION OF GENUINE SCORES

Dependence of quality scores on genuine scores is shown in Figure 43. OPS images have the least occlusion, for two main reasons: a) occluded images were rejected by the capture time quality check, and b) subjects were assisted by an operator. QFIRE A5 images have the highest occlusion.

100

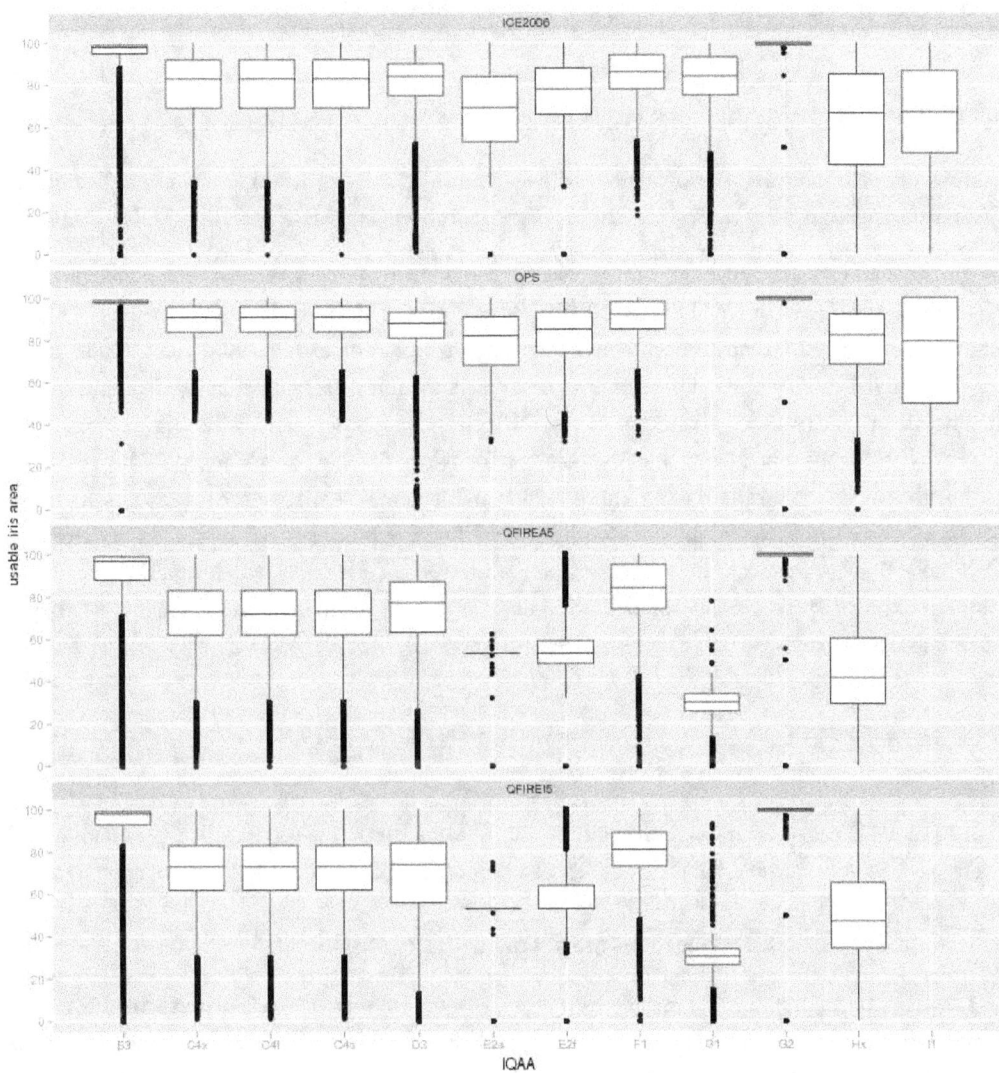

Figure 42: Box and whisker plots of the IQAAs that generate USABLE IRIS AREA scores.

For all IQAAs, images with high USABLE IRIS AREA result in low genuine score, which means that occlusion affects the genuine distribution; high occlusion shifts the genuine distribution to the right (i.e., towards the impostor distribution).

The biggest rate of change is for IQAA Hx USABLE IRIS AREA scores followed by C4s and E2.

Note the very similar behavior of IQAA C4x and Hx.

RELATIONSHIP WITH THE DISTRIBUTION OF IMPOSTOR SCORES

Figure 44 indicates occlusion affects impostor distribution as well. Low usable iris area (i.e., high occlusion) results in low impostor scores; that is, the distribution is shifted to the left (i.e., towards the genuine distribution). The effect on impostor distribution is smaller than on the genuine distribution; nonetheless, the shift in both impostor and genuine distribution means that both FNMR and FMR are affected by USABLE IRIS AREA .

RANKED DET:: DO LOW-QUALITY IMAGES PRODUCE HIGH FNMR OR FMR?

Figure 45 shows the comparative performance of images with 15% lowest usable iris area, 15% highest usable area and the rest. The difference can be as high as one order of magnitude (IQAA Hx, B3, C4s and C4f). USABLE IRIS AREA scores generated by IQAA I1 do not relate to performance, making I1 the least effective IQAA .

Except for IQAA B3, the DET curves of the ICE2006 images with the highest 15% USABLE IRIS AREA is very flat, suggesting a well-separated impostor distribution. However, it shows higher error rates than the ICE2006 images with medium (the middle 70%) USABLE IRIS AREA area. Other comparators exhibit different behavior. Comparators A2a ranked-DET curves are shown in Figure 46. The ranking of the DET curves are as expected; the highest performance is observed for the images with the least occlusion and the least performance for the images with the highest degree of occlusion. Also note that the false match rate of comparator A2a is stable across the three sets of images with low, mid, and high USABLE IRIS AREA areas as is evident by the straightness of the brown lines connecting the DET curves at the same score threshold values. That means occlusion increases comparator A2a's false non-match rate but not its false match rate. In contrast, for comparator Hz1, both false match and false non-match rates are increased as the USABLE IRIS AREA area is decreased due to occlusions.

EFFECT OF QUALITY ON FNMR : HOW QUICKLY FNMR IMPROVES WHEN POOR QUALITY SAMPLES ARE REJECTED?

Rejection of ICE2006 images with low USABLE IRIS AREA scores improves FNMR quickly, as shown in Figure 47. A 2% rejection reduces FNMR by almost 10% (IQAA C4s and comparator C4s). On ICE2006 images, IQAAs Hx and C4s, C4f and C4x are the best performers, regardless of the comparators. Following closely behind are IQAAs F1, G2, G1, E2f, and B3. IQAAs I1 and D3 USABLE IRIS AREA scores are not predictive of FNMR at all.

Predictive power of USABLE IRIS AREA scores drops for QFIRE I5 images. IQAA C4s performs best for comparators Hz1 and its mated comparator, C4s, particularly for rejection rate less than 2%. B3 USABLE IRIS AREA scores is the best predictive power of its mated comparator. No other IQAA USABLE IRIS AREA scores are a reasonable predictor of B3 comparator. IQAA G1 is effective for all comparators only when the rejection rate is larger than 5%. TEST OF SIGNIFICANCE ::

DO THE IMAGES INVOLVED IN SUCCESSFUL VERIFICATION ATTEMPTS HAVE SIGNIFICANTLY HIGHER QUALITY SCORES THAN THOSE INVOLVED IN FAILED VERIFICATION ATTEMPTS?

Tables 17 and 18 indicate that:
USABLE IRIS AREA significantly affects genuine and impostor distributions, and
IQAAs E2a, E2f and G2 are not effective predictor performance on QFIRE I5 or QFIRE A5 images.

EFFECT OF VARIATION BETWEEN THE TWO SAMPLES:: DOES SAMENESS MATTER?

Figure 48 confirms conclusions of Figure 43 that occlusion elevates FNMR . IQAAs Hx, C4s, F1 and G1 are effective in identifying the images that cause false non-match due to a high percentage of occlusion. Hx and C4s perform better than the other two on QFIRE I5 images.

A2a=NEUROTECHNOLOGY-a	B3=CROSSMATCH	C4s=CAMBRIDGE-s	D3=AWARE	E2a=IRITECH-a	G1=IRISID-1	I1=KYNEN	Hz1=L1-z1
A2f=NEUROTECHNOLOGY-f	C4x=CAMBRIDGE-x	C4f=CAMBRIDGE-f	F1=MORPHO	E2f=IRITECH-f	G2=IRISID-2	Hx=L1-x	Hz2=L1-z2

The influence of the difference in USABLE IRIS AREA scores on FNMR is more noticeable for QFIRE I5 images than the ICE2006.

OBSERVATIONS AND CONCLUSIONS

USABLE IRIS AREA greatly influences performance. The difference between FNMR of images with the lowest USABLE IRIS AREA and the highest USABLE IRIS AREA can be as large as two orders of magnitude (IQAA E2a and G1 – Dataset ICE2006). The effect on FMR is greater for some comparators; Hz1 gives higher FMR on highly occluded images, whe re comparator A2a FMR is more stable.

Implementations from all IQCE participants except one organization measured USABLE IRIS AREA . This large support suggests that USABLE IRIS AREA can be measured universally, however, the wide range of the IQAAs performance implies that reliable measurement of USABLE IRIS AREA is a challenge and requires dedicated image processing including a good segmentation of iris texture.

Overall, IQAAs Hx and C4s USABLE IRIS AREA scores are the best predictor of the match-ability of an iris image for their native iris recognition algorithm as well as other comparators. IQAA I1 is the worst performer.

| A2a=NEUROTECHNOLOGY-a | B3=CROSSMATCH | C4s=CAMBRIDGE-s | D3=AWARE | E2a=IRITECH-a | G1=IRISID-1 | I1=KYNEN | Hz1=L1-z1 |
| A2f=NEUROTECHNOLOGY-f | C4x=CAMBRIDGE-x | C4f=CAMBRIDGE-f | F1=MORPHO | E2f=IRITECH-f | G2=IRISID-2 | Hx=L1-x | Hz2=L1-z2 |

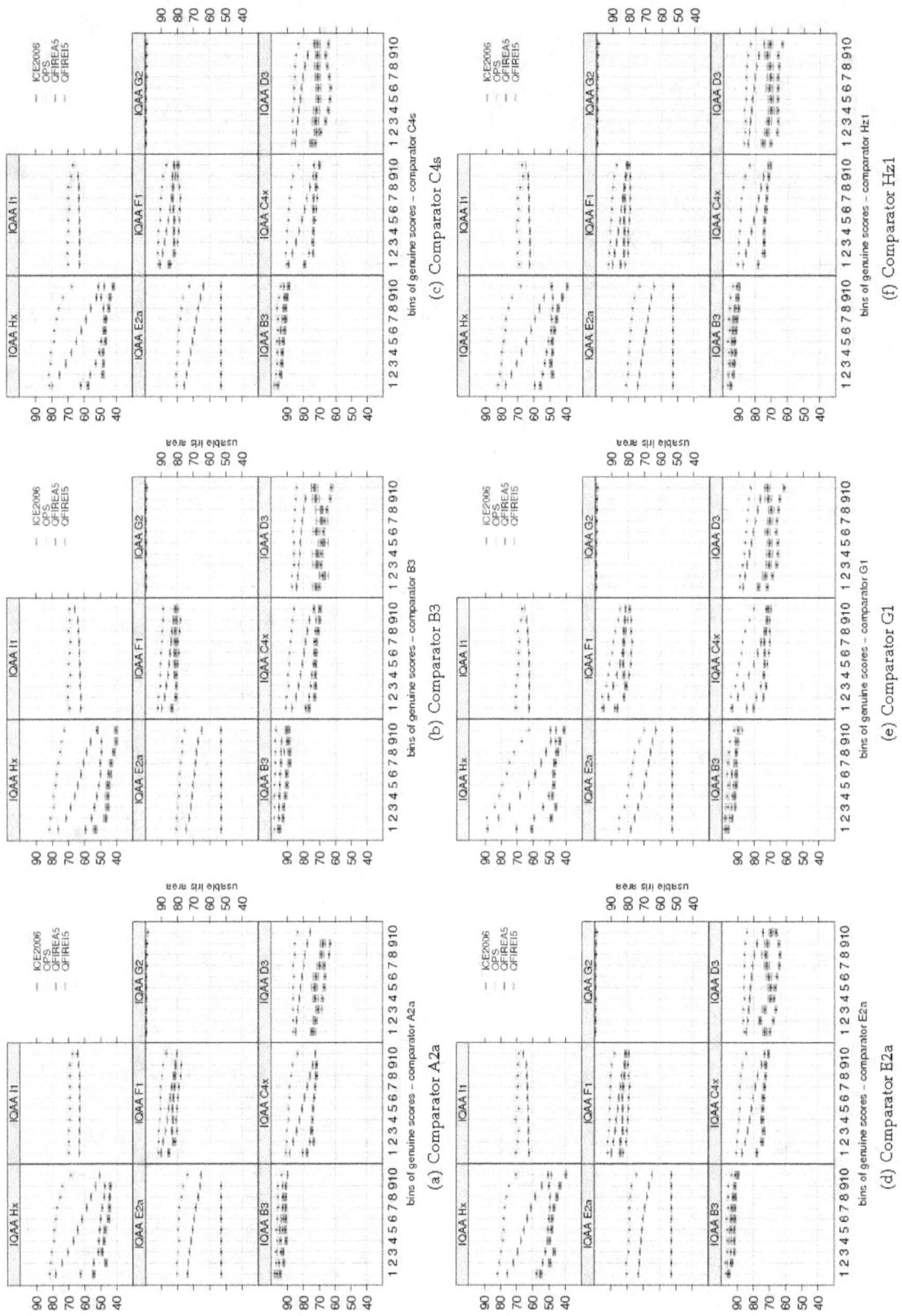

Figure 43: Pairwise USABLE IRIS AREA scores vs. genuine score for the primary Class Z submissions of each participant. Each plot shows quality scores computed by different IQAA. Genuine scores are divided equally into ten groups. Groups overlap by 5 percent, meaning 5% of the data in one bin also belongs to the next bin. The bootstrapped pairwise quality for each group is shown in a box and whisker plot. Pairwise quality is computed as geometric mean of the quality of the two samples being compared. Occlusion shifts the genuine distribution to the right, as a result higher FNMR is observed for images with low usable iris area, as is shown in Figure 48. IQAAs Hx and C4s exhibit the higher change in USABLE IRIS AREA score vs. the genuine score than other IQAAs.

| A2a=NEUROTECHNOLOGY-a | B3=CROSSMATCH | C4s=CAMBRIDGE-s | D3=AWARE | E2a=IRITECH-a | G1=IRISID-1 | I1=KYNEN | Hz1=L1-z1 |
| A2f=NEUROTECHNOLOGY-f | | C4x=CAMBRIDGE-x | C4f=CAMBRIDGE-f | F1=MORPHO | E2f=IRITECH-f | G2=IRISID-2 | Hx=L1-x | Hz2=L1-z2 |

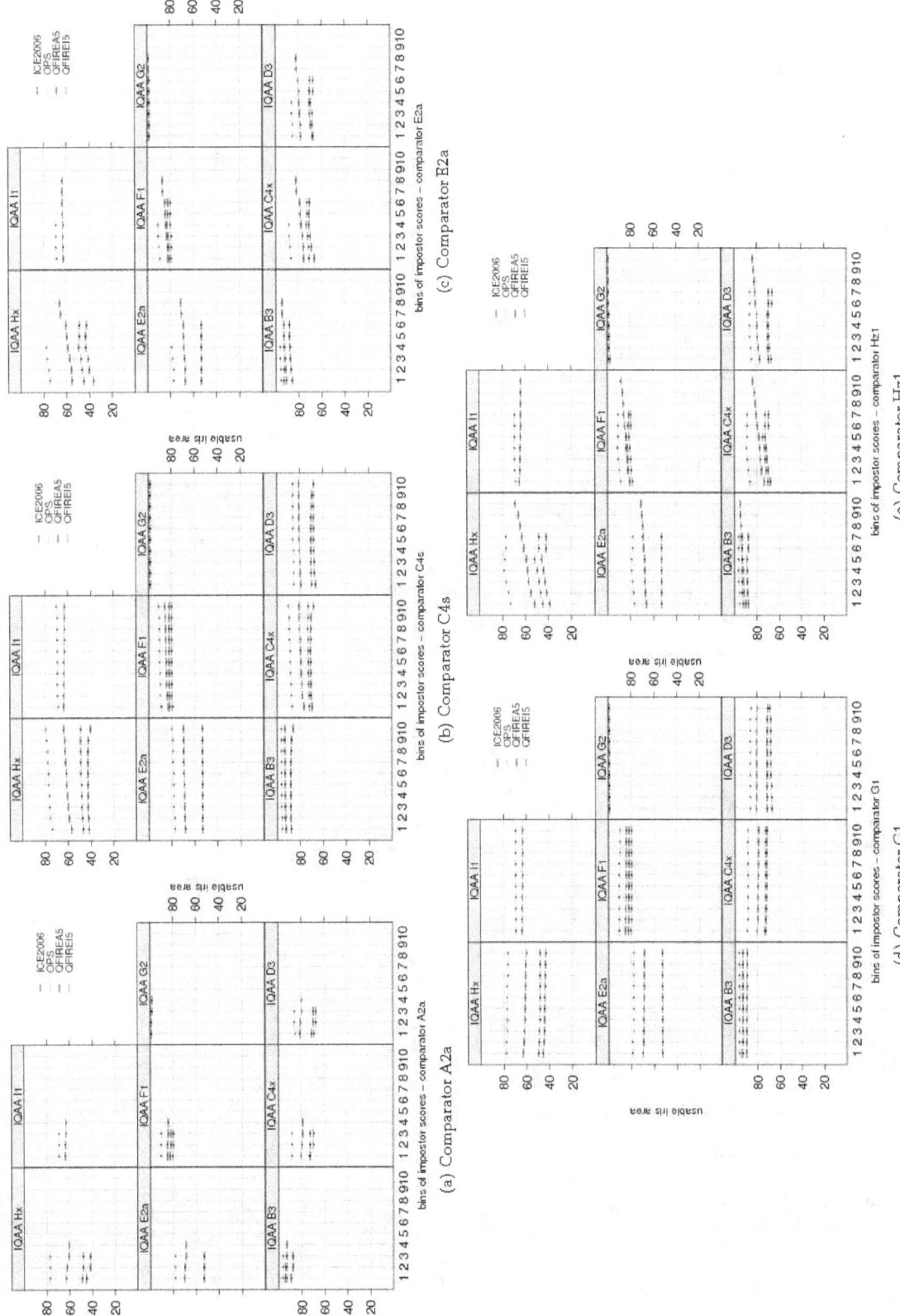

Figure 44: Pairwise USABLE IRIS AREA scores vs. impostor scores for the primary Class Z submissions of each participant. Each plot shows quality scores computed by different IQAA. Similar to plots of figure 43, impostor scores are divided equally into ten groups, overlapping by 5 percent. The bootstrapped pairwise quality for each group is shown in a box and whisker plot. Pairwise quality is computed as geometric mean of the quality of the two samples being compared. Occlusion causes lower impostors scores and therefore elevates FMR .

A2a=NEUROTECHNOLOGY-a	B3=CROSSMATCH	C4s=CAMBRIDGE-s	D3=AWARE	E2a=IRITECH-a	G1=IRISID-1	I1=KYNEN	Hz1=L1-z1
A2f=NEUROTECHNOLOGY-f	C4x=CAMBRIDGE-x	C4f=CAMBRIDGE-f	F1=MORPHO	E2f=IRITECH-f	G2=IRISID-2	Hx=L1-x	Hz2=L1-z2

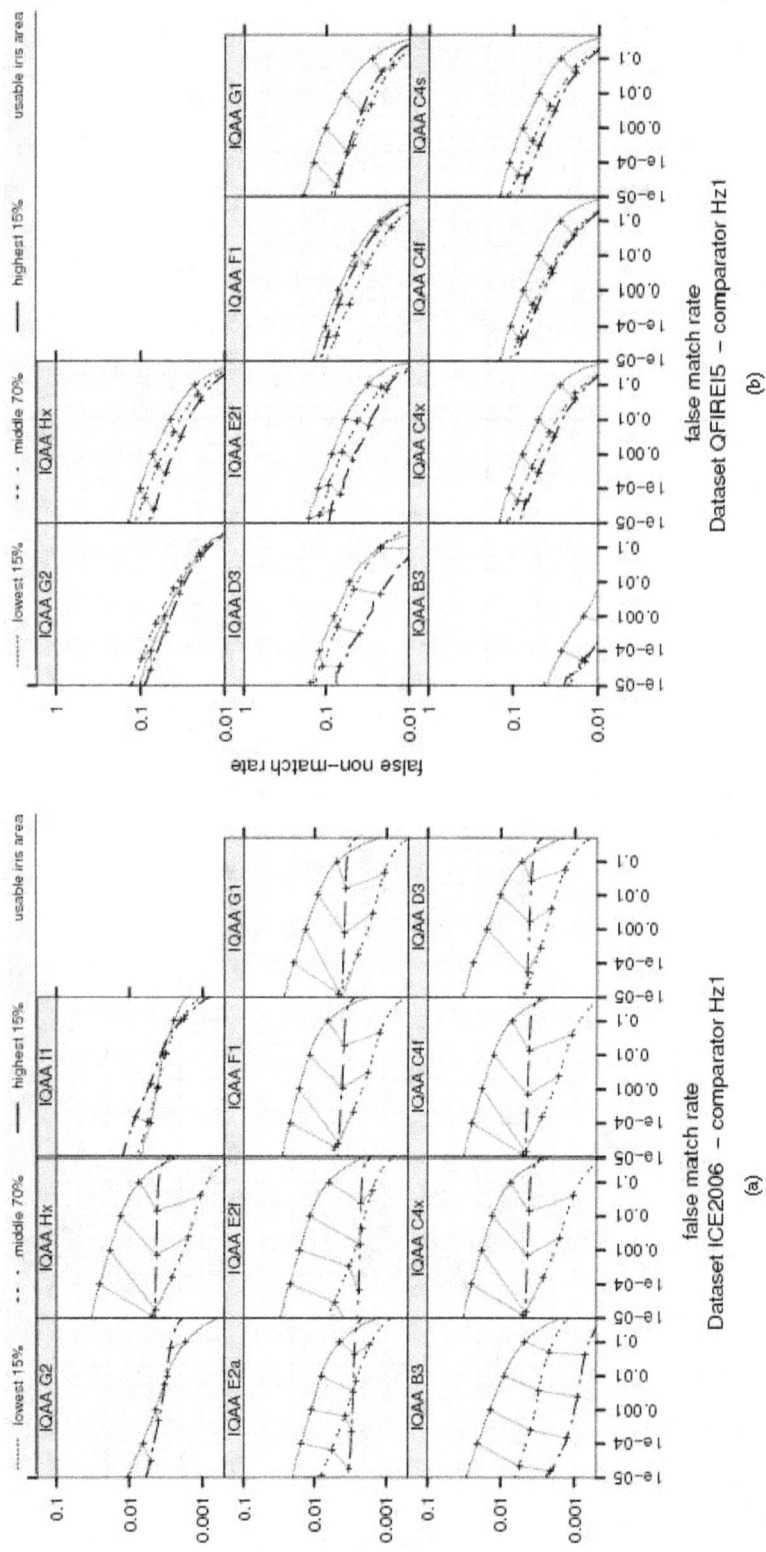

Figure 45: Ranked DET curves for comparator Hz1 and Datasets ICE2006 and QFIRE15 . The set of all comparisons are partitioned into three groups based on the pair-wise USABLE IRIS AREA quality of the images being compared. The lowest quality set contains comparisons with pairwise quality in the lowest 15 percentile. The highest quality set contains comparisons with pairwise quality in the highest 15 percentile. The rest of the comparisons, namely the middle 70%, make up the third set. The DETs are connected at the same score threshold values (brown lines). Lower FNMR and FMR are expected for higher quality images. ICE2006 images with small USABLE IRIS AREA scores inflate comparator Hz1 false non-match rate. Image with high USABLE IRIS AREA scores show higher error rate than the images with medium USABLE IRIS AREA scores except for IQAA B3. This behavior is unexpected, and is not observed for other comparators, for example A2a, as shown in the next figure.

| A2a=NEUROTECHNOLOGY-a | B3=CROSSMATCH | C4s=CAMBRIDGE-s | D3=AWARE | E2a=IRITECH-a | G1=IRISID-1 | I1=KYNEN | Hz1=L1-z1 |
| A2f=NEUROTECHNOLOGY-f | C4x=CAMBRIDGE-x | C4f=CAMBRIDGE-f | F1=MORPHO | E2f=IRITECH-f | G2=IRISID-2 | Hx=L1-x | Hz2=L1-z2 |

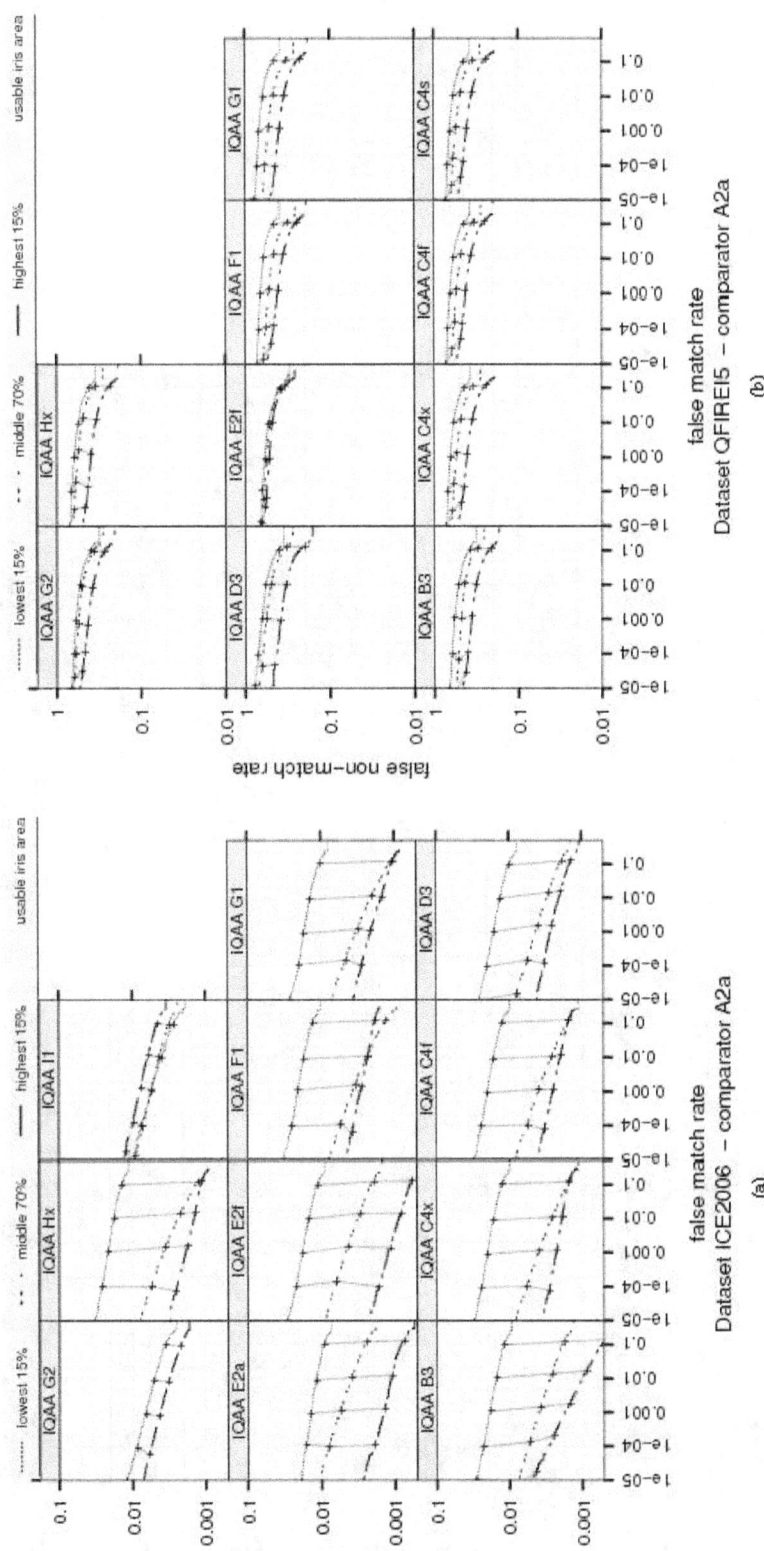

Figure 46: Ranked DET curves for comparator A2a and Datasets ICE2006 and QFIRE15 . The set of all comparisons are partitioned into three groups based on the pair-wise USABLE IRIS AREA quality of the images being compared. ahe lowest quality set contains comparisons with pairwise quality in the lowest 15 percentile. The highest quality set contains comparisons with pairwise quality in the highest 15 percentile. The rest of the comparisons, namely the middle 70%, make up the third set. The DETs are connected at the same score threshold values (brown lines). Lower FNMR and FMR are expected for higher quality images.

| A2a=NEUROTECHNOLOGY-a | B3=CROSSMATCH | C4s=CAMBRIDGE-s | D3=AWARE | E2a=IRITECH-a | G1=IRISID-1 | I1=KYNEN | Hz1=L1-z1 |
| A2f=NEUROTECHNOLOGY-f | C4x=CAMBRIDGE-x | C4f=CAMBRIDGE-f | F1=MORPHO | E2f=IRITECH-f | G2=IRISID-2 | Hx=L1-x | Hz2=L1-z2 |

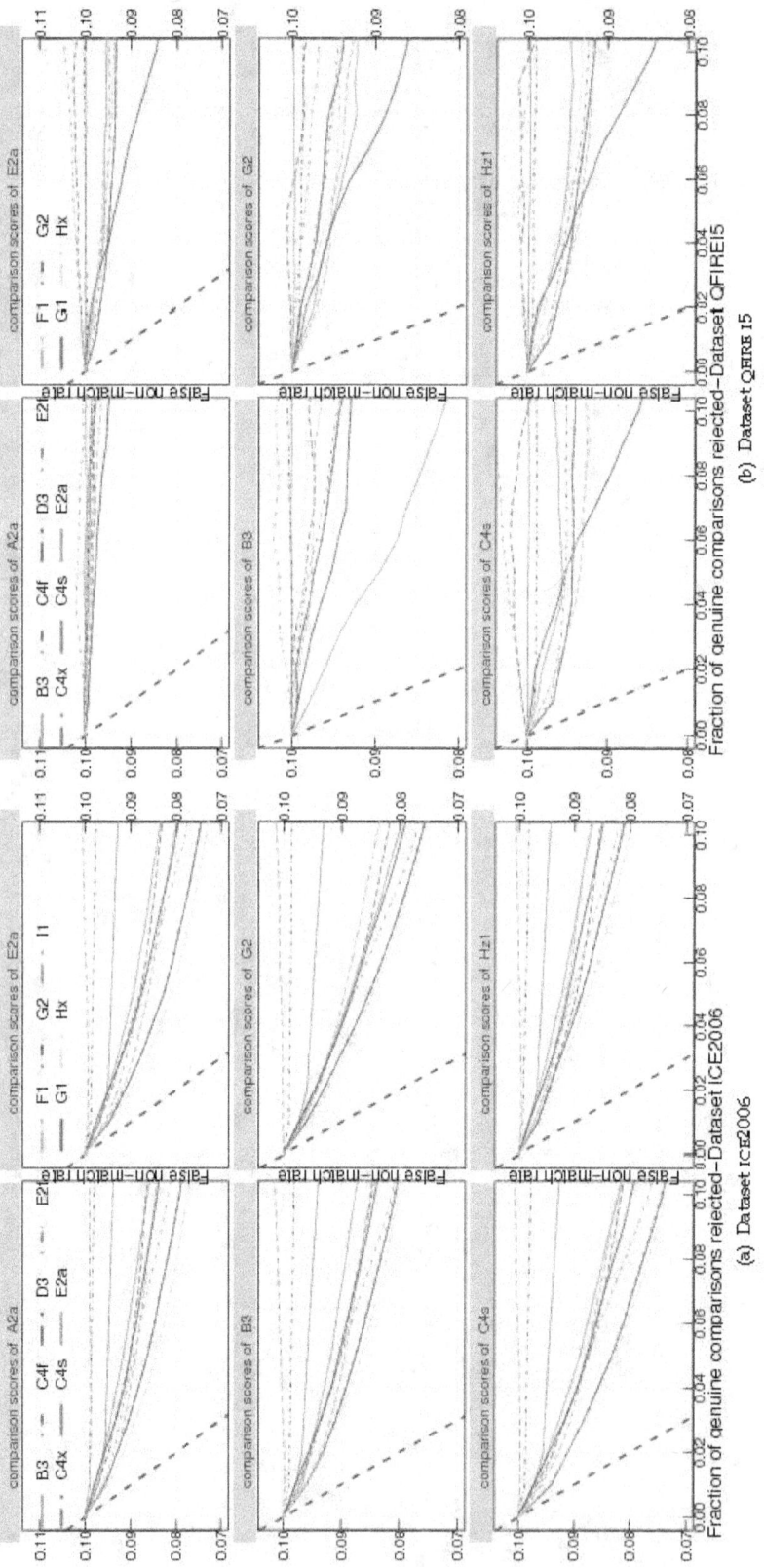

(a) Dataset ICE2006

(b) Dataset QFIRE I5

Figure 47: FNMR vs. reject curves for USABLE IRIS AREA scores on datasets ICE2006 and QFIRE I5. The threshold is set to give an initial FNMR = 0.1. The gray dotted line shows the ideal case where the rejection of the comparisons with the lowest ten percent quality results in zero FNMR.

| A2a=NEUROTECHNOLOGY-a | B3=CROSSMATCH | C4s=CAMBRIDGE-s | D3=AWARE | E2a=IRITECH-a | G1=IRISID-1 | I1=KYNEN | Hz1=L1-z1 |
| A2f=NEUROTECHNOLOGY-f | C4x=CAMBRIDGE-x | C4f=CAMBRIDGE-f | F1=MORPHO | E2f=IRITECH-f | G2=IRISID-2 | Hx=L1-x | Hz2=L1-z2 |

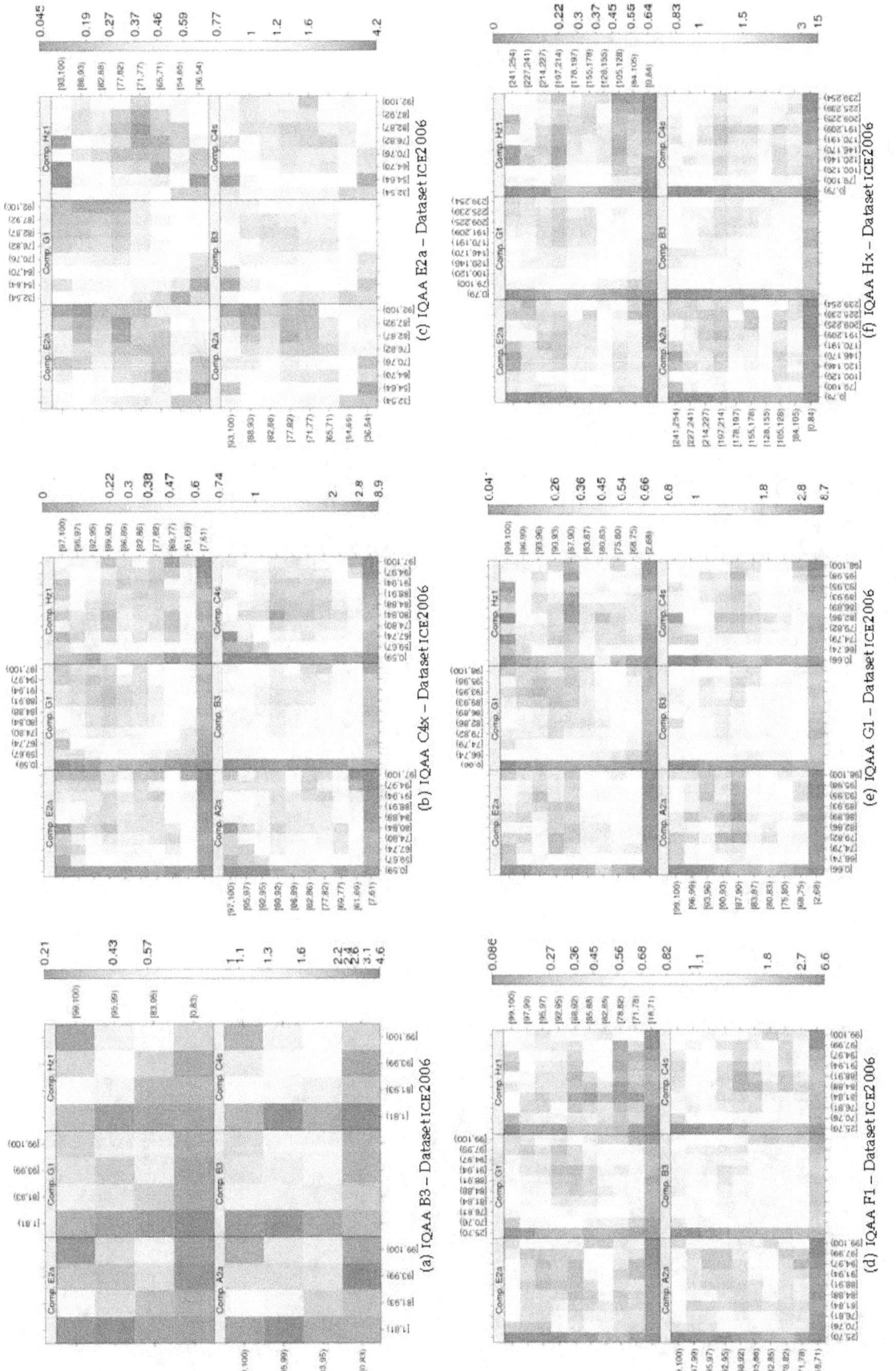

Figure 48: USABLE IRIS AREA computed by primary IQAA submissions and FNMR for IQCE comparators for ICE2006 images. The y-axis represents enrollment samples' quality with verification samples' on the x-axis. The USABLE IRIS AREA scores are quantized into 10 quantiles. The color scale plots $\frac{FNMR}{FNMR_0}$ for comparisons with verification and enrollment qualities ($q_{verification}, q_{enrollment}$). $FNMR_0$ is the nominal FNMR which is the false non-match rate computed over all the images at the same comparison score threshold, in this case at FMR = 0.001. Yellow/Green color represent an improvement in FNMR. Blue color represent a degradation of FNMR. White color means no change in FNMR.

109

| A2a=NEUROTECHNOLOGY-a | B3=CROSSMATCH | C4s=CAMBRIDGE-s | D3=AWARE | E2a=IRITECH-a | G1=IRISID-1 | I1=KYNEN | Hz1=L1-z1 |
| A2f=NEUROTECHNOLOGY-f | C4x=CAMBRIDGE-x | C4f=CAMBRIDGE-f | F1=MORPHO | E2f=IRITECH-f | G2=IRISID-2 | Hx=L1-x | Hz2=L1-z2 |

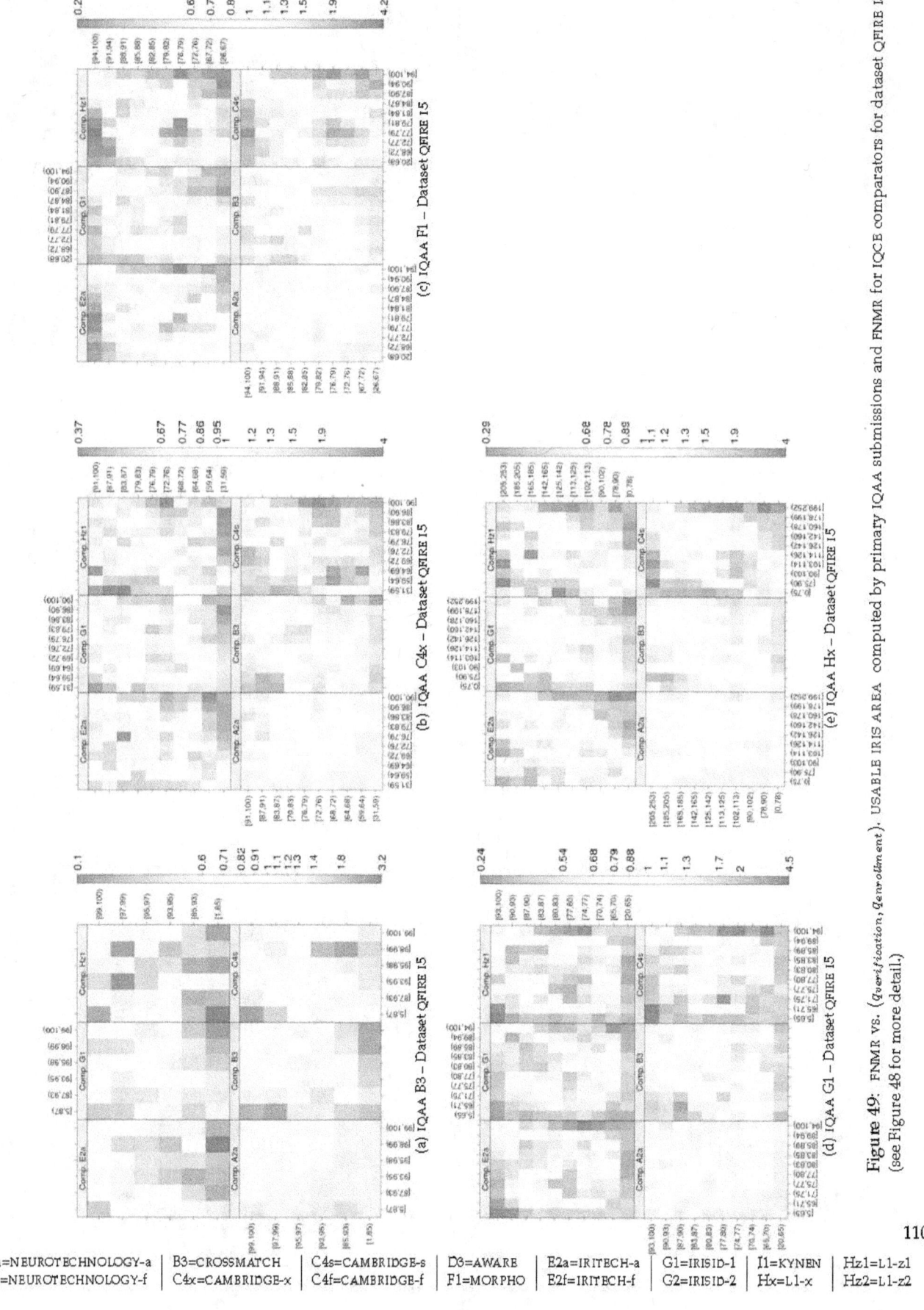

Figure 49: FNMR vs. (*qverification, qenroliment*). USABLE IRIS AREA computed by primary IQAA submissions and FNMR for IQCE comparators for dataset QFIRE I5 . (see Figure 48 for more detail.)

A2a=NEUROTECHNOLOGY-a	B3=CROSSMATCH	C4s=CAMBRIDGE-s	D3=AWARE	E2a=IRITECH-a	G1=IRISID-1	I1=KYNEN	Hz1=L1-z1
A2f=NEUROTECHNOLOGY-f	C4x=CAMBRIDGE-x	C4f=CAMBRIDGE-f	F1=MORPHO	E2f=IRITECH-f	G2=IRISID-2	Hx=L1-x	Hz2=L1-z2

Dataset	comparator	IQAA B3	IQAA C4x	IQAA E2a	IQAA E2f	IQAA F1	IQAA G1	IQAA G2	IQAA Hx
ICE2006	A2a	(8.99,9.21)	(12.58,12.88)	(8.04,8.34)	(10.99,11.26)	(9.70,9.93)	(10.11,10.39)	(1.38,1.42)	(21.25,21.76)
ICE2006	B3	(8.81,8.90)	(9.00,9.13)	(5.95,6.09)	(7.59,7.72)	(5.09,5.19)	(6.87,7.00)	(0.64,0.66)	(14.03,14.26)
ICE2006	C4s	(9.58,9.74)	(14.55,14.77)	(5.99,6.21)	(8.66,8.87)	(7.12,7.28)	(8.02,8.23)	(1.28,1.31)	(15.90,16.28)
ICE2006	E2a	(10.66,10.88)	(15.17,15.47)	(8.73,9.04)	(11.92,12.21)	(10.39,10.62)	(10.36,10.67)	(0.48,0.53)	(23.50,24.02)
ICE2006	G2	(9.84,9.94)	(13.47,13.62)	(8.50,8.65)	(11.35,11.49)	(7.13,7.24)	(11.07,11.20)	(0.36,0.38)	(21.62,21.87)
ICE2006	Hz1	(6.45,6.71)	(8.95,9.31)	(5.24,5.59)	(7.67,7.99)	(6.84,7.11)	(5.39,5.72)	(0.60,0.65)	(12.74,13.33)
OPS	A2a	(6.00,13.73)	(1.03,6.02)	(4.25,11.93)	(1.94,8.54)	(-0.05,4.30)	(1.12,6.24)	(8.52,11.00)	(2.50,11.94)
OPS	B3	(1.25,2.15)	(-0.11,1.98)	(1.93,5.14)	(0.95,3.71)	(-0.78,1.04)	(0.87,2.99)	(1.47,2.42)	(0.79,4.73)
OPS	C4s	(1.58,7.82)	(0.51,4.52)	(4.30,10.47)	(3.45,8.76)	(0.54,4.04)	(0.27,4.39)	(-1.24,0.84)	(2.55,10.14)
OPS	E2a	(-4.52,4.59)	(-0.72,5.14)	(3.73,12.75)	(0.48,8.23)	(-1.41,3.71)	(-2.38,3.64)	(-1.73,1.31)	(-2.65,8.44)
OPS	G2	(5.61,10.59)	(6.88,10.11)	(9.48,14.46)	(9.91,14.18)	(4.59,7.41)	(8.93,12.09)	(-0.01,0.26)	(12.72,18.81)
OPS	Hz1	(-1.74,5.60)	(-1.74,2.96)	(3.68,10.93)	(2.98,9.20)	(-1.34,2.76)	(-1.80,3.02)	(0.77,3.18)	(-1.43,7.46)
QFIREA5	A2a	(0.84,1.50)	(2.14,2.67)	(-0.00,0.00)	(0.43,2.98)	(1.66,2.17)	(1.44,2.00)	(-0.08,0.01)	(3.96,4.82)
QFIREA5	B3	(1.64,2.65)	(2.38,3.24)	(-0.00,0.00)	(1.32,5.63)	(0.19,1.00)	(2.17,3.02)	(-0.01,0.14)	(5.13,6.43)
QFIREA5	C4s	(2.52,3.40)	(3.33,4.08)	(0.00,0.00)	(-0.02,3.66)	(0.22,0.92)	(1.54,2.30)	(-0.09,0.01)	(5.19,6.40)
QFIREA5	E2a	(1.87,2.47)	(1.77,2.29)	(-0.00,0.00)	(1.36,4.02)	(1.15,1.63)	(1.69,2.22)	(-0.04,0.03)	(4.17,5.01)
QFIREA5	G2	(1.89,2.54)	(2.32,2.87)	(-0.00,0.00)	(0.36,2.94)	(0.72,1.23)	(2.22,2.78)	(-0.05,0.03)	(6.05,6.95)
QFIREA5	Hz1	(1.09,2.17)	(3.38,4.31)	(0.00,0.00)	(-1.57,2.65)	(1.13,1.99)	(3.07,4.02)	(-0.12,0.01)	(8.02,9.52)
QFIREI5	A2a	(1.68,1.97)	(3.69,3.92)	(-0.00,0.00)	(0.99,2.30)	(3.05,3.25)	(4.05,4.27)	(0.13,0.15)	(5.68,6.05)
QFIREI5	B3	(5.02,5.24)	(1.96,2.20)	(-0.00,0.00)	(-0.48,1.45)	(1.49,1.70)	(2.23,2.45)	(-0.00,0.02)	(1.90,2.29)
QFIREI5	C4s	(1.00,1.96)	(0.22,0.51)	(-0.00,-0.00)	(-1.44,0.57)	(-0.39,-0.14)	(1.60,1.88)	(0.12,0.16)	(0.21,0.68)
QFIREI5	E2a	(2.56,3.55)	(0.75,1.06)	(0.00,0.00)	(-2.36,-0.50)	(-0.90,-0.64)	(2.21,2.50)	(-0.03,0.01)	(0.87,1.37)
QFIREI5	G2	(2.81,3.26)	(1.82,2.08)	(0.00,0.00)	(2.46,4.18)	(1.00,1.21)	(2.88,3.13)	(0.14,0.17)	(2.81,3.23)
QFIREI5	Hz1	(3.16,4.39)	(1.89,2.27)	(-0.00,-0.00)	(-0.46,1.65)	(0.29,0.60)	(2.79,3.15)	(0.00,0.05)	(2.35,2.95)

Table 17: Tukey HSD mean difference in USABLE IRIS AREA . Each cell shows the 95% confidence level in the difference in the mean pairwise quality for images verified correctly (i.e., genuine score equal or less than threshold) and those rejected falsely (i.e., genuine score larger than threshold). Quality scores were computed by the SDK identified by the column header and comparison scores were generated by the SDK identified by the row header. If the interval does not contain zero, the difference in mean is significant. Cells where difference in mean is not significant have pink background. For monotonic quality components (all except DILATION , and depending on quality implementation GRAY SCALE SPREAD), the expected behavior is to have higher quality scores for pair of enrollment verification images that result in genuine comparison scores less than threshold. Pairwise quality is computed as geometric mean of the quality of two samples being compared. Threshold is set to give false match rate of 0.001.

A2a=NEUROTECHNOLOGY-a	B3=CROSSMATCH	C4s=CAMBRIDGE-s	D3=AWARE	E2a=IRITECH-a	G1=IRISID-1	I1=KYNEN	Hz1=L1-z1
A2f=NEUROTECHNOLOGY-f	C4x=CAMBRIDGE-x	C4f=CAMBRIDGE-f	F1=MORPHO	E2f=IRITECH-f	G2=IRISID-2	Hx=L1-x	Hz2=L1-z2

Dataset	comparator	IQAA B3	IQAA C4x	IQAA E2a	IQAA E2f	IQAA F1	IQAA G1	IQAA G2	IQAA Hx
ICE2006	A2a	(-2.09,-1.48)	(-2.45,-1.81)	(-2.55,-1.90)	(-2.83,-2.25)	(-1.48,-0.99)	(-2.05,-1.31)	(-0.65,-0.17)	(-5.15,-4.07)
ICE2006	B3	(17.22,17.57)	(16.32,16.79)	(5.98,6.44)	(9.35,9.77)	(8.10,8.45)	(13.45,13.98)	(3.89,4.23)	(22.73,23.51)
ICE2006	C4s	(3.21,3.68)	(5.78,6.28)	(1.41,1.91)	(2.65,3.10)	(3.56,3.94)	(4.78,5.36)	(0.71,1.08)	(8.82,9.65)
ICE2006	E2a	(5.83,6.31)	(7.52,8.02)	(3.56,4.07)	(6.06,6.51)	(5.21,5.59)	(7.06,7.64)	(1.90,2.28)	(10.74,11.60)
ICE2006	G2	(-1.64,-1.15)	(-3.04,-2.52)	(-2.29,-1.77)	(-3.07,-2.61)	(-1.94,-1.55)	(-2.42,-1.89)	(-0.13,-0.06)	(-6.02,-5.16)
ICE2006	Hz1	(5.05,5.57)	(7.61,8.17)	(2.12,2.68)	(4.12,4.62)	(4.85,5.27)	(9.35,9.98)	(3.62,4.03)	(11.37,12.30)
OPS	A2a	(-0.25,0.68)	(-0.34,0.18)	(-0.87,-0.05)	(-0.71,-0.01)	(-0.11,0.35)	(-0.06,0.49)	(-0.11,0.20)	(-1.13,-0.10)
OPS	B3	(4.19,4.38)	(6.38,6.81)	(4.17,4.84)	(4.65,5.21)	(4.07,4.45)	(4.79,5.24)	(0.51,0.74)	(11.52,12.36)
OPS	C4s	(1.40,2.17)	(4.32,4.75)	(2.83,3.50)	(3.31,3.89)	(3.04,3.42)	(3.37,3.82)	(0.02,0.28)	(7.59,8.44)
OPS	E2a	(0.04,0.81)	(1.25,1.69)	(0.72,1.41)	(1.04,1.63)	(1.14,1.53)	(1.17,1.64)	(-0.05,0.21)	(2.07,2.93)
OPS	G2	(-0.39,0.38)	(-1.55,-1.12)	(-1.86,-1.18)	(-2.33,-1.75)	(-1.35,-0.97)	(-1.37,-0.94)	(-0.08,-0.04)	(-3.14,-2.30)
OPS	Hz1	(1.05,1.82)	(4.13,4.56)	(2.89,3.56)	(3.33,3.90)	(3.39,3.87)	(3.81,4.27)	(0.43,0.68)	(7.42,8.26)
QFIREA5	A2a	(5.33,6.52)	(4.71,5.48)	(-0.00,0.00)	(-1.51,1.50)	(-2.70,-2.00)	(-0.27,0.07)	(0.08,0.23)	(3.56,4.58)
QFIREA5	C4s	(0.84,1.88)	(3.63,4.33)	(-0.00,0.00)	(-0.18,2.45)	(1.34,1.97)	(0.40,0.69)	(0.02,0.15)	(3.42,4.35)
QFIREA5	E2a	(-7.34,-6.33)	(1.38,2.07)	(-0.00,0.00)	(-2.68,0.19)	(4.00,4.63)	(0.64,0.91)	(-0.34,-0.21)	(10.47,11.39)
QFIREA5	G2	(0.39,1.40)	(-0.36,0.31)	(0.00,0.01)	(-3.04,-0.33)	(-1.69,-1.07)	(-0.66,-0.38)	(-0.05,0.08)	(-1.70,-0.77)
QFIREA5	Hz1	(0.96,2.01)	(6.61,7.30)	(-0.00,0.00)	(-1.10,1.77)	(2.78,3.41)	(1.28,1.59)	(-0.09,0.05)	(10.88,11.80)
QFIREI5	A2a	(-0.20,0.28)	(-1.28,-0.91)	(0.00,0.00)	(-1.74,0.83)	(-0.93,-0.63)	(-0.31,0.04)	(-0.04,0.00)	(-1.40,-0.82)
QFIREI5	C4s	(0.91,1.33)	(2.38,2.70)	(0.00,0.00)	(-1.14,1.03)	(1.33,1.60)	(1.80,2.10)	(0.05,0.08)	(3.78,4.28)
QFIREI5	E2a	(1.62,2.03)	(2.56,2.88)	(0.00,0.00)	(-0.28,1.34)	(0.35,0.61)	(2.05,2.36)	(0.04,0.07)	(5.54,6.04)
QFIREI5	G2	(-2.09,1.06)	(-3.44,-1.01)	(-0.00,-0.00)	(-5.75,5.21)	(-1.50,0.47)	(-2.45,-0.19)	(-0.17,0.07)	(-4.12,-0.34)
QFIREI5	Hz1	(2.71,3.13)	(3.48,3.80)	(0.00,0.00)	(-0.05,1.80)	(1.94,2.20)	(4.08,4.38)	(0.13,0.16)	(4.58,5.08)

Table 18: Tukey HSD mean difference in USABLE IRIS AREA scores. Each cell shows the 95% confidence level in difference in mean of pairwise quality for images correctly rejected (i.e., the impostor score equal or greater than threshold) and those falsely matched (i.e., the impostor score less than threshold). Quality scores were computed by the SDK identified by the column header and comparison scores were generated by the SDK identified by the row header. If the interval does not contain zero, the difference in mean is significant. Cells where difference in mean is not significant are shaded in pink. For monotonic increasing quality components (all except DILATION, and depending on quality implementation GRAY SCALE SPREAD), the expected behavior is to have higher quality scores for the pair of (enrollment, verification) images that result in impostor comparison scores equal or greater than threshold. Pairwise quality is computed as geometric mean of the quality of two samples being compared. Threshold is set to give false match rate of 0.001.

9.5 Iris_sclera contrast

The source of variation in IRIS SCLERA CONTRAST can be extrinsic (illumination wavelength and other capture device characteristics), or intrinsic (eye disease such as albinism, shadow of eyelash on iris, etc.). Nevertheless, insufficient IRIS SCLERA CONTRAST is believed to affect the accuracy of segmentation and feature extraction.

Eight vendors (A, C, D, E, F, G, H, and I) submitted SDKs that generate IRIS SCLERA CONTRAST scores. IQCE examined the effect of these IQAAS' IRIS SCLERA CONTRAST scores on performance. The distribution of the IRIS SCLERA CONTRAST scores is shown in Figure 50, and the quantitative results follows. In order to make the boxplots more readable, quality scores in [0–254] range were linearly scaled back to [0–100].

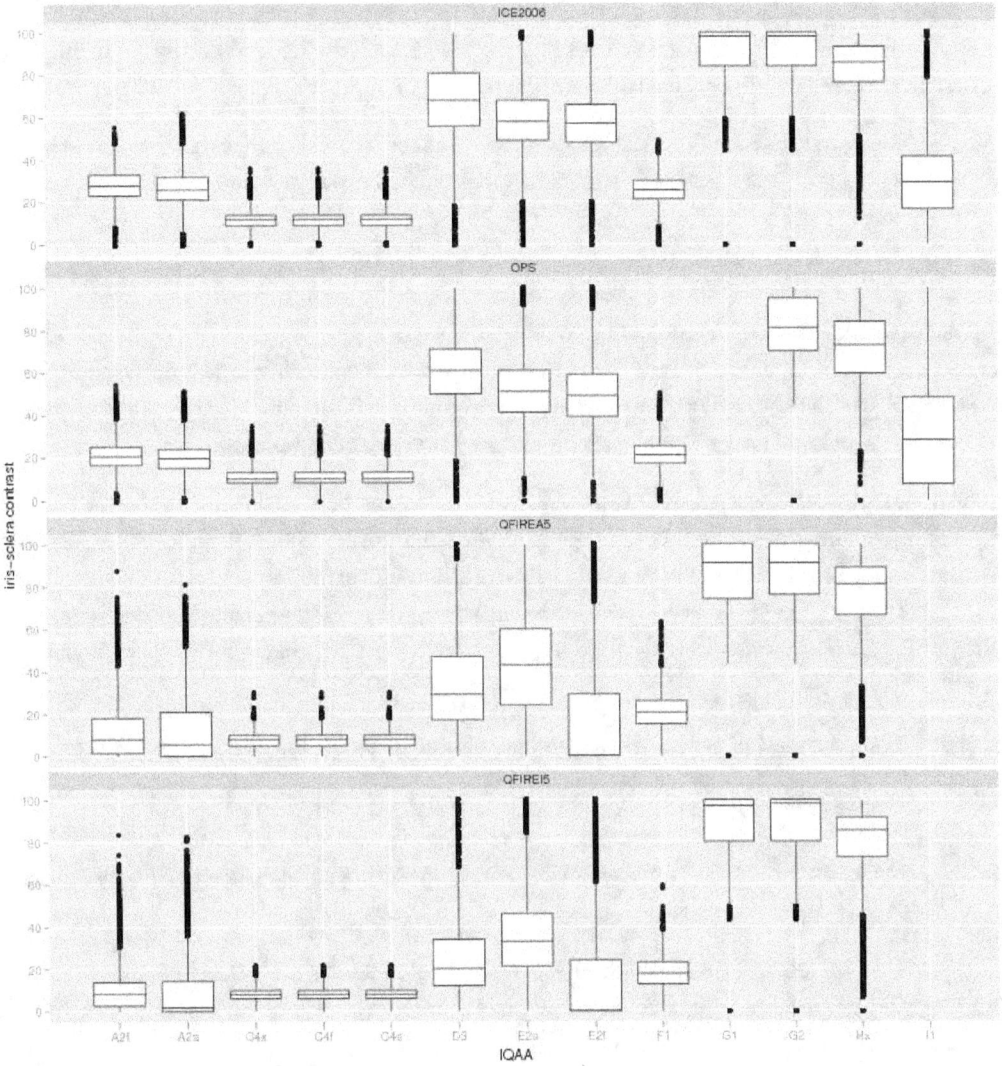

Figure 50: Box and whisker plots of the IQAAS that generate IRIS SCLERA CONTRAST scores.

RELATIONSHIP WITH THE DISTRIBUTION OF GENUINE SCORES

113

| A2a=NEUROTECHNOLOGY-a | B3=CROSSMATCH | C4s=CAMBRIDGE-s | D3=AWARE | E2a=IRITECH-a | G1=IRISID-1 | I1=KYNEN | Hz1=L1-z1 |
| A2f=NEUROTECHNOLOGY-f | C4x=CAMBRIDGE-x | C4f=CAMBRIDGE-f | F1=MORPHO | E2f=IRITECH-f | G2=IRISID-2 | Hx=L1-x | Hz2=L1-z2 |

The IRIS SCLERA CONTRAST scores vs. genuine scores for primary comparators are shown in Figure 51. The first observation is that the range of IRIS SCLERA CONTRAST scores of different IQAAs are vastly different. The range can be as low as [0-20] (IQAA C4x) and as high as [60-100] (IQAA Hx). The second observation is that images in the ICE2006 dataset have the highest IRIS SCLERA CONTRAST scores, except for IQAA F1 which gives the highest IRIS SCLERA CONTRAST scores to QFIRE I5 images. The lowest scores occur for QFIRE I5 images except for IQAA Hx, where OPS images have the lowest IRIS SCLERA CONTRAST scores. The biggest spread across datasets is given by IQAA E2a.

Generally, high IRIS SCLERA CONTRAST scores are associated with low genuine scores, although the rate of change is small.

RELATIONSHIP WITH THE DISTRIBUTION OF IMPOSTOR SCORES

Figure 52 shows the relationship between IRIS SCLERA CONTRAST and the impostor scores of primary comparators. IRIS SCLERA CONTRAST scores are almost constant for different bins of impostor scores.

Figures 51 and 52 suggest that the IRIS SCLERA CONTRAST effect on FNMR is greater than on FMR. This result is not surprising as, IRIS SCLERA CONTRAST mostly affects segmentation accuracy and therefore FNMR.

RANKED DET:: DO LOW-QUALITY IMAGES PRODUCE HIGH FNMR OR FMR?

ICE2006 images with the lowest 15% IRIS SCLERA CONTRAST scores give significantly higher FNMR than the images in the upper 15 percentile. The effect on FMR is smaller as shown by the almost vertical brown lines connecting the DET curves of Figure 53(a). The best ranking of performance occurs for IQAAs E2a, E2f, C4x, and C4f. IQAAs Hx and I1 IRIS SCLERA CONTRAST scores are not effective in predicting performance of comparator Hz1.

On QFIRE I5 images, IQAAs C4x, C4f, and Hx give reasonable ranking of performance as seen in Figure 53(b). However, the difference in performance of the three groups is smaller than of ICE2006 images. IQAA E2a shows IRIS SCLERA CONTRAST scores give high FNMR, but its upper 15 percentile does not exhibit lower FNMR than the images with medium IRIS SCLERA CONTRAST (mid 70%) scores. The slope of the brown lines connecting the DET curves of Figure 53(b) is smaller than of Figure 53(a), suggesting that the IRIS SCLERA CONTRAST effect on FMR is greater for QFIRE I5 images than ICE2006.

IQAAs A2f and D3 are the least effective, where the undesirable behavior that the upper 15 percentile gives the lowest performance.

EFFECT OF QUALITY ON FNMR : HOW QUICKLY FNMR IMPROVES WHEN POOR QUALITY SAMPLES ARE REJECTED?

Rejection of as low as 4% ICE2006 images with the lowest IRIS SCLERA CONTRAST scores improves FNMR by more than 10% (IQAA C4s, and its mated comparator) as shown in Figure 54(a). Among all comparators, C4s and G2 show the biggest improvement in FNMR when images with low IRIS SCLERA CONTRAST are rejected. Except for comparator Hz1, the best performance is for IQAA C4s, followed by IQAAs E2a, E2f, D3, Hx, F1, G1, and G2. This group's performance is quite similar. The largest reduction in FNMR of comparator Hz1 happens for IQAA E2a and E2f, where C4s, D3, Hx, G1, G2, and F1 are in the second place. Rejection of IQAA I1 low IRIS SCLERA CONTRAST scores does not improve performance.

| A2a=NEUROTECHNOLOGY-a | B3=CROSSMATCH | C4s=CAMBRIDGE-s | D3=AWARE | E2a=IRITECH-a | G1=IRISID-1 | I1=KYNEN | Hz1=L1-z1 |
| A2f=NEUROTECHNOLOGY-f | | C4x=CAMBRIDGE-x | C4f=CAMBRIDGE-f | F1=MORPHO | E2f=IRITECH-f | G2=IRISID-2 | Hx=L1-x | Hz2=L1-z2 |

Rejection of QFIRE I5 images with low IRIS SCLERA CONTRAST scores improves FNMR , particularly for comparators C4s and Hz1. For both comparators, IQAA C4s is most effective, followed by Hx, E2a, and G1. IQAA E2a performs better for high rejection rates (larger than 4%). IQAA E2a and G2 are the best performers for their own mated comparators. IQAA A2a is the least effective; note that I1 failed to compute the quality score for QFIRE I5 images.

TEST OF SIGNIFICANCE :: DO THE IMAGES INVOLVED IN SUCCESSFUL VERIFICATION ATTEMPTS HAVE SIGNIFICANTLY HIGHER QUALITY SCORES THAN THOSE INVOLVED IN FAILED VERIFICATION ATTEMPTS?

Table 19 shows that IRIS SCLERA CONTRAST is a significant factor for ICE 2006; images verified correctly have a higher IRIS SCLERA CONTRAST score than those involved in a failed verification attempt (i.e., falsely rejected). A similar observation is made for QFIRE images, despite a few cells shaded in pink (mostly for comparator A2a - recall A2a recognition performance drops on QFIRE images.)

As for the effect of IRIS SCLERA CONTRAST on FMR, Table 20 shows that the IRIS SCLERA CONTRAST scores of ICE 2006 images that result in false matches are significantly different from those correctly rejected. There is no significant difference between IQAA E2f IRIS SCLERA CONTRAST scores of falsely matched and correctly rejected QFIRE images, nor for impostor scores of comparator G2. For other IQAA and comparator combinations, there exists a small but significant difference between IRIS SCLERA CONTRAST scores of images involved in false matches and those correctly rejected.

EFFECT OF VARIATION BETWEEN THE TWO SAMPLES:: DOES SAMENESS MATTER?

The heatmaps of Figures 55 and 56 indicate that while images with high values of IRIS SCLERA CONTRAST give low FNMR, dissimilarity between IRIS SCLERA CONTRAST scores of two images being compared elevates FNMR, particularly for comparators B3 and G1. The heatmap of QFIRE I5 images is more chaotic than that of the ICE 2006 images; however, the pattern of blue colors in the corners (indicating higher FNMR for images with low or dissimilar IRIS SCLERA CONTRAST) can be detected.

OBSERVATIONS AND CONCLUSIONS

IRIS SCLERA CONTRAST greatly influences performance of iris recognition algorithms.

Images with low IRIS SCLERA CONTRAST give high FNMR. The difference in FNMR can be up to two orders of magnitude (IQAA C4x – Dataset QFIRE I5 and ICE2006).

The effect on FMR is small, but significant.

Comparisons of images with similar IRIS SCLERA CONTRAST scores give lower FNMR than when the images' IRIS SCLERA CONTRAST scores differ from each other. The change in FNMR is the largest for IQAA Hx.

IQAA C4s, C4x and E2a IRIS SCLERA CONTRAST scores performed the best. The least effective are IQAA I1 and A2f.

| A2a=NEUROTECHNOLOGY-a | B3=CROSSMATCH | C4s=CAMBRIDGE-s | D3=AWARE | E2a=IRITECH-a | G1=IRISID-1 | I1=KYNEN | Hz1=L1-z1 |
| A2f=NEUROTECHNOLOGY-f | C4x=CAMBRIDGE-x | C4f=CAMBRIDGE-f | F1=MORPHO | E2f=IRITECH-f | G2=IRISID-2 | Hx=L1-x | Hz2=L1-z2 |

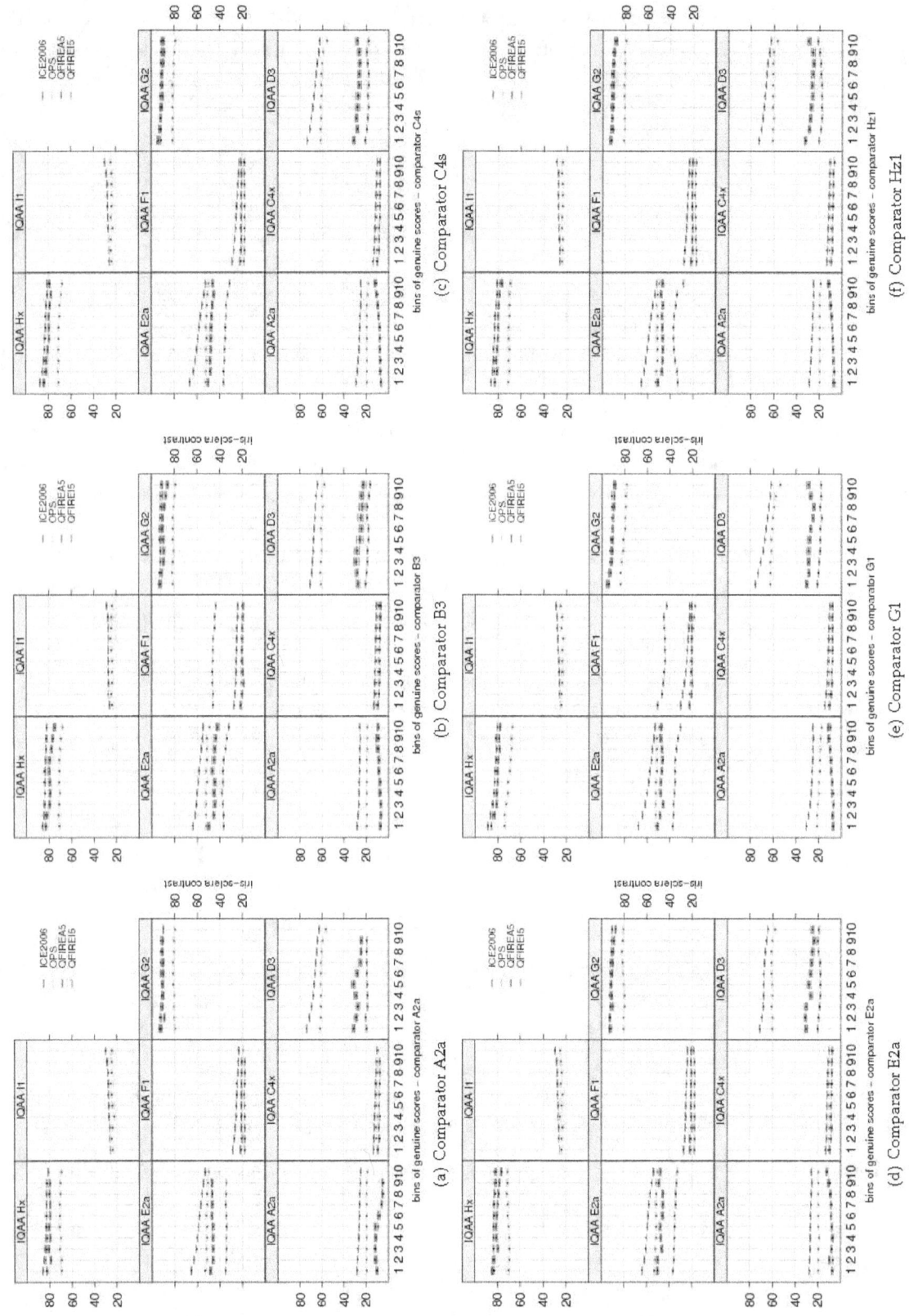

Figure 51: Pairwise IRIS SCLERA CONTRAST scores vs. genuine score for the primary Class Z submissions of each participants. Each plot shows quality scores computed by different IQAA. Genuine scores are divided equally into ten groups. Groups overlap by 5 percent. Bootstrapped pairwise quality for each group is shown in a box and whisker plot. Pairwise quality is computed as geometric mean of the quality of the two samples being compared.

| A2a=NEUROTECHNOLOGY-a | B3=CROSSMATCH | C4s=CAMBRIDGE-s | D3=AWARE | E2a=IRITECH-a | G1=IRISID-1 | I1=KYNEN | Hz1=L1-z1 |
| A2f=NEUROTECHNOLOGY-f | C4x=CAMBRIDGE-x | C4f=CAMBRIDGE-f | F1=MORPHO | E2f=IRITECH-f | G2=IRISID-2 | Hx=L1-x | Hz2=L1-z2 |

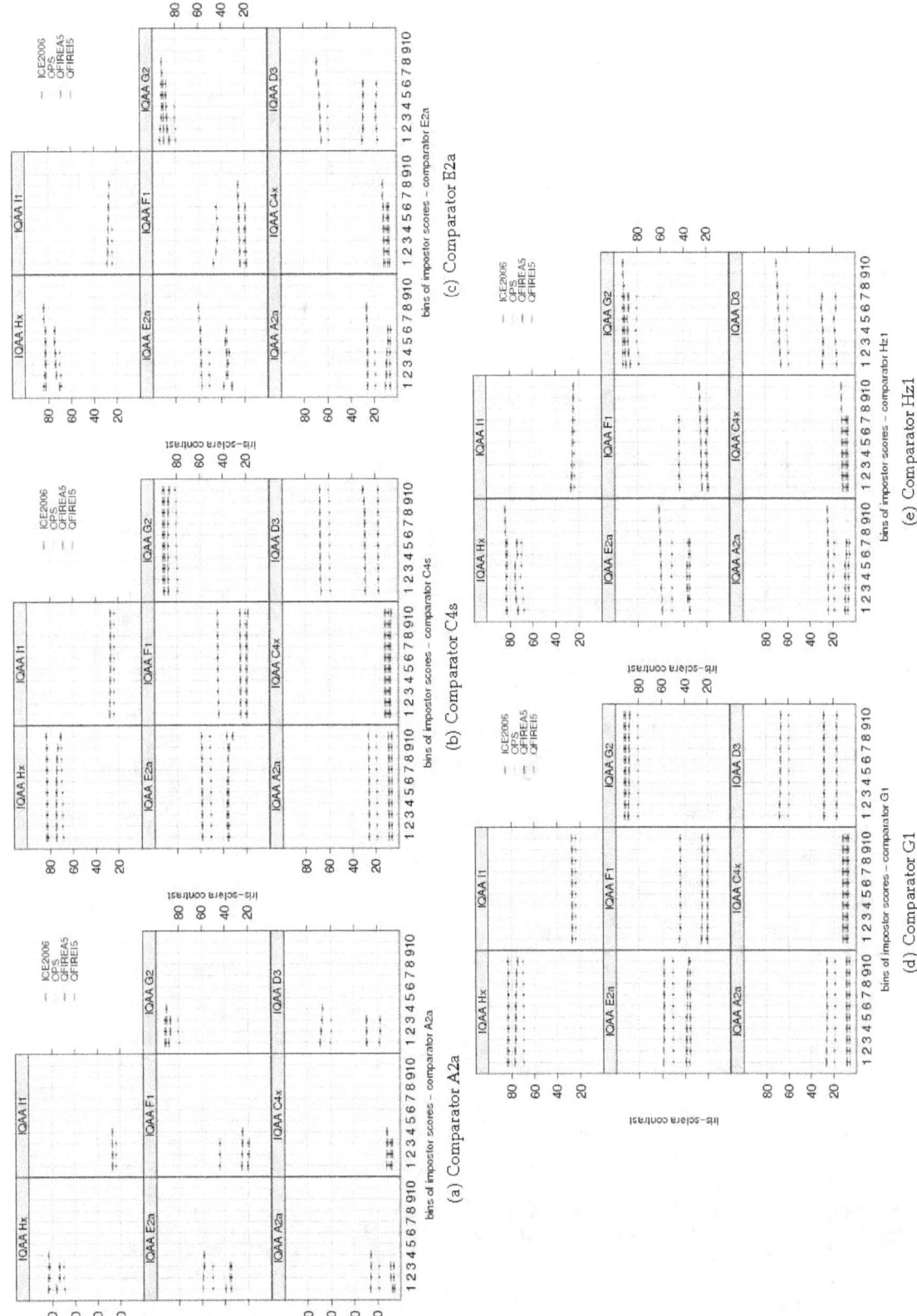

Figure 52: Pairwise IRIS SCLERA CONTRAST scores *vs.* impostor scores for the primary Class Z submissions of each participants. Each plot shows quality scores computed by different IQAA. Similar to plots of Figure 52, impostor scores are divided equally into ten groups. Groups overlap by 5 percent. Bootstrapped pairwise quality for each group is shown in a box and whisker plot. Pairwise quality is computed as geometric mean of the quality of the two samples being compared.

| A2a=NEUROTECHNOLOGY-a | B3=CROSSMATCH | C4s=CAMBRIDGE-s | D3=AWARE | E2a=IRITECH-a | G1=IRISID-1 | I1=KYNEN | Hz1=L1-z1 |
| A2f=NEUROTECHNOLOGY-f | C4x=CAMBRIDGE-x | C4f=CAMBRIDGE-f | F1=MORPHO | E2f=IRITECH-f | G2=IRISID-2 | Hx=L1-x | Hz2=L1-z2 |

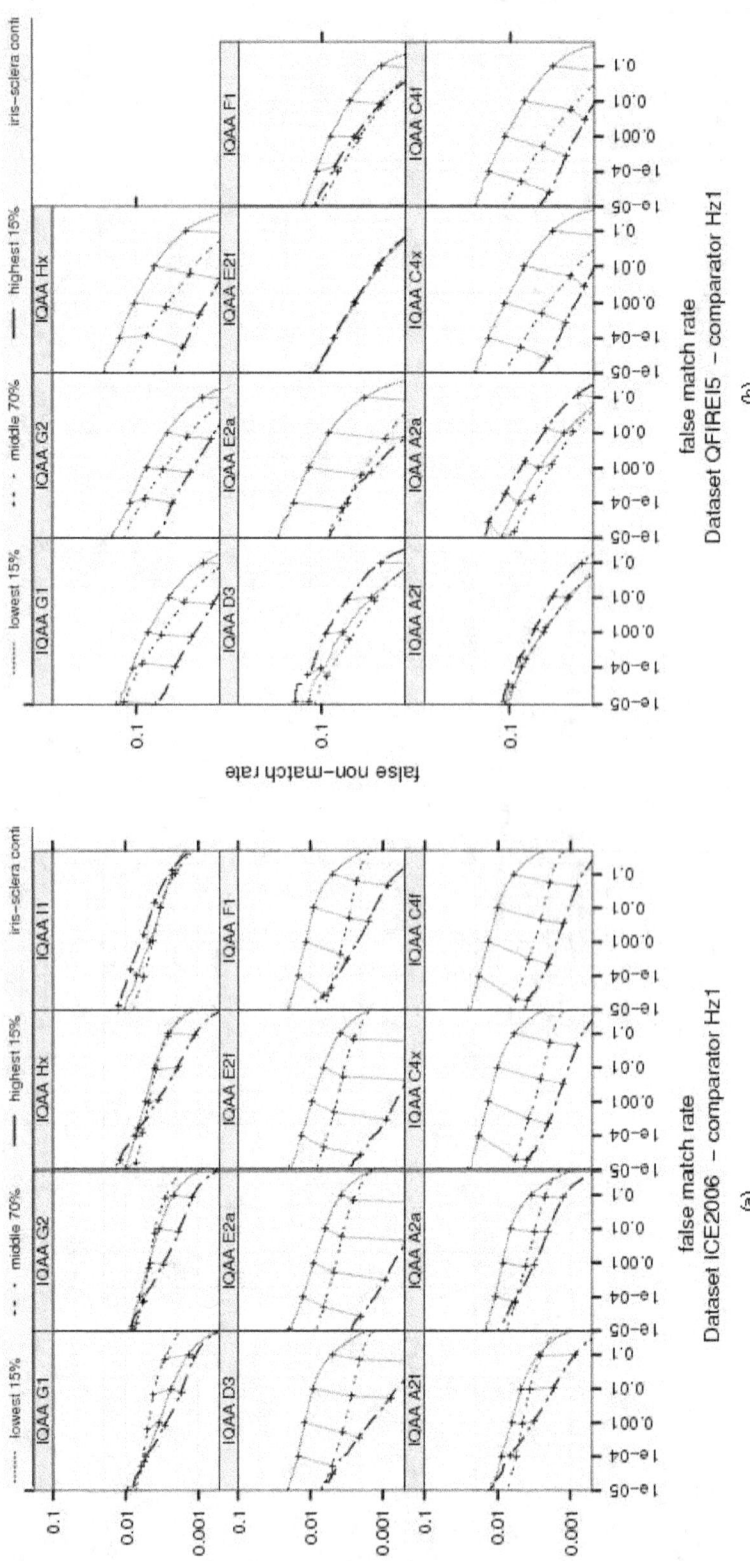

Figure 53: Ranked DET curves for comparator Hz1 and Datasets ICE2006 and QFIRE15 . The set of all comparisons were partitioned into three groups based on the pair-wise IRIS SCLERA CONTRAST quality of the images being compared. The lowest quality set contains comparisons with pairwise quality in the lower 15 percentile. The highest quality set contains comparisons with pairwise quality in the upper 15 percentile. The rest of the comparisons, namely the middle 70%, made up the third set. The DETs are connected at the same score threshold values (brown lines). Lower FNMR and FMR rates are expected for better quality images.

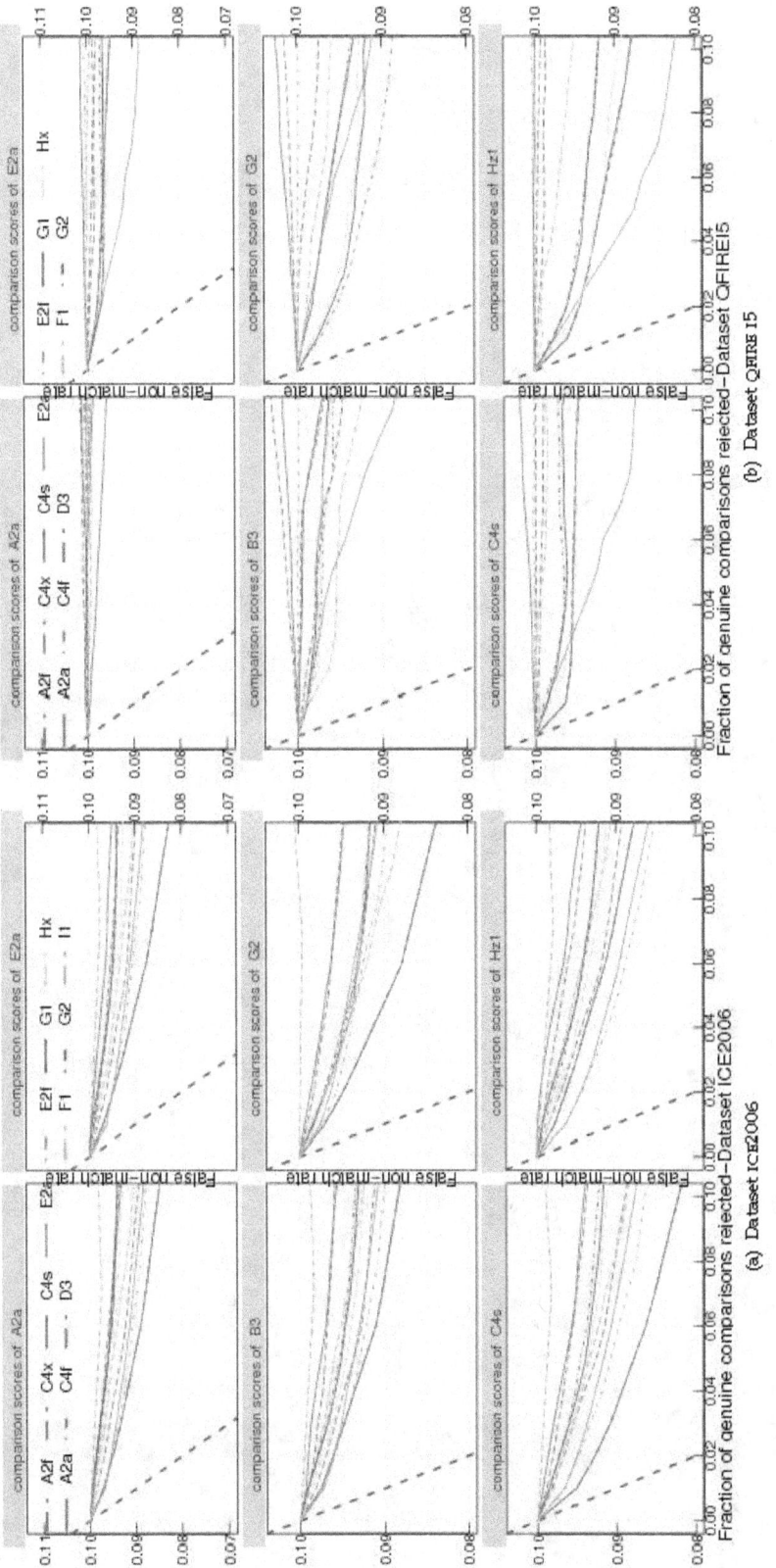

Figure 54: FNMR vs. reject curves for IRIS SCLERA CONTRAST scores on datasets ICE2006 and QFIRE I5. The threshold is set to give an initial FNMR = 0.1. The gray dotted line shows the ideal case where the rejection of the comparisons with the lowest ten percent quality results in zero FNMR.

119

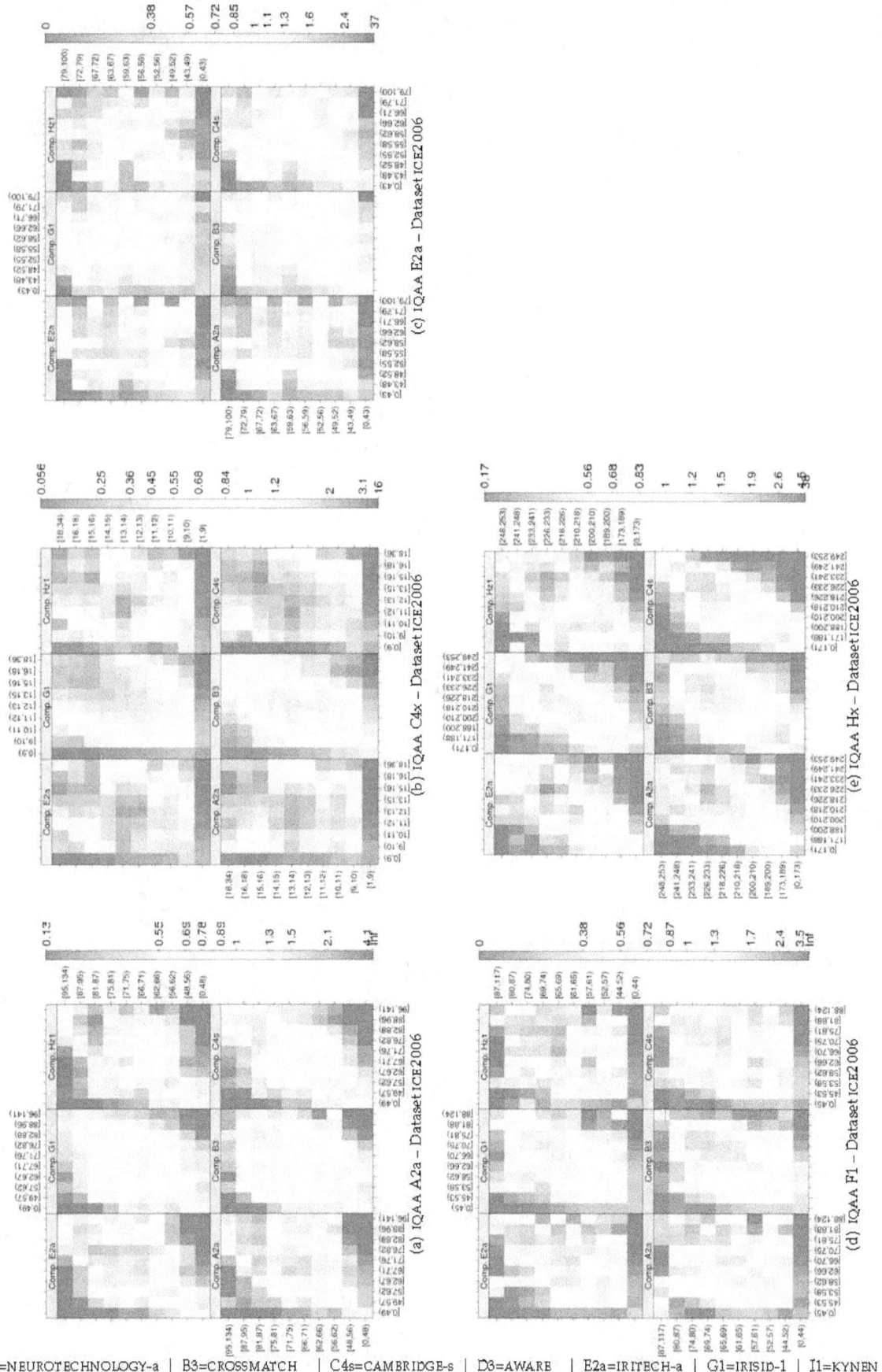

Figure 55: IRIS SCLERA CONTRAST computed by primary IQAA submissions and FNMR for IQCE comparators for dataset ICE2006 . The y-axis represents enrollment samples' quality with verification samples' on the x-axis. The IRIS SCLERA CONTRAST scores are quantized into 10 quantiles. The color scale plots $\frac{FNMR}{FNMR_0}$ for comparisons with verification and enrollment qualities ($q_{verification}, q_{enrollment}$). $FNMR_0$ is the nominal FNMR which is the false non-match rate computed over all the images at the same comparison score threshold, in this case at FMR = 0.001. Yellow/Green color represent an improvement in FNMR. Blue color represent a degradation of FNMR. White color means no change in FNMR.

120

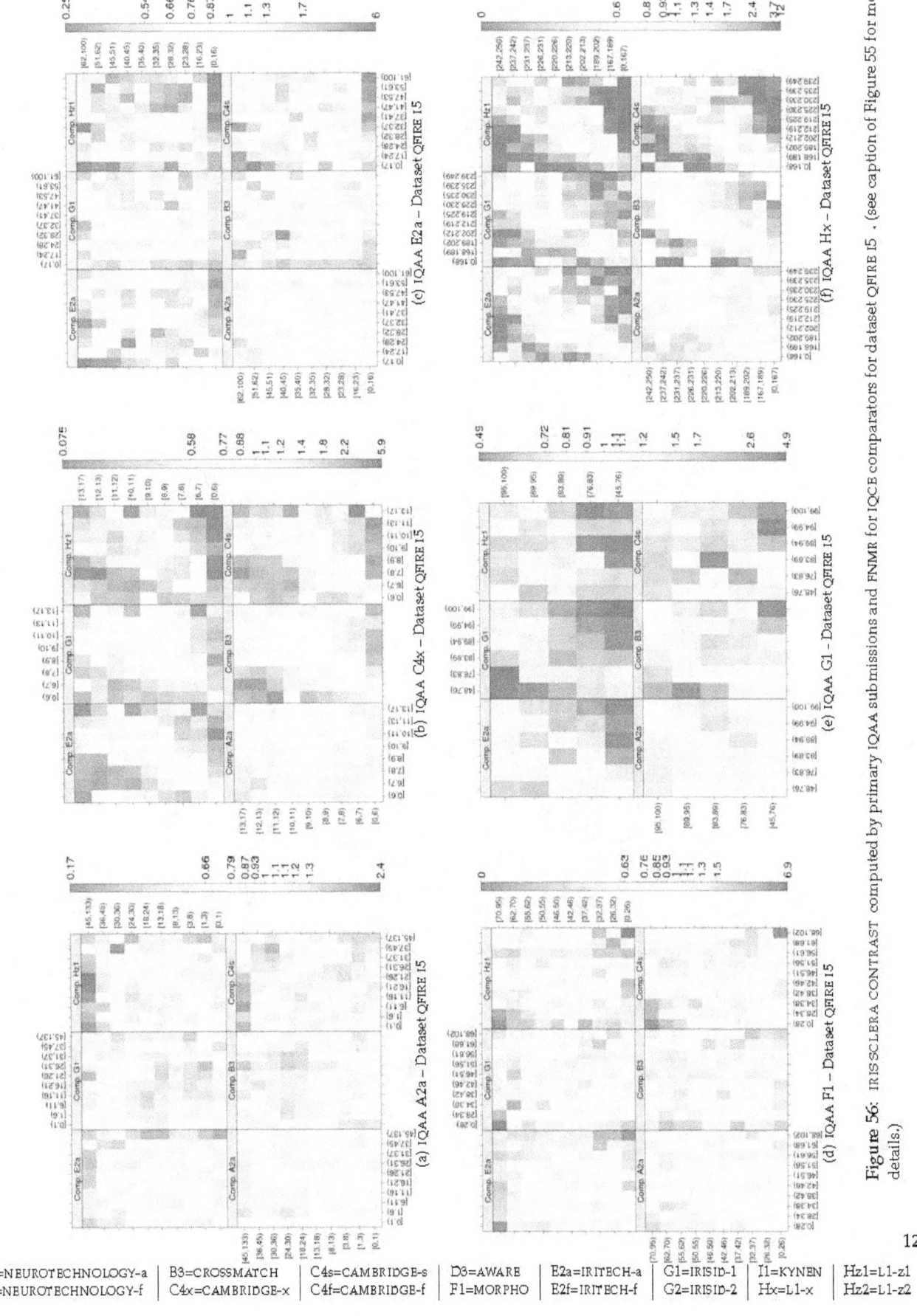

Figure 56: IRISSCLERA CONTRAST computed by primary IQAA submissions and FNMR for IQCE comparators for dataset QFIRE I5 . (see caption of Figure 55 for more details.)

A2a=NEUROTECHNOLOGY-a | B3=CROSSMATCH | C4s=CAMBRIDGE-s | D3=AWARE | E2a=IRITECH-a | G1=IRISID-1 | I1=KYNEN | Hz1=L1-z1
A2f=NEUROTECHNOLOGY-f | C4x=CAMBRIDGE-x | C4f=CAMBRIDGE-f | F1=MORPHO | E2f=IRITECH-f | G2=IRISID-2 | Hx=L1-x | Hz2=L1-z2

Dataset	comparator	IQAA A2f	IQAA C4x	IQAA E2a	IQAA E2f	IQAA F1	IQAA G1	IQAA G2	IQAA Hx
ICE2006	A2a	(2.97,3.12)	(2.49,2.57)	(10.22,10.54)	(11.81,12.13)	(4.09,4.25)	(3.16,3.42)	(3.85,4.09)	(6.06,6.33)
ICE2006	B3	(-0.77,-0.70)	(0.89,0.92)	(2.55,2.70)	(3.12,3.27)	(0.88,0.96)	(-0.06,0.05)	(-0.21,-0.10)	(-0.23,-0.10)
ICE2006	C4s	(1.64,1.76)	(3.08,3.14)	(6.77,7.00)	(7.62,7.86)	(4.08,4.20)	(2.08,2.28)	(0.91,1.09)	(2.45,2.65)
ICE2006	E2a	(2.15,2.31)	(2.34,2.42)	(10.39,10.72)	(12.32,12.65)	(3.62,3.78)	(1.00,1.27)	(1.93,2.19)	(3.46,3.73)
ICE2006	G2	(0.39,0.47)	(2.27,2.31)	(6.52,6.68)	(7.30,7.46)	(3.10,3.18)	(3.00,3.12)	(2.63,2.75)	(3.38,3.52)
ICE2006	Hz1	(1.91,2.09)	(1.86,1.95)	(7.49,7.85)	(8.42,8.78)	(3.03,3.21)	(0.75,1.03)	(1.25,1.53)	(1.81,2.12)
OPS	A2a	(0.55,4.23)	(0.66,2.53)	(2.66,11.04)	(3.34,11.55)	(0.66,4.28)	(-0.10,7.81)	(6.84,14.81)	(-0.09,9.28)
OPS	B3	(-0.21,1.32)	(0.04,0.81)	(1.66,5.17)	(2.21,5.64)	(0.11,1.63)	(1.24,4.53)	(1.44,4.75)	(0.47,4.38)
OPS	C4s	(-0.91,2.05)	(0.22,1.72)	(1.74,8.49)	(1.63,8.24)	(-0.35,2.56)	(-2.25,4.11)	(-2.05,4.38)	(-2.06,5.48)
OPS	E2a	(-1.74,2.58)	(-0.49,1.69)	(-1.83,8.02)	(-1.88,7.77)	(-0.81,3.44)	(-4.07,5.23)	(-4.16,5.22)	(-5.08,5.92)
OPS	G2	(-0.50,1.89)	(1.14,2.35)	(2.11,7.55)	(2.66,8.00)	(1.68,4.03)	(1.27,6.34)	(-2.31,2.72)	(-1.40,4.68)
OPS	Hz1	(-1.71,1.77)	(-0.25,1.51)	(0.18,8.10)	(-0.27,7.49)	(-0.67,2.75)	(-3.61,3.85)	(-1.89,5.64)	(-2.80,6.03)
QFIREA5	A2a	(-0.11,0.32)	(0.33,0.48)	(-0.77,0.31)	(-0.49,0.44)	(0.14,0.50)	(-0.22,0.37)	(-0.01,0.57)	(0.17,0.84)
QFIREA5	B3	(-2.02,-1.38)	(1.03,1.27)	(1.68,3.35)	(0.15,1.56)	(0.26,0.84)	(2.58,3.53)	(2.36,3.29)	(3.21,4.26)
QFIREA5	C4s	(-2.18,-1.59)	(0.63,0.84)	(0.47,1.91)	(-0.82,0.44)	(-0.53,-0.04)	(1.24,2.04)	(1.14,1.91)	(1.29,2.17)
QFIREA5	E2a	(-0.45,-0.04)	(0.75,0.89)	(1.21,2.21)	(0.13,1.00)	(0.17,0.51)	(1.74,2.29)	(1.55,2.08)	(2.08,2.69)
QFIREA5	G2	(-1.59,-1.16)	(0.67,0.82)	(-0.13,0.95)	(-0.35,0.59)	(-0.34,0.03)	(2.10,2.68)	(2.00,2.56)	(2.48,3.13)
QFIREA5	Hz1	(-2.12,-1.39)	(0.95,1.20)	(0.10,1.89)	(-0.63,0.93)	(-0.49,1.10)	(2.45,3.44)	(2.55,3.50)	(3.08,4.17)
QFIREI5	A2a	(-0.45,-0.32)	(0.57,0.63)	(-0.17,0.19)	(-0.72,-0.45)	(-0.03,0.10)	(-0.32,-0.10)	(-0.50,-0.27)	(-0.05,0.19)
QFIREI5	B3	(-0.95,-0.82)	(0.34,0.39)	(3.74,4.08)	(-0.12,0.16)	(1.96,2.28)	(0.44,0.67)	(0.53,0.77)	(1.04,1.29)
QFIREI5	C4s	(0.09,0.25)	(0.47,0.53)	(4.17,4.61)	(-0.60,-0.27)	(-0.03,0.12)	(0.68,0.96)	(0.57,0.86)	(2.01,2.32)
QFIREI5	E2a	(-0.08,0.08)	(0.50,0.56)	(1.68,2.15)	(-1.77,-1.42)	(-0.93,-0.77)	(1.04,1.34)	(1.07,1.38)	(1.56,1.89)
QFIREI5	G2	(0.02,0.16)	(0.72,0.77)	(4.91,5.30)	(0.39,0.69)	(0.80,0.93)	(2.38,2.63)	(2.49,2.74)	(2.93,3.20)
QFIREI5	Hz1	(-0.75,-0.55)	(1.02,1.11)	(8.82,9.38)	(-1.35,-0.92)	(0.95,1.14)	(3.01,3.37)	(3.08,3.45)	(4.99,5.39)

Table 19: Tukey HSD difference in mean of IRIS SCLERA CONTRAST scores. Each cell shows the 95% confidence level in difference in mean of pairwise quality for images verified correctly (i.e., the genuine score equal or less than threshold) and those rejected falsely (i.e., the genuine score larger than threshold). Quality scores were computed by the SDK identified by the column header and comparison scores were generated by the SDK identified by the row header. If the interval does not contain zero, the difference in mean is significant. Cells where difference in mean is not significant have pink background. For monotonically increasing quality components (all except DILATION, and depending on quality implementation GRAY SCALE SPREAD), the expected behavior is to have higher quality scores for the pair of enrollment and verification images that give genuine comparison scores less than threshold. The pairwise quality is computed as geometric mean of the quality of two samples being compared. Threshold is set to give false match rate of 0.001.

A2a=NEUROTECHNOLOGY-a	B3=CROSSMATCH	C4s=CAMBRIDGE-s	D3=AWARE	E2a=IRITECH-a	G1=IRISID-1	I1=KYNEN	Hz1=L1-z1
A2f=NEUROTECHNOLOGY-f	C4x=CAMBRIDGE-x	C4f=CAMBRIDGE-f	F1=MORPHO	E2f=IRITECH-f	G2=IRISID-2	Hx=L1-x	Hz2=L1-z2

Dataset	comparator	IQAA A2f	IQAA C4x	IQAA E2a	IQAA E2f	IQAA F1	IQAA G1	IQAA G2	IQAA Hx
ICE2006	A2a	(-0.81,-0.50)	(-0.70,-0.55)	(-2.51,-1.86)	(-2.39,-1.74)	(-1.50,-1.19)	(-1.72,-1.00)	(-1.57,-0.93)	(-1.59,-1.04)
ICE2006	B3	(-0.45,-0.22)	(1.49,1.60)	(5.29,5.76)	(6.13,6.60)	(4.63,4.86)	(3.71,4.22)	(2.82,3.28)	(-0.11,0.29)
ICE2006	C4s	(-0.50,-0.26)	(0.30,0.43)	(0.68,1.18)	(0.83,1.33)	(0.85,1.09)	(0.29,0.85)	(0.21,0.71)	(-0.61,-0.19)
ICE2006	E2a	(-1.23,-0.98)	(1.46,1.58)	(2.58,3.08)	(2.51,3.02)	(0.96,1.20)	(2.39,2.95)	(2.20,2.70)	(0.50,0.93)
ICE2006	G2	(-0.99,-0.74)	(-0.43,-0.30)	(-1.58,-1.06)	(-1.63,-1.11)	(-1.63,-1.38)	(-1.87,-1.37)	(-1.48,-1.11)	(-1.70,-1.26)
ICE2006	Hz1	(-0.45,-0.19)	(0.87,1.00)	(1.52,2.06)	(1.82,2.36)	(1.16,1.43)	(4.42,5.03)	(2.71,3.25)	(-0.57,-0.10)
OPS	A2a	(0.33,0.69)	(0.13,0.31)	(-0.23,0.60)	(0.07,0.87)	(-0.20,0.16)	(1.09,1.89)	(1.11,1.91)	(1.24,2.18)
OPS	B3	(0.69,0.98)	(0.64,0.79)	(1.12,1.79)	(1.44,2.10)	(2.33,2.63)	(2.50,3.14)	(2.72,3.37)	(3.12,3.89)
OPS	C4s	(0.52,0.82)	(0.39,0.54)	(0.26,0.93)	(0.36,1.03)	(1.55,1.85)	(1.85,2.50)	(1.87,2.53)	(2.32,3.10)
OPS	E2a	(0.46,0.76)	(0.20,0.36)	(-0.27,0.41)	(-0.23,0.44)	(0.77,1.08)	(1.21,1.87)	(1.27,1.94)	(1.61,2.40)
OPS	G2	(-0.48,-0.18)	(-0.14,0.01)	(-0.63,0.04)	(-0.58,0.09)	(-0.81,-0.52)	(-0.19,0.46)	(-0.17,0.46)	(-0.34,-0.44)
OPS	Hz1	(0.69,0.98)	(0.49,0.64)	(0.67,1.34)	(0.87,1.53)	(1.47,1.77)	(2.18,2.84)	(2.35,3.00)	(2.56,3.34)
QFIREA5	A2a	(0.78,1.31)	(0.47,0.66)	(6.44,7.94)	(0.76,1.70)	(1.04,1.48)	(0.19,1.04)	(1.34,2.11)	(6.21,7.26)
QFIREA5	C4s	(-0.35,0.13)	(0.22,0.39)	(2.19,3.55)	(-0.06,0.79)	(0.61,1.01)	(0.75,1.47)	(1.05,1.71)	(1.26,2.21)
QFIREA5	E2a	(-1.02,-0.54)	(-0.96,-0.79)	(-13.45,-12.09)	(-1.29,-0.45)	(-0.33,0.08)	(-1.07,-0.40)	(-0.67,-0.03)	(-3.48,-2.53)
QFIREA5	G2	(-0.57,-0.07)	(-0.29,-0.11)	(0.32,1.71)	(-0.86,0.04)	(-0.48,-0.07)	(-1.28,-0.60)	(-0.54,0.09)	(0.09,1.02)
QFIREA5	Hz1	(-0.92,-0.43)	(0.76,0.93)	(1.76,3.13)	(-0.01,0.85)	(2.13,2.54)	(3.56,4.34)	(4.03,4.72)	(5.90,6.85)
QFIREI5	A2a	(0.51,0.76)	(-0.21,-0.13)	(0.21,0.86)	(0.36,0.89)	(-1.21,-0.68)	(0.05,0.43)	(0.06,0.44)	(-0.30,0.11)
QFIREI5	C4s	(-1.46,-1.25)	(0.48,0.55)	(0.01,0.57)	(-0.09,0.37)	(1.42,1.88)	(2.49,2.82)	(2.34,2.67)	(2.93,3.30)
QFIREI5	E2a	(1.78,1.99)	(0.72,0.79)	(-7.67,-7.10)	(-2.76,-2.31)	(-6.41,-5.95)	(-0.27,0.06)	(-0.34,-0.01)	(0.20,0.56)
QFIREI5	G2	(-2.83,-1.18)	(-0.41,0.13)	(-3.43,0.84)	(-1.41,2.05)	(-3.72,-0.23)	(-0.97,1.48)	(-0.91,1.54)	(-1.00,1.17)
QFIREI5	Hz1	(-1.00,-0.78)	(0.91,0.98)	(2.99,3.56)	(-0.47,-0.01)	(0.72,1.18)	(1.03,1.36)	(0.87,1.20)	(1.89,2.26)

Table 20: Tukey HSD mean difference in IRIS SCLERA CONTRAST scores. Each cell shows the 95% confidence level in difference in mean of pairwise quality for images correctly rejected (i.e., the impostor score equal or greater than threshold) and those falsely matched (i.e., the impostor score less than threshold). Quality scores were computed by the SDK identified by the column header and comparison scores were generated by the SDK identified by the row header. If the interval does not contain zero, the difference in mean is significant. Cells where difference in mean is not significant are shaded in pink. For monotonic increasing quality components (all except DILATION, and depending on quality implementation GRAY SCALE SPREAD), the expected behavior is to have higher quality scores for the pair of (enrollment, verification) images that result in impostor comparison scores equal or greater than threshold. Pairwise quality is computed as geometric mean of the quality of two samples being compared. Threshold is set to give false match rate of 0.001.

A2a=NEUROTECHNOLOGY-a	B3=CROSSMATCH	C4s=CAMBRIDGE-s	D3=AWARE	E2a=IRITECH-a	G1=IRISID-1	I1=KYNEN	Hz1=L1-z1
A2f=NEUROTECHNOLOGY-f	C4x=CAMBRIDGE-x	C4f=CAMBRIDGE-f	F1=MORPHO	E2f=IRITECH-f	G2=IRISID-2	Hx=L1-x	Hz2=L1-z2

9.6 Iris_pupil contrast

IRIS PUPIL CONTRAST is a measure of the image characteristics at the boundary between the iris region and the pupil. There is usually a lower texture contrast between iris and pupil than iris and sclera, making iris pupil detection the more difficult task. Iris segmentation algorithms are known to be sensitive to noise, specular reflection on iris-pupil boundary, or extrinsic lighting conditions, all which could affect segmentation failure or degrade its accuracy.

The intrinsic IRIS PUPIL CONTRAST varies among human irises. Certain medical conditions such as cataracts or intraocular lenses may impact IRIS PUPIL CONTRAST . It is also affected by capture device characteristics.

IQCE examined the effect of IRIS PUPIL CONTRAST on performance. All submissions except B3 generate IRIS PUPIL CONTRAST scores. The distribution of their IRIS PUPIL CONTRAST scores is shown in Figure 57. In order to make the boxplots more readable, quality scores in [0–254] range were linearly scaled back to [0–100].

The following sections detail the dependence of recognition error rates on IRIS PUPIL CONTRAST .

RELATIONSHIP WITH THE DISTRIBUTION OF GENUINE SCORES

IRIS PUPIL CONTRAST score of primary IQAA vs. primary IQCE comparators are shown in Figure 58.

Noteworthy observations follow:
The range of IRIS PUPIL CONTRAST scores varies among the IQAAS; the interquartile range is as low as [0-20] for A2a and as high as [40-100] for Hx. This difference in IRIS PUPIL CONTRAST scores of different IQAAs adversely affects interoperability of the IRIS PUPIL CONTRAST scores.
ICE2006 images give the highest IRIS PUPIL CONTRAST scores, followed by OPS. QFIRE I5 images have the lowest IRIS PUPIL CONTRAST scores (in the absence of any well defined cross-algorithm calibration or normalization).
Generally low IRIS PUPIL CONTRAST is observed for high genuine scores.
The biggest change in IRIS PUPIL CONTRAST score for different bins of genuine scores is seen for IQAAs Hx, C4x, and E2a.

RELATIONSHIP WITH THE DISTRIBUTION OF IMPOSTOR SCORES

Figure 59 suggest that the impostor distribution of IQCE comparators is not affected by IRIS PUPIL CONTRAST scores of any IQAAS.

RANKED DET:: DO LOW-QUALITY IMAGES PRODUCE HIGH FNMR OR FMR?

As shown in Figure 60(a), images with low IRIS PUPIL CONTRAST scores cause false non-match. The largest gap in FNMR between ICE2006 images in the lowest and highest 15 percentile of IRIS PUPIL CONTRAST scores occurs for IQAAs C4f, C4x, Hx and the smallest for IQAA I1, E2a, and E2f.

Except for IQAA A2f and D3, recognition performance is similar for ICE2006 images in the upper 15% and the 70% in the middle. FMR of comparator Hz1is affected but not as greatly as FNMR .

Similar observations can be made from Figure 60(b). The highest FNMR and FMR are observed for QFIRE I5 images with the lowest IRIS PUPIL CONTRAST scores. Images with the highest value of IRIS PUPIL CONTRAST score give lower FNMR

| A2a=NEUROTECHNOLOGY-a | B3=CROSSMATCH | C4s=CAMBRIDGE-s | D3=AWARE | E2a=IRITECH-a | G1=IRISID-1 | I1=KYNEN | Hz1=L1-z1 |
| A2f=NEUROTECHNOLOGY-f | | C4x=CAMBRIDGE-x | C4f=CAMBRIDGE-f | F1=MORPHO | E2f=IRITECH-f | G2=IRISID-2 | Hx=L1-x | Hz2=L1-z2 |

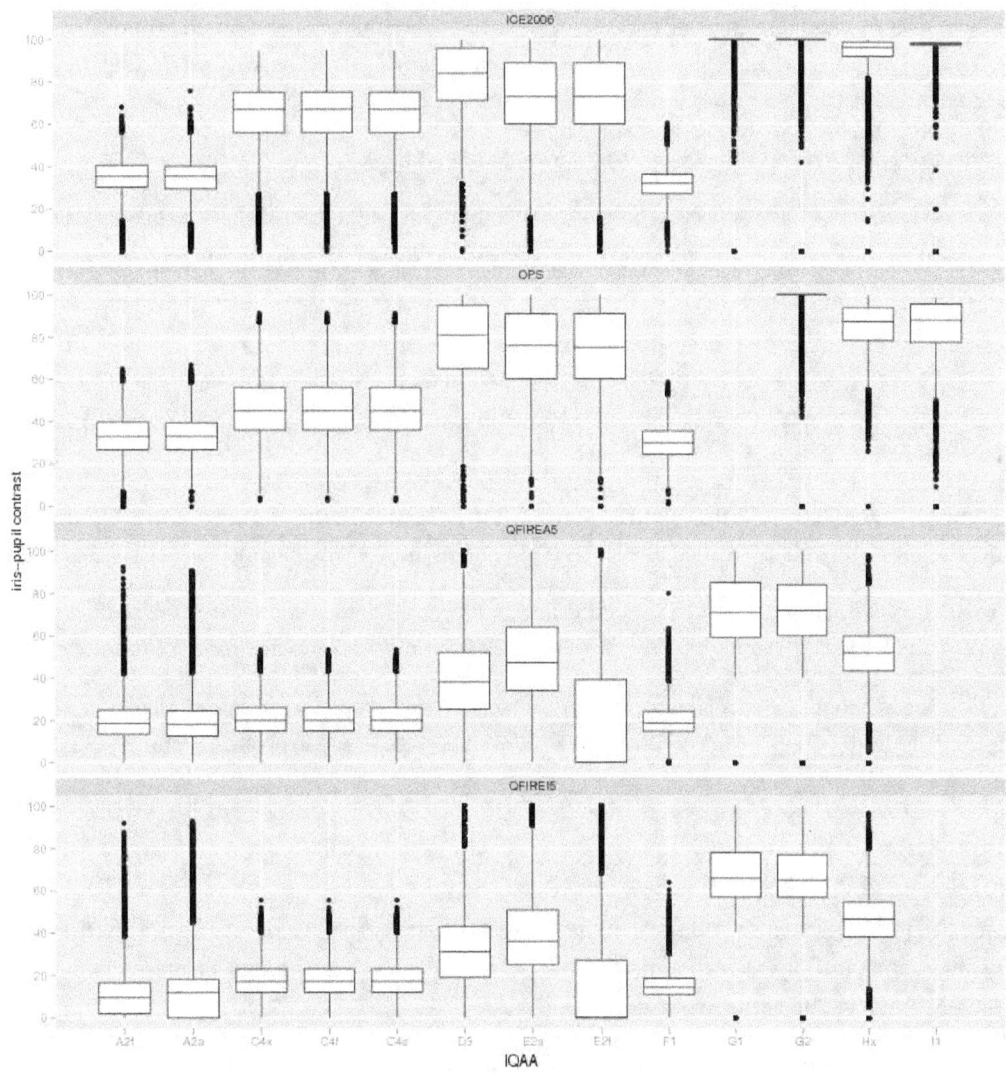

Figure 57: Box and whisker plots of the IQAAs that generate IRIS PUPIL CONTRAST scores.

and FMR. (See the connected points of IQAA C4f DET at FMR =0.0001. The difference in error rates of the three sets are close to an order of magnitude).

The best performance ranking occurs for IQAA C4x, C4f, and Hx. IRIS PUPIL CONTRAST scores of IQAA A2f, A2a and F1 do not lead to any ranking of performance.

EFFECT OF QUALITY ON FNMR : HOW QUICKLY FNMR IMPROVES WHEN POOR QUALITY SAMPLES ARE REJECTED?

Rejection of images with low IRIS PUPIL CONTRAST improves FNMR as demonstrated in Figure 61. On ICE2006 images IQAA C4s is the best performer, for all IQCE comparators, where rejection of the 6% lowest IRIS PUPIL CONTRAST reduced FNMR to 0.085 from its original value of 0.1. Very similar performance is observed for IQAAs Hx, E2a, E2f, and F1.

A2a=NEUROTECHNOLOGY-a	B3=CROSSMATCH	C4s=CAMBRIDGE-s	D3=AWARE	E2a=IRITECH-a	G1=IRISID-1	I1=KYNEN	Hz1=L1-z1
A2f=NEUROTECHNOLOGY-f	C4x=CAMBRIDGE-x	C4f=CAMBRIDGE-f	F1=MORPHO	E2f=IRITECH-f	G2=IRISID-2	Hx=L1-x	Hz2=L1-z2

IQAA G1 seems to be more accurate in its IRIS PUPIL CONTRAST quality assessment when the contrast is very low. Rejecting 0-3% of its lowest IRIS PUPIL CONTRAST images improve FNMR; however, rejecting more than 3% does not improve FNMR any further.

IQAA I1 is the least effective in predicting performance, followed by A2f.

On QFIRE I5 images, IQAA C4s is the most effective for comparators Hz1 and E2a. For the same rejection rates, it results in a larger reduction in FNMR than their mated IQAA. IQAA E2f, which performs reasonably well on the ICE2006 dataset, is the least effective on QFIRE I5.

TEST OF SIGNIFICANCE :: DO THE IMAGES INVOLVED IN SUCCESSFUL VERIFICATION ATTEMPTS HAVE SIGNIFICANTLY HIGHER QUALITY SCORES THAN THOSE INVOLVED IN FAILED VERIFICATION ATTEMPTS?

Table 21 shows that for all combinations of IQAA and comparator, the mean of pairwise IRIS PUPIL CONTRAST scores is significantly larger for the ICE2006 images that result in successful verification and those that are falsely rejected.

On OPS images, IRIS PUPIL CONTRAST is a significant factor for all comparators except E2a. The reason might be that E2a has a very small FNMR, meaning that the number of data points were too few for a robust statistical test.

On QFIRE I5 images, ignoring IQAA E2 which IRIS PUPIL CONTRAST scores are not predictive of performance, successful verification generally involves images with higher IRIS PUPIL CONTRAST scores than comparisons that result in false rejects.

EFFECT OF VARIATION BETWEEN THE TWO SAMPLES:: DOES SAMENESS MATTER?

The heatmaps of Figures 62 and 63 indicate that images with low IRIS PUPIL CONTRAST score give high FNMR. The strong symmetry across diagonal of each cell indicates that "sameness" matters as FNMR increases as the difference between IRIS PUPIL CONTRAST values of the two images being compared increases.

The lowest FNMR is achieved when both images have high IRIS PUPIL CONTRAST (the top right corner of each cell.)

OBSERVATIONS AND CONCLUSIONS

IQCE concludes that IRIS PUPIL CONTRAST has a significant effect on FNMR and FMR. Among IQAAs, C4s performs the best and it can predict recognition performance its native iris recognition algorithm as well as other non-native ones. IQAAs Hx and E2a are the second best performers. IQAA I1 and A2f are the least effective.

| A2a=NEUROTECHNOLOGY-a | B3=CROSSMATCH | C4s=CAMBRIDGE-s | D3=AWARE | E2a=IRITECH-a | G1=IRISID-1 | I1=KYNEN | Hz1=L1-z1 |
| A2f=NEUROTECHNOLOGY-f | C4x=CAMBRIDGE-x | C4f=CAMBRIDGE-f | F1=MORPHO | E2f=IRITECH-f | G2=IRISID-2 | Hx=L1-x | Hz2=L1-z2 |

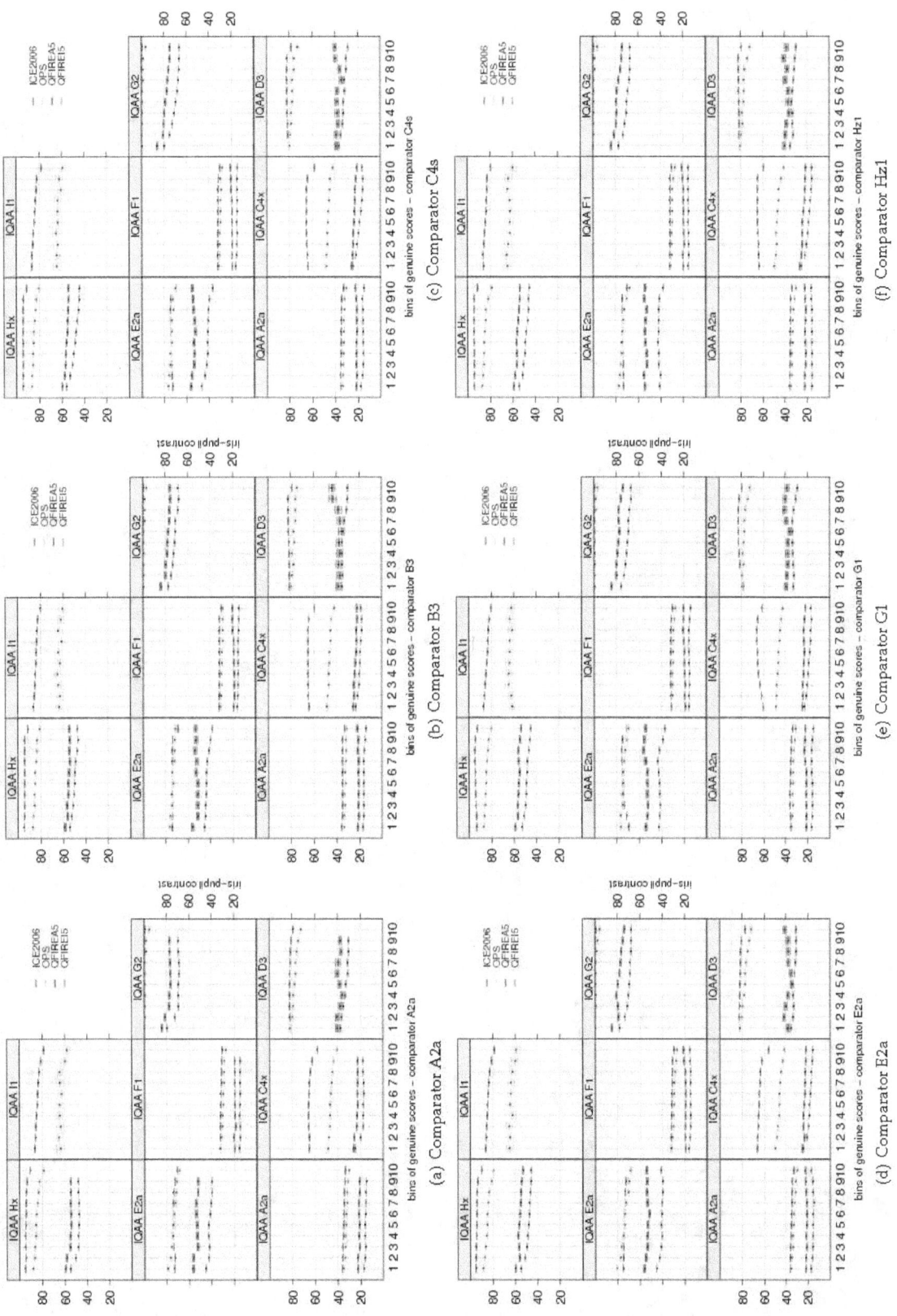

Figure 58: Pairwise IRIS PUPIL CONTRAST scores vs. genuine score for the primary Class Z submissions of each participant. Each plot shows quality scores computed by different IQAA. Genuine scores are divided equally into ten groups. Groups overlap by 5 percent, meaning 5% of the data in one bin also belongs to the next bin. The bootstrapped pairwise quality for each group is shown in a box and whisker plot. Pairwise quality is computed as geometric mean of the quality of the two samples being compared.

127

A2a=NEUROTECHNOLOGY-a	B3=CROSSMATCH	C4s=CAMBRIDGE-s	D3=AWARE	E2a=IRITECH-a	G1=IRISID-1	I1=KYNEN	Hz1=L1-z1
A2f=NEUROTECHNOLOGY-f	C4x=CAMBRIDGE-x	C4f=CAMBRIDGE-f	F1=MORPHO	E2f=IRITECH-f	G2=IRISID-2	Hx=L1-x	Hz2=L1-z2

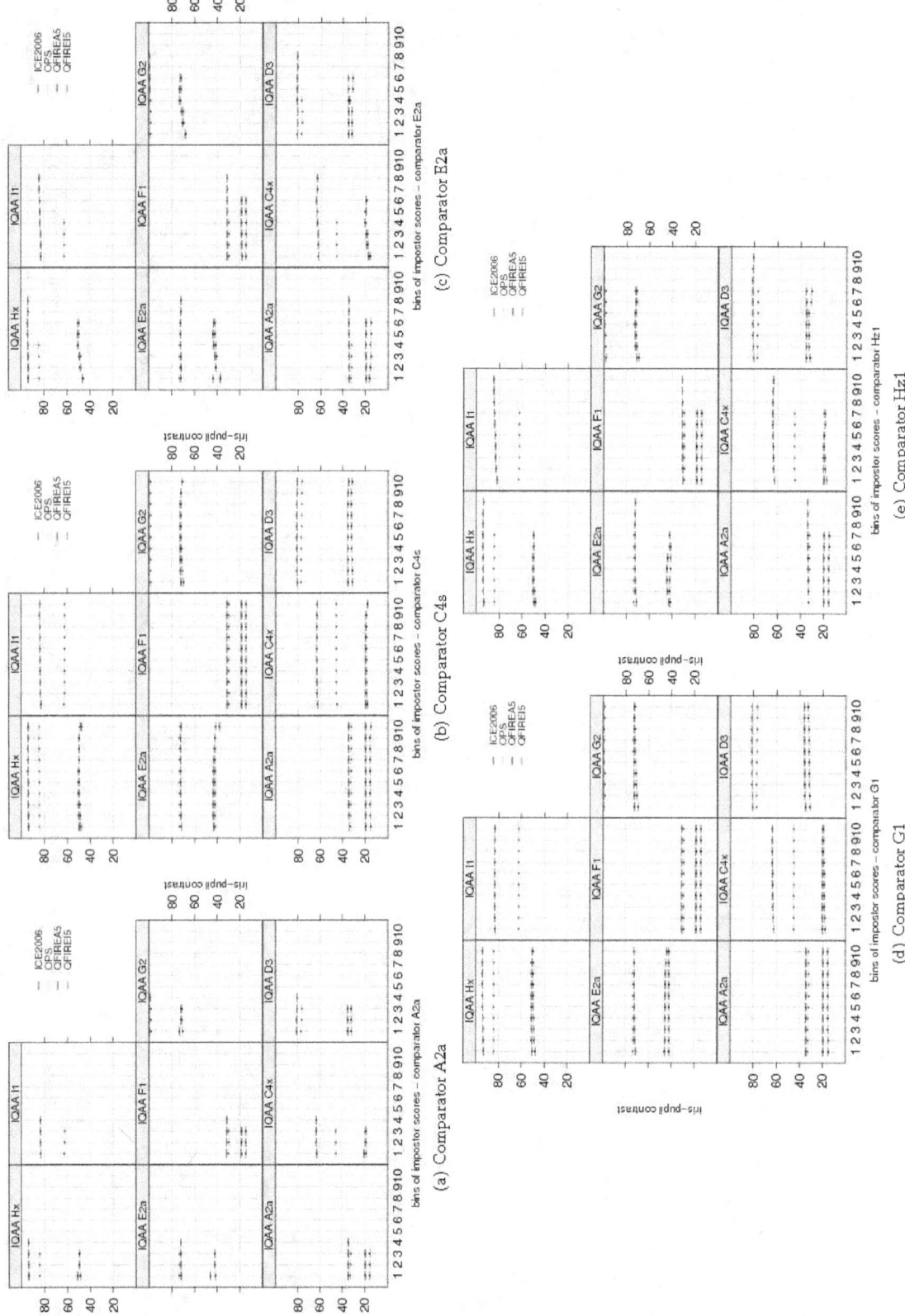

Figure 59: Pairwise IRIS PUPIL CONTRAST scores vs. impostor scores for the primary Class Z submissions of each participants. Each plot shows quality scores computed by different IQAA. Similar to plots of Figure 51, impostor scores are divided equally into ten groups. Groups overlap by 5 percent. Bootstrapped pairwise quality for each group is shown in a box and whisker plot. Pairwise quality is computed as geometric mean of the quality of the two samples being compared.

(a) Comparator A2a

(b) Comparator C4s

(c) Comparator E2a

(d) Comparator G1

(e) Comparator Hz1

| A2a=NEUROTECHNOLOGY-a | B3=CROSSMATCH | C4s=CAMBRIDGE-s | D3=AWARE | E2a=IRITECH-a | G1=IRISID-1 | I1=KYNEN | Hz1=L1-z1 |
| A2f=NEUROTECHNOLOGY-f | C4x=CAMBRIDGE-x | C4f=CAMBRIDGE-f | F1=MORPHO | E2f=IRITECH-f | G2=IRISID-2 | Hx=L1-x | Hz2=L1-z2 |

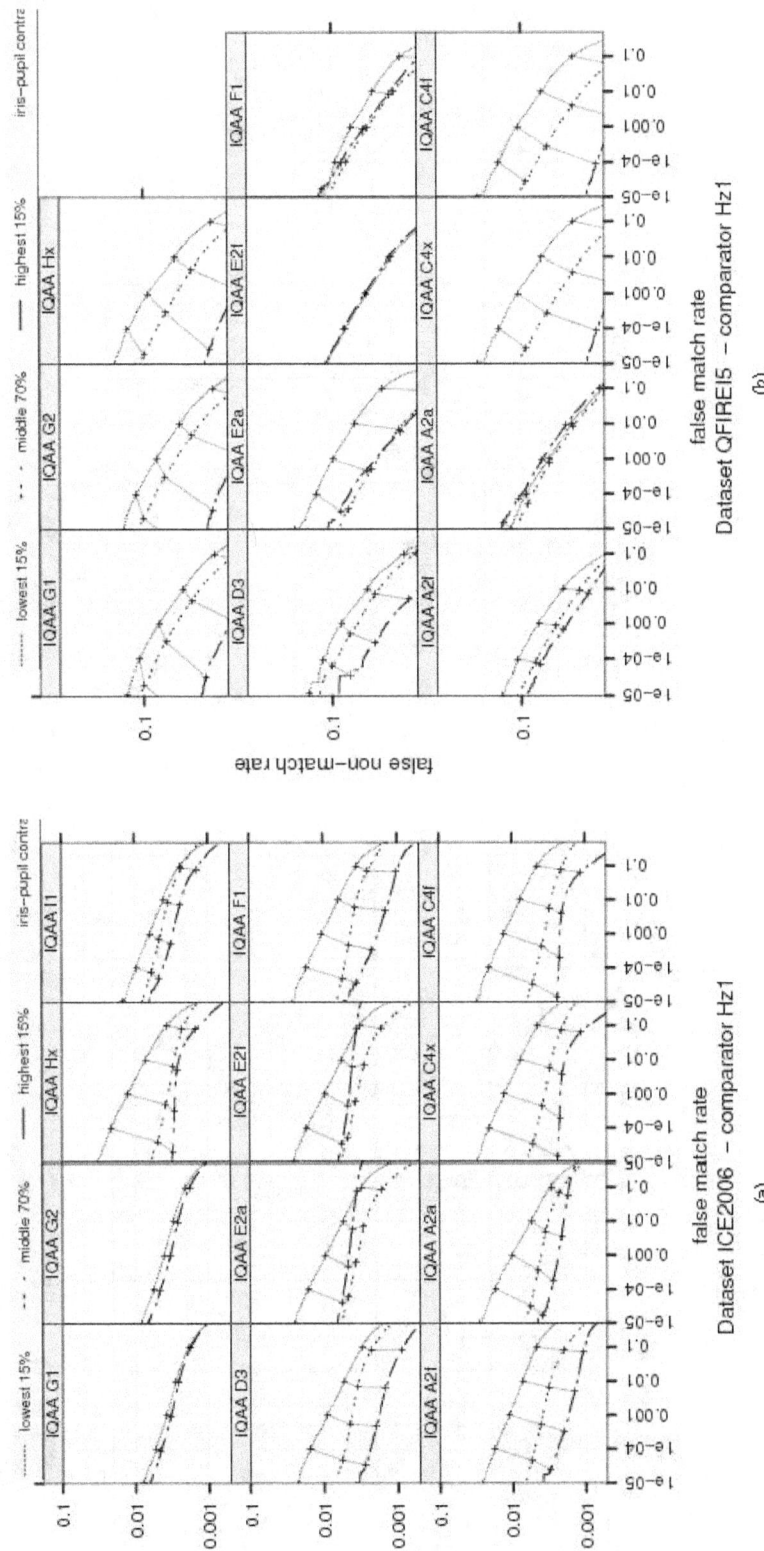

Figure 60: Ranked DET curves for comparator Hz1 and Datasets ICE2006 and QFIRE 15 . The set of all comparisons were partitioned into three groups based on the pair-wise IRIS PUPIL CONTRAST quality of the images being compared. The lowest quality set contains comparisons with pairwise quality in the lower 15 percentile. The highest quality set contains comparisons with pairwise quality in the upper 15 percentile. The rest of the comparisons, namely the middle 70%, made up the third set. The DETs are connected at the same score threshold values (brown lines). Lower FNMR and FMR rates are expected for better quality images.

| A2a=NEUROTECHNOLOGY-a | B3=CROSSMATCH | C4s=CAMBRIDGE-s | D3=AWARE | E2a=IRITECH-a | G1=IRISID-1 | I1=KYNEN | Hz1=L1-z1 |
| A2f=NEUROTECHNOLOGY-f | C4x=CAMBRIDGE-x | C4f=CAMBRIDGE-f | F1=MORPHO | E2f=IRITECH-f | G2=IRISID-2 | Hx=L1-x | Hz2=L1-z2 |

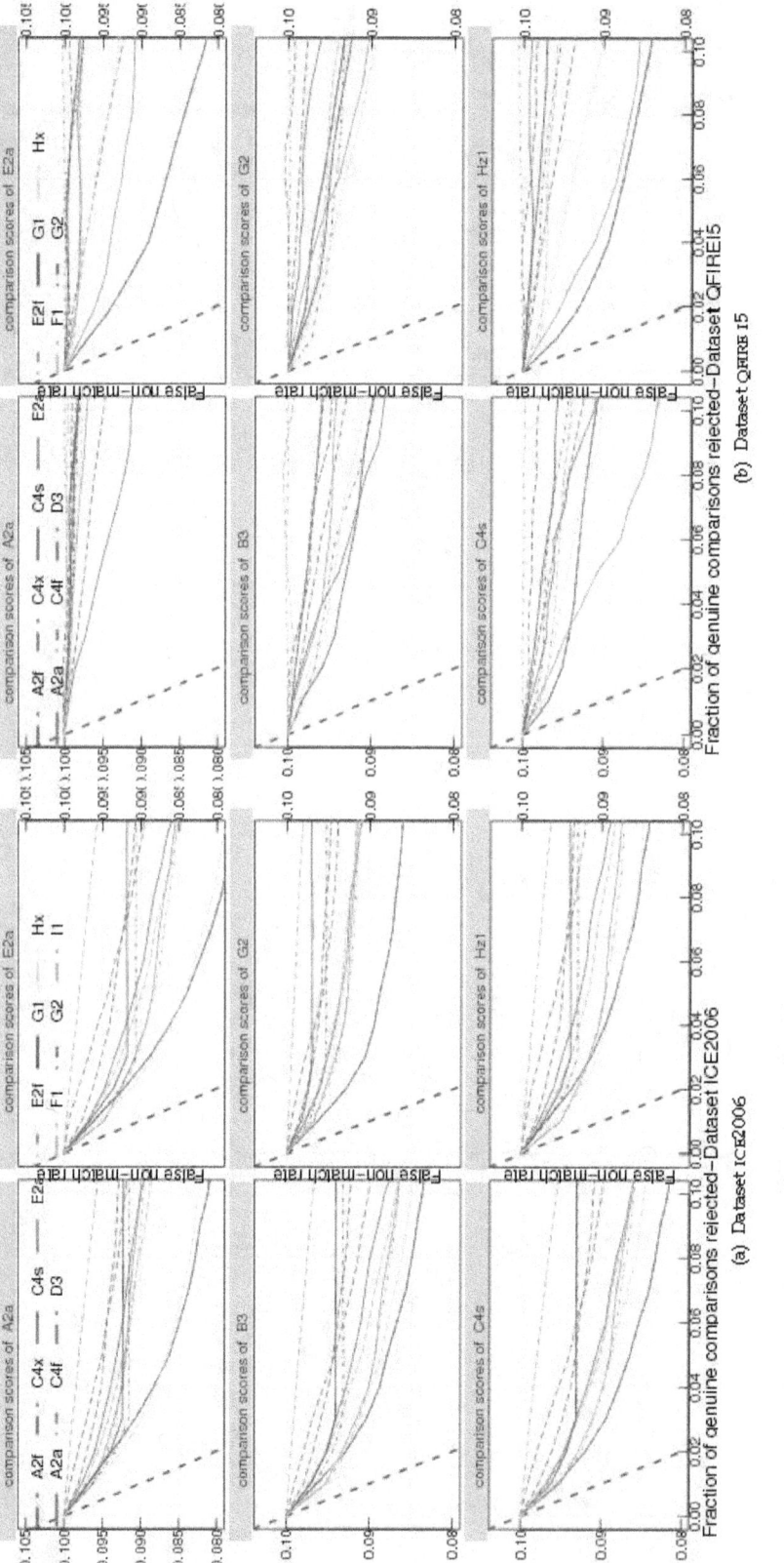

Figure 61: FNMR vs. reject curves for IRIS PUPIL CONTRAST scores on datasets ICE2006 and QFIRE15. The threshold is set to give an initial FNMR = 0.1. The gray dotted line shows the ideal case where the rejection of the comparisons with the lowest ten percent quality results in zero FNMR.

A2a=NEUROTECHNOLOGY-a | B3=CROSSMATCH | C4s=CAMBRIDGE-s | D3=AWARE | E2a=IRITECH-a | G1=IRISID-1 | I1=KYNEN | Hz1=L1-z1
A2f=NEUROTECHNOLOGY-f | C4x=CAMBRIDGE-x | C4f=CAMBRIDGE-f | F1=MORPHO | E2f=IRITECH-f | G2=IRISID-2 | Hx=L1-x | Hz2=L1-z2

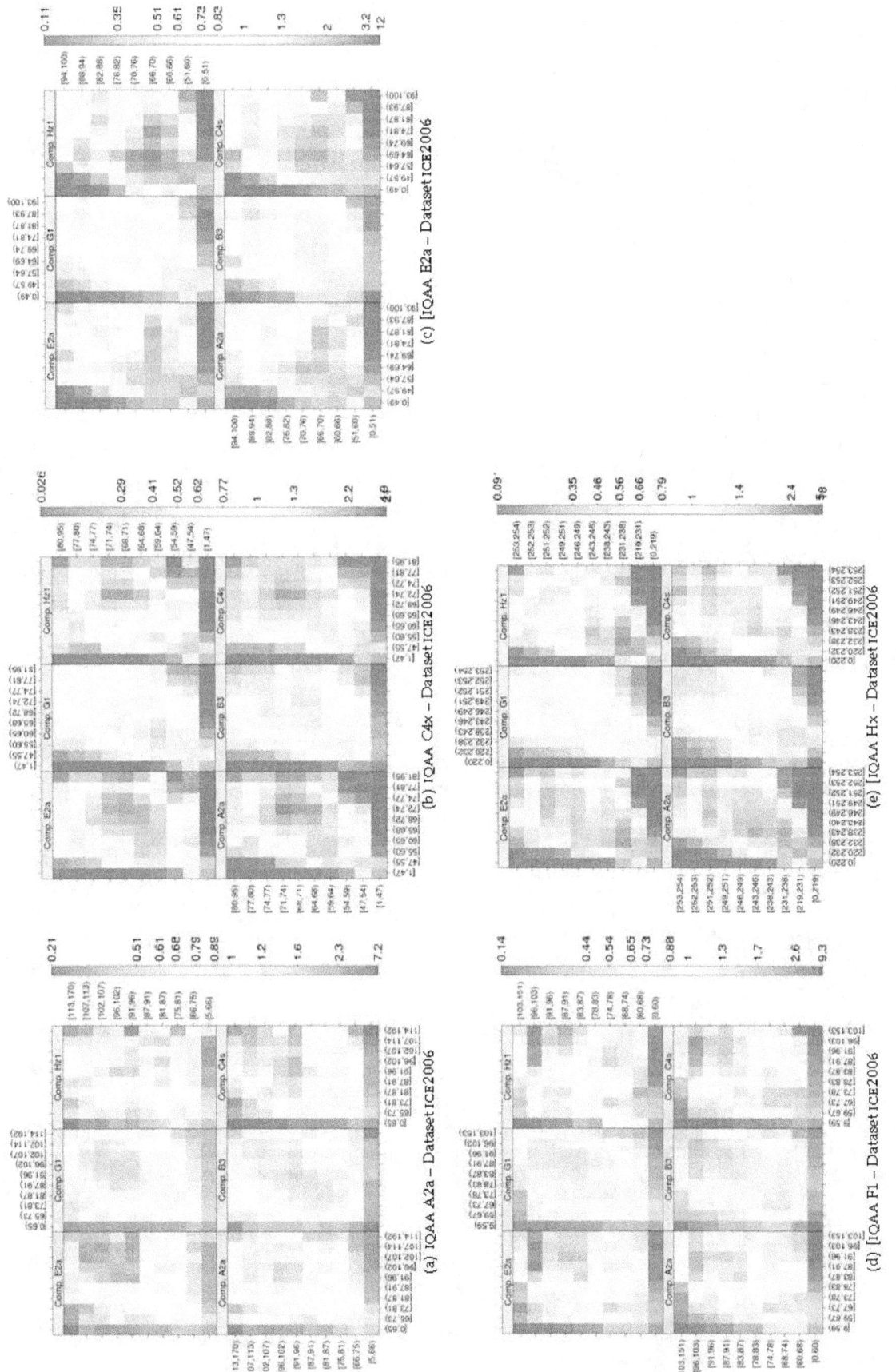

Figure 62: IRIS PUPIL CONTRAST computed by primary IQAA submissions and FNMR for IQCE comparators for dataset ICE2006. The y-axis represents enrollment samples' quality with verification samples' on the x-axis. The IRIS PUPIL CONTRAST scores are quantized into 10 quantiles. The color scale plots $\frac{FNMR}{FNMR_0}$ for comparisons with verification and enrollment qualities ($q_{verification}, q_{enrollment}$). $FNMR_0$ is the nominal FNMR which is the false non-match rate computed over all the images at the same comparison score threshold, in this case at FMR = 0.0001. Yellow/Green color represent an improvement in FNMR. Blue color represent a degradation of FNMR. White color means no change in FNMR.

131

A2a=NEUROTECHNOLOGY-a | B3=CROSSMATCH | C4s=CAMBRIDGE-s | D3=AWARE | E2a=IRITECH-a | G1=IRISID-1 | I1=KYNEN | Hz1=L1-z1
A2f=NEUROTECHNOLOGY-f | C4x=CAMBRIDGE-x | C4f=CAMBRIDGE-f | F1=MORPHO | E2f=IRITECH-f | G2=IRISID-2 | Hx=L1-x | Hz2=L1-z2

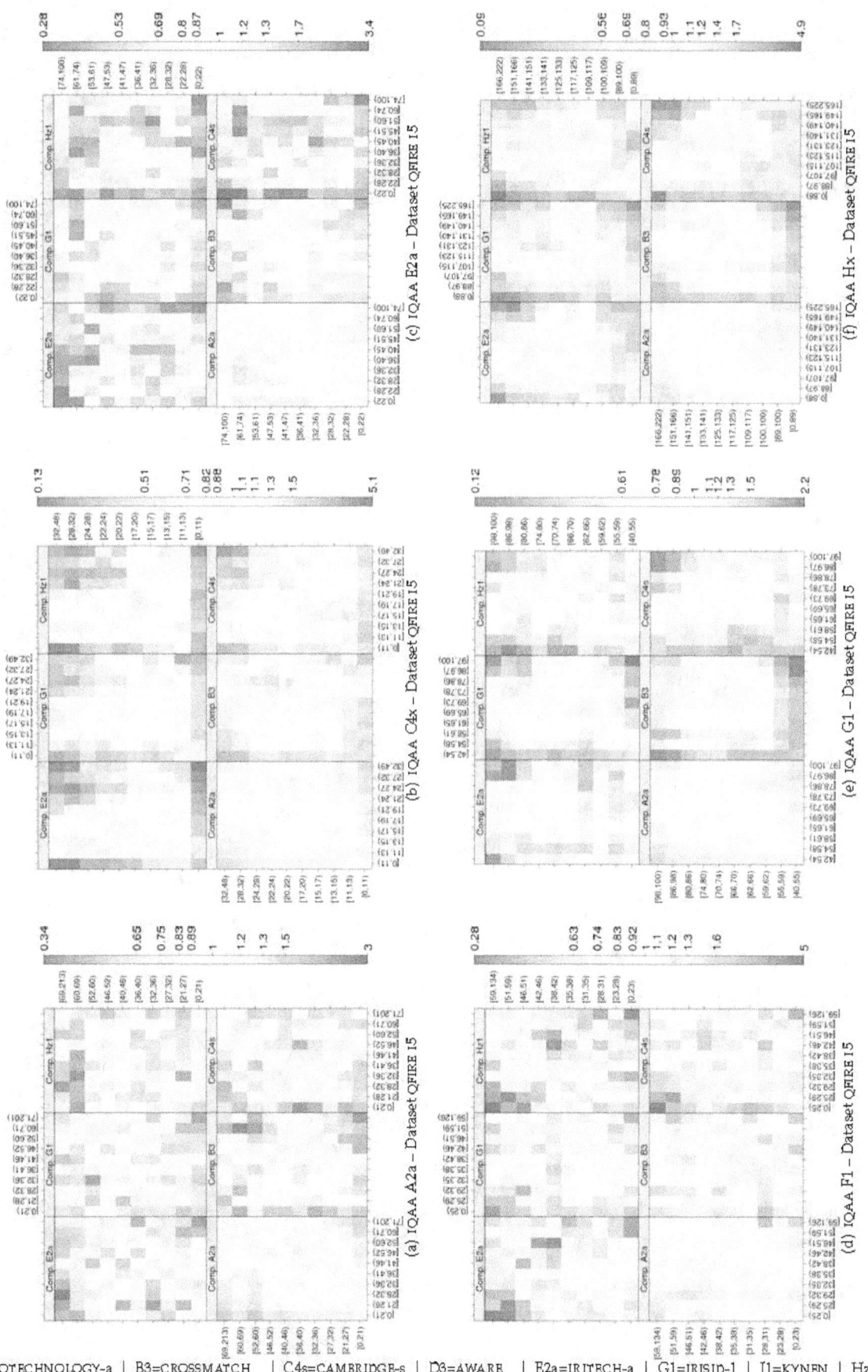

Figure 63: IRIS PUPIL CONTRAST computed by primary IQAA submissions and FNMR for IQCE comparators for dataset QFIRE I5 . (see Figure 62 for more detail.)

132

A2a=NEUROTECHNOLOGY-a   B3=CROSSMATCH   C4s=CAMBRIDGE-s   D3=AWARE   E2a=IRITECH-a   G1=IRISID-1   I1=KYNEN   Hz1=L1-z1
A2f=NEUROTECHNOLOGY-f   C4x=CAMBRIDGE-x   C4f=CAMBRIDGE-f   F1=MORPHO   E2f=IRITECH-f   G2=IRISID-2   Hx=L1-x   Hz2=L1-z2

Dataset	comparator	IQAA A2f	IQAA C4x	IQAA E2a	IQAA E2f	IQAA F1	IQAA G1	IQAA G2	IQAA Hx
ICE2006	A2a	(4.14,4.31)	(12.90,13.20)	(11.22,11.63)	(10.96,11.37)	(2.64,2.78)	(2.13,2.17)	(2.67,2.71)	(8.44,8.59)
ICE2006	B3	(4.69,4.77)	(11.12,11.26)	(10.56,10.75)	(10.65,10.84)	(4.05,4.12)	(1.21,1.22)	(1.33,1.34)	(6.15,6.21)
ICE2006	C4s	(5.75,5.87)	(15.81,16.03)	(10.78,11.08)	(10.20,10.51)	(3.91,4.01)	(3.66,3.69)	(1.95,1.98)	(6.88,6.99)
ICE2006	E2a	(4.98,5.15)	(13.58,13.88)	(14.24,14.66)	(13.92,14.33)	(3.76,3.91)	(2.37,2.42)	(2.82,2.86)	(9.04,9.19)
ICE2006	G2	(2.21,2.30)	(8.63,8.78)	(5.84,6.04)	(5.77,5.98)	(1.71,1.78)	(0.91,0.93)	(1.44,1.46)	(3.97,4.04)
ICE2006	Hz1	(3.15,3.35)	(7.17,7.53)	(4.26,4.73)	(4.00,4.46)	(1.96,2.13)	(0.81,0.86)	(1.09,1.14)	(3.50,3.68)
OPS	A2a	(1.66,6.52)	(2.37,9.70)	(1.61,11.96)	(1.42,11.79)	(0.72,4.83)	(6.10,9.43)	(11.15,14.57)	(3.97,10.00)
OPS	B3	(1.53,3.56)	(4.45,7.51)	(2.87,7.20)	(2.74,7.07)	(0.89,2.61)	(4.44,5.78)	(4.33,5.69)	(4.98,7.50)
OPS	C4s	(0.95,4.86)	(3.60,9.48)	(1.10,9.42)	(1.32,9.66)	(0.00,3.31)	(3.22,5.91)	(3.38,6.20)	(3.83,8.68)
OPS	E2a	(0.51,6.23)	(-1.64,6.96)	(-1.17,10.99)	(-1.18,10.99)	(-0.44,4.39)	(-0.97,2.97)	(-1.17,2.95)	(-0.74,6.35)
OPS	G2	(4.81,7.97)	(5.36,10.12)	(6.61,13.34)	(6.66,13.40)	(2.81,5.48)	(8.56,10.42)	(6.07,7.64)	(6.88,10.79)
OPS	Hz1	(0.96,5.55)	(0.14,7.04)	(3.11,12.85)	(2.32,12.08)	(0.14,4.01)	(1.73,4.87)	(3.50,6.77)	(3.29,8.96)
QFIREA5	A2a	(0.40,0.84)	(1.24,1.63)	(1.09,2.16)	(-0.75,0.39)	(-0.25,0.09)	(2.05,2.76)	(1.76,2.45)	(1.36,1.92)
QFIREA5	B3	(-0.03,0.63)	(1.47,2.04)	(-1.36,0.21)	(-0.74,0.99)	(-1.52,-1.00)	(2.68,3.71)	(2.73,3.73)	(1.21,2.02)
QFIREA5	C4s	(-0.68,-0.07)	(2.55,3.06)	(-1.64,-0.20)	(-0.94,0.61)	(-1.38,-0.91)	(3.78,4.73)	(3.82,4.73)	(1.84,2.58)
QFIREA5	E2a	(-0.17,0.25)	(1.37,1.72)	(0.90,1.89)	(-0.28,0.79)	(-0.47,-0.14)	(3.84,4.49)	(3.79,4.42)	(2.27,2.79)
QFIREA5	G2	(-0.85,-0.40)	(1.22,1.60)	(-2.00,-0.94)	(-0.69,0.47)	(-1.32,-0.97)	(3.66,4.36)	(4.13,4.80)	(1.89,2.44)
QFIREA5	Hz1	(-1.27,-0.52)	(2.04,2.68)	(-0.42,1.36)	(-0.58,1.34)	(-1.56,-0.97)	(4.19,5.38)	(4.04,5.18)	(2.22,3.14)
QFIRE15	A2a	(1.91,2.08)	(2.02,2.17)	(2.55,2.93)	(-0.55,-0.21)	(0.19,0.28)	(2.85,3.11)	(3.02,3.28)	(2.36,2.57)
QFIRE15	B3	(2.97,3.15)	(1.80,1.95)	(4.41,4.78)	(0.22,0.58)	(0.83,0.93)	(4.34,4.61)	(4.40,4.67)	(3.57,3.78)
QFIRE15	C4s	(1.54,1.77)	(2.42,2.59)	(5.49,5.96)	(-0.28,0.15)	(0.72,0.84)	(3.82,4.14)	(4.34,4.66)	(4.49,4.75)
QFIRE15	E2a	(0.56,0.80)	(3.04,3.23)	(-0.37,0.13)	(-1.39,-0.95)	(-0.51,-0.37)	(2.20,2.54)	(2.79,3.13)	(3.16,3.43)
QFIRE15	G2	(1.18,1.38)	(2.16,2.32)	(4.31,4.73)	(0.36,0.73)	(0.55,0.67)	(3.51,3.80)	(3.75,4.02)	(3.65,3.88)
QFIRE15	Hz1	(1.14,1.42)	(2.89,3.11)	(5.81,6.41)	(-1.41,-0.87)	(0.06,0.22)	(2.61,3.02)	(3.07,3.48)	(3.49,3.82)

Table 21: Tukey HSD difference in mean of IRIS PUPIL CONTRAST scores. Each cell shows the 95% confidence level in difference in mean of pairwise quality for images verified correctly (i.e., the genuine score equal or less than threshold) and those rejected falsely (i.e, the genuine score larger than threshold). Quality scores were computed by the SDK identified by the column header and comparison scores were generated by the SDK identified by the row header. If the interval does not contain zero, the difference in mean is significant. Cells where difference in mean is not significant have pink background. For monotonically increasing quality components (all except DILATION, and depending on quality implementation GRAY SCALE SPREAD), the expected behavior is to have higher quality scores for the pair of enrollment and verification images that give genuine comparison scores less than threshold. The pairwise quality is computed as geometric mean of the quality of two samples being compared. Threshold is set to give false match rate of 0.001.

133

A2a=NEUROTECHNOLOGY-a B3=CROSSMATCH C4s=CAMBRIDGE-s D3=AWARE E2a=IRITECH-a G1=IRISID-1 I1=KYNEN Hz1=L1-z1
A2f=NEUROTECHNOLOGY-f C4x=CAMBRIDGE-x C4f=CAMBRIDGE-f F1=MORPHO E2f=IRITECH-f G2=IRISID-2 Hx=L1-x Hz2=L1-z2

Dataset	comparator	IQAA A2f	IQAA C4x	IQAA E2a	IQAA E2f	IQAA F1	IQAA G1	IQAA G2	IQAA Hx
OPS	A2a	(-1.48,-0.96)	(-0.20,0.60)	(-2.53,-1.45)	(-2.58,-1.49)	(-1.37,-0.93)	(-0.22,0.16)	(-0.18,0.22)	(-0.49,0.16)
OPS	B3	(0.40,0.82)	(2.49,3.14)	(0.80,1.69)	(0.82,1.70)	(0.28,0.64)	(0.67,0.97)	(0.98,1.29)	(2.20,2.72)
OPS	C4s	(-0.07,0.36)	(1.49,2.14)	(0.27,1.16)	(0.24,1.13)	(-0.13,0.23)	(0.23,0.55)	(0.26,0.59)	(1.14,1.67)
OPS	E2a	(-1.07,-0.64)	(-0.09,0.57)	(-2.16,-1.26)	(-2.17,-1.26)	(-0.99,-0.63)	(-0.15,0.17)	(-0.06,0.28)	(-0.14,0.39)
OPS	G2	(-0.96,-0.54)	(0.26,0.92)	(-1.43,-0.54)	(-1.44,-0.54)	(-0.95,-0.59)	(-0.03,0.24)	(-0.00,0.22)	(-0.04,0.49)
OPS	Hz1	(0.00,0.43)	(1.89,2.54)	(0.67,1.55)	(0.61,1.50)	(-0.10,0.25)	(0.33,0.65)	(0.50,0.83)	(1.40,1.92)

Table 22: Tukey HSD mean difference in IRIS PUPIL CONTRAST scores. Each cell shows the 95% confidence level in difference in mean of pairwise quality for images correctly rejected (i.e., the impostor score equal or greater than threshold) and those falsely matched (i.e., the impostor score less than threshold). Quality scores were computed by the SDK identified by the column header and comparison scores were generated by the SDK identified by the row header. If the interval does not contain zero, the difference in mean is significant. Cells where difference in mean is not significant are shaded in pink. For monotonic increasing quality components (all except DILATION , and depending on quality implementation GRAY SCALE SPREAD), the expected behavior is to have higher quality scores for the pair of (enrollment, verification) images that result in impostor comparison scores equal or greater than threshold. Pairwise quality is computed as geometric mean of the quality of two samples being compared. Threshold is set to give false match rate of 0.001.

134

A2a=NEUROTECHNOLOGY-a	B3=CROSSMATCH	C4s=CAMBRIDGE-s	D3=AWARE	E2a=IRITECH-a	G1=IRISID-1	I1=KYNEN	Hz1=L1-z1
A2f=NEUROTECHNOLOGY-f		C4x=CAMBRIDGE-x	C4f=CAMBRIDGE-f	F1=MORPHO	E2f=IRITECH-f	G2=IRISID-2	Hx=L1-x	Hz2=L1-z2

9.7 Iris shape

IRIS SHAPE is defined as the shape of iris-sclera boundary. The shape of an iris is very often not a circle or even an ellipse. The non-circularity could be either intrinsic (i.e., subject character) due to natural anatomical variation or be caused by subject behavior such as non-frontal gaze. Other than some medical condition and surgical procedure that can affect it, the IRIS SHAPE , is believed to stay stable over the period of a human life.

The earlier academic publications on iris recognition [6, 24] used circle-fitting methods to estimate the IRIS SHAPE . However, the circularity assumption is not always true; consequently, the accuracy of these methods drops when dealing with iris images with off-axis angle or non-circular for other reasons (including intrinsically non-circle irises). There are many published technical papers documenting methods for detection of iris-sclera boundary (as part of iris segmentation) [8], and some do not make the circularity assumption [8].

IQCE invited submission of SDKs that measure the IRIS SHAPE and did not specify it as a measure of circularity. IQCE received nine submissions from six organizations. The distribution of their IRIS SHAPE scores is shown in Figure 64. In order to make the boxplots more readable, quality scores in [0–254] range were linearly scaled back to [0–100].

The quantitative results of the effect of IRIS SHAPE on performance follows.

Note that IQAA D3's IRIS SHAPE is highly correlated with its USABLE IRIS AREA scores. The Spearman rank correlation of 0.82 suggests either D3's IRIS SHAPE or its USABLE IRIS AREA is not a faithful computation of the image properties that its measurement was intended. The result of IQAA D3 IRIS SHAPE is included here, but it should not be considered as a separate and statistically independent quality component than its USABLE IRIS AREA scores.

RELATIONSHIP WITH THE DISTRIBUTION OF GENUINE SCORES

Figure 65 shows that, for all comparators, IRIS SHAPE scores change with the genuine scores.

IQAA C4x IRIS SHAPE scores trend in the wrong direction for images in QFIRE and OPS datasets; high IRIS SHAPE scores are observed when genuine scores are large (recall that low genuine scores are desirable since they are dissimilarity scores).

Among the datasets, the biggest rate of change is seen for QFIRE A5 images, which is expected given that QFIRE A5 contains images with a diverse range of off-axis angle.

Among the comparators, A2a's genuine scores is the least affected.

The last remark is regarding the range of IRIS SHAPE scores of different IQAAs. IQAA C4x IRIS SHAPE scores are less than 50 while IQAA Hx scores are all larger than 60, indicating that the IRIS SHAPE scores of IQAA Hx and C4x are not interoperable.

RELATIONSHIP WITH THE DISTRIBUTION OF IMPOSTOR SCORES

Impostor distribution is not nearly as affected as the genuine distribution, as show by almost flat boxes in Figure 66.

Among the comparators, E2a's impostor scores seem the most affected, particularly for QFIRE A5 and ICE2006 images.

| A2a=NEUROTECHNOLOGY-a | B3=CROSSMATCH | C4s=CAMBRIDGE-s | D3=AWARE | E2a=IRITECH-a | G1=IRISID-1 | I1=KYNEN | Hz1=L1-z1 |
| A2f=NEUROTECHNOLOGY-f | C4x=CAMBRIDGE-x | C4f=CAMBRIDGE-f | F1=MORPHO | E2f=IRITECH-f | G2=IRISID-2 | Hx=L1-x | Hz2=L1-z2 |

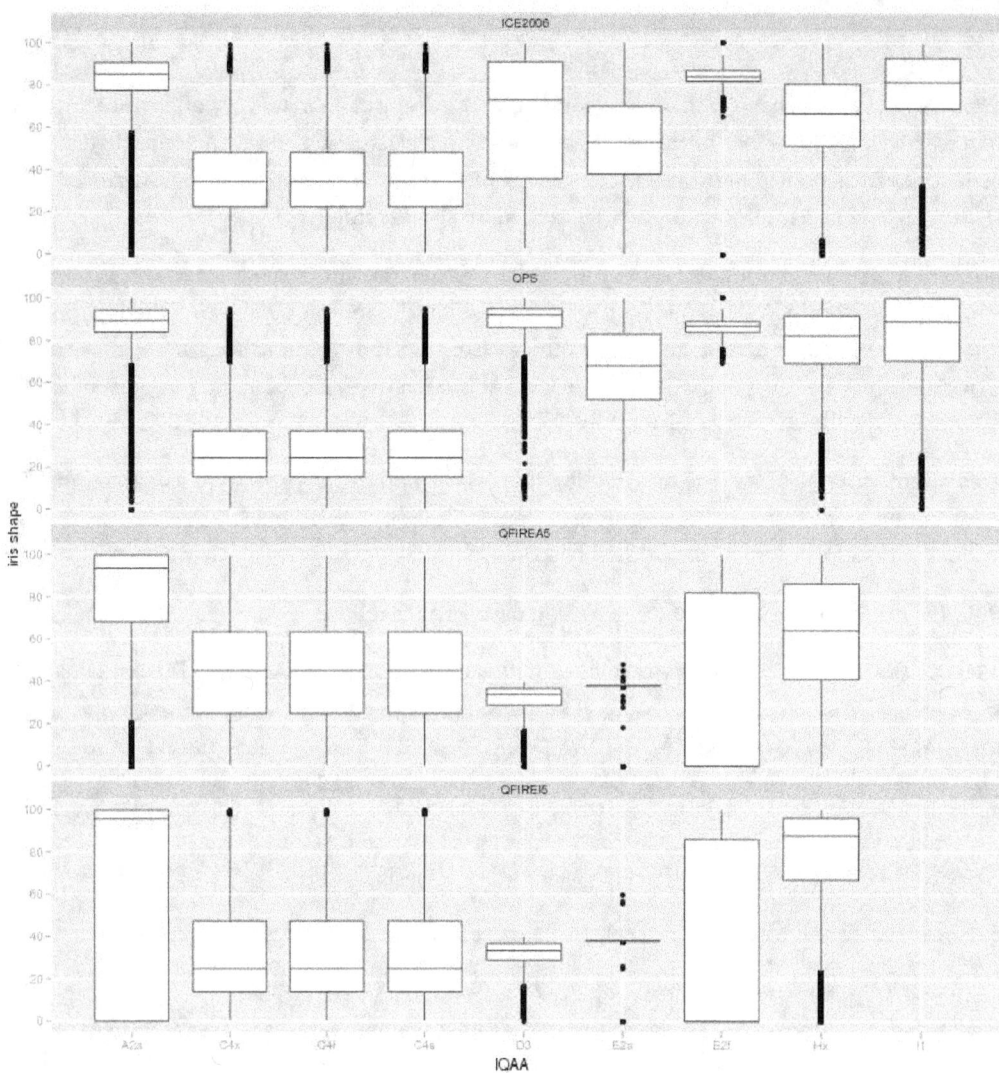

Figure 64: Box and whisker plots of the IQAAs that generate IRIS SHAPE scores.

The least affected are comparators G1 and C4s.

RANKED DET:: DO LOW-QUALITY IMAGES PRODUCE HIGH FNMR OR FMR?

Figure 67 shows comparator Hz1's ranked DET.

For most of the IQAA's performance on the ICE2006 images with low, mid and high IRIS SHAPE scores are similar. IQAAs C4x, C4f, E2f, Hx, and I1 give almost identical performance for the three groups of the images. The ICE2006 images in the lowest 15 percentile IRIS SHAPE scores of IQAAs D3 and E2a give higher FNMR than the remaining images. However, the observed FNMR of images with IRIS SHAPE in the highest 15 percentile and middle 70% are comparable. The rank ordering of IQAA A2a is reverse, the lowest 15 percentile IRIS SHAPE give the best performance, and the lowest performance occurs for images in its highest 15 percentile.

On QFIRE A5 images (Figure 67(b)), only IQAAs C4x, C4f, and Hx IRIS SHAPE scores give an ordered indication of performance. As mentioned before, the rankings of the DET curves are reversed for C4x and C4f; images with low IRIS SHAPE give lower FNMR than those with high IRIS SHAPE scores.

The effect on FMR is much smaller, for either ICE2006 or QFIRE A5 datasets.

EFFECT OF QUALITY ON FNMR : HOW QUICKLY FNMR IMPROVES WHEN POOR QUALITY SAMPLES ARE REJECTED?

Rejection of images with low IRIS SHAPE scores only slightly improves FNMR.

On ICE2006 images, the best FNMR improvement is observed for IQAA D3. However because IQAA D3 IRIS SHAPE scores are highly correlated with its USABLE IRIS AREA scores (see Figure 119), it is not clear if the IQAA D3 IRIS SHAPE scores are a faithful measurement of iris-sclera boundary quality. Nonetheless it should not be considered as a separate (and statistically independent) quality component than its USABLE IRIS AREA scores.

Rejection of the ICE2006 images with low IRIS SHAPE scores as computed by IQAAs E2a, Hx, or A2a (for comparators G2 and B3) improves the FNMR, though the improvement is small.

Results on QFIRE A5 images are not encouraging. Rejection of images with poor IRIS SHAPE scores as computed by IQAAs C4s, C4x, or Hx improves FNMR slightly. No other IQAA is effective.

Given that IQAA C4x's, C4s's, and C4f's high IRIS SHAPE scores mean low-quality rejection curves of IQAAs C4x, C4s, and C4f are computed by rejecting the high scoring images.

TEST OF SIGNIFICANCE :: DO THE IMAGES INVOLVED IN SUCCESSFUL VERIFICATION ATTEMPTS HAVE SIGNIFICANTLY HIGHER QUALITY SCORES THAN THOSE INVOLVED IN FAILED VERIFICATION ATTEMPTS?

Table 23 shows that

a) there is a significant difference in the mean of pairwise IRIS SHAPE scores when computed by IQAAs C4x and Hx; and

b) the sense of IQAA C4x IRIS SHAPE score is inverted; images that have high IRIS SHAPE scores give high FNMR.

No other IQAA's IRIS SHAPE scores are statistically significant.

Per Table 24, there is not a significant difference in the mean of pairwise IRIS SHAPE scores between OPS or QFIRE images that are falsely matched and those correctly rejected.

EFFECT OF VARIATION BETWEEN THE TWO SAMPLES:: DOES SAMENESS MATTER?

The heatmaps of Figure 69-71 show that images with low IRIS SHAPE scores (or high in case of IQAAs C4s and A2a) give slightly higher FNMR than the remaining images.

Like other quality components, comparators B3 and G1 prefer similarity between IRIS SHAPE scores of the two images being compared. Other comparators are not sensitive to this difference.

| A2a=NEUROTECHNOLOGY-a | B3=CROSSMATCH | C4s=CAMBRIDGE-s | D3=AWARE | E2a=IRITECH-a | G1=IRISID-1 | I1=KYNEN | Hz1=L1-z1 |
| A2f=NEUROTECHNOLOGY-f | C4x=CAMBRIDGE-x | C4f=CAMBRIDGE-f | F1=MORPHO | E2f=IRITECH-f | G2=IRISID-2 | Hx=L1-x | Hz2=L1-z2 |

The effect of IRIS SHAPE on FNMR is, quite expectedly, more pronounced for QFIRE A5 images.

IQAA C4s, Hx, and A2a perform better than other IQAAs for all three datasets.

OBSERVATIONS AND CONCLUSIONS

For some IQAA , their IRIS SHAPE scores correlates highly with other quality components, for example the IRIS SHAPE scores of IQAA D3 are highly correlated with its USABLE IRIS AREA scores. This high correlation suggests that IRIS SHAPE is not statistically independent of other quality components, and its effect on performance has already accounted for by other quality components. Rejection of up to 10% of the lowest paiewise quality, improves FNMR by no more than 0.01 from its baseline value of 0.1.

For these reasons, IQCE recommends exclusion of IRIS SHAPE as a quality component.

| A2a=NEUROTECHNOLOGY-a | B3=CROSSMATCH | C4s=CAMBRIDGE-s | D3=AWARE | E2a=IRITECH-a | G1=IRISID-1 | I1=KYNEN | Hz1=L1-z1 |
| A2f=NEUROTECHNOLOGY-f | C4x=CAMBRIDGE-x | C4f=CAMBRIDGE-f | F1=MORPHO | E2f=IRITECH-f | G2=IRISID-2 | Hx=L1-x | Hz2=L1-z2 |

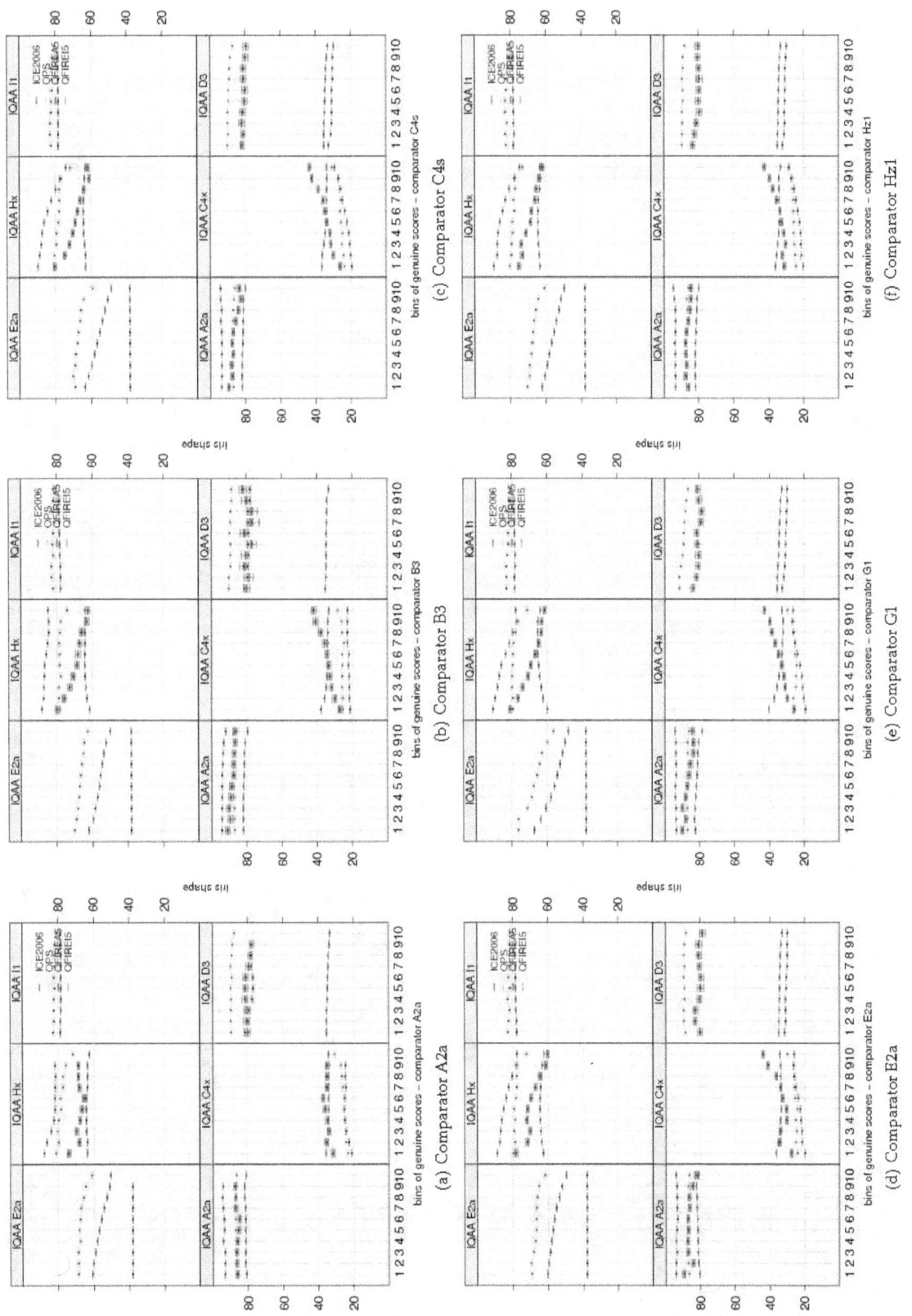

Figure 65: Pairwise IRIS SHAPE scores vs. genuine score for the primary Class Z submissions of each participant. Each plot shows quality scores computed by different IQAA. Genuine scores are divided equally into ten groups. Groups overlap by 5 percent, meaning 5% of the data in one bin also belongs to the next bin. The bootstrapped pairwise quality for each group is shown in a box and whisker plot. Pairwise quality is computed as geometric mean of the quality of the two samples being compared. The change in IRIS SHAPE scores are wide and the complete separation of boxes indicates that the change is significant. For all comparators, IRIS SHAPE scores change with the genuine scores.

A2a=NEUROTECHNOLOGY-a	B3=CROSSMATCH	C4s=CAMBRIDGE-s	D3=AWARE	E2a=IRITECH-a	G1=IRISID-1	I1=KYNEN	Hz1=L1-z1
A2f=NEUROTECHNOLOGY-f	C4x=CAMBRIDGE-x	C4f=CAMBRIDGE-f	F1=MORPHO	E2f=IRITECH-f	G2=IRISID-2	Hx=L1-x	Hz2=L1-z2

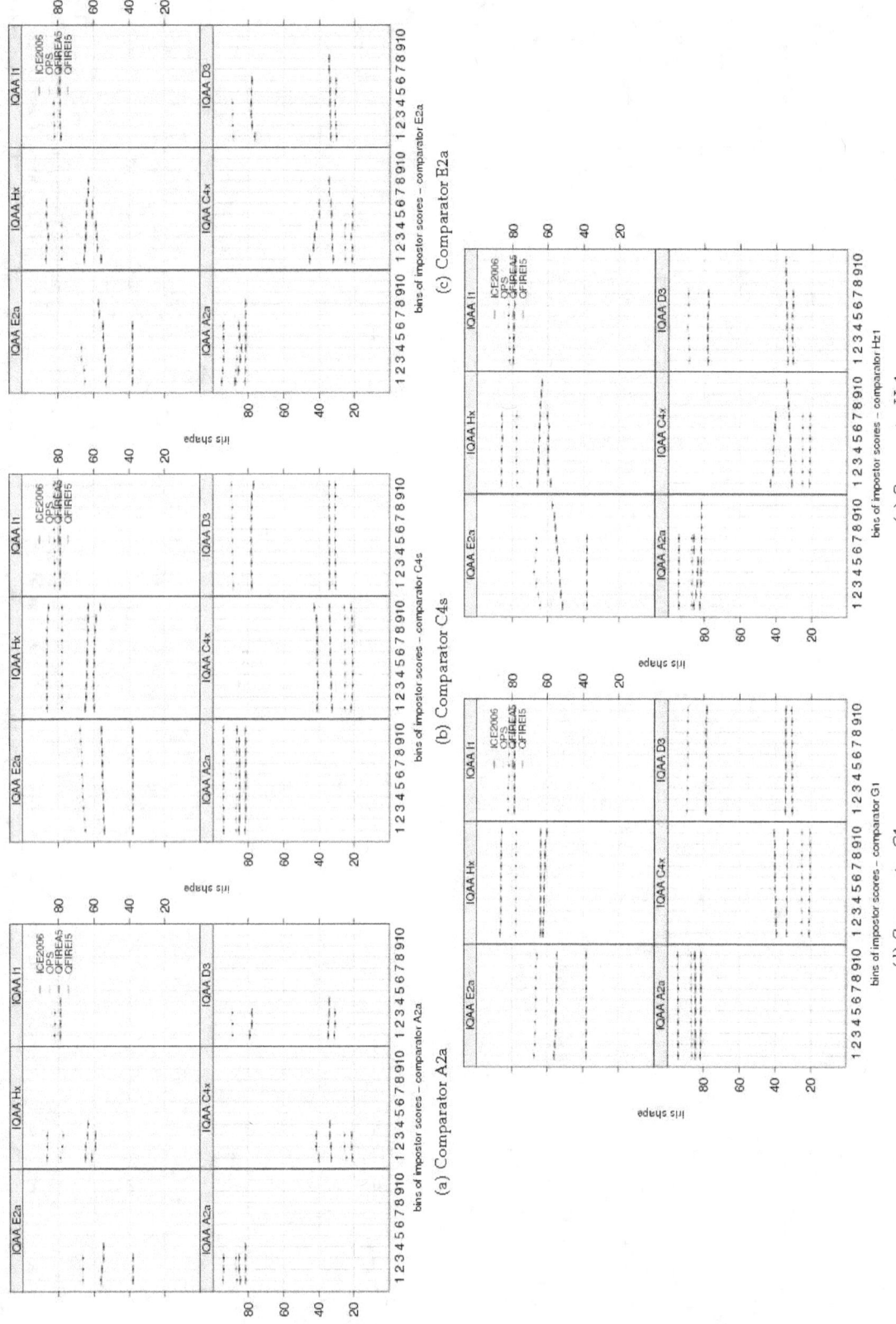

Figure 66: Pairwise IRIS SHAPE scores vs. impostor scores for the primary Class Z submissions of each participants. Each plot shows quality scores computed by different IQAA. Similar to plots of Figure 65, impostor scores are divided equally into ten groups. Groups overlap by 5 percent. Bootstrapped pairwise quality for each group is shown in a box and whisker plot. Pairwise quality is computed as geometric mean of the quality of the two samples being compared. Only a small change in IRIS SHAPE scores is observes over the range of the impostor scores.

A2a=NEUROTECHNOLOGY-a   B3=CROSSMATCH   C4s=CAMBRIDGE-s   D3=AWARE   E2a=IRITECH-a   G1=IRISID-1   I1=KYNEN   Hz1=L1-z1
A2f=NEUROTECHNOLOGY-f   C4x=CAMBRIDGE-x   C4f=CAMBRIDGE-f   F1=MORPHO   E2f=IRITECH-f   G2=IRISID-2   Hx=L1-x   Hz2=L1-z2

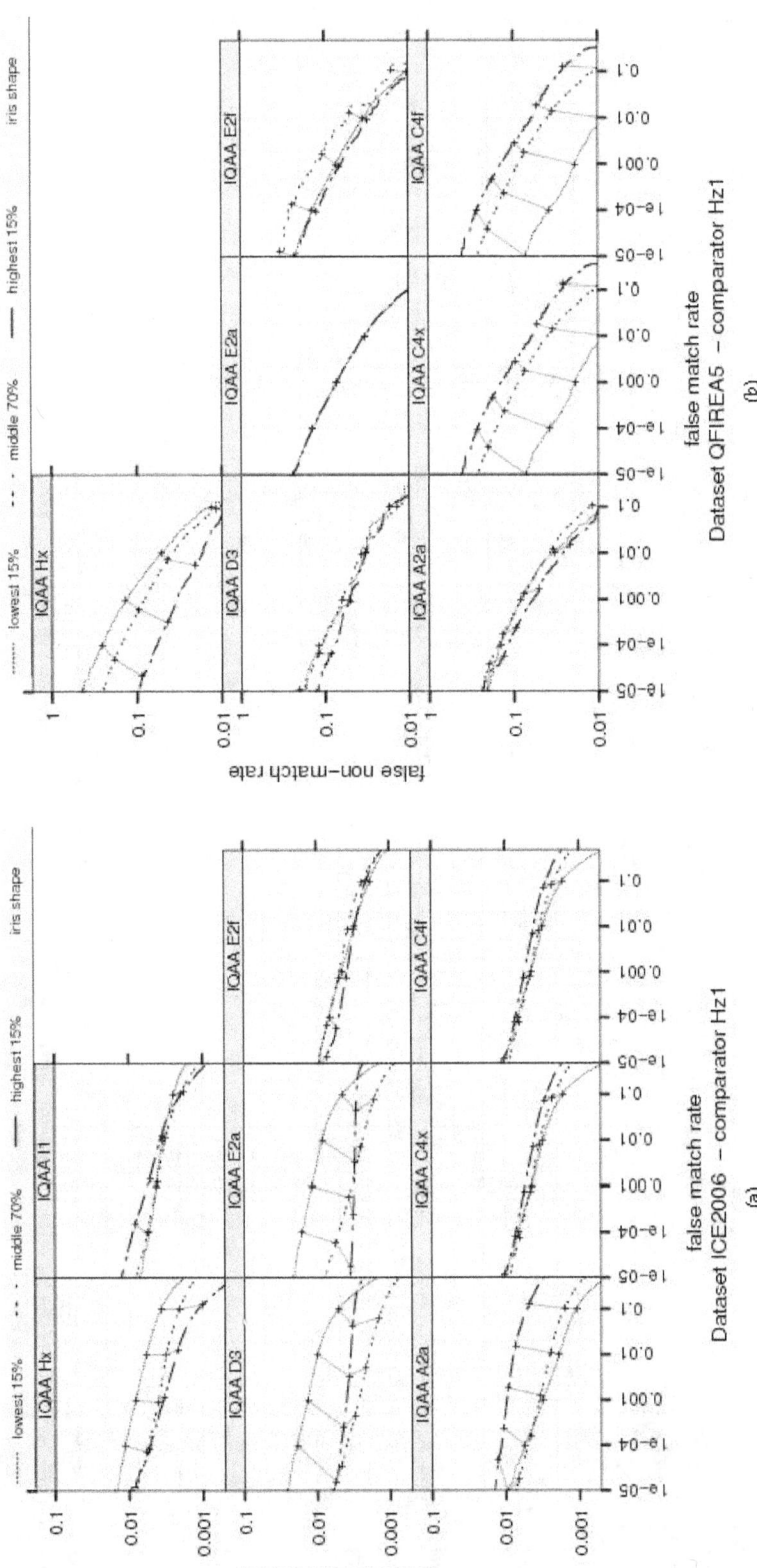

Figure 67: Ranked DET curves for comparator Hz1 and Datasets ICE2006 and QFIRE A5 . The set of all comparisons were partitioned into three groups based on the pair-wise IRIS SHAPE quality of the images being compared. The lowest quality set contains comparisons with pairwise quality in the lower 15 percentile. The highest quality set contains comparisons with pairwise quality in the upper 15 percentile. The rest of the comparisons, namely the middle 70%, made up the third set. The DETs are connected at the same score threshold values (brown lines). Lower FNMR and FMR rates are expected for better quality images. On QFIRE A5 images, only IQAAs C4x, C4f and Hx IRIS SHAPE scores are effective. Images with high IRIS SHAPE scores of IQAAs C4x or C4f give lower FNMR than other images. The change in FMR is very small.

141

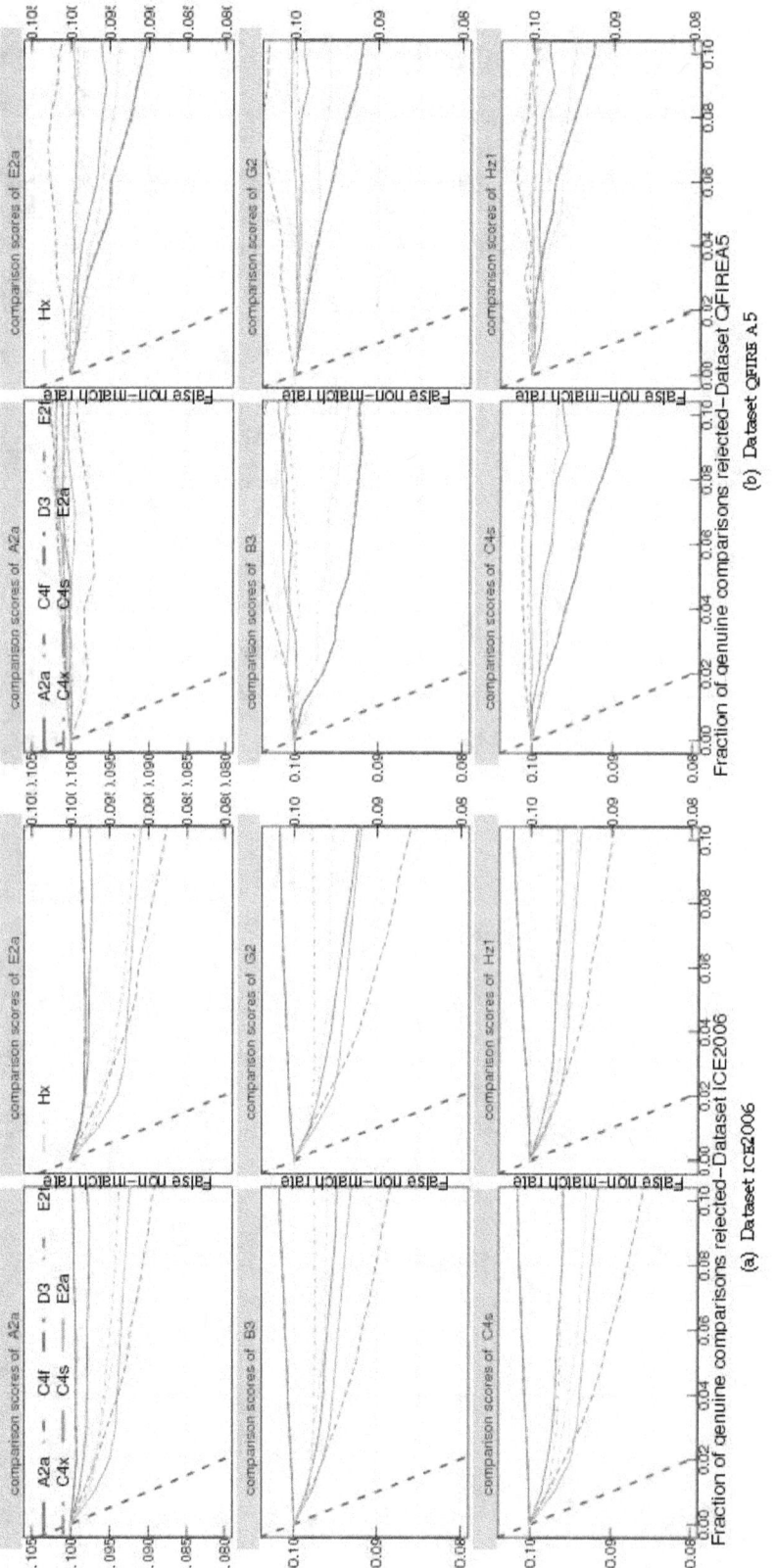

Figure 68: FNMR vs. reject curves for IRIS SHAPE scores on datasets ICE2006 and QFIRE 15. The threshold is set to give an initial FNMR = 0.1. The gray dotted line shows the ideal case where the rejection of the comparisons with the lowest ten percent quality results in zero FNMR. No IQAA shows a strong improvement in FNMR after rejecting images with its low IRIS SHAPE scores.

| A2a=NEUROTECHNOLOGY-a | B3=CROSSMATCH | C4s=CAMBRIDGE-s | D3=AWARE | E2a=IRITECH-a | G1=IRISID-1 | I1=KYNEN | Hz1=L1-z1 |
| A2f=NEUROTECHNOLOGY-f | C4x=CAMBRIDGE-x | C4f=CAMBRIDGE-f | F1=MORPHO | E2f=IRITECH-f | G2=IRISID-2 | Hx=L1-x | Hz2=L1-z2 |

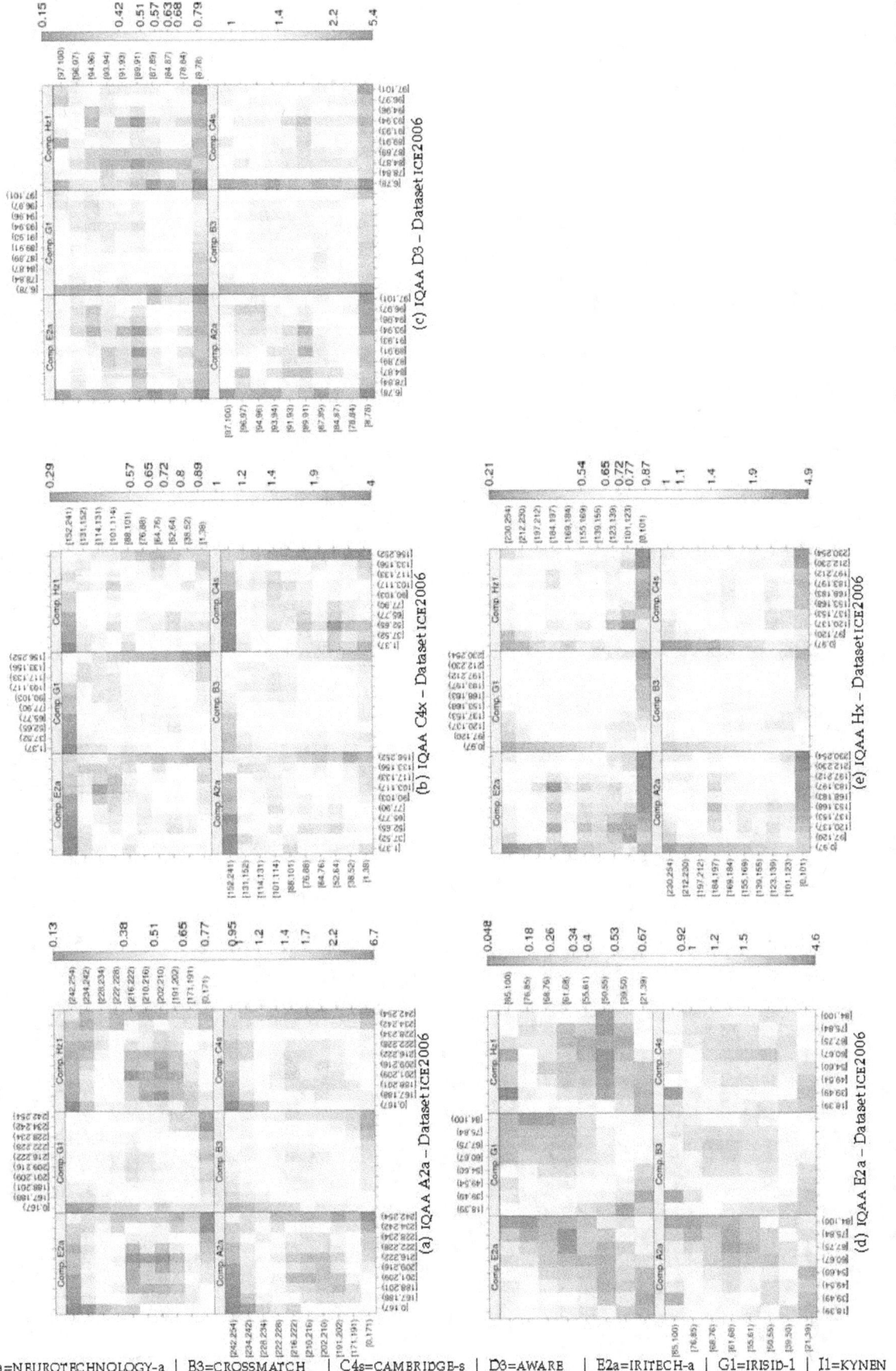

Figure 69: IRIS SHAPE computed by primary IQAA submissions and FNMR for IQCE comparators for dataset ICE2006 . The y-axis represents enrollment samples' quality with verification samples' on the x-axis. The color scale plots $\frac{FNMR}{FNMR_0}$ for comparisons with verification and enrollment qualities ($q_{verification}, q_{enrollment}$). FNMR$_0$ is the nominal FNMR which is the false non-match rate computed over all the images at the same comparison score threshold, in this case at FMR = 0.001. Yellow/Green color represent an improvement in FNMR. Blue color represent a degradation of FNMR. White color means no change in FNMR.

143

| A2a=NEUROTECHNOLOGY-a | B3=CROSSMATCH | C4s=CAMBRIDGE-s | D3=AWARE | E2a=IRITECH-a | G1=IRISID-1 | I1=KYNEN | Hz1=L1-z1 |
| A2f=NEUROTECHNOLOGY-f | C4x=CAMBRIDGE-x | C4f=CAMBRIDGE-f | F1=MORPHO | E2f=IRITECH-f | G2=IRISID-2 | Hx=L1-x | Hz2=L1-z2 |

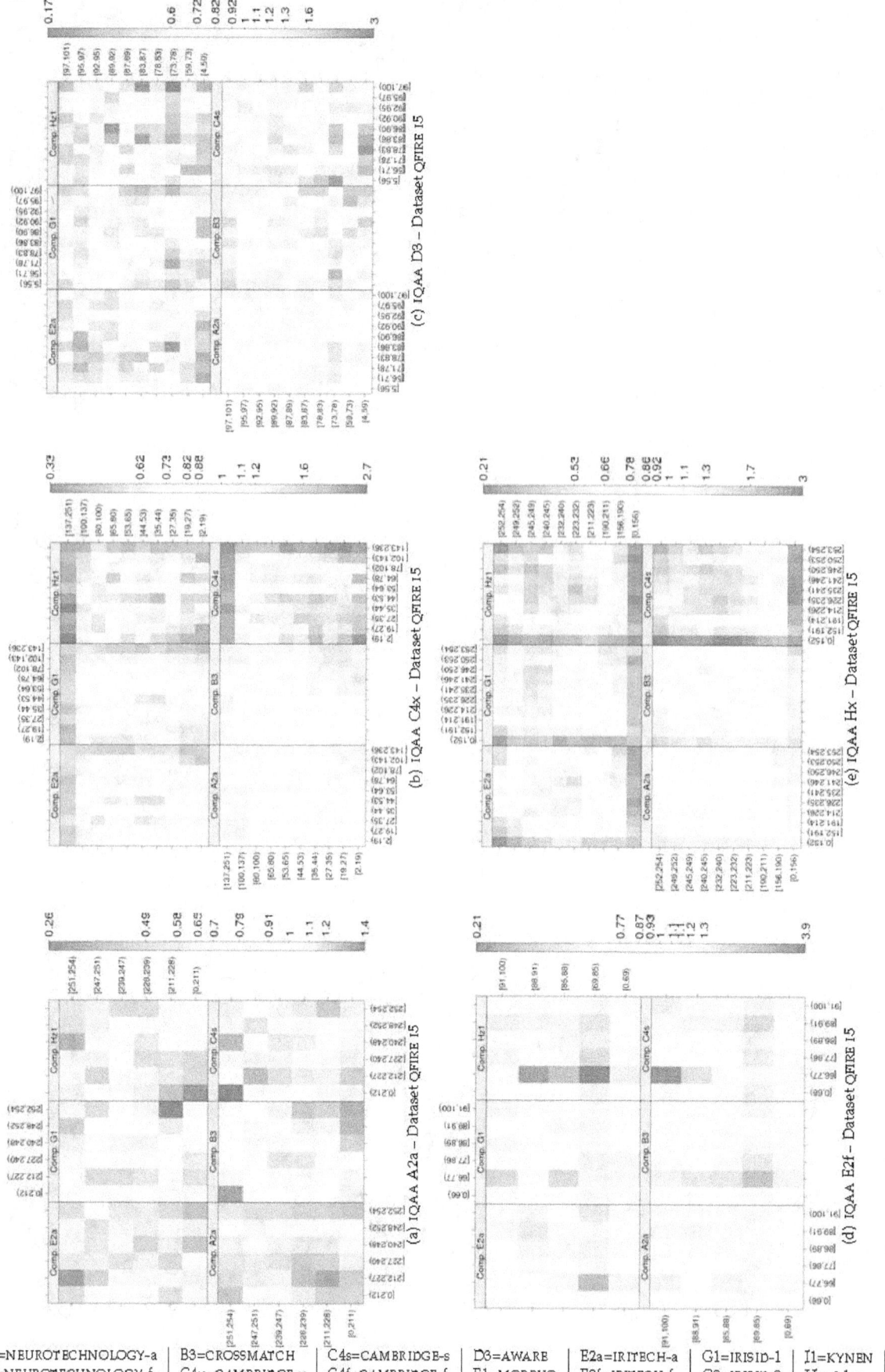

Figure 70: IRIS SHAPE computed by primary IQAA submissions and FNMR for IQCE comparators for dataset QFIRE 15 . The y-axis represents enrollment samples' quality with verification samples' on the x-axis. The IRIS SCLERA CONTRAST scores are quantized into 10 quantiles. The color scale plots $\frac{FNMR}{FNMR_0}$ for comparisons with verification and enrollment qualities ($q_{verification}, q_{enrollment}$). FNMR$_0$ is the nominal FNMR which is the false non-match rate computed over all the images at the same comparison score threshold, in this case at FMR = 0.001. Yellow/Green color represent an improvement in FNMR. Blue color represent a degradation of FNMR. White color means no change in FNMR.

144

| A2a=NEUROTECHNOLOGY-a | B3=CROSSMATCH | C4s=CAMBRIDGE-s | D3=AWARE | E2a=IRITECH-a | G1=IRISID-1 | I1=KYNEN | Hz1=L1-z1 |
| A2f=NEUROTECHNOLOGY-f | C4x=CAMBRIDGE-x | C4f=CAMBRIDGE-f | F1=MORPHO | E2f=IRITECH-f | G2=IRISID-2 | Hx=L1-x | Hz2=L1-z2 |

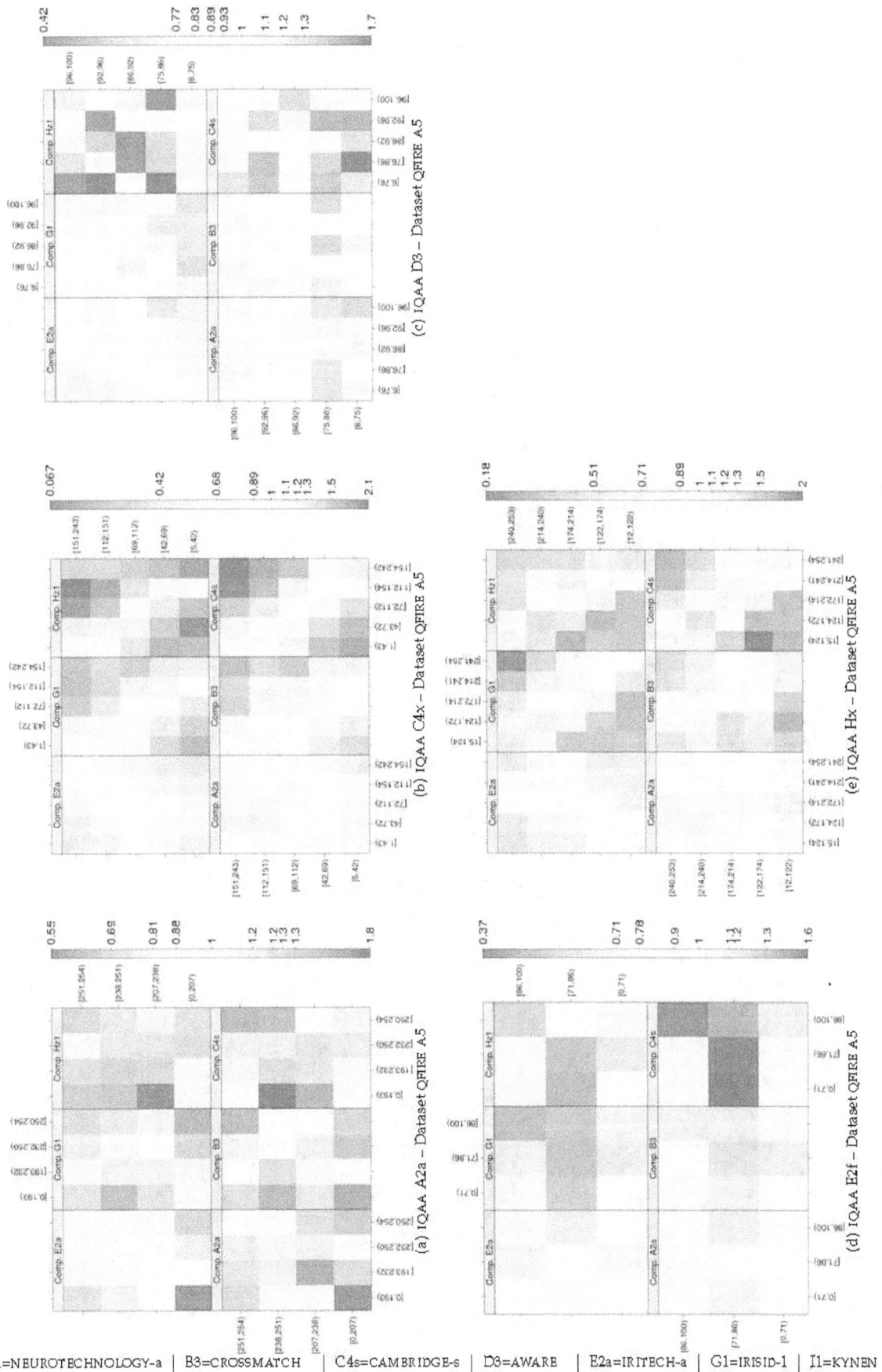

Figure 71: IRIS SHAPE computed by primary IQAA submissions and FNMR for IQCB comparators for dataset QFIRE A5 . The y-axis represents enrollment samples' quality with verification samples' on the x-axis. The IRIS SCLERA CONTRAST scores are quantized into 10 quantiles. The color scale plots $\frac{\text{FNMR}}{\text{FNMR}_0}$ for comparisons with verification and enrollment qualities ($q_{verification}, q_{enrollment}$). FNMR_0 is the nominal FNMR which is the false non-match rate computed over all the images at the same comparison score threshold, in this case at FMR = 0.001. Yellow/Green color represent an improvement in FNMR. Blue color represent a degradation of FNMR. White color means no change in FNMR.

(a) IQAA A2a – Dataset QFIRE A5

(b) IQAA C4x – Dataset QFIRE A5

(c) IQAA D3 – Dataset QFIRE A5

(d) IQAA E2f – Dataset QFIRE A5

(e) IQAA Hx – Dataset QFIRE A5

A2a=NEUROTECHNOLOGY-a	B3=CROSSMATCH	C4s=CAMBRIDGE-s	D3=AWARE	E2a=IRITECH-a	G1=IRISID-1	I1=KYNEN	Hz1=L1-z1
A2f=NEUROTECHNOLOGY-f	C4x=CAMBRIDGE-x	C4f=CAMBRIDGE-f	F1=MORPHO	E2f=IRITECH-f	G2=IRISID-2	Hx=L1-x	Hz2=L1-z2

Dataset	comparator	IQAA C4x	IQAA E2a	IQAA E2f	IQAA Hx
ICE2006	A2a	(-2.35,-2.01)	(9.30,9.66)	(0.87,0.94)	(8.23,8.62)
ICE2006	B3	(1.59,1.75)	(6.70,6.87)	(-0.12,-0.08)	(0.41,0.59)
ICE2006	C4s	(-5.55,-5.30)	(6.61,6.87)	(0.14,0.20)	(5.46,5.74)
ICE2006	E2a	(-2.35,-2.00)	(10.12,10.49)	(0.93,1.00)	(9.22,9.61)
ICE2006	G2	(0.07,0.24)	(9.87,10.05)	(0.06,0.09)	(3.18,3.37)
ICE2006	Hz1	(-1.80,-1.38)	(5.92,6.33)	(0.26,0.35)	(3.43,3.90)
OPS	A2a	(-9.05,-1.22)	(5.27,15.15)	(-0.36,1.47)	(0.36,8.91)
OPS	B3	(-7.26,-4.00)	(1.92,6.05)	(0.52,1.28)	(4.71,8.27)
OPS	C4s	(-12.44,-6.15)	(4.79,12.72)	(1.01,2.48)	(7.29,14.16)
OPS	E2a	(-10.29,-1.10)	(4.11,15.71)	(0.05,2.20)	(-0.05,9.99)
OPS	G2	(-12.54,-7.46)	(11.28,17.68)	(0.73,1.92)	(9.65,15.18)
OPS	Hz1	(-10.98,-3.60)	(4.13,13.44)	(0.37,2.09)	(7.69,15.74)
QFIREA5	A2a	(-1.28,-0.32)	(-0.00,0.00)	(-1.40,-0.34)	(0.38,1.44)
QFIREA5	B3	(-8.56,-7.19)	(-0.00,0.00)	(-1.01,1.66)	(7.14,8.67)
QFIREA5	C4s	(-10.51,-9.26)	(-0.00,-0.00)	(-1.61,0.73)	(7.44,8.86)
QFIREA5	E2a	(-4.30,-3.42)	(-0.00,0.00)	(-0.75,0.87)	(6.26,7.23)
QFIREA5	G2	(-9.05,-8.13)	(-0.00,0.00)	(-0.89,0.86)	(8.70,9.74)
QFIREA5	Hz1	(-9.60,-8.04)	(-0.00,-0.00)	(-0.76,2.15)	(6.24,8.01)
QFIREI5	A2a	(-1.28,-0.96)	(-0.00,0.00)	(-1.84,-1.16)	(3.00,3.34)
QFIREI5	B3	(-0.91,-0.62)	(0.00,0.00)	(-1.22,-0.50)	(1.79,2.09)
QFIREI5	C4s	(-6.86,-6.48)	(-0.00,0.00)	(-0.83,0.04)	(10.62,11.03)
QFIREI5	E2a	(-2.81,-2.40)	(-0.00,0.00)	(-2.40,-1.49)	(5.97,6.41)
QFIREI5	G2	(-4.51,-4.18)	(-0.00,0.00)	(-0.47,0.30)	(7.61,7.97)
QFIREI5	Hz1	(-5.54,-5.06)	(-0.00,0.00)	(-3.57,-2.47)	(9.70,10.23)

Table 23: Tukey HSD difference in mean of IRIS SHAPE scores. Each cell shows the 95% confidence level in difference in mean of pairwise quality for images verified correctly (i.e., the genuine score equal or less than threshold) and those rejected falsely (i.e., the genuine score larger than threshold). Quality scores were computed by the SDK identified by the column header and comparison scores were generated by the SDK identified by the row header. If the interval does not contain zero, the difference in mean is significant. Cells where difference in mean is not significant have pink background. For monotonically increasing quality components (all except DILATION, and depending on quality implementation GRAY SCALE SPREAD), the expected behavior is to have higher quality scores for the pair of enrollment and verification images that give genuine comparison scores less than threshold. The pairwise quality is computed as geometric mean of the quality of two samples being compared. Threshold is set to give false match rate of 0.001.

146

A2a=NEUROTECHNOLOGY-a | B3=CROSSMATCH | C4s=CAMBRIDGE-s | D3=AWARE | E2a=IRITECH-a | G1=IRISID-1 | I1=KYNEN | Hz1=L1-z1
A2f=NEUROTECHNOLOGY-f | C4x=CAMBRIDGE-x | C4f=CAMBRIDGE-f | F1=MORPHO | E2f=IRITECH-f | G2=IRISID-2 | Hx=L1-x | Hz2=L1-z2

Dataset	comparator	IQAA C4x	IQAA E2a	IQAA E2f	IQAA Hx
ICE2006	A2a	(0.38,1.15)	(-2.97,-2.22)	(0.15,0.31)	(-2.60,-1.72)
ICE2006	B3	(3.03,3.59)	(6.52,7.07)	(-0.83,-0.71)	(-3.08,-2.45)
ICE2006	C4s	(1.51,2.11)	(1.68,2.26)	(-0.20,-0.07)	(-2.10,-1.42)
ICE2006	E2a	(0.05,0.66)	(3.86,4.45)	(0.00,0.13)	(-1.28,-0.59)
ICE2006	G2	(-1.99,-1.37)	(-2.77,-2.17)	(0.26,0.39)	(0.44,1.15)
ICE2006	Hz1	(-0.06,0.60)	(2.62,3.26)	(0.17,0.32)	(-0.45,0.30)
OPS	A2a	(1.06,1.90)	(-0.77,0.28)	(-0.27,-0.07)	(-1.97,-1.01)
OPS	B3	(-0.57,0.11)	(4.97,5.83)	(0.17,0.34)	(0.89,1.67)
OPS	C4s	(0.30,0.98)	(3.57,4.44)	(0.01,0.18)	(-0.56,0.23)
OPS	E2a	(-0.17,0.53)	(0.83,1.71)	(-0.02,0.15)	(-0.07,0.73)
OPS	G2	(-0.42,0.27)	(-2.50,-1.62)	(-0.16,0.01)	(-0.44,0.35)
OPS	Hz1	(-0.11,0.58)	(3.78,4.64)	(0.10,0.27)	(0.03,0.81)
QFIREA5	A2a	(-1.15,0.01)	(0.00,0.00)	(-1.42,0.70)	(4.00,5.37)
QFIREA5	C4s	(-1.17,-0.12)	(-0.00,0.00)	(-0.80,1.11)	(0.64,1.88)
QFIREA5	E2a	(-11.37,-10.31)	(-0.00,0.00)	(1.04,2.94)	(2.49,3.72)
QFIREA5	G2	(-0.77,0.32)	(0.00,0.01)	(-1.88,0.11)	(0.93,2.19)
QFIREA5	Hz1	(-7.71,-6.65)	(-0.00,0.00)	(0.07,1.99)	(6.27,7.51)
QFIREI5	A2a	(-1.20,-0.67)	(-0.00,0.00)	(0.76,2.18)	(-0.00,0.58)
QFIREI5	C4s	(-3.63,-3.16)	(-0.00,0.00)	(-1.30,-0.06)	(1.43,1.93)
QFIREI5	E2a	(-0.89,-0.43)	(-0.00,0.00)	(-4.98,-3.74)	(0.44,0.94)
QFIREI5	G2	(-3.66,-0.17)	(-0.00,0.00)	(-5.71,3.56)	(-2.10,1.65)
QFIREI5	Hz1	(-4.45,-3.98)	(-0.00,0.00)	(-4.33,-3.10)	(2.74,3.24)

Table 24: Tukey HSD mean difference in IRIS SHAPE scores. Each cell shows the 95% confidence level in difference in mean of pairwise quality for images correctly rejected (i.e., the impostor score equal or greater than threshold) and those falsely matched (i.e., the impostor score less than threshold). Quality scores were computed by the SDK identified by the column header and comparison scores were generated by the SDK identified by the row header. If the interval does not contain zero, the difference in mean is significant. Cells where difference in mean is not significant are shaded in pink. For monotonic increasing quality components (all except DILATION, and depending on quality implementation GRAY SCALE SPREAD), the expected behavior is to have higher quality scores for the pair of (enrollment, verification) images that result in impostor comparison scores equal or greater than threshold. Pairwise quality is computed as geometric mean of the quality of two samples being compared. Threshold is set to give false match rate of 0.001.

147

9.8 Pupil shape

Given that the iris portion just around the pupil has high information content, the accurate detection of iris-pupil boundary is of the utmost importance.

The non-circularity could be either natural anatomical variation (subject character) or due to non-frontal gaze (subject behavior) or both. Certain medical conditions will induce highly non-circular pupils. PUPIL SHAPE is mostly affected by characteristic of the subject than the capture device or capture environment. As such, iris recognition technologies have to adapt to the population characteristic.

A good number of iris segmentation algorithms consider pupil as a circle and as such, fit a circle to model iris-pupil boundary. However, PUPIL SHAPE is not circular, and not even elliptical. Segmentation accuracy of algorithms based on circularity assumption are severely degraded when iris-pupil boundary is occluded by reflections (from illumination or eyeglasses) or when the pupil has an usual shape. Several recent publications propose iris-pupil boundary detection algorithms that are not constrained to circle fitting; the most cited is [8].

Nine IQCE submissions (from six organizations) generate PUPIL SHAPE scores. The distribution of their PUPIL SHAPE scores is shown in Figure 72. In order to make the boxplots more readable, quality scores in [0–254] range were linearly scaled back to [0–100].

Results on quantitative analysis of the effect of PUPIL SHAPE on performance follows.

RELATIONSHIP WITH THE DISTRIBUTION OF GENUINE SCORES

Box plots of Figure 73 PUPIL SHAPE show substantial variations in PUPIL SHAPE scores across bins of the genuine scores. PUPIL SHAPE scores generated by IQAAs Hx and C4x exhibit the largest slope, though C4x slope is negative indicating that IQAA C4x's low PUPIL SHAPE score means high quality. The smallest belongs to IQAAS' A2a and E2a.

PUPIL SHAPE scores of IQAA C4x, similar to its IRIS SHAPE scores, increase as the genuine scores increase, meaning that images with high PUPIL SHAPE score can give high FNMR.

Behavior of each IQAA is similar across the comparators. Comparator A2a's genuine scores are the least affected by PUPIL SHAPE scores.

Among the datasets, the largest variation takes place for QFIRE images, particularly for QFIRE A5, where most IQAAs have significantly different PUPIL SHAPE scores across bins of the genuine scores. The least variation happens for OPS images.

The OPS dataset has the highest PUPIL SHAPE scores, followed by ICE2006, QFIRE I5, and finally QFIRE A5. This ranking of the datasets is logical and expected as occlusion and off-axis make QFIRE images the "most difficult to match" and OPS images are the "easiest to match" due to their selection procedure (see Section 4).

QFIRE I5 images have a high degree of occlusion mostly because of specular reflections, which often happens at iris-pupil boundaries. QFIRE A5 images, for the most part, have non-frontal gaze.

RELATIONSHIP WITH THE DISTRIBUTION OF IMPOSTOR SCORES

148

| A2a=NEUROTECHNOLOGY-a | B3=CROSSMATCH | C4s=CAMBRIDGE-s | D3=AWARE | E2a=IRITECH-a | G1=IRISID-1 | I1=KYNEN | Hz1=L1-z1 |
| A2f=NEUROTECHNOLOGY-f | C4x=CAMBRIDGE-x | C4f=CAMBRIDGE-f | F1=MORPHO | E2f=IRITECH-f | G2=IRISID-2 | Hx=L1-x | Hz2=L1-z2 |

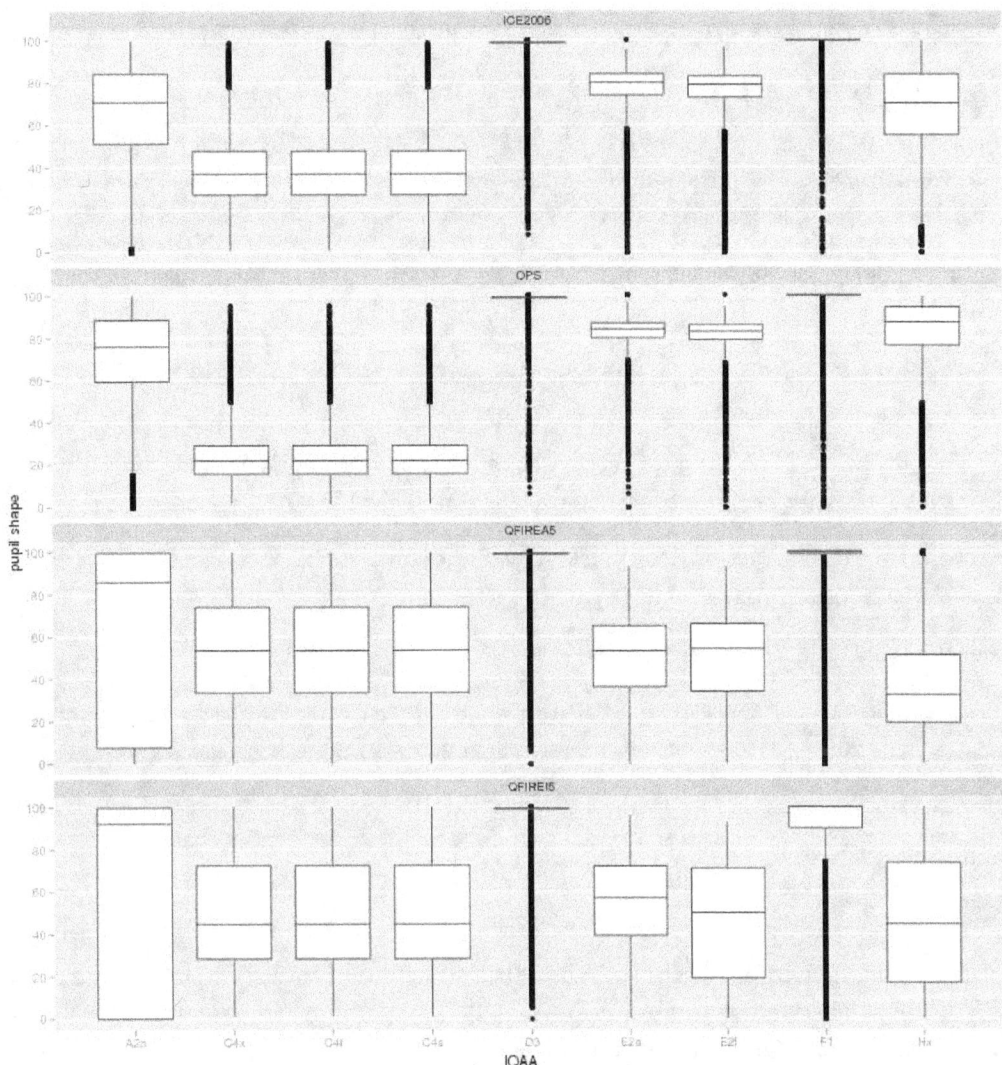

Figure 72: Box and whisker plots of the IQAAs that generate PUPIL SHAPE scores.

Figure 74 shows PUPIL SHAPE scores vary across different bins of the impostor scores, but the variation between PUPIL SHAPE and the impostor scores is smaller than the genuine scores.

PUPIL SHAPE scores of IQAA Hx gives the largest separation among the datasets.

RANKED DET:: DO LOW-QUALITY IMAGES PRODUCE HIGH FNMR OR FMR?

Poor PUPIL SHAPE scores inflates FNMR as shown in Figure 75.

As mentioned before, "the higher, the better" assumption is not valid for IQAA's A2a, C4x, and C4s; images with higher A2a, C4x or C4f PUPIL SHAPE scores give higher FNMR than the other images.

On ICE2006 images, the difference between FNMR observed for the images with the worst 15 percentile PUPIL SHAPE scores and the mid 70% is larger than between the mid 70% and the best 15 percentile.

IQAAs E2a, E2f, and Hx give the best performance ranking on the ICE2006 image.

On QFIRE A5 and QFIRE I5 images, IQAAs A2a, D3, or F1 PUPIL SHAPE scores are not a predictor of performance, since the same recognition error is observed for the three different levels of PUPIL SHAPE scores. The best performance ranking is achieved by IQAAs C4x, C4s, Hx and E2a.

The change in FMR is significantly smaller than the change in FNMR, and is almost constant for ICE2006 images.

EFFECT OF QUALITY ON FNMR : HOW QUICKLY FNMR IMPROVES WHEN POOR QUALITY SAMPLES ARE REJECTED?

Figure 76 shows that IQAA C4x is the most effective since it exhibits the largest negative derivative at the low rejection rates. It performs the best for its mated comparator, and is almost ideal on QFIRE A5 dataset.

The second best performers are IQAAs E2a and Hx. IQAA F1 performs similar to E2a and Hx on ICE2006 images, but its performance drops on QFIRE images.

Comparator C4s is the most sensitive to PUPIL SHAPE .

Rejection curves of IQAAs A2a, C4s, C4x, and C4f are generated by rejecting the images with their highest PUPIL SHAPE scores because, as mentioned before, FNMR increases as their PUPIL SHAPE scores increase.

TEST OF SIGNIFICANCE :: DO THE IMAGES INVOLVED IN SUCCESSFUL VERIFICATION ATTEMPTS HAVE SIGNIFICANTLY HIGHER QUALITY SCORES THAN THOSE INVOLVED IN FAILED VERIFICATION ATTEMPTS?

Table 25 shows that the difference in mean of pairwise PUPIL SHAPE score between images involved in correct verification and those involved in false rejection are significant when PUPIL SHAPE scores are generated by IQAAs C4x, E2a, E2f, and Hx. Therefore, PUPIL SHAPE significantly affects FNMR.

Table 26 suggests that PUPIL SHAPE has a significant effect on FMR, and the magnitude of the effect depends on the datasets and comparators. On QFIRE images, there is significant difference in mean of IQAAs C4x's and Hx's PUPIL SHAPE scores between images involved in comparisons result in correct rejection (i.e., impostor scores greater than threshold) and those involved in false match (i.e., impostor scores less than or equal to threshold). But this is not the case for IQAA E2f. On ICE2006 images, IQAAs C4x's, E2a's and E2f's PUPIL SHAPE scores pass the test of significance, but Hx's failed on two comparators.

EFFECT OF VARIATION BETWEEN THE TWO SAMPLES:: DOES SAMENESS MATTER?

Figures 77-79 confirm the earlier findings that PUPIL SHAPE affects performance, and that IQAA Hx and C4x are the best performers.

Images with the worst PUPIL SHAPE scores elevate FNMR.

Whether the difference in PUPIL SHAPE scores of the images being compared affect FNMR or not, depends on the IQAA that measures the PUPIL SHAPE and the dataset used. On ICE2006 images, sameness matters when PUPIL SHAPE is

| A2a=NEUROTECHNOLOGY-a | B3=CROSSMATCH | C4s=CAMBRIDGE-s | D3=AWARE | E2a=IRITECH-a | G1=IRISID-1 | I1=KYNEN | Hz1=L1-z1 |
| A2f=NEUROTECHNOLOGY-f | C4x=CAMBRIDGE-x | C4f=CAMBRIDGE-f | F1=MORPHO | E2f=IRITECH-f | G2=IRISID-2 | Hx=L1-x | Hz2=L1-z2 |

measured by IQAA A2a or C4x. On QFIRE I5 images, sameness does not matter, regardless of the IQAA . On QFIRE A5 images only IQAA A2a's measurement of PUPIL SHAPE is sensitive to the difference of the two images being compared. For PUPIL SHAPE scores of IQAAs E2a and Hx, sameness does not matter, regardless of the dataset. High FNMR is observed if at least one of the images has poor PUPIL SHAPE score.

OBSERVATIONS AND CONCLUSIONS

PUPIL SHAPE significantly affects the genuine score distributions. Images with poor PUPIL SHAPE inflate FNMR.

Images with the lowest PUPIL SHAPE scores result in up two orders of magnitude higher FNMR than the images with the highest GAZE ANGLE scores (IQAA C4x – Dataset QFIRE I5, IQAA C4x, and Hx – Dataset QFIRE A5 and IQAAs E2a, Hx and A2a – Dataset ICE2006). FNMR is not affected by the difference in PUPIL SHAPE scores of the two images being compared.

The effect on FMR is small.

IQAA C4x, E2a and Hx perform better than other IQAAS.

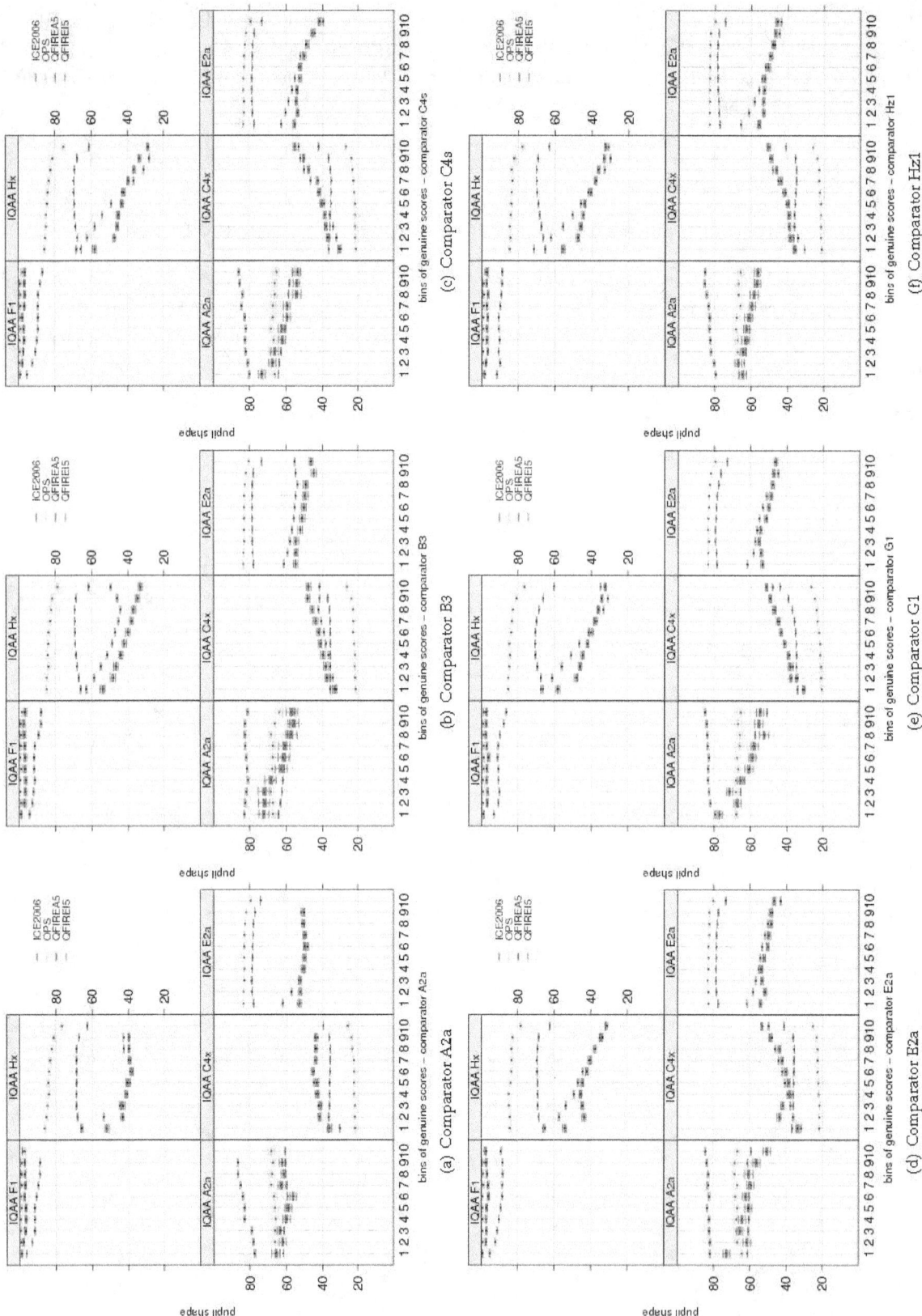

Figure 73: Pairwise PUPIL SHAPE scores vs. genuine score for the primary Class Z submissions of each participant. Each plot shows quality scores computed by different IQAA. Genuine scores are divided equally into ten groups. Groups overlap by 5 percent, meaning 5% of the data in one bin also belongs to the next bin. The bootstrapped pairwise quality for each group is shown in a box and whisker plot. Pairwise quality is computed as geometric mean of the quality of the two samples being compared. The distribution of the genuine scores are affected by PUPIL SHAPE score. The non-over lapping boxes of QFIRE images, indicate a significant effect.

| A2a=NEUROTECHNOLOGY-a | B3=CROSSMATCH | C4s=CAMBRIDGE-s | D3=AWARE | E2a=IRITECH-a | G1=IRISID-1 | I1=KYNEN | Hz1=L1-z1 |
| A2f=NEUROTECHNOLOGY-f | C4x=CAMBRIDGE-x | C4f=CAMBRIDGE-f | F1=MORPHO | E2f=IRITECH-f | G2=IRISID-2 | Hx=L1-x | Hz2=L1-z2 |

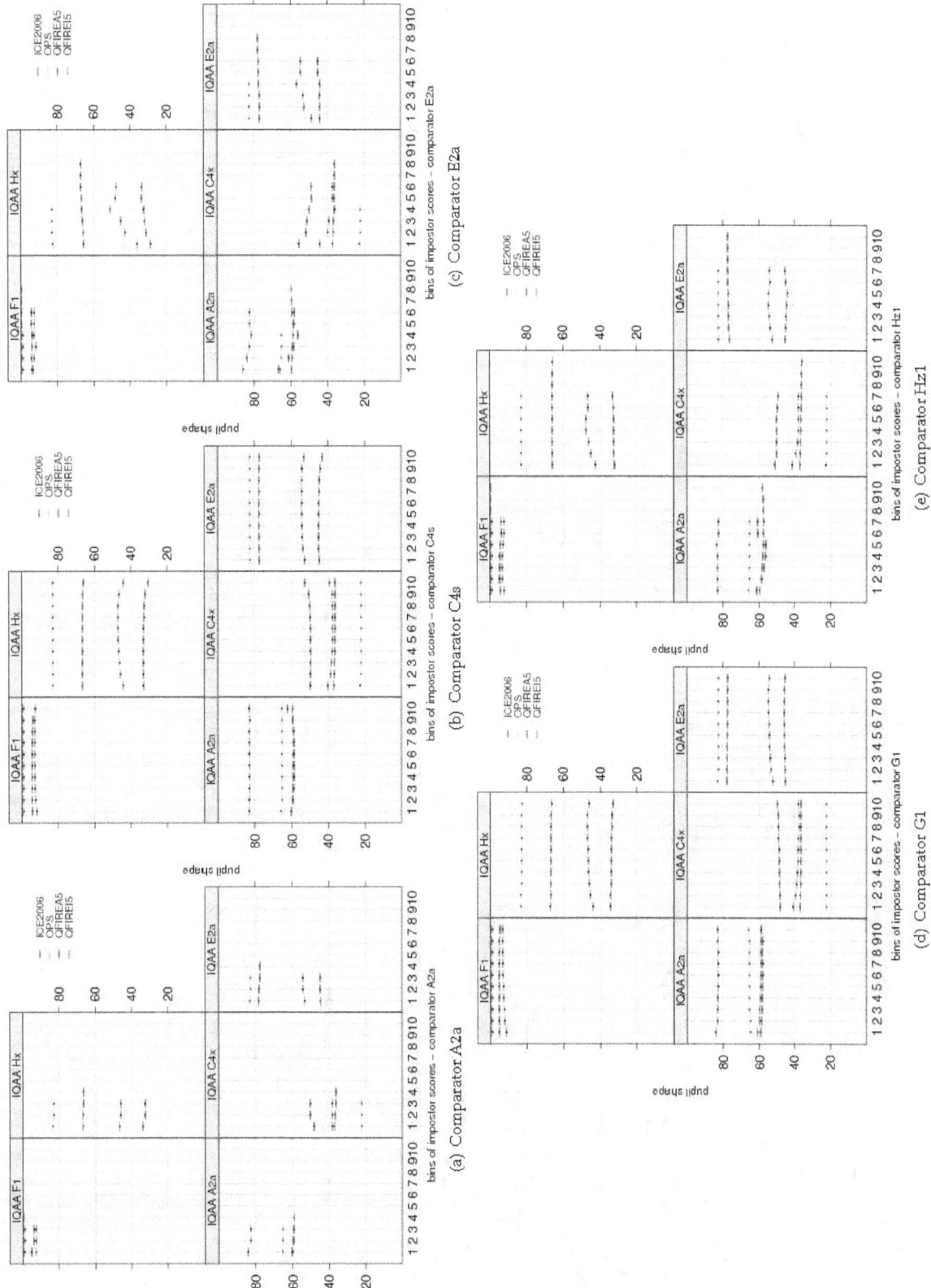

Figure 74: Pairwise PUPIL SHAPE scores vs. impostor scores for the primary Class Z submissions of each participants. Each plot shows quality scores computed by different IQAA. Similar to plots of Figure 73, impostor scores are divided equally into ten groups. Groups overlap by 5 percent. Bootstrapped pairwise quality for each group is shown in a box and whisker plot. Pairwise quality is computed as geometric mean of the quality of the two samples being compared.

153

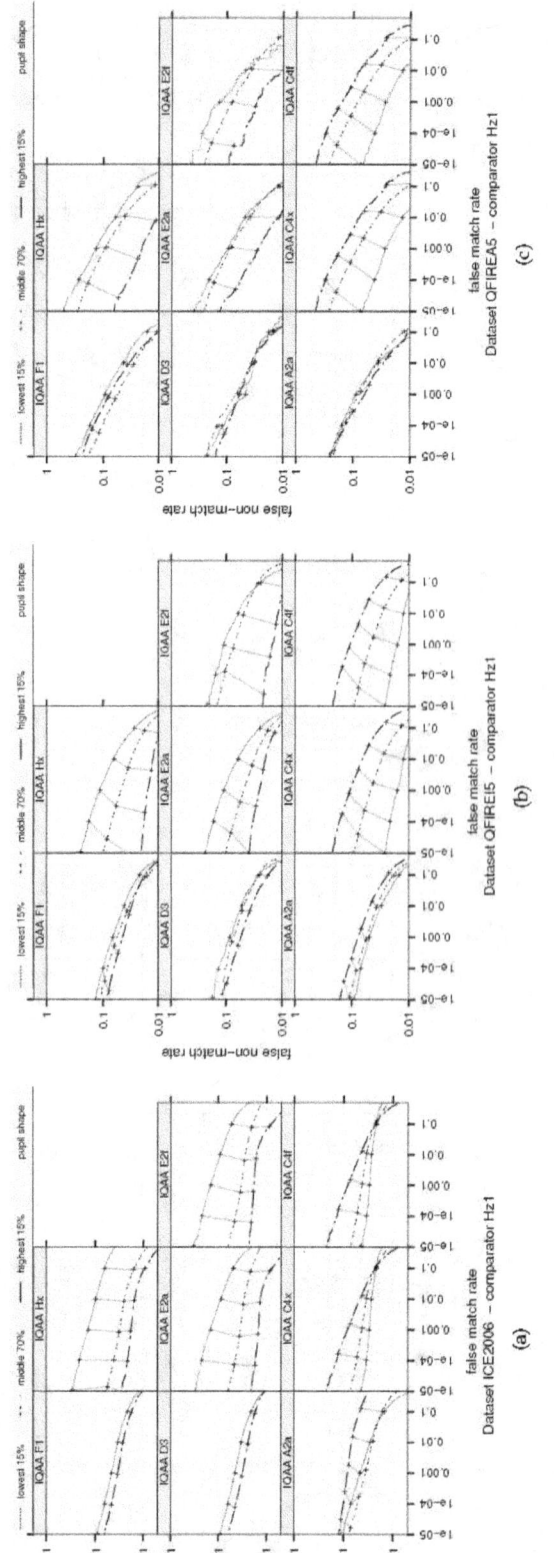

Figure 75: Ranked DET curves for comparator Hz1 and Datasets ICE2006, QFIRE I5 and QFIRE A5. The set of all comparisons were partitioned into three groups based on the pair-wise PUPIL SHAPE quality of the images being compared. The lowest quality set contains comparisons with pairwise quality in the lower 15 percentile. The highest quality set contains comparisons with pairwise quality in the upper 15 percentile. The rest of the comparisons, namely the middle 70%, made up the third set. The DETs are connected at the same score threshold values (brown lines). Lower FNMR and FMR rates are expected for better quality images. PUPIL SHAPE affect performance, images with poor PUPIL SHAPE values computed by IQAAs C4x, C4f, E2a, E2f, and Hx elevate FNMR. The effect on FMR is smaller. Note that high PUPIL SHAPE scores of IQAAs A2a C4x and C4s are associated with low-quality (in the sense of PUPIL SHAPE) and high PUPIL SHAPE score with low-quality.

| A2a=NEUROTECHNOLOGY-a | B3=CROSSMATCH | C4s=CAMBRIDGE-s | D3=AWARE | E2a=IRITECH-a | G1=IRISID-1 | I1=KYNEN | Hz1=L1-z1 |
| A2f=NEUROTECHNOLOGY-f | C4x=CAMBRIDGE-x | C4f=CAMBRIDGE-f | F1=MORPHO | E2f=IRITECH-f | G2=IRISID-2 | Hx=L1-x | Hz2=L1-z2 |

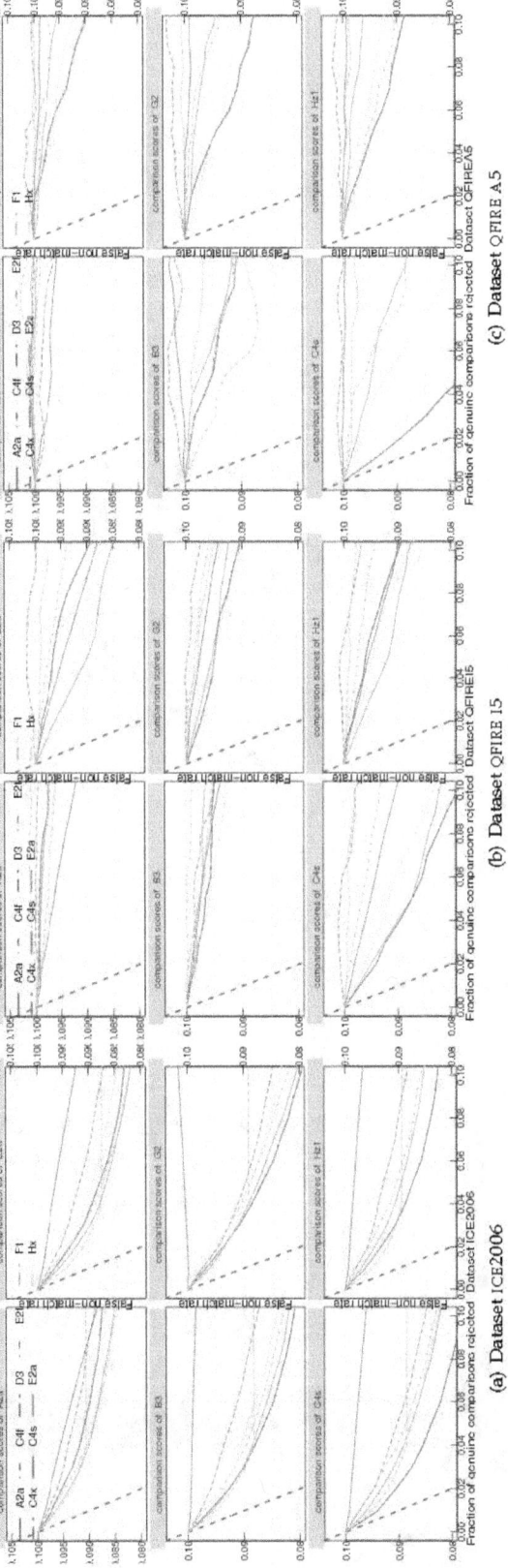

(a) Dataset ICE2006

(b) Dataset QFIRE 15

(c) Dataset QFIRE A5

Figure 76: FNMR vs. reject curves for PUPIL SHAPE scores on datasets ICE2006, QFIRE 15 and QFIRE A5. The threshold is set to give an initial FNMR = 0.1. The gray dotted line shows the ideal case where the rejection of the comparisons with the lowest ten percent quality results in zero FNMR. Rejection of images with the lowest PUPIL SHAPE reduces FNMR. Note its near ideal performance on QFIRE A5 images using its mated (i.e. C4s comparator).

155

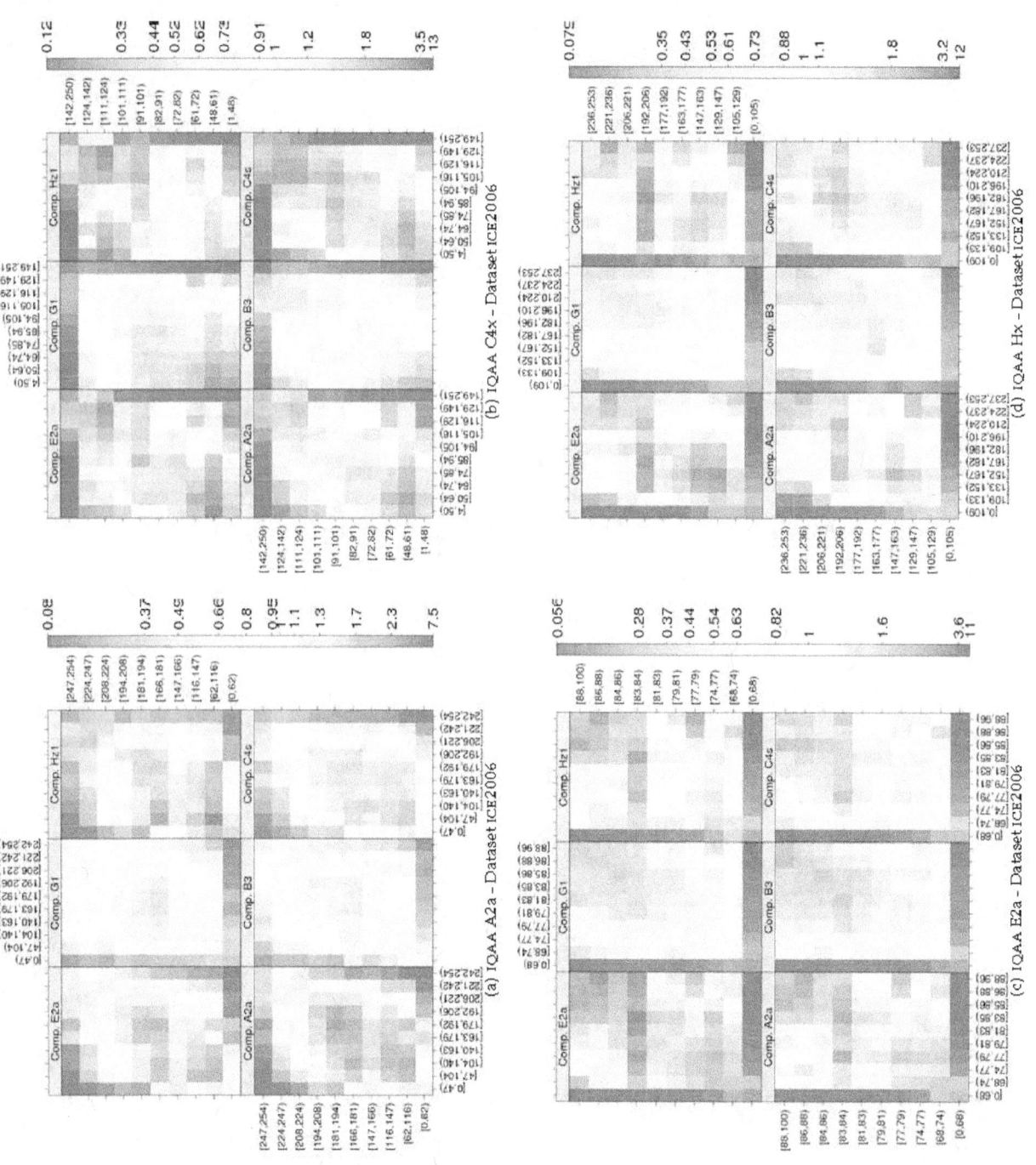

Figure 77: PUPIL SHAPE computed by primary IQAA submissions and FNMR for IQCE comparators for dataset ICE2006 . The y-axis represents enrollment samples' quality with verification samples' on the x-axis. The color scale plots $\frac{FNMR}{FNMR_0}$ for comparisons with verification and enrollment qualities ($q_{verification}, q_{enrollment}$). $FNMR_0$ is the nominal FNMR which is the false non-match rate computed over all the images at the same comparison score threshold, in this case at FMR = 0.001. Yellow/Green color represent an improvement in FNMR. Blue color represent a degradation of FNMR. White color means no change in FNMR.

| A2a=NEUROTECHNOLOGY-a | B3=CROSSMATCH | D3=AWARE | E2a=IRITECH-a | G1=IRISID-1 | I1=KYNEN | Hz1=L1-z1 |
| A2f=NEUROTECHNOLOGY-f | C4x=CAMBRIDGE-x | C4f=CAMBRIDGE-f | F1=MORPHO | E2f=IRITECH-f | G2=IRISID-2 | Hx=L1-x | Hz2=L1-z2 |

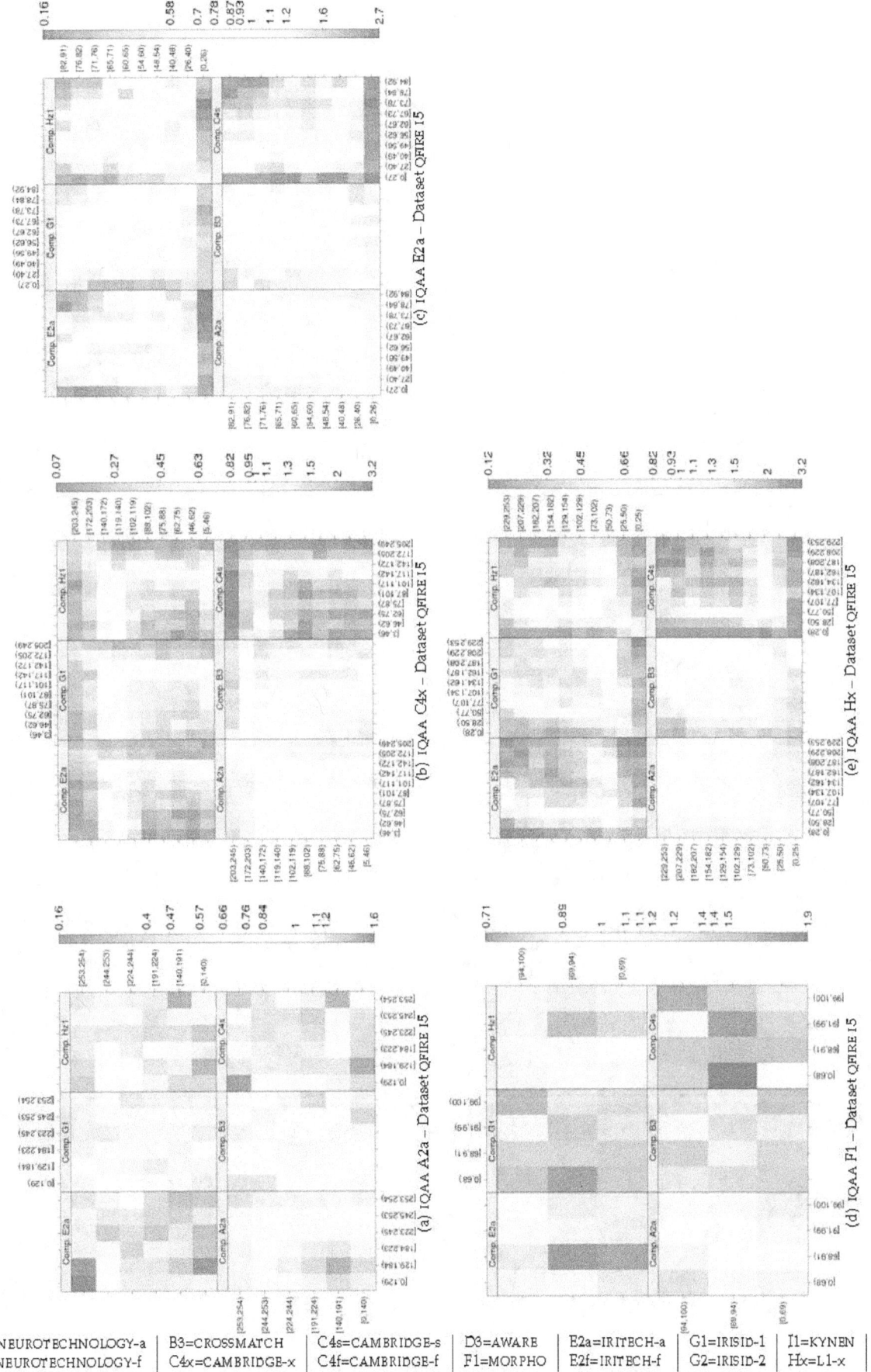

Figure 78: FNMR vs. (qverification, qenrollment). PUPIL SHAPE computed by primary IQAA submissions and FNMR for IQCB comparators for dataset QFIRE I5 . (see caption of Figure 77 for more detail.) Poor PUPIL SHAPE elevates FNMR. Sameness does not matter. Low IQAA C4x PUPIL SHAPE scores means "good quality" since they give low FNMR.

(a) IQAA A2a – Dataset QFIRE I5
(b) IQAA C4x – Dataset QFIRE I5
(c) IQAA E2a – Dataset QFIRE I5
(d) IQAA F1 – Dataset QFIRE I5
(e) IQAA Hx – Dataset QFIRE I5

| A2a=NEUROTECHNOLOGY-a | B3=CROSSMATCH | C4s=CAMBRIDGE-s | D3=AWARE | E2a=IRITECH-a | G1=IRISID-1 | I1=KYNEN | Hz1=L1-z1 |
| A2f=NEUROTECHNOLOGY-f | C4x=CAMBRIDGE-x | C4f=CAMBRIDGE-f | F1=MORPHO | E2f=IRITECH-f | G2=IRISID-2 | Hx=L1-x | Hz2=L1-z2 |

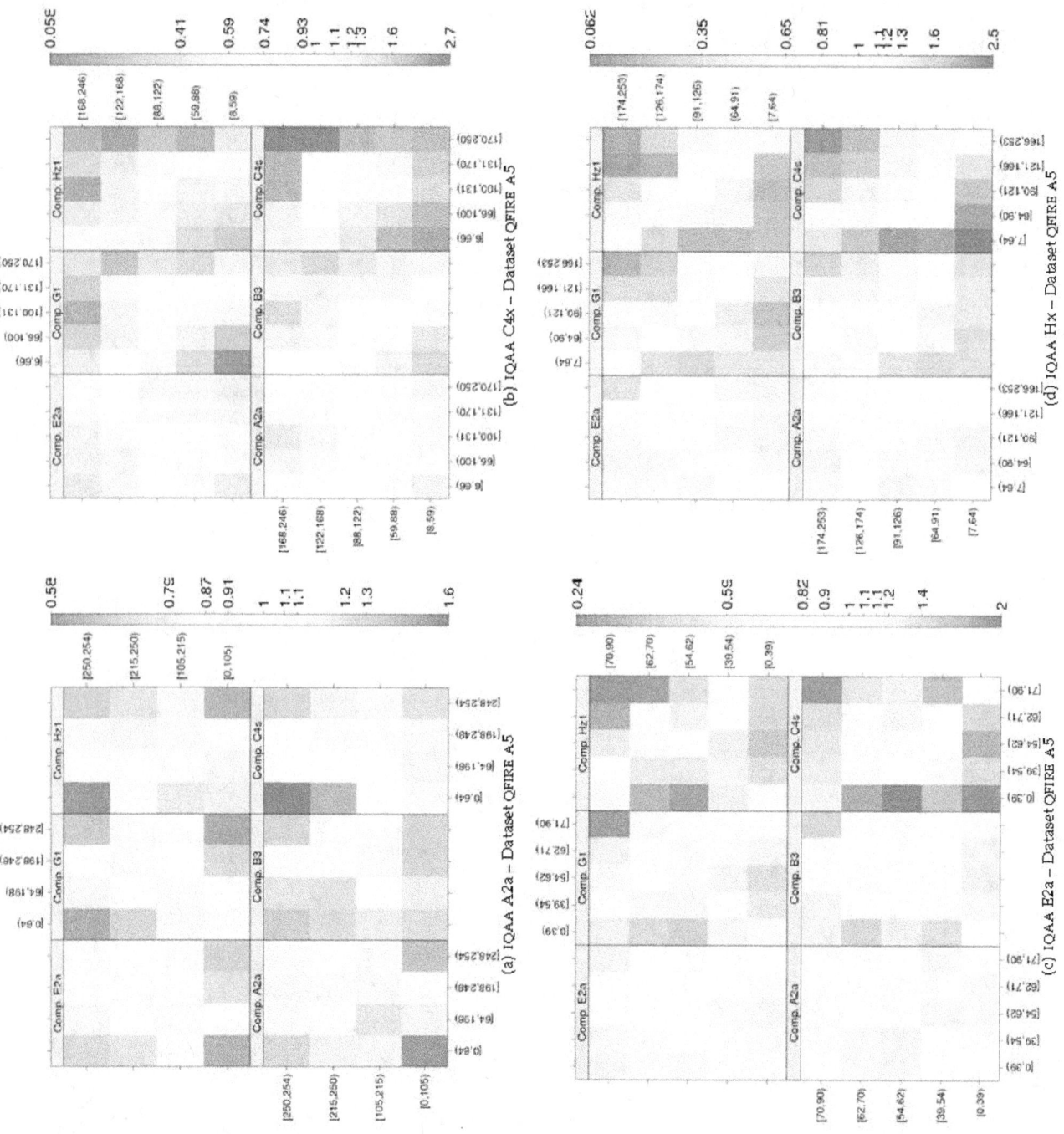

Figure 79: FNMR vs. (*verification; enrollment*). PUPIL SHAPE computed by primary IQAA submissions and FNMR for IQCE comparators for dataset QFIRE I5. (see 77 for more detail.) Poor PUPIL SHAPE elevates FNMR. Sameness does not matter. Low IQAA C4x PUPIL SHAPE scores means "good quality" since they give low FNMR.

Dataset	comparator	IQAA C4x	IQAA E2a	IQAA E2f	IQAA Hx
ICE2006	A2a	(-6.55,-6.23)	(16.92,17.12)	(16.89,17.11)	(13.57,13.98)
ICE2006	B3	(-8.88,-8.73)	(10.42,10.51)	(9.96,10.06)	(13.43,13.62)
ICE2006	C4s	(-9.26,-9.03)	(12.33,12.48)	(12.06,12.22)	(13.21,13.51)
ICE2006	E2a	(-7.89,-7.56)	(18.07,18.28)	(18.30,18.52)	(16.30,16.72)
ICE2006	G2	(-9.55,-9.39)	(11.42,11.52)	(10.97,11.07)	(12.68,12.88)
ICE2006	Hz1	(-3.14,-2.78)	(9.17,9.42)	(8.73,9.00)	(9.34,9.83)
OPS	A2a	(-9.33,-3.80)	(2.70,6.07)	(2.03,6.05)	(2.74,10.57)
OPS	B3	(-5.37,-3.05)	(2.65,4.04)	(2.11,3.79)	(3.43,6.71)
OPS	C4s	(-12.01,-7.55)	(6.14,8.85)	(5.08,8.31)	(7.77,14.06)
OPS	E2a	(-4.89,1.63)	(0.81,4.78)	(0.08,4.82)	(-2.49,6.72)
OPS	G2	(-12.63,-9.04)	(7.58,9.76)	(8.14,10.74)	(14.42,19.49)
OPS	Hz1	(-8.43,-3.20)	(5.93,9.10)	(4.66,8.46)	(3.53,10.91)
QFIREA5	A2a	(-3.22,-2.26)	(0.91,1.94)	(-3.85,3.04)	(3.58,4.59)
QFIREA5	B3	(-8.46,-7.14)	(4.77,6.27)	(8.21,18.46)	(9.13,10.61)
QFIREA5	C4s	(-14.84,-13.59)	(9.13,10.50)	(9.81,18.00)	(13.72,15.06)
QFIREA5	E2a	(-4.59,-3.69)	(3.01,3.97)	(2.82,8.89)	(7.75,8.68)
QFIREA5	G2	(-10.22,-9.29)	(5.00,6.02)	(4.27,10.04)	(10.56,11.55)
QFIREA5	Hz1	(-10.41,-8.82)	(5.03,6.75)	(4.38,13.94)	(9.53,11.23)
QFIREI5	A2a	(-4.79,-4.42)	(4.65,5.09)	(1.38,5.39)	(8.18,8.70)
QFIREI5	B3	(-4.42,-4.07)	(1.62,2.04)	(3.73,8.61)	(3.97,4.51)
QFIREI5	C4s	(-13.03,-12.57)	(14.99,15.54)	(9.70,15.09)	(18.60,19.25)
QFIREI5	E2a	(-9.39,-8.91)	(11.21,11.79)	(9.10,14.09)	(16.04,16.73)
QFIREI5	G2	(-8.14,-7.74)	(7.12,7.61)	(7.85,12.37)	(12.57,13.15)
QFIREI5	Hz1	(-8.38,-7.80)	(8.10,8.81)	(7.36,13.01)	(13.46,14.30)

Table 25: Tukey HSD difference in mean of PUPIL SHAPE scores. Each cell shows the 95% confidence level in difference in mean of pairwise quality for images verified correctly (i.e., the genuine score equal or less than threshold) and those rejected falsely (i.e., the genuine score larger than threshold). Quality scores were computed by the SDK identified by the column header and comparison scores were generated by the SDK identified by the row header. If the interval does not contain zero, the difference in mean is significant. Cells where difference in mean is not significant have pink background. For monotonically increasing quality components (all except DILATION, and depending on quality implementation GRAY SCALE SPREAD), the expected behavior is to have higher quality scores for the pair of enrollment and verification images that give genuine comparison scores less than threshold. The pairwise quality is computed as geometric mean of the quality of two samples being compared. Threshold is set to give false match rate of 0.001.

159

Dataset	comparator	IQAA C4x	IQAA E2a	IQAA E2f	IQAA Hx
ICE2006	A2a	(-2.78,-2.13)	(-1.08,-0.61)	(-1.06,-0.56)	(-0.32,0.55)
ICE2006	B3	(-3.52,-3.06)	(4.82,5.15)	(4.67,5.02)	(3.38,4.01)
ICE2006	C4s	(-2.04,-1.54)	(0.65,1.01)	(0.66,1.04)	(0.54,1.22)
ICE2006	E2a	(-3.63,-3.13)	(2.52,2.88)	(2.89,3.28)	(4.37,5.06)
ICE2006	G2	(-1.86,-1.34)	(-0.85,-0.48)	(-0.76,-0.36)	(-0.44,0.27)
ICE2006	Hz1	(-1.90,-1.35)	(1.27,1.68)	(1.39,1.82)	(0.58,1.33)
OPS	A2a	(-0.56,0.01)	(-0.58,-0.21)	(-0.65,-0.20)	(-1.47,-0.63)
OPS	B3	(-2.00,-1.54)	(0.43,0.72)	(0.61,0.98)	(1.90,2.58)
OPS	C4s	(-1.02,-0.56)	(-0.00,0.30)	(0.08,0.45)	(0.53,1.22)
OPS	E2a	(-0.51,-0.04)	(0.30,0.61)	(0.52,0.90)	(0.83,1.53)
OPS	G2	(-0.44,0.03)	(-0.57,-0.27)	(-0.55,-0.18)	(-1.16,-0.46)
OPS	Hz1	(-1.26,-0.80)	(0.06,0.36)	(0.07,0.44)	(0.31,1.00)
QFIREA5	A2a	(-5.03,-3.86)	(3.18,4.53)	(7.51,16.14)	(3.75,4.85)
QFIREA5	C4s	(-2.84,-1.77)	(0.34,1.56)	(-0.69,7.82)	(0.79,1.78)
QFIREA5	E2a	(-17.51,-16.45)	(-6.39,-5.17)	(-14.20,-4.58)	(2.18,3.17)
QFIREA5	G2	(-1.75,-0.66)	(2.09,3.35)	(4.17,12.72)	(0.17,1.19)
QFIREA5	Hz1	(-8.76,-7.69)	(-1.18,0.05)	(-7.44,0.95)	(3.12,4.11)
QFIREI5	A2a	(-3.64,-2.97)	(3.01,3.83)	(2.61,10.97)	(1.04,2.03)
QFIREI5	C4s	(-9.02,-8.44)	(5.02,5.72)	(7.07,14.13)	(7.62,8.47)
QFIREI5	E2a	(-20.45,-19.87)	(12.23,12.94)	(13.89,19.15)	(24.72,25.58)
QFIREI5	G2	(-10.71,-6.34)	(2.25,7.58)	(-10.14,54.56)	(5.56,12.04)
QFIREI5	Hz1	(-9.64,-9.06)	(5.18,5.89)	(11.08,17.09)	(6.30,7.15)

Table 26: Tukey HSD mean difference in PUPIL SHAPE scores. Each cell shows the 95% confidence level in difference in mean of pairwise quality for images correctly rejected (i.e., the impostor score equal or greater than threshold) and those falsely matched (i.e., the impostor score less than threshold). Quality scores were computed by the SDK identified by the column header and comparison scores were generated by the SDK identified by the row header. If the interval does not contain zero, the difference in mean is significant. Cells where difference in mean is not significant are shaded in pink. For monotonic increasing quality components (all except DILATION, and depending on quality implementation GRAY SCALE SPREAD), the expected behavior is to have higher quality scores for the pair of (enrollment, verification) images that result in impostor comparison scores equal or greater than threshold. Pairwise quality is computed as geometric mean of the quality of two samples being compared. Threshold is set to give false match rate of 0.001.

160

9.9 Margin

Five IQCE submissions (A2a, A2f, D3, E2a, E2f) from three organizations generated MARGIN scores.

The distribution of their MARGIN scores is shown in Figure 80. In order to make the boxplots more readable, quality scores in [0–254] range were linearly scaled back to [0–100].

IQCE did not repeat IREX1 study on margin, and only evaluated the effectiveness of the submitted MARGIN scores in prediction of performance. High MARGIN score and no effect on performance is expected for QFIRE images, since these images were prepared per requirements for [1] KIND CROPPED.

No effect on performance is expected on OPS images either, mainly because of its selection procedure, and secondly, visual inspection confirmed that the images do have sufficient margins.

IQAA A2a's MARGIN scores are highly correlated with its IRIS SIZE on ICE2006 images and DILATION on QFIRE I5 images.

RELATIONSHIP WITH THE DISTRIBUTION OF GENUINE SCORES

Figures 81 shows that MARGIN does not affect the genuine score distributions. All IQAAs give comparable scores to ICE2006 and OPS datasets. Ditto the QFIRE A5 and QFIRE I5 datasets.

All IQAAs give ICE2006 and OPS images higher MARGIN scores than QFIRE images.

RELATIONSHIP WITH THE DISTRIBUTION OF IMPOSTOR SCORES

Impostor distribution is not affected by MARGIN as shown in Figure 82.

RANKED DET:: DO LOW-QUALITY IMAGES PRODUCE HIGH FNMR OR FMR?

The ranked DET of Figure 83 shows that MARGIN scores of IQAAs D3, E2a, and E2f do not give any ranking of performance. IQAA A2a gives three distinct but overlapping DET curves.

EFFECT OF QUALITY ON FNMR : HOW QUICKLY FNMR IMPROVES WHEN POOR QUALITY SAMPLES ARE REJECTED?

Rejection of images with low IQAA A2a's MARGIN only slightly improves FNMR for ICE2006 images. OPS and QFIRE I5 are not affected. IQAAs D3, E2a, and E2f MARGIN scores are not predictor of performance.

TEST OF SIGNIFICANCE :: DO THE IMAGES INVOLVED IN SUCCESSFUL VERIFICATION ATTEMPTS HAVE SIGNIFICANTLY HIGHER QUALITY SCORES THAN THOSE INVOLVED IN FAILED VERIFICATION ATTEMPTS?

Results of Tukey HSD test for the difference in pairwise MARGIN scores between images involved in comparisons that result in correct match and those that caused false reject are shown in Table 27.

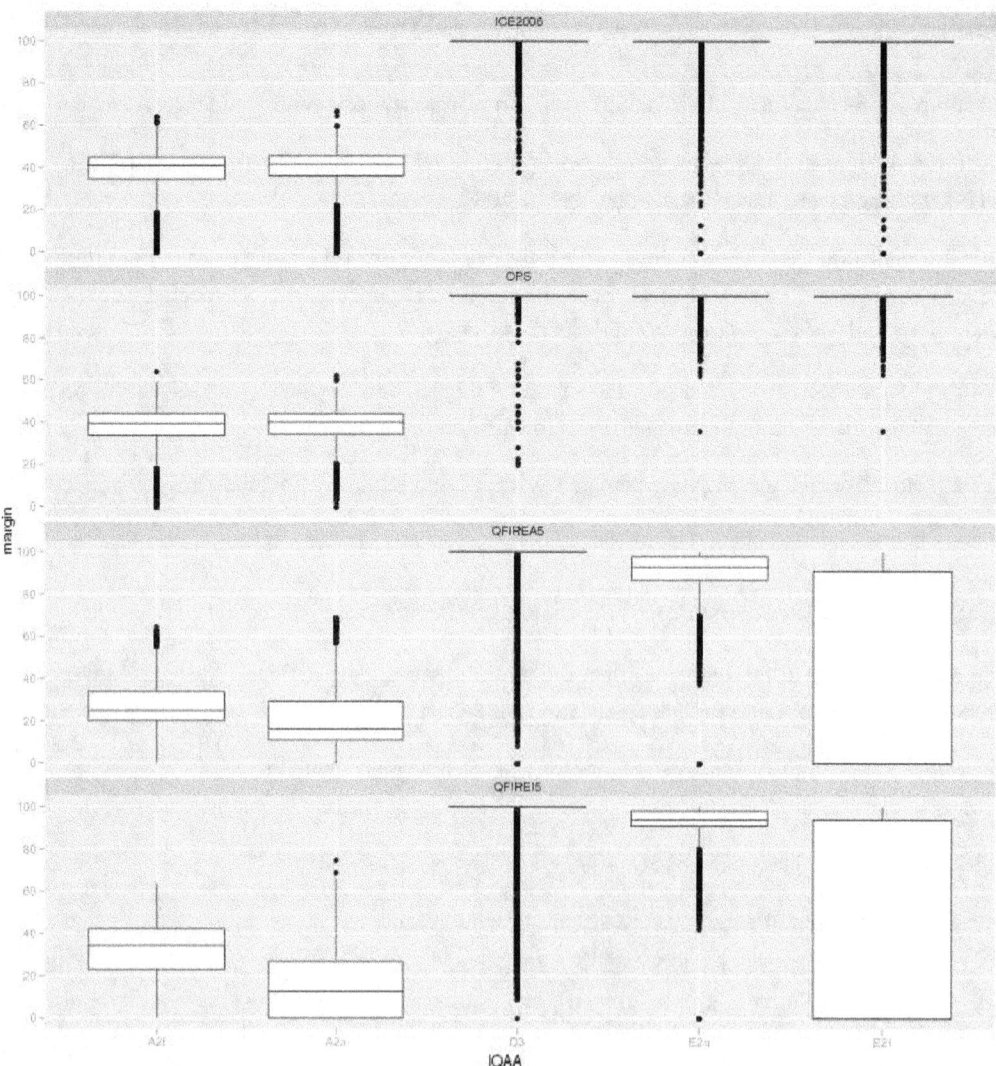

Figure 80: Box and whisker plots of the IQAAs that generate MARGIN scores.

On OPS image, neither of IQAAs give significantly different MARGIN scores.

There is a significant, but small, difference for MARGIN scores generated by IQAA A2a, however, A2a's MARGIN scores are highly correlated with its IRIS SIZE on ICE2006 images and DILATION on QFIRE I5 images.

IQAA E2f's MARGIN scores of images successfully verified are not significantly different from the images that are falsely rejected.

Also, the negative sign for IQAAs E2a and E2f on QFIRE images indicates that the pairwise MARGIN scores' of images that are successfully verified are lower than those results in false reject. This behavior does not concur with the IQAAs behavior on ICE2006 images, where the difference in mean of the two groups are positive numbers.

Table 28 shows that the difference in pairwise MARGIN scores of images correctly rejected (i.e., the impostor score equal or greater than threshold) and those falsely matched (i.e., the impostor score less than threshold) are not significant.

EFFECT OF VARIATION BETWEEN THE TWO SAMPLES:: DOES SAMENESS MATTER?

Figure 85 confirms the earlier findings that on ICE2006 images, IQAA A2a's MARGIN scores has a small effect on FNMR. However, sameness does not matter.

No change in FNMR is observed for OPS and QFIRE images.

Results for IQAAs D3, E2a, and E2f are not shown because the number of distinct scores generated by them were too few to make the binning possible.

OBSERVATIONS AND CONCLUSIONS

As expected, MARGIN scores do not affect the performance of QFIRE or OPS images.

On ICE2006 images, images with low MARGIN scores increase FNMR slightly.

Since, for the existing range of margins in the IQCE test data, MARGIN scores of the IQCE submissions do not affect performance, we conclude that the margin requirements recommended by IREXI and already incorporated in [1] are adequate.

| A2a=NEUROTECHNOLOGY-a | B3=CROSSMATCH | C4s=CAMBRIDGE-s | D3=AWARE | E2a=IRITECH-a | G1=IRISID-1 | I1=KYNEN | Hz1=L1-z1 |
| A2f=NEUROTECHNOLOGY-f | C4x=CAMBRIDGE-x | C4f=CAMBRIDGE-f | F1=MORPHO | E2f=IRITECH-f | G2=IRISID-2 | Hx=L1-x | Hz2=L1-z2 |

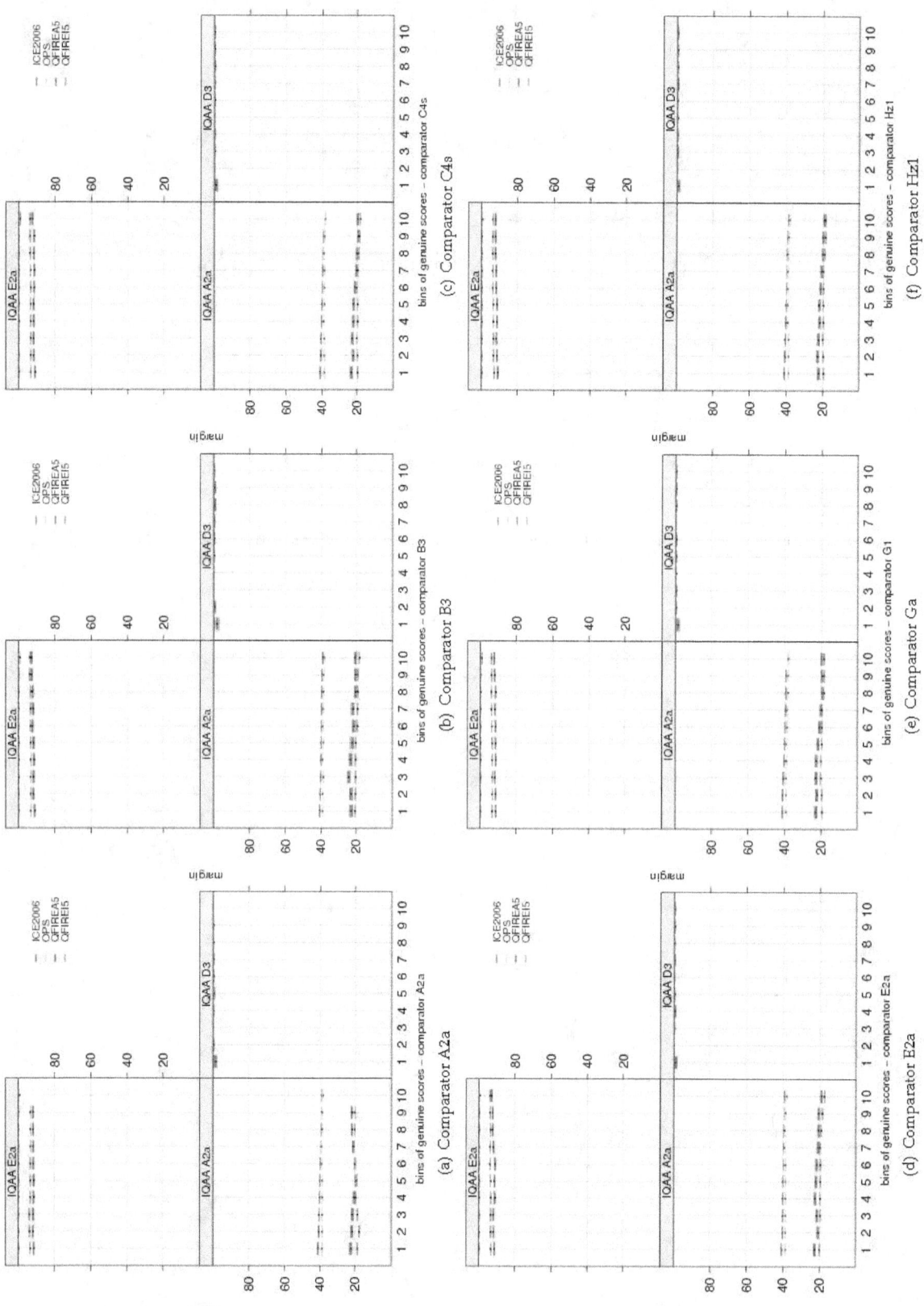

Figure 81: Pairwise MARGIN scores vs. genuine score for the primary Class Z submissions of each participant. Each plot shows quality scores computed by different IQAA.. Genuine scores are divided equally into ten groups. Groups overlap by 5 percent. Bootstrapped pairwise quality for each group is shown in a box and whisker plot. Pairwise quality is computed as geometric mean of the quality of the two samples being compared. The genuine distributions are not affected by MARGIN .

A2a=NEUROTECHNOLOGY-a | B3=CROSSMATCH | C4s=CAMBRIDGE-s | D3=AWARE | E2a=IRITECH-a | G1=IRISID-1 | I1=KYNEN | Hz1=L1-z1
A2f=NEUROTECHNOLOGY-f | C4x=CAMBRIDGE-x | C4f=CAMBRIDGE-f | F1=MORPHO | E2f=IRITECH-f | G2=IRISID-2 | Hx=L1-x | Hz2=L1-z2

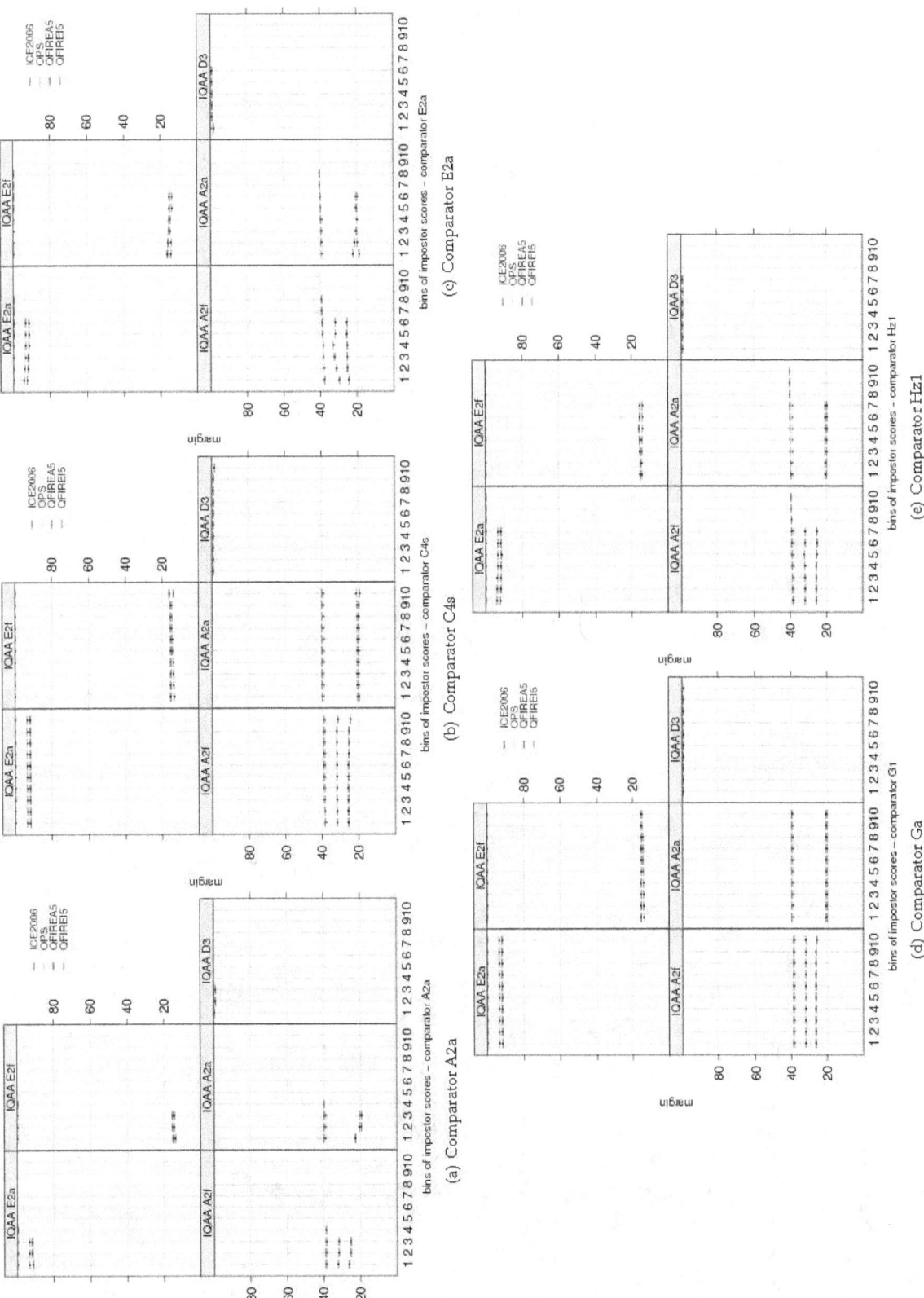

Figure 82: Pairwise MARGIN scores vs. impostor scores for the primary Class Z submissions of each participants. Each plot shows quality scores computed by different IQAA. Similar to plots of Figure 81, impostor scores are divided equally into ten groups. Groups overlap by 5 percent. Bootstrapped pairwise quality for each group is shown in a box and whisker plot. Pairwise quality is computed as geometric mean of the quality of the two samples being compared. The impostor distributions are not affected by MARGIN.

165

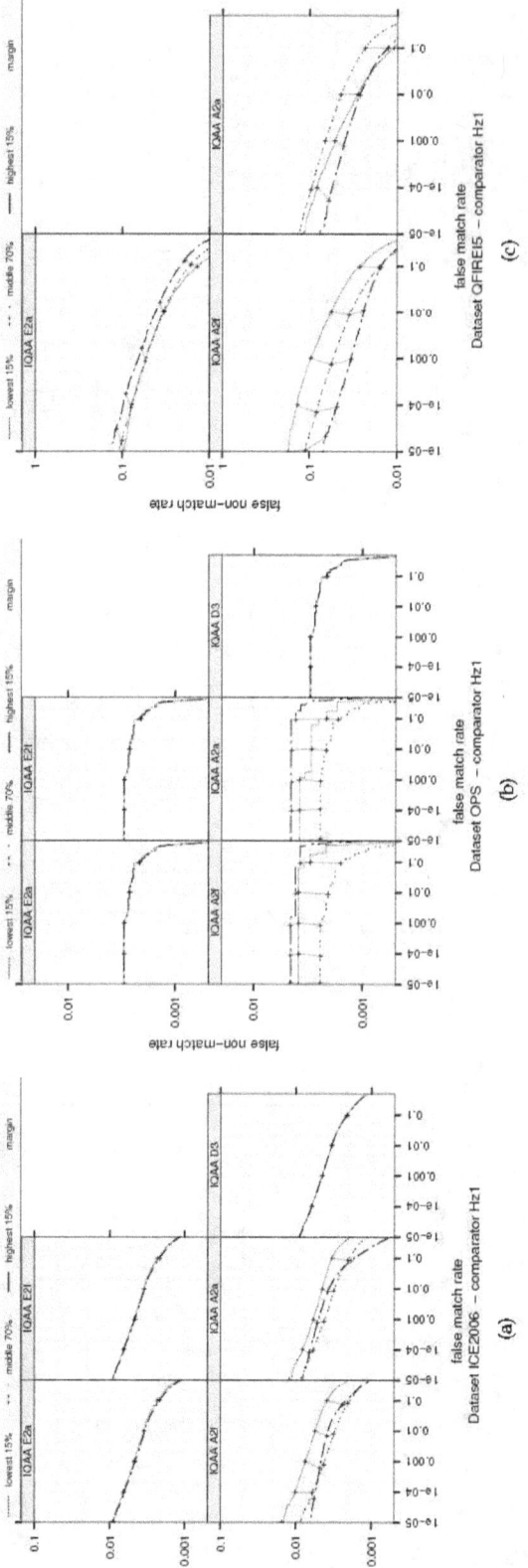

Figure 83: Ranked DET curves for comparator Hz1 and Data sets ICE2006 and OPS . The set of all comparisons were partitioned into three groups based on the pair-wise MARGIN quality of the images being compared. The lowest quality set contains comparisons with pairwise quality in the lower 15 percentile. The highest quality set contains comparisons with pairwise quality in the upper 15 percentile. The rest of the comparisons, namely the middle 70%, made up the third set. The DETs are connected at the same score threshold values (brown lines). Lower FNMR and FMR rates are expected for better quality images. Only IQAA A2a MARGIN scores give three distinct DET curves, but the performance of the images with its low, mid or high MARGIN scores are quite comparable.

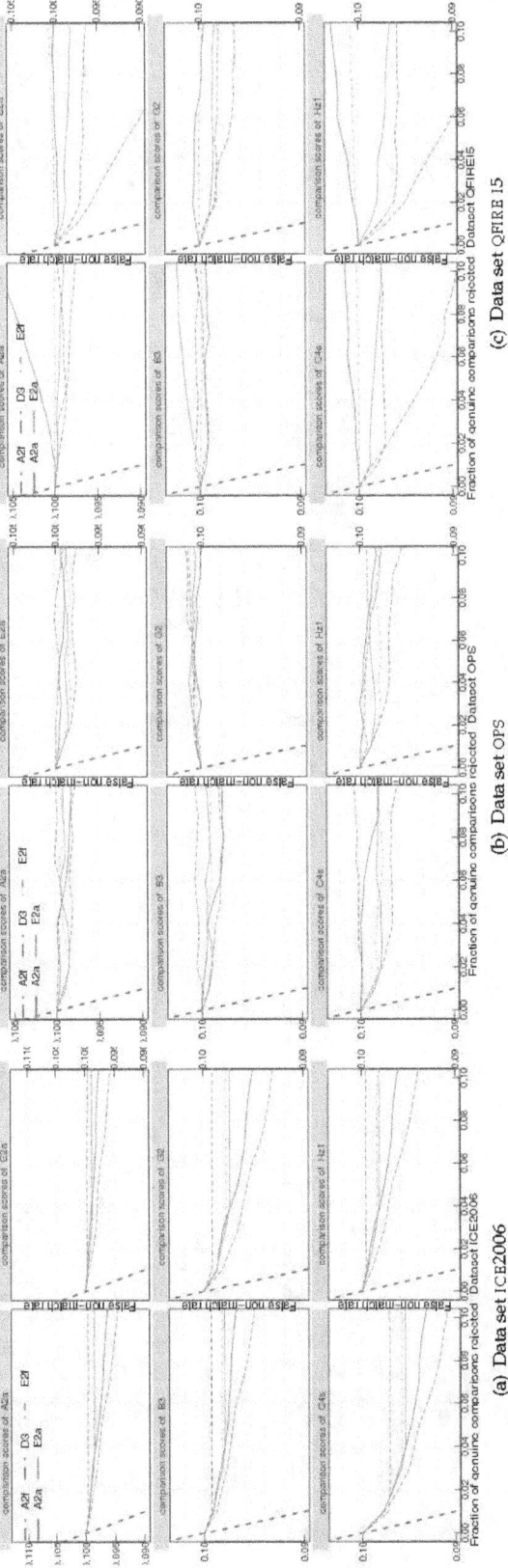

Figure 84: FNMR vs. reject curves for MARGIN scores on datasets ICE2006 and QFIRE 15. The threshold is set to give an initial FNMR = 0.1. The gray dotted line shows the ideal case where the rejection of the comparisons with the lowest ten percent quality results in zero FNMR. Rejection of images with low IQAA A2a's MARGIN scores slightly improves FNMR. IQAAs D3, E2a and E2f do not show any improvement in FNMR after rejecting images with their low MARGIN scores.

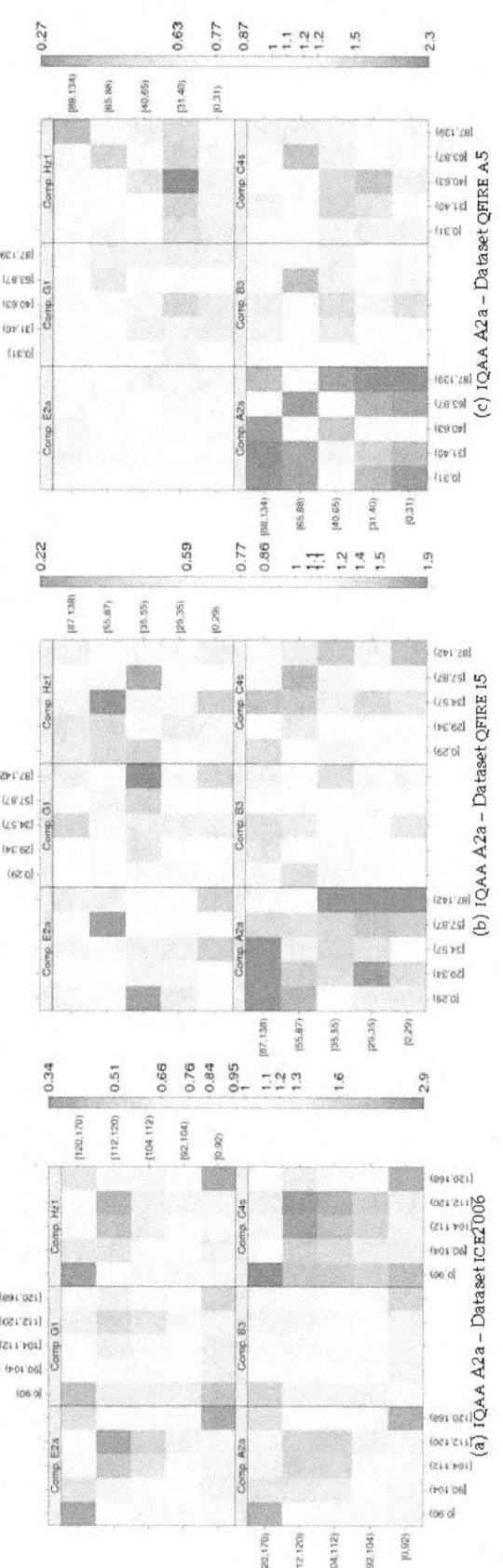

Figure 85: MARGIN computed by primary IQAA submissions and FNMR for IQCE comparators for datasets OPS and ICE2006. The y-axis represents enrollment samples' quality with verification samples' quality on the x-axis. The MARGIN scores are quantized into 10 quantiles. The color scale plots $\frac{FNMR}{FNMR_0}$ for comparisons with verification and enrollment qualities (q_{verification}, q_{enrollment}). $FNMR_0$ is the nominal FNMR which is the false non-match rate computed over all the images at the same comparison score threshold, in this case at FMR = 0.001. Yellow/Green color represent an improvement in FNMR. Blue color represent a degradation of FNMR. White color means no change in FNMR.

(a) IQAA A2a – Dataset ICE2006

(b) IQAA A2a – Dataset QFIRE 15

(c) IQAA A2a – Dataset QFIRE A5

| A2a=NEUROTECHNOLOGY-a | B3=CROSSMATCH | C4s=CAMBRIDGE-s | D3=AWARE | E2a=IRITECH-a | G1=IRISID-1 | I1=KYNEN | Hz1=L1-z1 |
| A2f=NEUROTECHNOLOGY-f | C4x=CAMBRIDGE-x | C4f=CAMBRIDGE-f | F1=MORPHO | E2f=IRITECH-f | G2=IRISID-2 | Hx=L1-x | Hz2=L1-z2 |

Dataset	comparator	IQAA A2f	IQAA E2a	IQAA E2f
ICE2006	A2a	(1.89,2.06)	(0.62,0.67)	(0.52,0.57)
ICE2006	B3	(2.35,2.43)	(0.74,0.76)	(0.73,0.75)
ICE2006	C4s	(7.82,7.94)	(4.07,4.11)	(3.94,3.98)
ICE2006	E2a	(2.39,2.57)	(0.63,0.68)	(0.61,0.66)
ICE2006	G2	(3.78,3.86)	(1.19,1.21)	(1.13,1.15)
ICE2006	Hz1	(1.50,1.71)	(0.39,0.46)	(0.28,0.34)
OPS	A2a	(-0.10,3.55)	(-0.13,0.44)	(-0.11,0.43)
OPS	B3	(-0.25,1.28)	(-0.07,0.17)	(-0.08,0.14)
OPS	C4s	(-0.84,2.09)	(0.03,0.49)	(0.05,0.49)
OPS	E2a	(-0.81,3.49)	(-0.09,0.58)	(-0.09,0.55)
OPS	G2	(0.32,2.70)	(0.57,0.94)	(0.57,0.92)
OPS	Hz1	(-1.64,1.81)	(-0.13,0.39)	(-0.12,0.38)
QFIREA5	A2a	(-0.25,0.13)	(-0.26,0.01)	(-1.50,0.38)
QFIREA5	B3	(-0.53,0.02)	(-1.04,-0.64)	(-1.37,1.51)
QFIREA5	C4s	(0.72,1.24)	(-1.00,-0.63)	(-2.11,0.41)
QFIREA5	E2a	(0.69,1.05)	(-0.36,-0.10)	(-0.94,0.81)
QFIREA5	G2	(0.36,0.74)	(-0.81,-0.53)	(-1.24,0.64)
QFIREA5	Hz1	(1.21,1.86)	(-1.00,-0.54)	(-1.08,2.05)
QFIREI5	A2a	(0.53,0.71)	(0.37,0.44)	(-1.82,-1.08)
QFIREI5	B3	(-1.88,-1.70)	(-0.53,-0.45)	(-1.53,-0.75)
QFIREI5	C4s	(2.34,2.56)	(-0.26,-0.17)	(-0.92,0.02)
QFIREI5	E2a	(2.92,3.15)	(-0.36,-0.26)	(-2.54,-1.54)
QFIREI5	G2	(0.04,0.23)	(-0.46,-0.38)	(-0.65,0.18)
QFIREI5	Hz1	(3.22,3.50)	(-0.08,0.04)	(-3.87,-2.67)

Table 27: Tukey HSD difference in mean of MARGIN scores. Each cell shows the 95% confidence level in difference in mean of pairwise quality for images verified correctly (i.e., the genuine score equal or less than threshold) and those rejected falsely (i.e., the genuine score larger than threshold). Quality scores were computed by the SDK identified by the column header and comparison scores were generated by the SDK identified by the row header. If the interval does not contain zero, the difference in mean is significant. Cells where difference in mean is not significant have pink background. For monotonically increasing quality components (all except DILATION, and depending on quality implementation GRAY SCALE SPREAD), the expected behavior is to have higher quality scores for the pair of enrollment and verification images that give genuine comparison scores less than threshold. The pairwise quality is computed as geometric mean of the quality of two samples being compared. Threshold is set to give false match rate of 0.001.

Dataset	comparator	IQAA A2f	IQAA E2a	IQAA E2f
ICE2006	A2a	(-0.15,0.25)	(-0.12,0.01)	(-0.12,0.01)
ICE2006	B3	(3.80,4.09)	(0.17,0.26)	(0.17,0.26)
ICE2006	C4s	(0.99,1.31)	(-0.04,0.07)	(-0.03,0.08)
ICE2006	E2a	(3.02,3.34)	(0.07,0.17)	(0.11,0.21)
ICE2006	G2	(-0.16,0.16)	(-0.10,0.00)	(-0.09,0.02)
ICE2006	Hz1	(0.93,1.28)	(0.08,0.19)	(0.12,0.23)
OPS	A2a	(-0.20,0.24)	(-0.05,0.02)	(-0.04,0.02)
OPS	B3	(1.00,1.35)	(0.12,0.17)	(0.09,0.15)
OPS	C4s	(0.28,0.63)	(0.02,0.08)	(0.02,0.07)
OPS	E2a	(-0.41,-0.05)	(-0.03,0.03)	(-0.03,0.03)
OPS	G2	(-0.41,-0.06)	(-0.06,-0.00)	(-0.02,-0.00)
OPS	Hz1	(0.19,0.55)	(0.02,0.08)	(0.02,0.07)
QFIREA5	A2a	(1.32,1.82)	(1.45,1.81)	(-1.15,1.14)
QFIREA5	C4s	(0.07,0.52)	(-0.10,0.23)	(-0.68,1.40)
QFIREA5	E2a	(0.08,0.53)	(-4.88,-4.55)	(0.54,2.61)
QFIREA5	G2	(0.65,1.10)	(0.07,0.39)	(-1.89,0.28)
QFIREA5	Hz1	(0.34,0.79)	(-1.43,-1.10)	(-0.05,2.04)
QFIREI5	A2a	(-0.19,0.15)	(0.33,0.46)	(0.75,2.29)
QFIREI5	C4s	(0.04,0.34)	(0.35,0.46)	(-1.49,-0.15)
QFIREI5	E2a	(2.75,3.04)	(-1.35,-1.24)	(-5.36,-4.02)
QFIREI5	G2	(-0.31,1.94)	(-0.01,0.84)	(-6.50,3.51)
QFIREI5	Hz1	(-0.82,-0.53)	(-0.60,-0.48)	(-4.91,-3.58)

Table 28: Tukey HSD mean difference in MARGIN scores. Each cell shows the 95% confidence level in difference in mean of pairwise quality for images correctly rejected (i.e., the impostor score equal or greater than threshold) and those falsely matched (i.e., the impostor score less than threshold). Quality scores were computed by the SDK identified by the column header and comparison scores were generated by the SDK identified by the row header. If the interval does not contain zero, the difference in mean is significant. Cells where difference in mean is not significant are shaded in pink. For monotonic increasing quality components (all except DILATION, and depending on quality implementation GRAY SCALE SPREAD), the expected behavior is to have higher quality scores for the pair of (enrollment, verification) images that result in impostor comparison scores equal or greater than threshold. Pairwise quality is computed as geometric mean of the quality of two samples being compared. Threshold is set to give false match rate of 0.001.

170

| A2a=NEUROTECHNOLOGY-a | B3=CROSSMATCH | C4s=CAMBRIDGE-s | D3=AWARE | E2a=IRITECH-a | G1=IRISID-1 | I1=KYNEN | Hz1=L1-z1 |
| A2f=NEUROTECHNOLOGY-f | C4x=CAMBRIDGE-x | C4f=CAMBRIDGE-f | F1=MORPHO | E2f=IRITECH-f | G2=IRISID-2 | Hx=L1-x | Hz2=L1-z2 |

9.10   Sharpness

Defocus blur can result from many sources, but in general, defocus occurs when the object (an iris in this case) is outside the depth of field of the camera. The further an object is from the focal plane the higher the degree of defocus. Depth of field is affected by aperture size, the smaller the aperture size the greater the depth of field.

SHARPNESS and compression should not be confounded because they produce different degradations of the image. For example, very severe JPEG compression produces post-optical block quantisation artefacts (sharp edges) that can cause a high SHARPNESS scores.

Several methods for measuring the MOTION BLUR of an iris image have been reported in the academic literature: [8, 23, 15, 20, 14] etc.

All IQCE submissions except I1 supported measurement of SHARPNESS of the images. The distribution of their SHARP-NESS scores is shown in Figure 86. In order to make the boxplots more readable, quality scores in [0–254] range were linearly scaled back to [0–100].

RELATIONSHIP WITH THE DISTRIBUTION OF GENUINE SCORES

The genuine score distributions of all the IQCE comparators are affected by SHARPNESS scores as shown in Figure 87. Images with large (i.e., good) SHARPNESS scores give low genuine scores.

The largest change in SHARPNESS scores vs. the genuine scores is observed for IQAAs A2a, C4x, followed by G2, and F1. The non-overlapping boxes suggest that the change in these IQAAS' SHARPNESS score is significant. The smallest change is observed for IQAA E2a, and B3.

Among the datasets, QFIRE I5 gets the lowest SHARPNESS score and the largest negative derivative, which is expected given its collection protocol as explained in Section 4. The OPS dataset get the highest SHARPNESS score and the least change across the genuine scores.

The range of SHARPNESS scores differs among the IQAAS, indicating the SHARPNESS scores of different IQAA are not interoperable.

RELATIONSHIP WITH THE DISTRIBUTION OF IMPOSTOR SCORES

Figure 88 indicates that SHARPNESS scores affect the impostor distributions; however, the effect is smaller than of the genuine scores.

Expectedly, the lowest SHARPNESS scores and the biggest change is observed for QFIRE I5 images.

RANKED DET:: DO LOW-QUALITY IMAGES PRODUCE HIGH FNMR OR FMR?

Not surprisingly, SHARPNESS affects both FNMR and FMR as shown in the ranked DET curves of Figure 89. The difference in FNMR can be as high as an order of magnitude (IQAA C4x - QFIRE I5 dataset).

On ICE2006 images IQAAs C4x, C4f, and Hx give the best separation in performance between the images in the lowest 15 percentile SHARPNESS scores and those in the highest 15 percentile.

| A2a=NEUROTECHNOLOGY-a | B3=CROSSMATCH | C4s=CAMBRIDGE-s | D3=AWARE | E2a=IRITECH-a | G1=IRISID-1 | I1=KYNEN | Hz1=L1-z1 |
| A2f=NEUROTECHNOLOGY-f | C4x=CAMBRIDGE-x | C4f=CAMBRIDGE-f | F1=MORPHO | E2f=IRITECH-f | G2=IRISID-2 | Hx=L1-x | Hz2=L1-z2 |

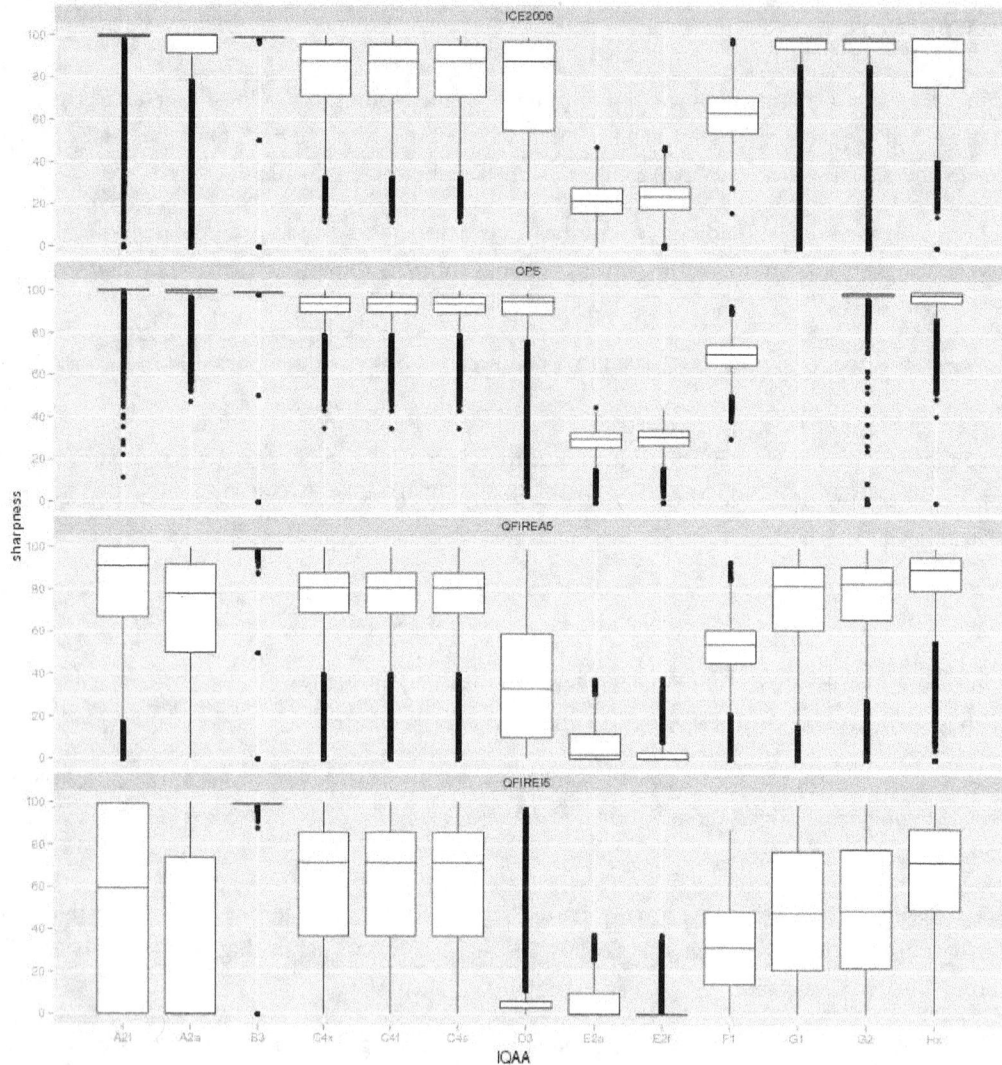

Figure 86: Box and whisker plots of the IQAAs that generate SHARPNESS scores.

IQAA B3's SHARPNESS scores are not predictive of performance of comparator Hz1.

QFIRE I5 dataset has a wide range of defocus. SHARPNESS scores of IQAAs C4x, C4f and A2a (FOLLOWED BY F1) give the best performance ranking, with an order of magnitude difference between images in the lowest and the highest 15 percentile. SHARPNESS scores of IQAA Hx, D3, and B3 are not effective.

EFFECT OF QUALITY ON FNMR : HOW QUICKLY FNMR IMPROVES WHEN POOR QUALITY SAMPLES ARE REJECTED?

As shown in figure 90, IQAA A2a is the best performer on ICE2006 images for all IQCE comparators, and near ideal for its mates comparator. Rejection of the worst 4% SHARPNESS scores of IQAA A2a reduces its FNMR to 0.08 from its original 0.1 value (i.e., 20 percent reduction). The performance of IQAAs E2a, E2f, F1, D3, C4x, and Hx on ICE2006 images are quite comparable. IQAA G1 is the least effective. Reject curves of IQAAs C4x, C4f and Hz are identical.

On QFIRE I5 images, IQAA C4x is the most effective for all the comparators, particularly for comparators C4s, Hz1, and E2a.

TEST OF SIGNIFICANCE :: DO THE IMAGES INVOLVED IN SUCCESSFUL VERIFICATION ATTEMPTS HAVE SIGNIFICANTLY HIGHER QUALITY SCORES THAN THOSE INVOLVED IN FAILED VERIFICATION ATTEMPTS?

Table 29 shows that there is a significant difference between the mean of pairwise SHARPNESS quality for images verified correctly (i.e., the genuine score equal or less than threshold) and those rejected falsely (i.e., the genuine score larger than threshold) for all datasets except OPS. The difference is larger for IQAAs A2f C4x, F1, G1, G2 and Hx than IQAA B3 or E2f. IQAAs A2f, C4x, F1, G1 and G2 show larger difference for QFIRE I5 images than other dataset, which is the desired behavior.

Likewise, neglecting the OPS dataset, Table 30 shows that the difference in mean of pairwise SHARPNESS scores of images correctly rejected (i.e., the impostor score equal or greater than threshold) and those falsely matched (i.e., the impostor score less than threshold) for all IQAAs except B3. The biggest difference is observed for IQAAs A2a, C4x, F1, and G1 (or G2).

EFFECT OF VARIATION BETWEEN THE TWO SAMPLES:: DOES SAMENESS MATTER?

Figure 92 shows that images with low SHARPNESS scores elevate FNMR. Variation of SHARPNESS scores between the two images being compared does not affect the FNMR, except when both images have the lowest possible SHARPNESS scores. FNMR is increased when at least one of the the images has low a SHARPNESS score. IQAAs D3 and E2a are the least effective. Also, the number of distinct SHARPNESS scores generated by these two are fewer than other IQAAS.

IQAA C4x, F1, and Hx are most effective in their assessment of SHARPNESS .

On ICE2006 images, no change in FNMR is observed across the range of any IQAA's SHARPNESS scores (see Figure 91). This can be explained by the lack of defocus impairment in ICE2006 images.

OBSERVATIONS AND CONCLUSIONS

SHARPNESS affects FNMR and FMR. Images with low SHARPNESS inflate FNMR and FMR . The difference between SHARPNESS scores of the two images being compared does not affect the FNMR, except when both images have the lowest possible SHARPNESS scores.

On the QFIRE I5 images, IQAA C4x and F1 are most effective in their assessment of SHARPNESS , for their native iris recognition algorithms as well as others. On the ICE2006 images, A2a and E2a are more effective.

QFIRE I5 dataset, by design, covers a wide range of SHARPNESS , which makes it most appropriate for assessment of IQAA's SHARPNESS scores.

173

| A2a=NEUROTECHNOLOGY-a | B3=CROSSMATCH | C4s=CAMBRIDGE-s | D3=AWARE | E2a=IRITECH-a | G1=IRISID-1 | I1=KYNEN | Hz1=L1-z1 |
| A2f=NEUROTECHNOLOGY-f | C4x=CAMBRIDGE-x | C4f=CAMBRIDGE-f | F1=MORPHO | E2f=IRITECH-f | G2=IRISID-2 | Hx=L1-x | Hz2=L1-z2 |

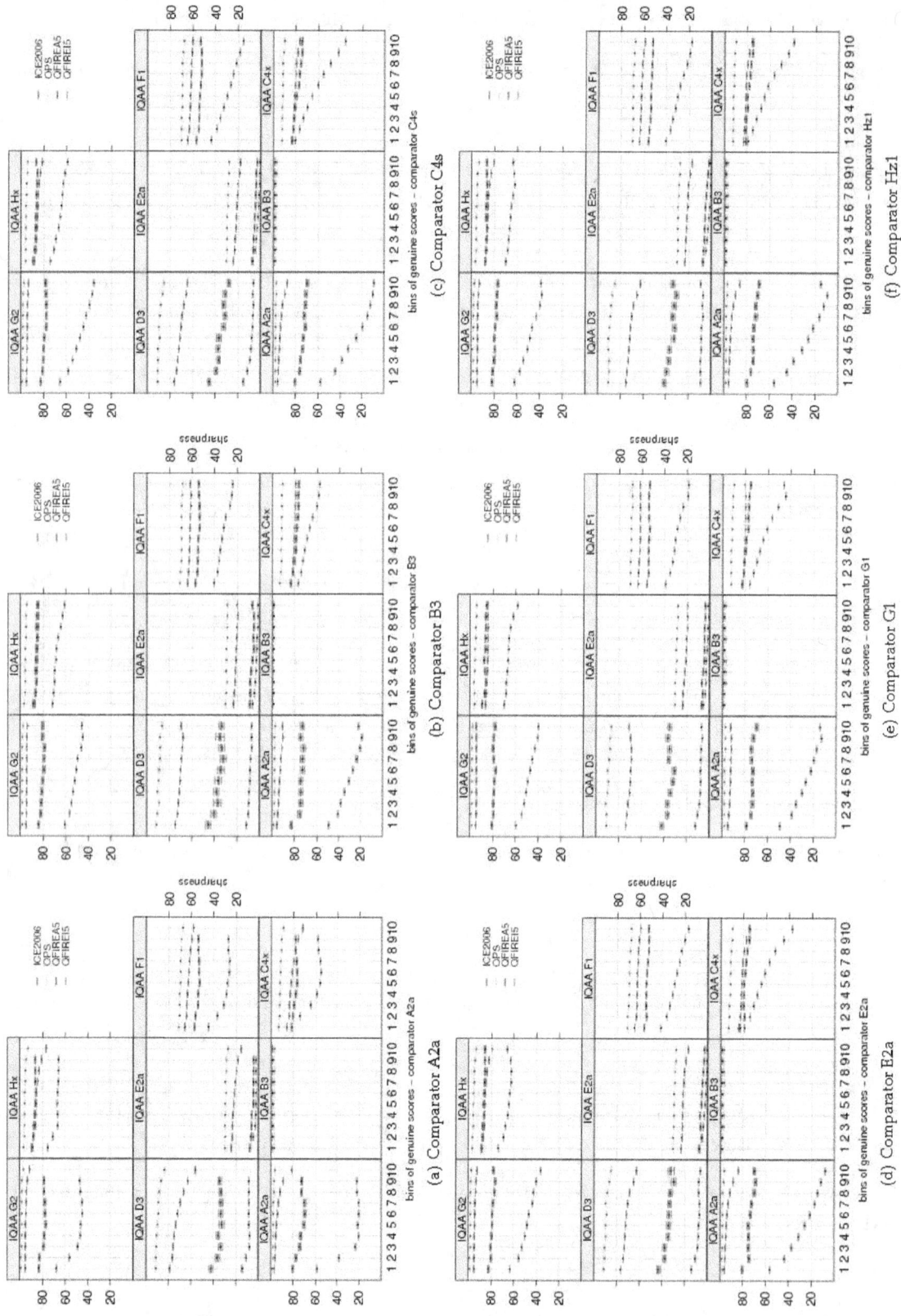

Figure 87: Pairwise SHARPNESS scores vs. genuine score for the primary Class Z submissions of each participant. Each plot shows quality scores computed by different IQAA. Genuine scores are divided equally into ten groups. Groups overlap by 5 percent, meaning 5% of the data in one bin also belongs to the next bin. The bootstrapped pairwise quality for each group is shown in a box and whisker plot. Pairwise quality is computed as geometric mean of the quality of the two samples being compared. The genuine score distributions are affected by SHARPNESS scores. IQAA E2a and B3 exhibit the smallest change.

174

A2a=NEUROTECHNOLOGY-a | B3=CROSSMATCH | C4s=CAMBRIDGE-s | D3=AWARE | E2a=IRITECH-a | G1=IRISID-1 | I1=KYNEN | Hz1=L1-z1
A2f=NEUROTECHNOLOGY-f | C4x=CAMBRIDGE-x | C4f=CAMBRIDGE-f | F1=MORPHO | E2f=IRITECH-f | G2=IRISID-2 | Hx=L1-x | Hz2=L1-z2

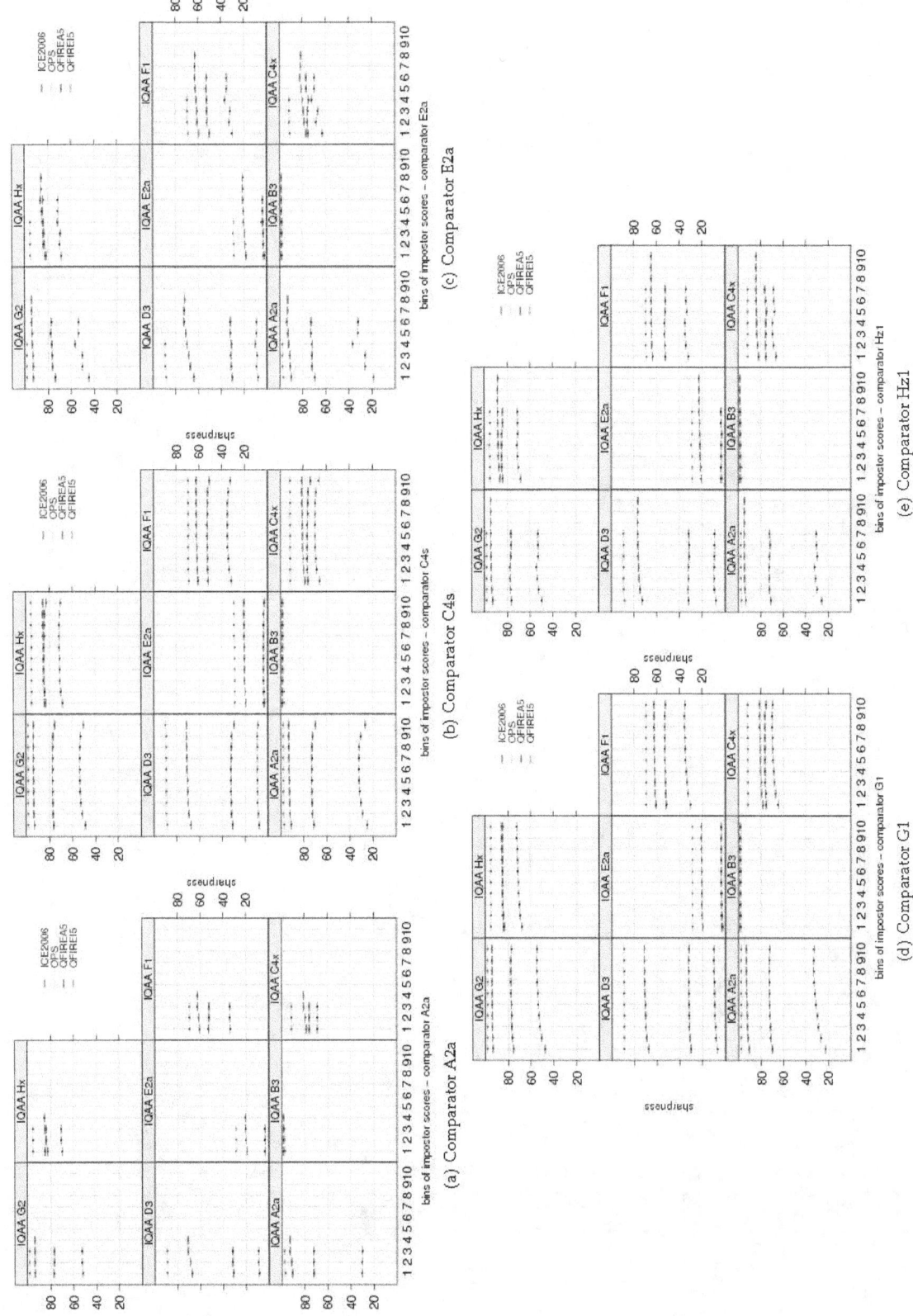

Figure 88: Pairwise SHARPNESS scores vs. impostor scores for the primary Class Z submissions of each participant. Each plot shows quality scores computed by different IQAA. Similar to plots of figure 87, impostor scores are divided equally into ten groups, overlapping by 5 percent. The bootstrapped pairwise quality for each group is shown in a box and whisker plot. Pairwise quality is computed as geometric mean of the quality of the two samples being compared.

| A2a=NEUROTECHNOLOGY-a | B3=CROSSMATCH | C4s=CAMBRIDGE-s | D3=AWARE | E2a=IRITECH-a | G1=IRISID-1 | I1=KYNEN | Hz1=L1-z1 |
| A2f=NEUROTECHNOLOGY-f | C4x=CAMBRIDGE-x | C4f=CAMBRIDGE-f | F1=MORPHO | E2f=IRITECH-f | G2=IRISID-2 | Hx=L1-x | Hz2=L1-z2 |

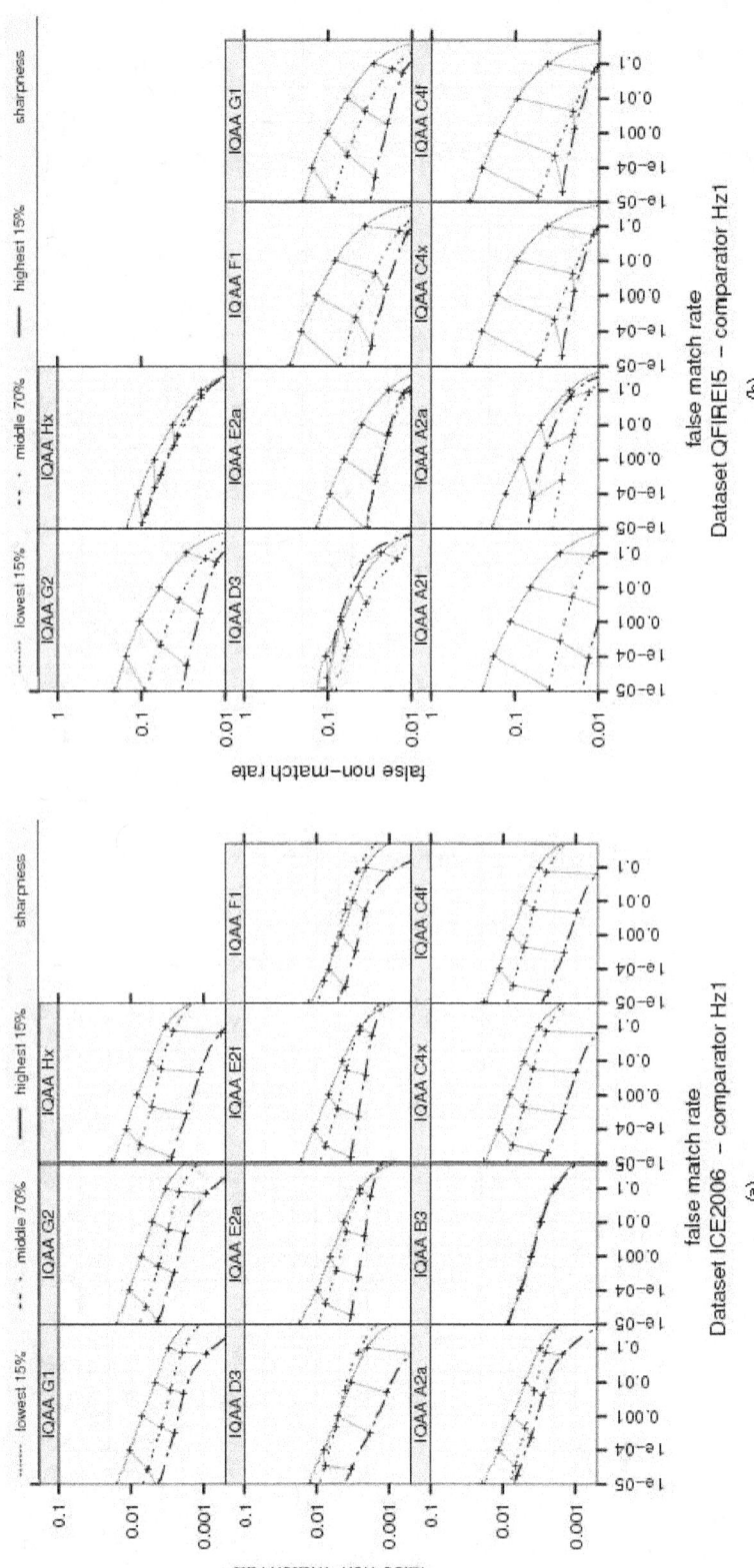

Figure 89: Ranked DET curves for comparator Hz1 and Datasets ICE2006 and QFIRE I5. The set of all comparisons were partitioned into three groups based on the pair-wise quality SHARPNESS of the images being compared. The lowest quality set contains comparisons with pairwise quality in the lower 15 percentile. The highest quality set contains comparisons with pairwise quality in the upper 15 percentile. The rest of the comparisons, namely the middle 70%, made up the third set. The DETs are connected at the same score threshold values (brown lines). Lower FNMR and FMR rates are expected for better quality images. Error rates observed for images with the lowest SHARPNESS scores generated of IQAAs C4x, C4f and A2a is an order of magnitude bigger than the images with the best SHARPNESS scores.

176

| A2a=NEUROTECHNOLOGY-a | B3=CROSSMATCH | C4s=CAMBRIDGE-s | D3=AWARE | E2a=IRITECH-a | G1=IRISID-1 | I1=KYNEN | Hz1=L1-z1 |
| A2f=NEUROTECHNOLOGY-f | C4x=CAMBRIDGE-x | C4f=CAMBRIDGE-f | F1=MORPHO | E2f=IRITECH-f | G2=IRISID-2 | Hx=L1-x | Hz2=L1-z2 |

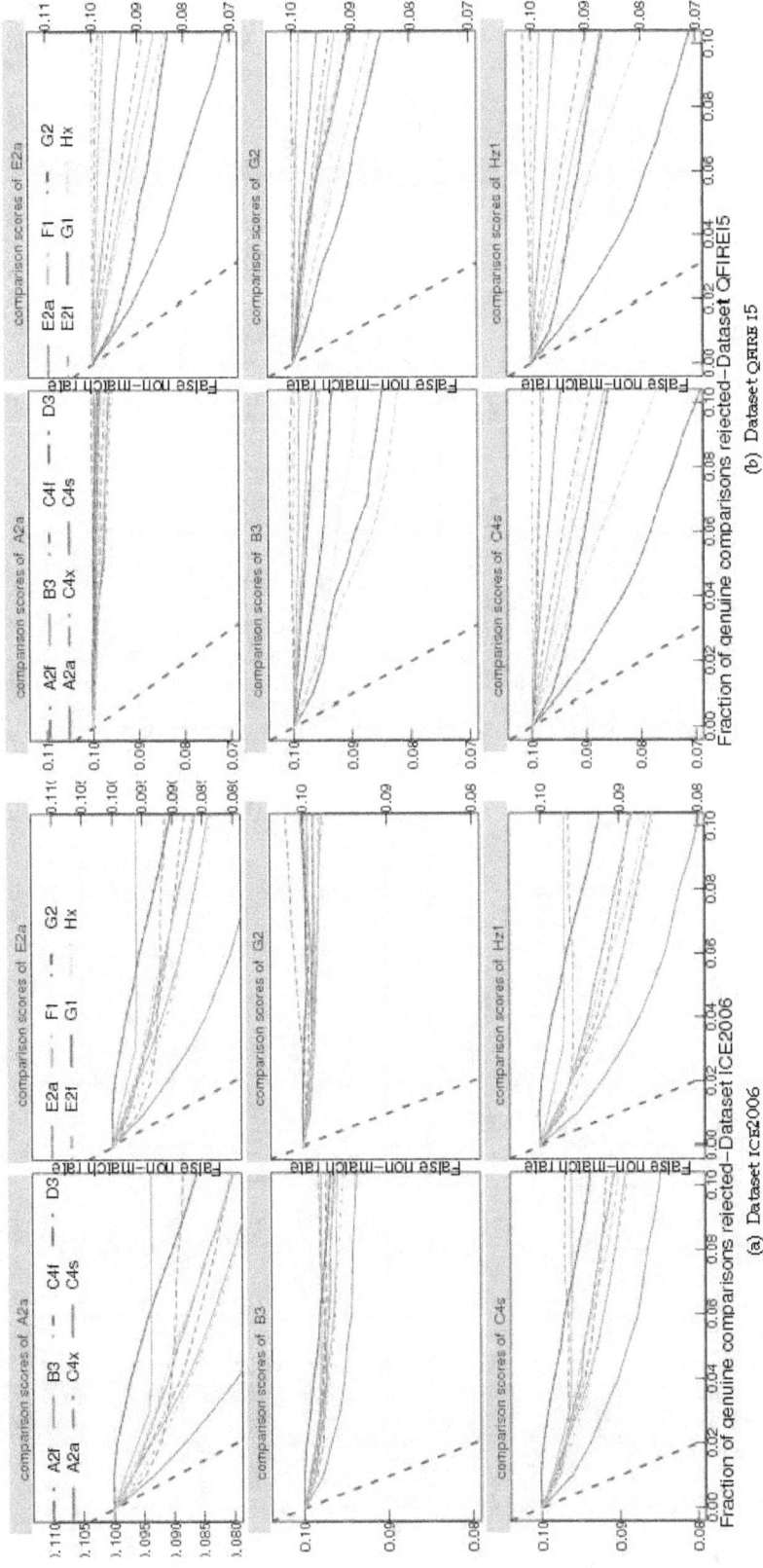

Figure 90: FNMR vs. reject curves for SHARPNESS scores on datasets ICE2006 and QFIRE 15. The threshold is set to give an initial FNMR = 0.1. The gray dotted line shows the ideal case where the rejection of the comparisons with the lowest ten percent quality results in zero FNMR. IQAA A2a performs the best on ICE2006 and IQAA C4x on QFIRE 15 images.

A2a=NEUROTECHNOLOGY-a	B3=CROSSMATCH	C4s=CAMBRIDGE-s	D3=AWARE	E2a=IRITECH-a	G1=IRISID-1	I1=KYNEN	Hz1=L1-z1
A2f=NEUROTECHNOLOGY-f	C4x=CAMBRIDGE-x	C4f=CAMBRIDGE-f	F1=MORPHO	E2f=IRITECH-f	G2=IRISID-2	Hx=L1-x	Hz2=L1-z2

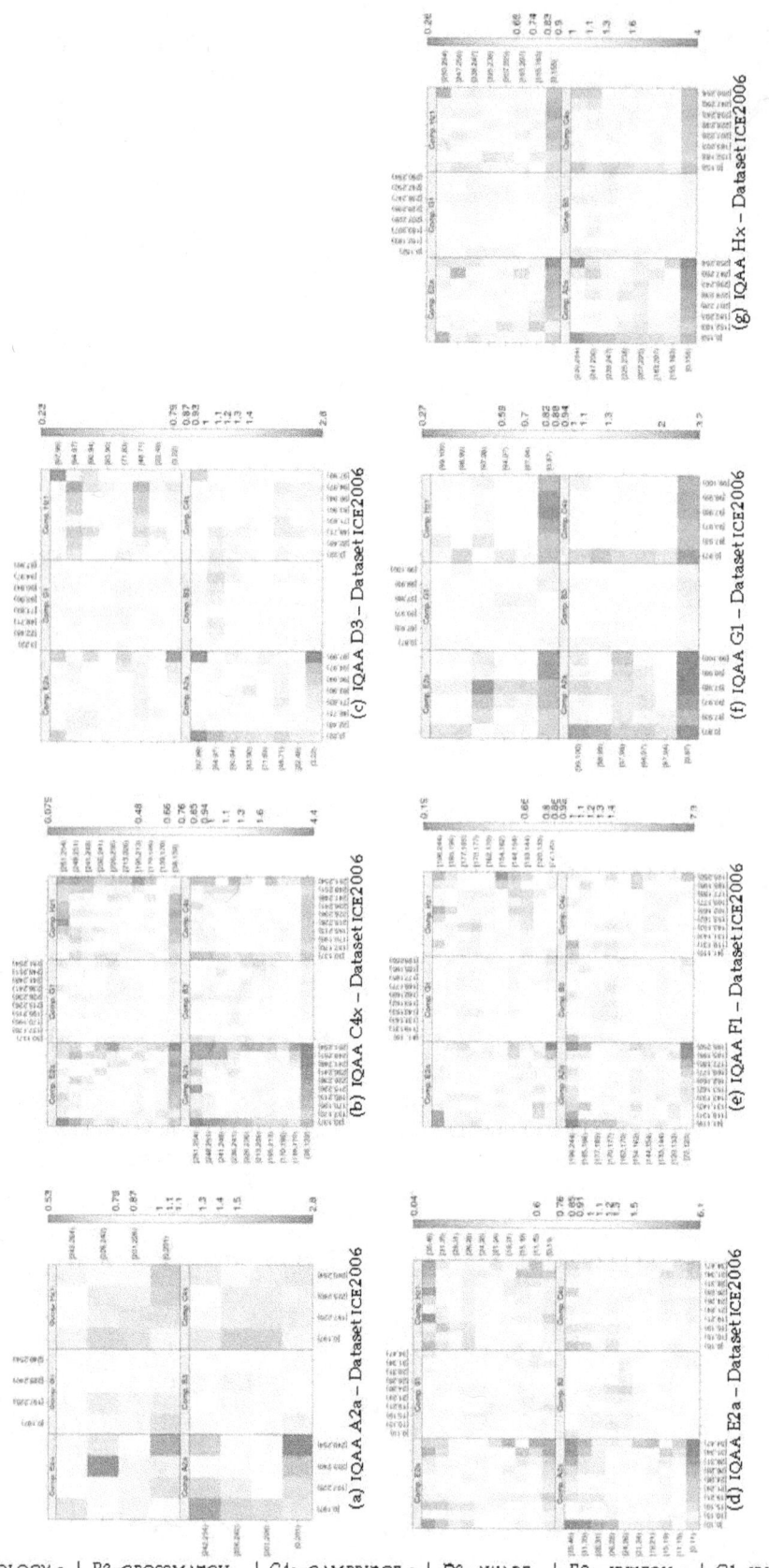

Figure 91: SHARPNESS computed by primary IQAA submissions and FNMR for IQCE comparators for dataset ICE2006 . The y-axis represents enrollment samples' quality with verification samples' on the x-axis. The SHARPNESS scores are quantized into 10 quantiles. The color scale plots $\frac{\text{FNMR}}{\text{FNMR}_0}$ for comparisons with verification and enrollment qualities ($q_{verification}, q_{enrollment}$). FNMR$_0$ is the nominal FNMR which is the false non-match rate computed over all the images at the same comparison score threshold, in this case at FMR = 0.001. Yellow/Green color represent an improvement in FNMR. Blue color represent a degradation of FNMR. White color means no change in FNMR. On ICE2006 image, no change in FNMR is observed across the range SHARPNESS vecqXl scores. This can be explained by the lack of defocus impairment in ICE2006 images.

178

A2a=NEUROTECHNOLOGY-a	B3=CROSSMATCH	C4s=CAMBRIDGE-s	D3=AWARE	E2a=IRITECH-a	G1=IRISID-1	I1=KYNEN	Hz1=L1-z1
A2f=NEUROTECHNOLOGY-f		C4x=CAMBRIDGE-x	F1=MORPHO	E2f=IRITECH-f	G2=IRISID-2	Hx=L1-x	Hz2=L1-z2
		C4f=CAMBRIDGE-f					

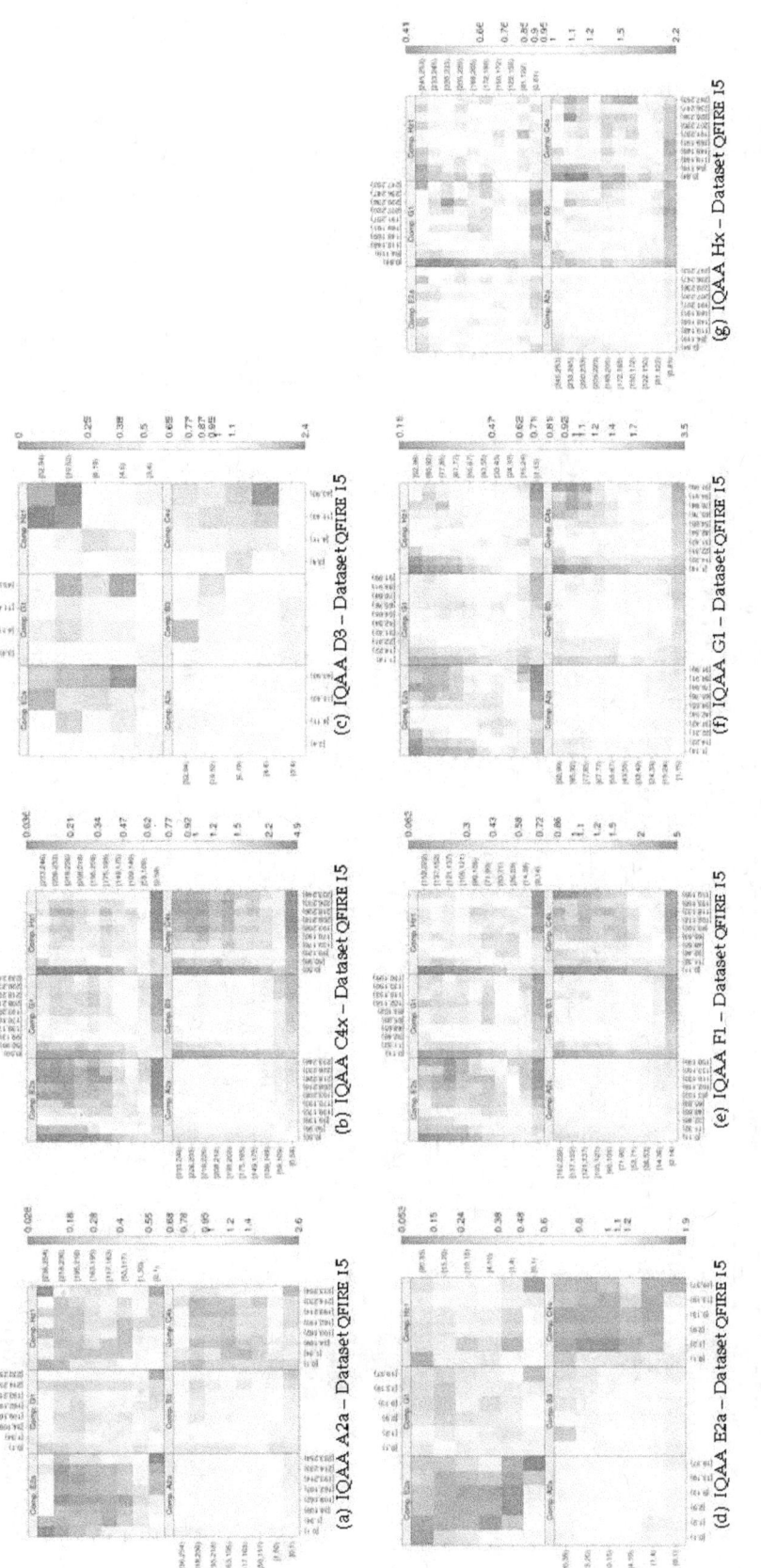

Figure 92: FNMR *vs.* ($q_{verification}$, $q_{enrollment}$). SHARPNESS computed by primary IQAA submissions and FNMR for IQCE comparators for dataset QFIRE I5 . (see Figure 91 caption for more detail). IQAA C4x, F1 and Hx are most effective in their assessment of SHARPNESS . Variation of SHARPNESS scores between the two images being compared does not affect the FNMR, except when both images have the lowest possible SHARPNESS scores.

(a) IQAA A2a – Dataset QFIRE I5

(b) IQAA C4x – Dataset QFIRE I5

(c) IQAA D3 – Dataset QFIRE I5

(d) IQAA E2a – Dataset QFIRE I5

(e) IQAA F1 – Dataset QFIRE I5

(f) IQAA G1 – Dataset QFIRE I5

(g) IQAA Hx – Dataset QFIRE I5

179

Dataset	comparator	IQAA A2f	IQAA B3	IQAA C4x	IQAA E2a	IQAA E2f	IQAA F1	IQAA G1	IQAA G2	IQAA Hx
ICE2006	A2a	(8.70,8.90)	(0.19,0.23)	(8.27,8.61)	(5.03,5.24)	(4.68,4.86)	(1.97,2.19)	(4.55,4.80)	(4.46,4.70)	(8.39,8.71)
ICE2006	B3	(1.63,1.72)	(0.27,0.29)	(1.14,1.30)	(-0.01,0.08)	(0.30,0.39)	(-0.74,-0.63)	(0.69,0.80)	(0.72,0.83)	(1.16,1.31)
ICE2006	C4s	(4.14,4.29)	(1.22,1.25)	(5.81,6.06)	(1.82,1.97)	(1.79,1.93)	(0.84,1.01)	(2.73,2.91)	(2.73,2.90)	(5.78,6.01)
ICE2006	E2a	(5.78,5.98)	(0.18,0.22)	(4.87,5.22)	(2.49,2.70)	(2.38,2.57)	(-0.14,0.08)	(2.52,2.78)	(2.44,2.69)	(5.32,5.64)
ICE2006	G2	(-0.15,-0.05)	(0.57,0.59)	(0.76,0.94)	(1.11,1.22)	(1.07,1.16)	(-0.38,-0.27)	(-0.27,-0.15)	(-0.12,0.00)	(0.81,0.97)
ICE2006	Hz1	(2.92,3.16)	(-0.02,0.03)	(2.45,2.87)	(0.87,1.12)	(0.93,1.15)	(0.14,0.41)	(0.62,0.93)	(0.80,1.11)	(2.16,2.55)
OPS	A2a	(-1.34,1.08)	(4.62,12.16)	(-0.61,2.84)	(-1.86,1.01)	(-1.50,1.16)	(-1.58,2.11)	(2.21,4.89)	(9.36,12.19)	(-0.65,2.45)
OPS	B3	(0.20,1.22)	(-0.06,0.06)	(0.99,2.42)	(0.55,1.74)	(0.65,1.76)	(0.49,2.03)	(1.98,3.05)	(1.95,3.06)	(1.22,2.52)
OPS	C4s	(0.63,2.57)	(0.24,6.33)	(-0.41,2.35)	(0.54,2.84)	(0.43,2.56)	(-0.53,2.44)	(-0.35,1.80)	(-0.48,1.87)	(-0.49,2.00)
OPS	E2a	(-1.30,1.54)	(-5.99,2.91)	(-2.42,1.62)	(-1.77,1.59)	(-1.31,1.81)	(-2.80,1.53)	(-0.30,2.85)	(-0.47,2.96)	(-2.25,1.39)
OPS	G2	(-0.33,1.24)	(1.61,6.48)	(1.03,3.26)	(0.17,2.03)	(-0.07,1.66)	(-0.42,1.98)	(4.17,5.53)	(0.35,1.31)	(0.91,2.90)
OPS	Hz1	(0.77,3.01)	(-2.93,4.25)	(-1.66,1.59)	(-0.22,2.47)	(-0.08,2.42)	(-1.08,2.40)	(-0.47,2.02)	(1.55,4.26)	(0.20,3.13)
QFIREA5	A2a	(1.77,3.19)	(0.00,0.01)	(0.81,1.42)	(1.40,1.83)	(0.10,0.34)	(0.96,1.47)	(0.87,1.74)	(0.80,1.65)	(0.26,0.82)
QFIREA5	B3	(0.75,2.87)	(0.01,0.02)	(2.95,3.84)	(1.37,2.04)	(0.15,0.54)	(0.70,1.43)	(1.04,2.29)	(1.08,2.30)	(0.71,1.52)
QFIREA5	C4s	(4.29,6.22)	(0.02,0.03)	(4.16,4.98)	(1.86,2.42)	(0.18,0.49)	(0.44,1.14)	(0.07,1.27)	(0.28,1.46)	(-0.02,0.73)
QFIREA5	E2a	(7.02,8.35)	(0.02,0.02)	(3.22,3.79)	(1.73,2.12)	(0.24,0.45)	(1.74,2.22)	(2.06,2.88)	(2.34,3.15)	(1.52,2.03)
QFIREA5	G2	(2.45,3.89)	(0.02,0.03)	(3.50,4.11)	(1.61,2.03)	(0.09,0.32)	(0.60,1.12)	(0.33,1.23)	(0.51,1.38)	(0.71,1.27)
QFIREA5	Hz1	(4.51,6.91)	(0.03,0.04)	(3.12,4.15)	(2.67,3.37)	(0.17,0.55)	(0.93,1.80)	(1.54,3.05)	(1.58,3.03)	(-0.39,0.54)
QFIREI5	A2a	(18.36,19.23)	(0.02,0.03)	(10.69,11.18)	(1.87,2.00)	(0.18,0.23)	(7.52,7.89)	(7.65,8.15)	(7.55,8.06)	(3.22,3.64)
QFIREI5	B3	(13.17,14.08)	(0.04,0.04)	(10.95,11.39)	(1.68,1.82)	(0.24,0.29)	(9.38,9.75)	(7.43,7.95)	(7.49,8.00)	(6.61,7.04)
QFIREI5	C4s	(34.44,35.52)	(0.10,0.12)	(27.17,27.77)	(2.14,2.29)	(0.27,0.33)	(14.61,15.07)	(12.98,13.61)	(12.89,13.53)	(7.44,7.98)
QFIREI5	E2a	(33.25,34.40)	(0.10,0.12)	(25.72,26.37)	(2.01,2.18)	(0.26,0.32)	(12.19,12.69)	(13.11,13.78)	(13.04,13.71)	(-0.68,-0.10)
QFIREI5	G2	(23.07,24.04)	(0.06,0.07)	(18.00,18.55)	(1.63,1.77)	(0.24,0.29)	(10.76,11.17)	(9.35,9.92)	(9.16,9.71)	(7.88,8.35)
QFIREI5	Hz1	(27.00,28.41)	(0.12,0.15)	(22.03,22.82)	(1.27,1.47)	(0.17,0.25)	(10.71,11.32)	(8.45,9.27)	(8.25,9.07)	(0.51,1.20)

Table 29: Tukey HSD difference in mean of SHARPNESS scores. Each cell shows the 95% confidence level in difference in mean of pairwise quality for images verified correctly (i.e., the genuine score equal or less than threshold) and those rejected falsely (i.e., the genuine score larger than threshold). Quality scores were computed by the SDK identified by the column header and comparison scores were generated by the SDK identified by the row header. If the interval does not contain zero, the difference in mean is significant. Cells where difference in mean is not significant have pink background. For monotonically increasing quality components (all except DILATION, and depending on quality implementation GRAY SCALE SPREAD), the expected behavior is to have higher quality scores for the pair of enrollment and verification images that give genuine comparison scores less than threshold. The pairwise quality is computed as geometric mean of the quality of two samples being compared. Threshold is set to give false match rate of 0.001.

180

A2a=NEUROTECHNOLOGY-a | B3=CROSSMATCH | C4s=CAMBRIDGE-s | D3=AWARE | E2a=IRITECH-a | G1=IRISID-1 | I1=KYNEN | Hz1=L1-z1
A2f=NEUROTECHNOLOGY-f | C4x=CAMBRIDGE-x | C4f=CAMBRIDGE-f | F1=MORPHO | E2f=IRITECH-f | G2=IRISID-2 | Hx=L1-x | Hz2=L1-z2

Dataset	comparator	IQAA A2f	IQAA B3	IQAA C4x	IQAA E2a	IQAA E2f	IQAA F1	IQAA G1	IQAA G2	IQAA Hx
ICE2006	A2a	(2.24,2.68)	(-0.37,0.03)	(8.27,9.09)	(3.85,4.32)	(3.43,3.84)	(4.83,5.33)	(1.45,2.24)	(1.63,2.34)	(7.75,8.51)
ICE2006	B3	(1.07,1.39)	(0.02,0.08)	(7.50,8.09)	(5.76,6.10)	(5.11,5.41)	(3.48,3.84)	(5.61,6.17)	(4.65,5.16)	(6.99,7.53)
ICE2006	C4s	(1.37,1.72)	(0.03,0.34)	(6.40,7.04)	(3.73,4.09)	(3.26,3.58)	(3.24,3.63)	(2.41,3.02)	(2.36,2.91)	(6.00,6.58)
ICE2006	E2a	(1.71,2.06)	(-0.19,0.13)	(11.10,11.74)	(6.02,6.39)	(5.37,5.69)	(6.75,7.14)	(4.34,4.96)	(4.20,4.76)	(10.37,10.97)
ICE2006	G2	(2.73,3.08)	(-0.20,0.11)	(6.15,6.81)	(2.69,3.07)	(2.50,2.84)	(3.63,4.03)	(1.17,1.73)	(1.58,2.03)	(5.78,6.39)
ICE2006	Hz1	(1.24,1.67)	(0.45,0.79)	(5.57,6.25)	(3.38,3.78)	(2.83,3.17)	(2.80,3.22)	(6.61,7.30)	(4.92,5.54)	(5.19,5.82)
OPS	A2a	(-0.35,-0.09)	(0.22,1.13)	(0.49,0.89)	(0.49,0.81)	(0.45,0.75)	(0.81,1.23)	(-0.12,0.21)	(-0.08,0.27)	(0.38,0.74)
OPS	B3	(-0.10,0.11)	(-0.01,0.02)	(1.40,1.72)	(1.25,1.50)	(1.17,1.41)	(1.23,1.57)	(0.38,0.63)	(0.67,0.94)	(1.35,1.65)
OPS	C4s	(-0.10,0.11)	(0.04,0.80)	(0.98,1.31)	(0.98,1.24)	(0.88,1.12)	(0.87,1.22)	(0.08,0.35)	(0.06,0.35)	(0.84,1.14)
OPS	E2a	(-0.03,0.18)	(-0.31,0.46)	(1.23,1.56)	(1.01,1.28)	(0.94,1.18)	(1.38,1.73)	(0.04,0.31)	(0.11,0.41)	(1.09,1.40)
OPS	G2	(0.09,0.30)	(-0.08,0.68)	(0.30,0.63)	(0.28,0.54)	(0.28,0.53)	(0.56,0.91)	(-0.07,0.15)	(-0.04,0.10)	(0.26,0.56)
OPS	Hz1	(-0.12,0.08)	(-0.06,0.69)	(1.26,1.59)	(1.18,1.44)	(1.04,1.28)	(1.22,1.56)	(0.32,0.58)	(0.47,0.76)	(1.05,1.35)
QFIREA5	A2a	(3.61,5.53)	(0.07,0.32)	(-0.53,0.34)	(-0.54,-0.16)	(-0.14,0.08)	(1.10,1.71)	(-2.74,-1.40)	(-0.87,0.30)	(0.90,1.79)
QFIREA5	C4s	(6.00,7.75)	(0.04,0.26)	(2.57,3.36)	(0.34,0.69)	(0.13,0.33)	(2.88,3.43)	(2.56,3.67)	(2.96,3.96)	(1.70,2.50)
QFIREA5	E2a	(-3.19,-1.45)	(-0.23,-0.02)	(-0.55,0.24)	(1.22,1.57)	(0.28,0.48)	(3.47,4.03)	(4.82,5.88)	(4.65,5.63)	(3.25,4.05)
QFIREA5	G2	(8.05,9.83)	(-0.06,0.12)	(4.95,5.74)	(0.88,1.25)	(0.09,0.30)	(3.73,4.29)	(4.16,5.22)	(4.90,5.85)	(2.27,3.03)
QFIREA5	Hz1	(7.54,9.28)	(-0.08,0.13)	(3.43,4.21)	(0.79,1.14)	(0.17,0.37)	(3.48,4.03)	(4.63,5.84)	(5.14,6.18)	(3.96,4.76)
QFIRE15	A2a	(10.99,12.74)	(0.02,0.03)	(3.50,4.34)	(0.35,0.63)	(0.10,0.21)	(2.80,3.50)	(3.68,4.69)	(3.79,4.79)	(1.76,2.54)
QFIRE15	C4s	(25.38,26.90)	(0.07,0.08)	(13.28,14.00)	(2.27,2.51)	(0.26,0.36)	(10.23,10.84)	(13.48,14.36)	(13.66,14.53)	(6.08,6.75)
QFIRE15	E2a	(33.57,35.09)	(0.16,0.17)	(21.21,21.94)	(2.61,2.86)	(0.31,0.40)	(12.84,13.44)	(22.12,23.00)	(22.19,23.07)	(3.37,4.04)
QFIRE15	G2	(19.58,31.11)	(0.05,0.12)	(13.56,19.02)	(1.31,3.17)	(-0.19,0.52)	(9.74,14.31)	(12.34,18.97)	(12.58,19.07)	(4.54,9.58)
QFIRE15	Hz1	(27.27,28.79)	(0.06,0.06)	(16.44,17.17)	(2.47,2.71)	(-0.26,0.35)	(12.49,13.09)	(15.31,16.20)	(15.80,16.68)	(11.05,11.72)

Table 30: Tukey HSD mean difference in SHARPNESS scores. Each cell shows the 95% confidence level in difference in mean of pairwise quality for images correctly rejected (i.e., the impostor score equal or greater than threshold) and those falsely matched (i.e., the impostor score less than threshold). Quality scores were computed by the SDK identified by the column header and comparison scores were generated by the SDK identified by the row header. If the interval does not contain zero, the difference in mean is significant. Cells where difference in mean is not significant are shaded in pink. For monotonic increasing quality components (all except DILATION, and depending on quality implementation GRAY SCALE SPREAD), the expected behavior is to have higher quality scores for the pair of (enrollment, verification) images that result in impostor comparison scores equal or greater than threshold. Pairwise quality is computed as geometric mean of the quality of two samples being compared. Threshold is set to give false match rate of 0.001.

181

9.11 Motion blur

MOTION BLUR is cause by motion of the camera or the iris, or both.

Only three of the IQCE submissions (D3, E2a, and E2f) generated MOTION BLUR scores. The distribution of their MOTION BLUR scores is shown in Figure 93.

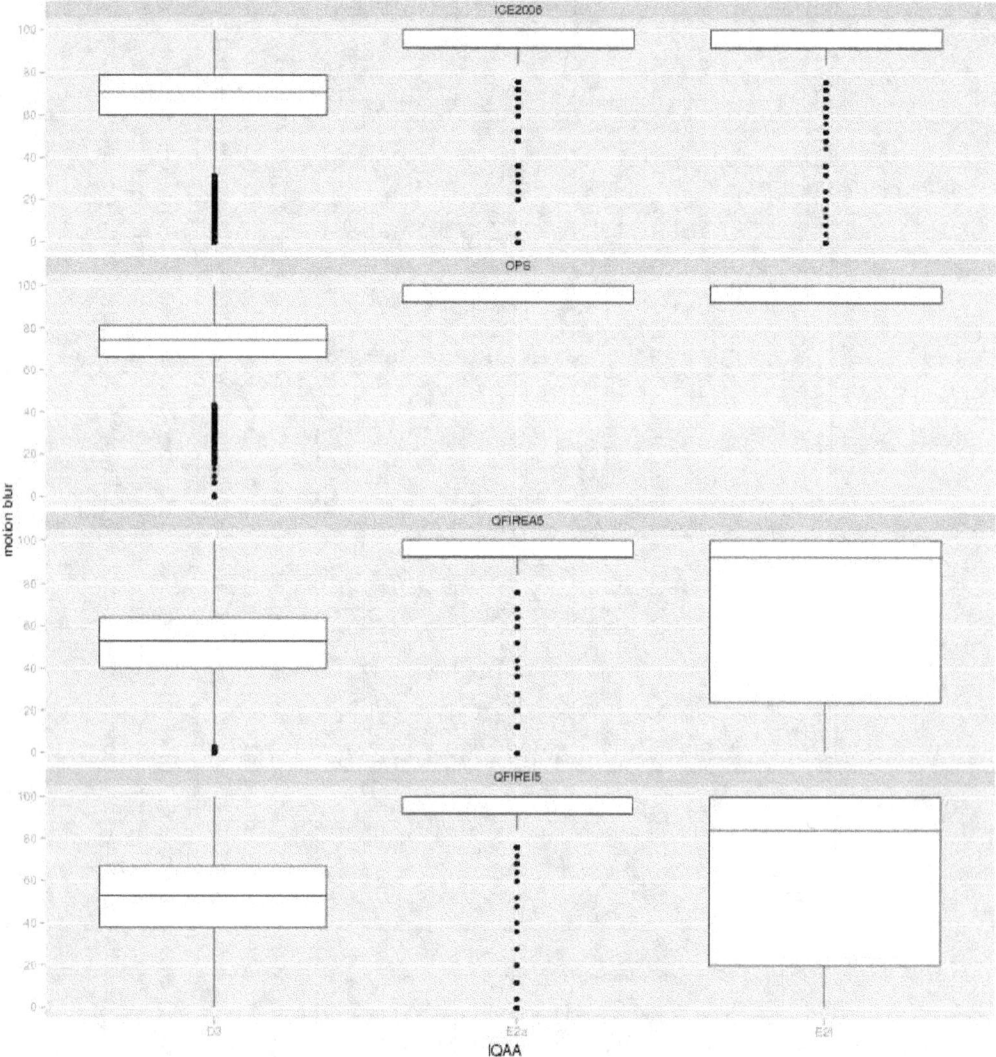

Figure 93: Box and whisker plots of the IQAAs that generate MOTION BLUR scores.

IQAAs E2a and E2f each generates only 22 distinct MOTION BLUR scores, and most of the images were give the same score.

IQAA E2a gave 93% of the ICE2006 a score 92 (48%) or 100 (45%).

IQAA E2f gave 69% of QFIRE I5 a score of either 0 (15%), or 92 (24%), or 100 (25%). IQAA E2a gave a score of 92 to 59% of the QFIRE I5 images and a score of 100 to the other 41%.

The very discrete distribution of IQAAs E2a and E2f MOTION BLUR scores might be either due to lack of MOTION BLUR impairment in the datasets or the inability of the IQAAs to accurately measure the extent of MOTION BLUR in the images.

RELATIONSHIP WITH THE DISTRIBUTION OF GENUINE SCORES

The genuine scores of OPS and ICE2006 images are not affected by the MOTION BLUR scores generated by IQAAs D3 E2a or E2f. A slight (but perhaps random) change is observed for QFIRE images.

RELATIONSHIP WITH THE DISTRIBUTION OF IMPOSTOR SCORES

Figure 95 indicates that the impostor scores are not affected by MOTION BLUR scores.

RANKED DET:: DO LOW-QUALITY IMAGES PRODUCE HIGH FNMR OR FMR?

IQAAs E2a and E2f MOTION BLUR scores are not predictive of performance for neither ICE2006 nor QFIRE I5 datasets. On QFIRE I5 images, the performance of the three sets of low, mid and high MOTION BLUR scores are identical. On ICE2006 images, the ranking of the DETS is not correct, images in the highest 15 percentile of IQAAs E2a or E2f MOTION BLUR scores give higher error rates than the middle 70%.

QFIRE I5 images within the lowest 15 percentile of IQAA D3's MOTION BLUR scores give higher FNMR and FMR than the remaining images. However, as shown in Figure 120, IQAA D3's quality scores on QFIRE I5 images are highly correlated, so its MOTION BLUR is not purely a measurement of the image signal to noise ratio. EFFECT OF QUALITY ON FNMR

: HOW QUICKLY FNMR IMPROVES WHEN POOR QUALITY SAMPLES ARE REJECTED?

Figure 97 confirms our earlier results that none of the IQAAS' MOTION BLUR score is effective in prediction of performance.

Rejection of the QFIRE I5 images with the lowest IQAA D3's MOTION BLUR score improves comparator Hz1's FNMR. However, as mentioned before, IQAA D3's score for the different quality components are highly correlated, which means its MOTION BLUR scores are not purely measurement of the signal to noise ratio of an image.

EFFECT OF VARIATION BETWEEN THE TWO SAMPLES:: DOES SAMENESS MATTER?

Given that IQAAs E2a and E2f's MOTION BLUR scores are mostly 92, 100 or 0, division of their scores into quantile and so generation of the heatmaps was not possible.

OBSERVATIONS AND CONCLUSIONS

None of the evaluated IQAAs generates MOTION BLUR scores that are predictive of performance. Two of them (IQAAs E2a and E2f) gave the same score to the majority of the images.

The few number of submissions implies that measurement of SIGNAL TO NOISE RATIO is not universal. Furthermore, their inability to compute distinct scores for the IQCE images suggests that either the imagery used do not represent a full range of MOTION BLUR impairment or computation of MOTION BLUR scores is a technical challenge not solved yet.

| A2a=NEUROTECHNOLOGY-a | B3=CROSSMATCH | C4s=CAMBRIDGE-s | D3=AWARE | E2a=IRITECH-a | G1=IRISID-1 | I1=KYNEN | Hz1=L1-z1 |
| A2f=NEUROTECHNOLOGY-f | C4x=CAMBRIDGE-x | C4f=CAMBRIDGE-f | F1=MORPHO | E2f=IRITECH-f | G2=IRISID-2 | Hx=L1-x | Hz2=L1-z2 |

As such, IQCE results on effect of MOTION BLUR on performance is inconclusive. IQCE recommends exclusion of SIGNAL TO NOISE RATIO from the ISO/IEC 29794-6 . The impairment caused by MOTION BLUR is similar to defocus blur, therefore measuring SHARPNESS could detect and flag poor quality images due to MOTION BLUR .

| A2a=NEUROTECHNOLOGY-a | B3=CROSSMATCH | C4s=CAMBRIDGE-s | D3=AWARE | E2a=IRITECH-a | G1=IRISID-1 | I1=KYNEN | Hz1=L1-z1 |
| A2f=NEUROTECHNOLOGY-f | C4x=CAMBRIDGE-x | C4f=CAMBRIDGE-f | F1=MORPHO | E2f=IRITECH-f | G2=IRISID-2 | Hx=L1-x | Hz2=L1-z2 |

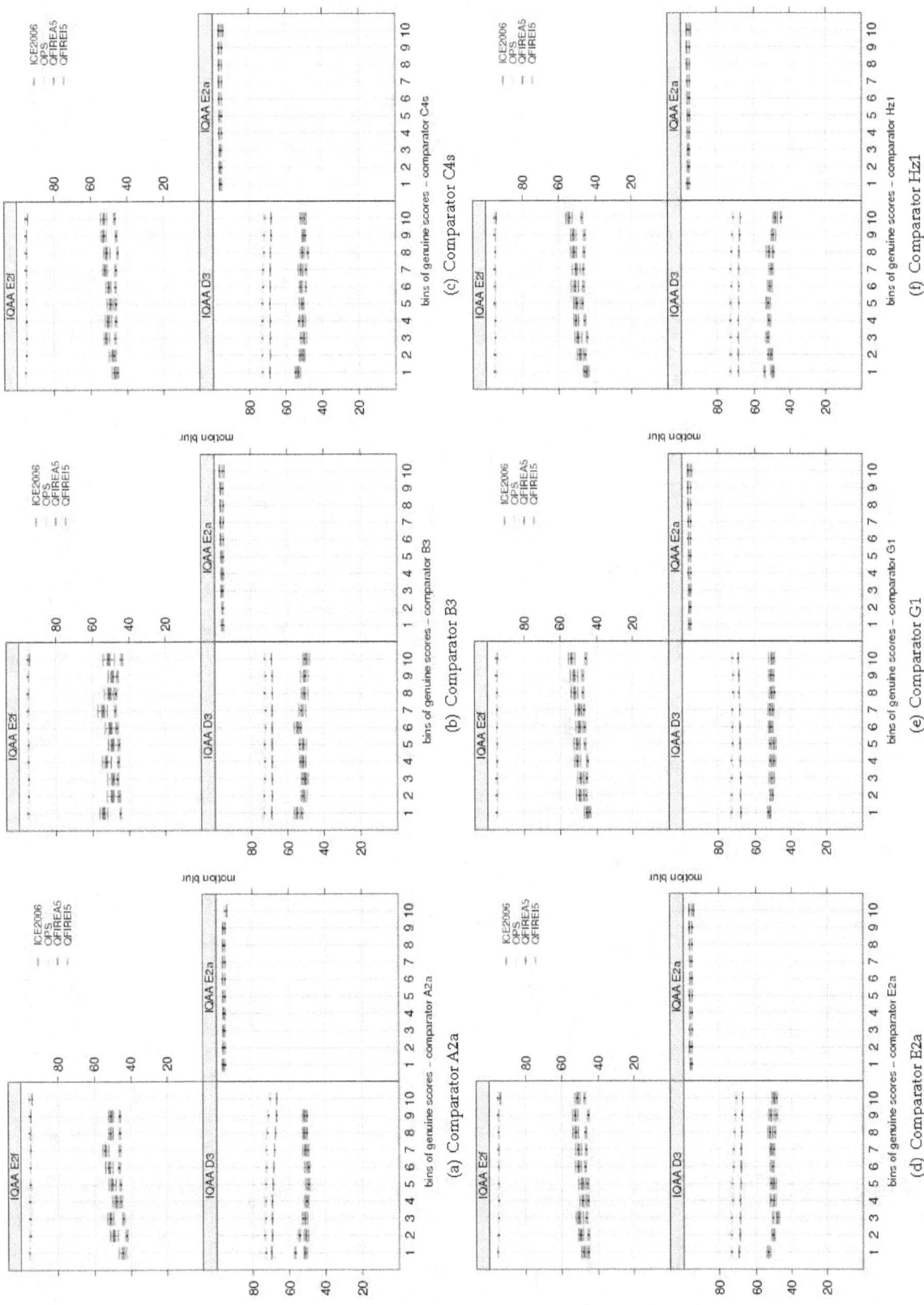

Figure 94: Pairwise MOTION BLUR scores vs. genuine score for the primary Class Z submissions of each participant. Each plot shows quality scores computed by different IQAA. Genuine scores are divided equally into ten groups. Groups overlap by 5 percent, meaning 5% of the data in one bin also belongs to the next bin. The bootstrapped pairwise quality for each group is shown in a box and whisker plot. Pairwise quality is computed as geometric mean of the quality of the two samples being compared.

185

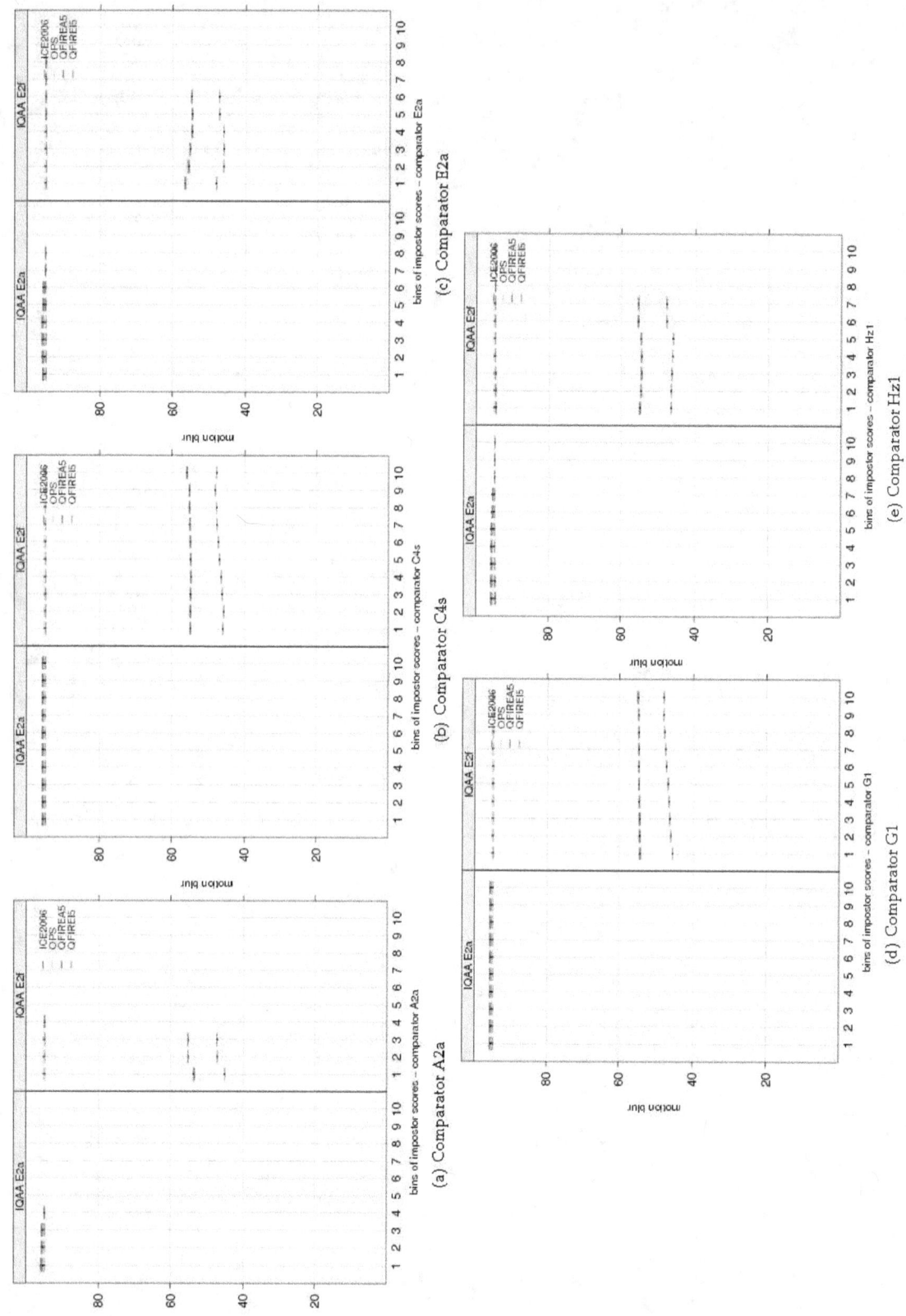

Figure 95: Pairwise MOTION BLUR scores vs. impostor scores for the primary Class Z submissions of each participant. Each plot shows quality scores computed by different IQAA. Similar to plots of figure 94, impostor scores are divided equally into ten groups, overlapping by 5 percent. The bootstrapped pairwise quality for each group is shown in a box and whisker plot. Pairwise quality is computed as geometric mean of the quality of the two samples being compared.

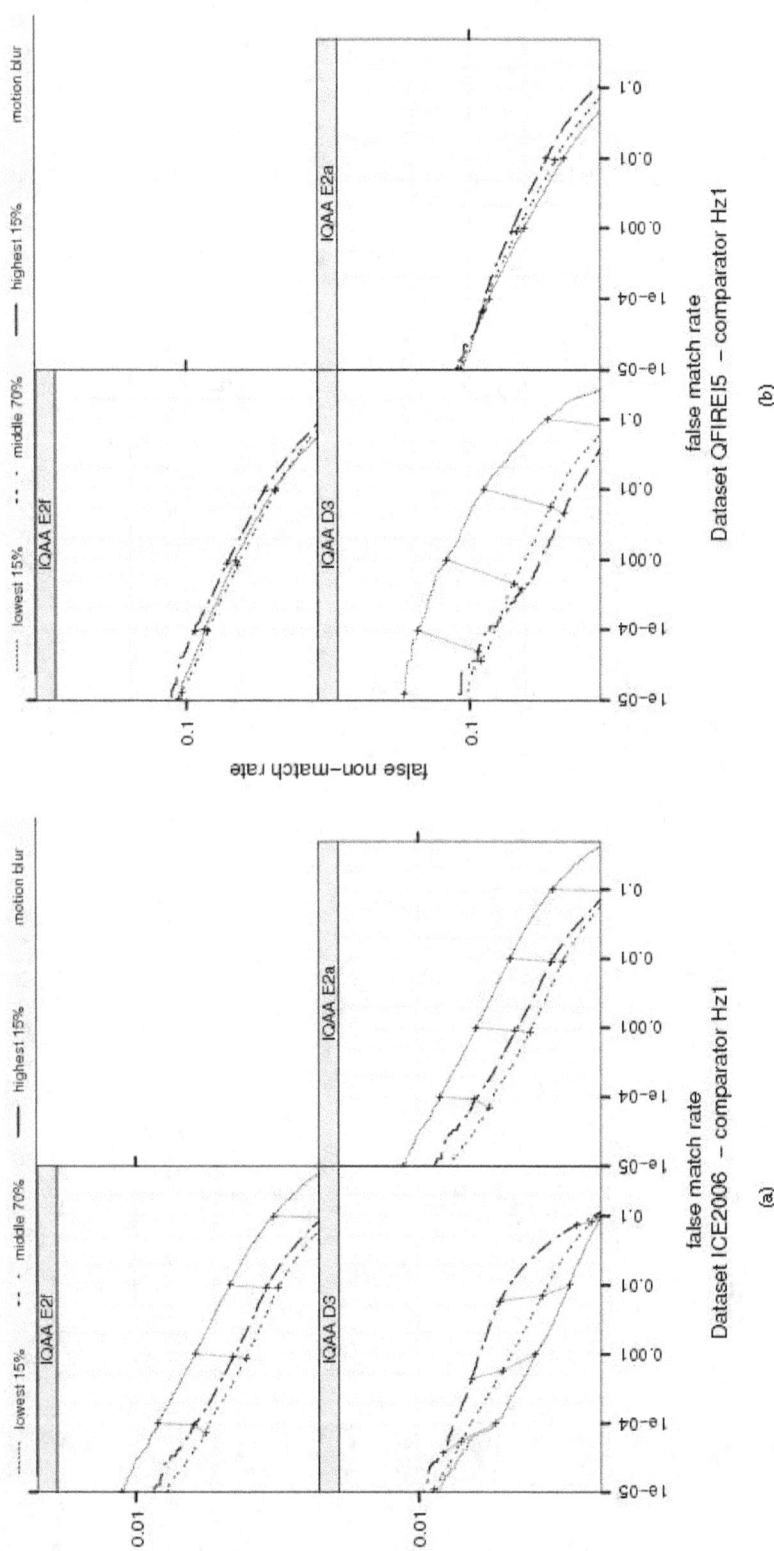

Figure 96: Ranked DET curves for comparator Hz1 and Datasets ICE2006 and QFIRE15 . The set of all comparisons were partitioned into three groups based on the pair-wise MOTION BLUR quality of the images being compared. The lowest quality set contains comparisons with pairwise quality in the lower 15 percentile. The highest quality set contains comparisons with pairwise quality in the upper 15 percentile. The rest of the comparisons, namely the middle 70%, made up the third set. The DETs are connected at the same score threshold values (brown lines). Lower FNMR and FMR rates are expected for better quality images. None of the IQAAS' MOTION BLUR score give a rank ordering of the performance of comparator Hz1.

187

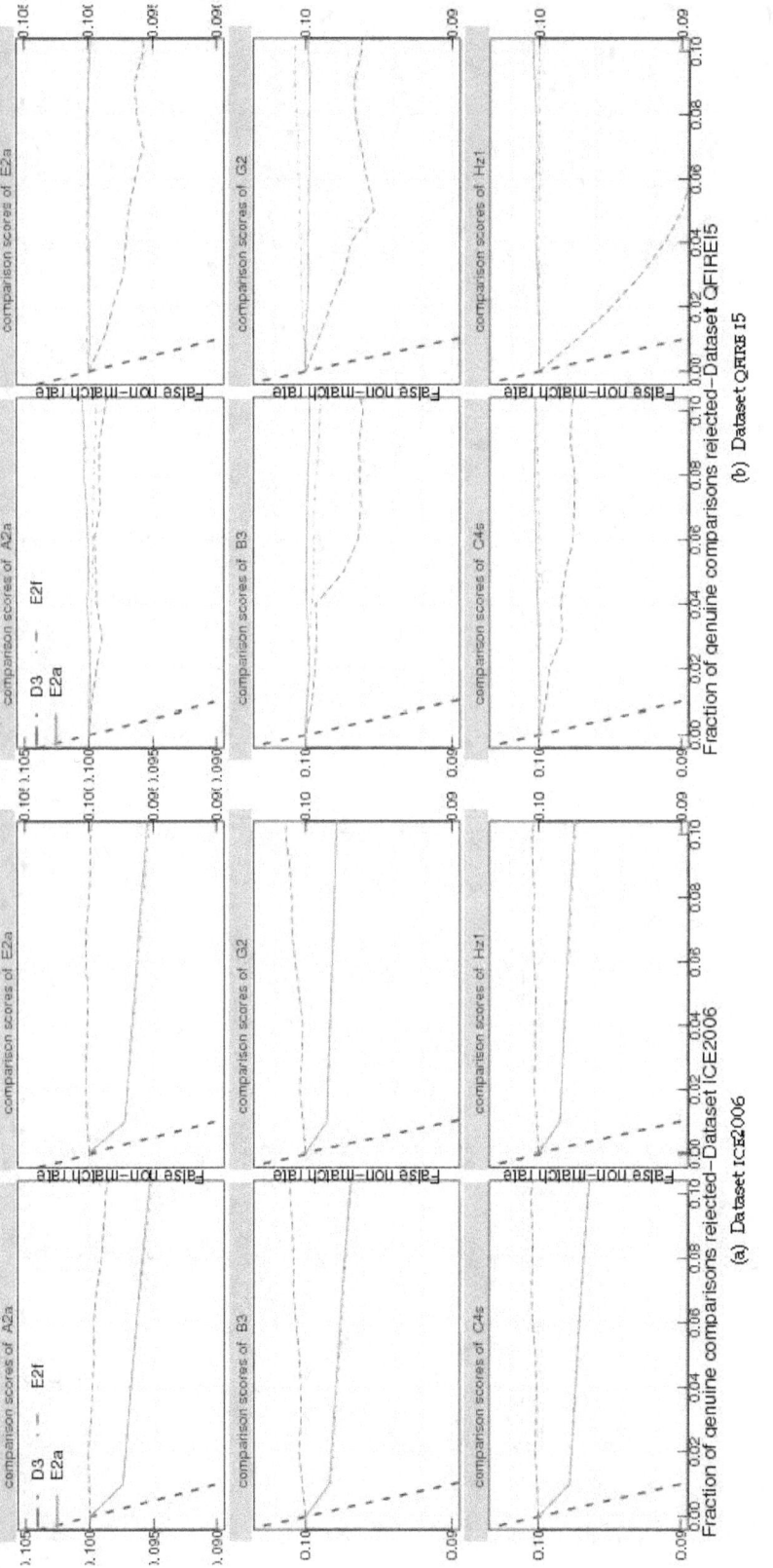

Figure 97: FNMR vs. reject curves for MOTION BLUR scores on datasets ICE2006 and QFIRE15. The threshold is set to give an initial FNMR = 0.1. The gray dotted line shows the ideal case where the rejection of the comparisons with the lowest ten percent quality results in zero FNMR. No IQAA shows a strong improvement in FNMR after rejecting images with its low IRIS SHAPE scores.

| A2a=NEUROTECHNOLOGY-a | B3=CROSSMATCH | C4s=CAMBRIDGE-s | D3=AWARE | E2a=IRITECH-a | G1=IRISID-1 | I1=KYNEN | Hz1=L1-z1 |
| A2f=NEUROTECHNOLOGY-f | C4x=CAMBRIDGE-x | C4f=CAMBRIDGE-f | F1=MORPHO | E2f=IRITECH-f | G2=IRISID-2 | Hx=L1-x | Hz2=L1-z2 |

9.12   Signal to noise ratio

ISO/IEC 19794-6 :2005 specifies SIGNAL TO NOISE RATIO requirement that the image signal-to-noise ratio should not be less than 40 dB inclusive of any noise introduced by image compression techniques. However it does not give any guidance on how to measure SIGNAL TO NOISE RATIO .

Measuring SIGNAL TO NOISE RATIO from an image is impossible if the noise model is not known. The major source of noise in an iris image is believed to be the sensor noise, which can be measured or modeled by imaging targets.

Nine IQCE submissions (A2a, A2f, D3, E2a, E2f, F1, G1, G2, and I1) from six organizations generated SIGNAL TO NOISE RATIO scores for each image. The distribution of their SIGNAL TO NOISE RATIO scores is shown in Figure 98. In order to make the boxplots more readable, quality scores in [0–254] range were linearly scaled back to [0–100].

Among the datasets, QFIRE I5 exhibits different range of SIGNAL TO NOISE RATIO , because the images are captured by different illumination intensity, specifically by varying levels of lights (based on LED arrays) positioned two feet from the subject. There is a total of eight LED-based lights which can be independently turned on/off (see Section 4).

RELATIONSHIP WITH THE DISTRIBUTION OF GENUINE SCORES

Figure 99 suggests that the SIGNAL TO NOISE RATIO scores do not affect the genuine scores distribution. SIGNAL TO NOISE RATIO scores are almost constant across the genuine scores, for all datasets.

IQAA E2a and E2f give the lowest SIGNAL TO NOISE RATIO scores to OPS and ICE2006 images. Other IQAAs give OPS and ICE2006 images the highest scores.

RELATIONSHIP WITH THE DISTRIBUTION OF IMPOSTOR SCORES

Impostor scores are not affected by any of the IQAAS' SIGNAL TO NOISE RATIO scores, as indicated by the non-changing boxes in Figure 100.

RANKED DET:: DO LOW-QUALITY IMAGES PRODUCE HIGH FNMR OR FMR?

The ranked DET curves of Figure 101 suggests that none of the IQAAS' SIGNAL TO NOISE RATIO score is able to give a significant rank ordering of the performance of comparator Hz1 on the QFIRE I5 dataset. On QFIRE I5 images, the DET curves of low, mid and high SIGNAL TO NOISE RATIO scores overlap for all IQAAS, except E2f. QFIRE I5 images with the lowest 15 percentile of IQAA E2f, give higher FNMR and FMR.

ICE2006 images with IQAAs A2a, A2f, E2a, and E2f's lowest SIGNAL TO NOISE RATIO scores result in higher FNMR than the images with mid or high SIGNAL TO NOISE RATIO scores. The change in FMR is negligible.

EFFECT OF QUALITY ON FNMR : HOW QUICKLY FNMR IMPROVES WHEN POOR QUALITY SAMPLES ARE REJECTED?

The fact that the IQAAS's performance is worse on QFIRE I5 than on the ICE2006 dataset, suggests that neither of the

| A2a=NEUROTECHNOLOGY-a | B3=CROSSMATCH | C4s=CAMBRIDGE-s | D3=AWARE | E2a=IRITECH-a | G1=IRISID-1 | I1=KYNEN | Hz1=L1-z1 |
| A2f=NEUROTECHNOLOGY-f | C4x=CAMBRIDGE-x | C4f=CAMBRIDGE-f | F1=MORPHO | E2f=IRITECH-f | G2=IRISID-2 | Hx=L1-x | Hz2=L1-z2 |

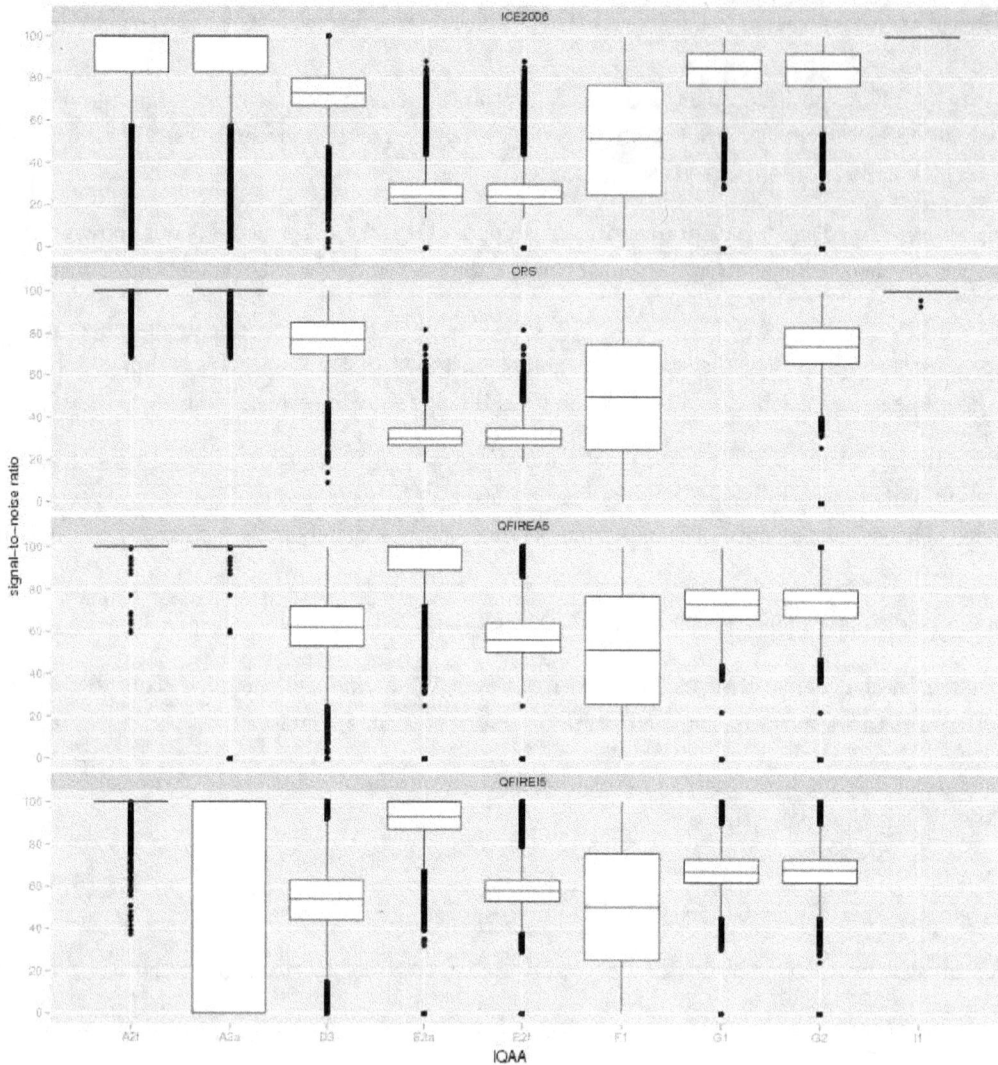

Figure 98: Box and whisker plots of the IQAAs that generate SIGNAL TO NOISE RATIO scores.

IQAAS's SIGNAL TO NOISE RATIO score is a faithful measurement of the SIGNAL TO NOISE RATIO .

EFFECT OF VARIATION BETWEEN THE TWO SAMPLES:: DOES SAMENESS MATTER?

Figures 103 and 104 shows that ICE2006 images with low SIGNAL TO NOISE RATIO scores of IQAAs E2a and A2a inflate FNMR. The performance of IQAA A2a and E2a sharply degrades on QFIRE I5 image. The variation of SIGNAL TO NOISE RATIO score does not affect FNMR.

OBSERVATIONS AND CONCLUSIONS

Technically speaking, measuring SIGNAL TO NOISE RATIO from an image is impossible if the noise model is not known. The major source of noise in an iris image is believed to be the camera noise, which can be measured or modeled by

190

imaging targets.

Nine IQCE submissions generate SIGNAL TO NOISE RATIO scores, but none of them were effective in prediction of performance. Their performance on QFIRE I5 images was worse than of the ICE2006 images, which suggests that the computed SIGNAL TO NOISE RATIO scores are not an accurate measurement of actual signal to noise ratio within the image.

The recommendation for the development of [2] is to consider SIGNAL TO NOISE RATIO as a capture device quality component instead of an image quality component. Sensor noise should be estimated by images appropriate, and perhaps dedicated test targets.

| A2a=NEUROTECHNOLOGY-a | B3=CROSSMATCH | C4s=CAMBRIDGE-s | D3=AWARE | E2a=IRITECH-a | G1=IRISID-1 | I1=KYNEN | Hz1=L1-z1 |
| A2f=NEUROTECHNOLOGY-f | C4x=CAMBRIDGE-x | C4f=CAMBRIDGE-f | F1=MORPHO | E2f=IRITECH-f | G2=IRISID-2 | Hx=L1-x | Hz2=L1-z2 |

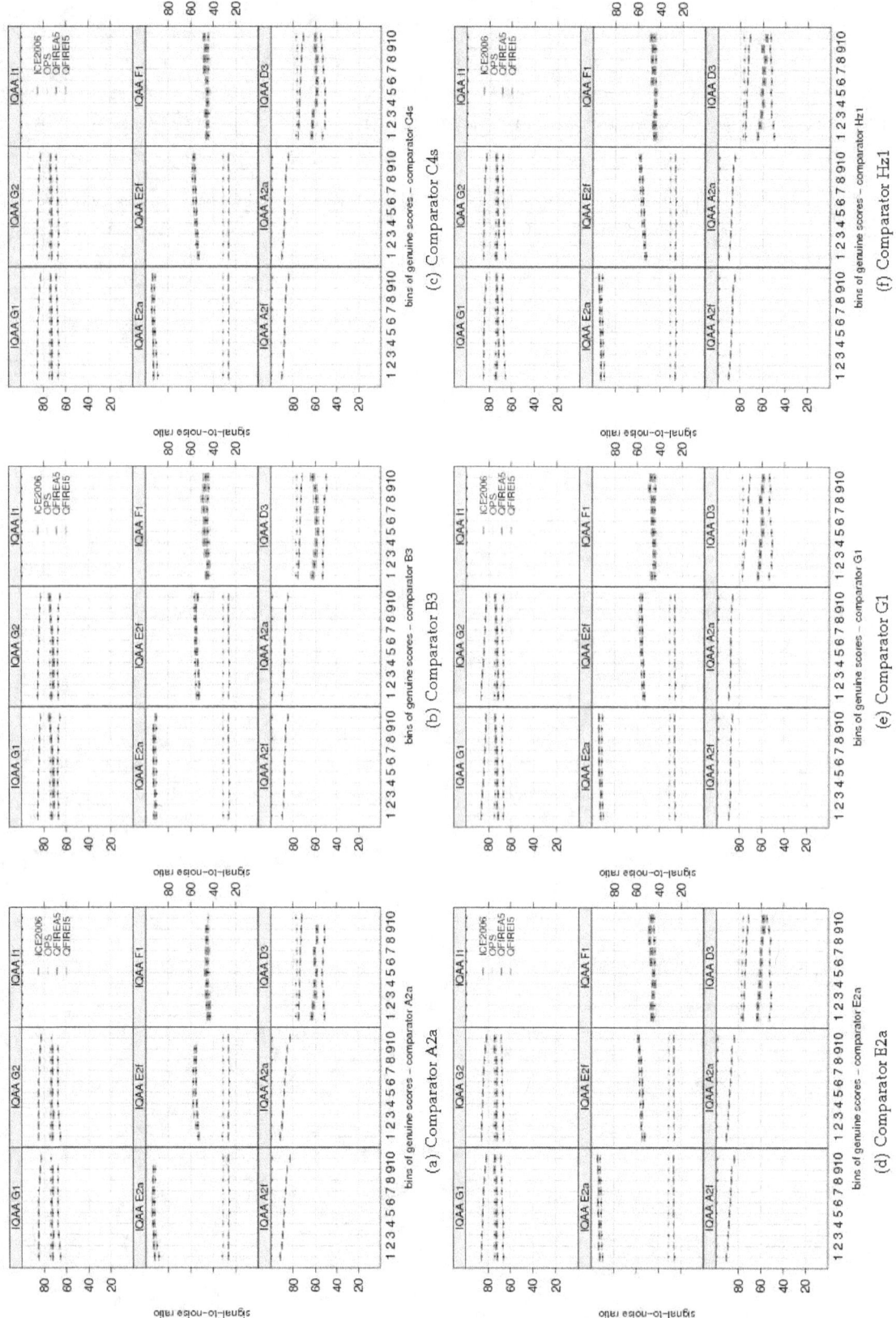

Figure 99: Pairwise SIGNAL TO NOISE RATIO scores vs. genuine score for the primary Class Z submissions of each participant. Each plot shows quality scores computed by different IQAA. Genuine scores are divided equally into ten groups. Groups overlap by 5 percent, meaning 5% of the data in one bin also belongs to the next bin. The bootstrapped pairwise quality for each group is shown in a box and whisker plot. Pairwise quality is computed as geometric mean of the quality of the two samples being compared. Genuine scores are not affected by the IQAAS' SIGNAL TO NOISE RATIO.

| A2a=NEUROTECHNOLOGY-a | B3=CROSSMATCH | C4s=CAMBRIDGE-s | D3=AWARE | E2a=IRITECH-a | G1=IRISID-1 | I1=KYNEN | Hz1=L1-z1 |
| A2f=NEUROTECHNOLOGY-f | C4x=CAMBRIDGE-x | C4f=CAMBRIDGE-f | F1=MORPHO | E2f=IRITECH-f | G2=IRISID-2 | Hx=L1-x | Hz2=L1-z2 |

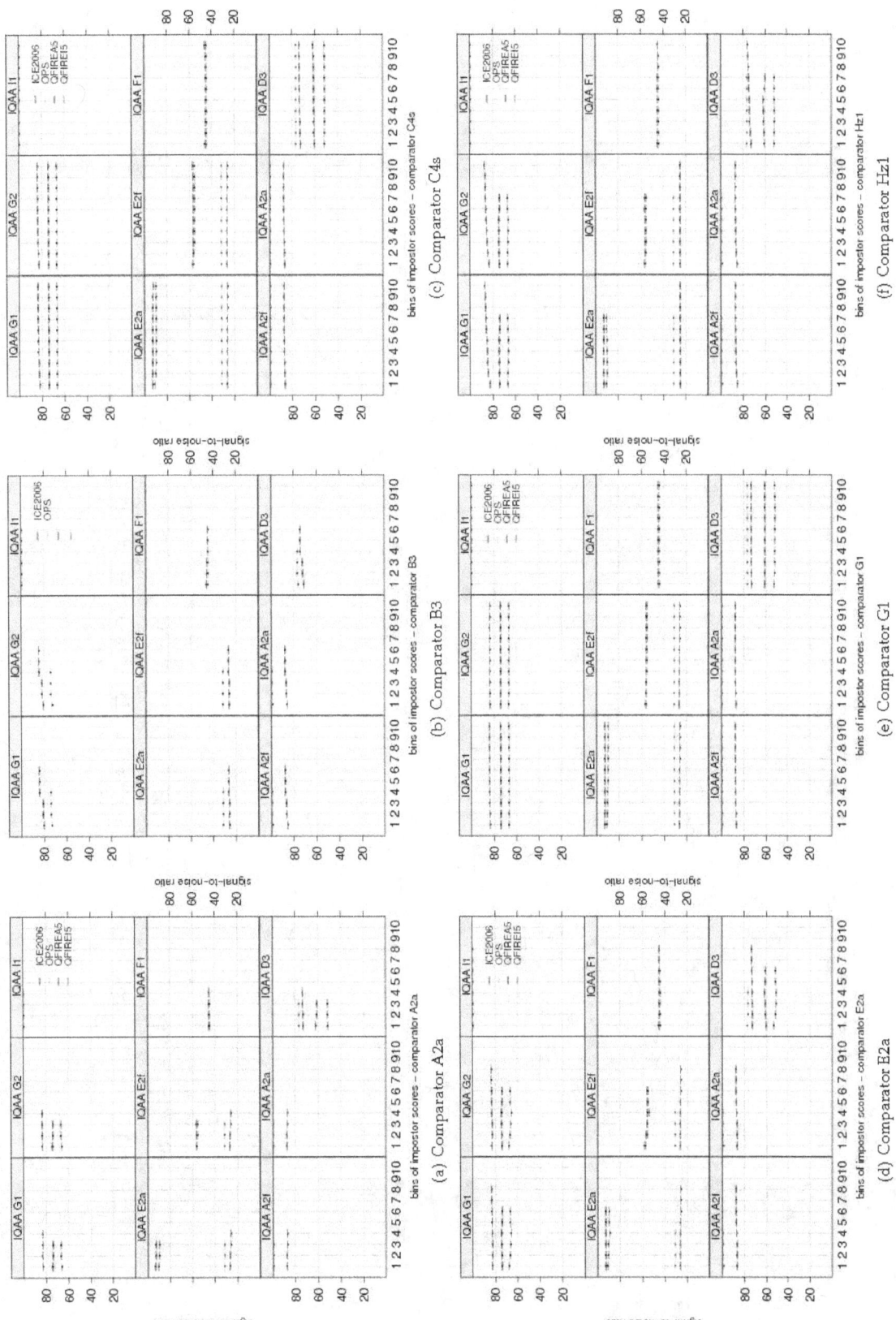

Figure 100: Pairwise SIGNAL TO NOISE RATIO scores vs. impostor scores for the primary Class Z submissions of each participant. Each plot shows quality scores computed by different IQAA. Similar to plots of figure 99, impostor scores are divided equally into ten groups, overlapping by 5 percent. The bootstrapped pairwise quality for each group is shown in a box and whisker plot. Pairwise quality is computed as geometric mean of the quality of the two samples being compared. Impostor scores are not affected by the IQAAS' SIGNAL TO NOISE RATIO .

193

| A2a=NEUROTECHNOLOGY-a | B3=CROSSMATCH | C4s=CAMBRIDGE-s | D3=AWARE | E2a=IRITECH-a | G1=IRISID-1 | I1=KYNEN | Hz1=L1-z1 |
| A2f=NEUROTECHNOLOGY-f | C4x=CAMBRIDGE-x | C4f=CAMBRIDGE-f | F1=MORPHO | E2f=IRITECH-f | G2=IRISID-2 | Hx=L1-x | Hz2=L1-z2 |

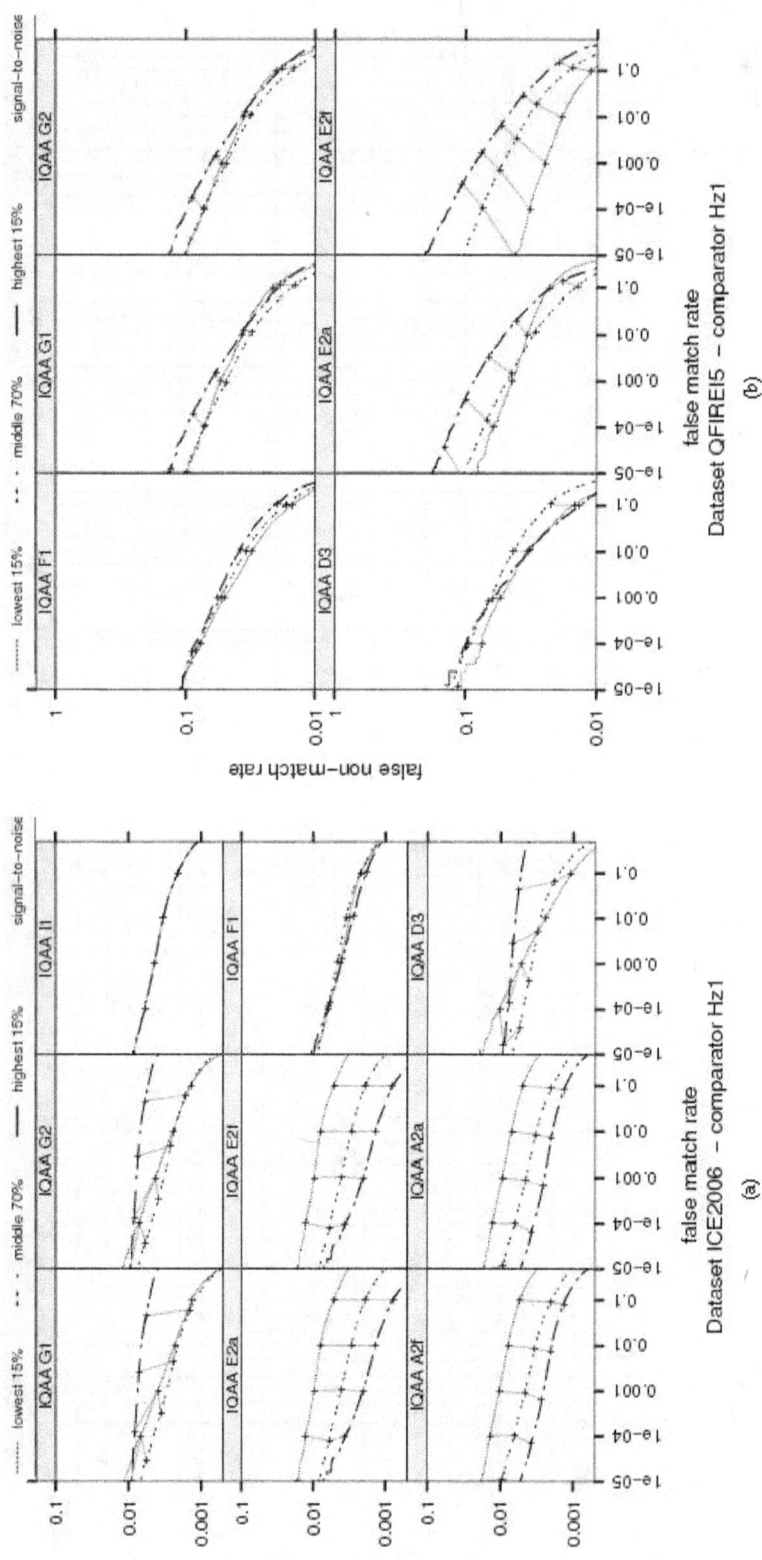

Figure 101: Ranked DET curves for comparator Hz1 and Datasets ICE2006 and QFIRE 15 . The set of all comparisons were partitioned into three groups based on the pair-wise quality of the images being compared. The lowest quality set contains comparisons with pairwise quality in the lower 15 percentile. The highest quality set contains comparisons with pairwise quality in the upper 15 percentile. The rest of the comparisons, namely the middle 70%, made up the third set. The DETs are connected at the same score threshold values (brown lines). Lower FNMR and FMR rates are expected for better quality images. None of the IQAAS' SIGNAL TO NOISE RATIO score is able to give a significant rank ordering of the performance of comparator Hz1 on QFIRE 15 dataset.

A2a=NEUROTECHNOLOGY-a   B3=CROSSMATCH   C4s=CAMBRIDGE-s   D3=AWARE   E2a=IRITECH-a   G1=IRISID-1   I1=KYNEN   Hz1=L1-z1
A2f=NEUROTECHNOLOGY-f   C4x=CAMBRIDGE-x   C4f=CAMBRIDGE-f   F1=MORPHO   E2f=IRITECH-f   G2=IRISID-2   Hx=L1-x   Hz2=L1-z2

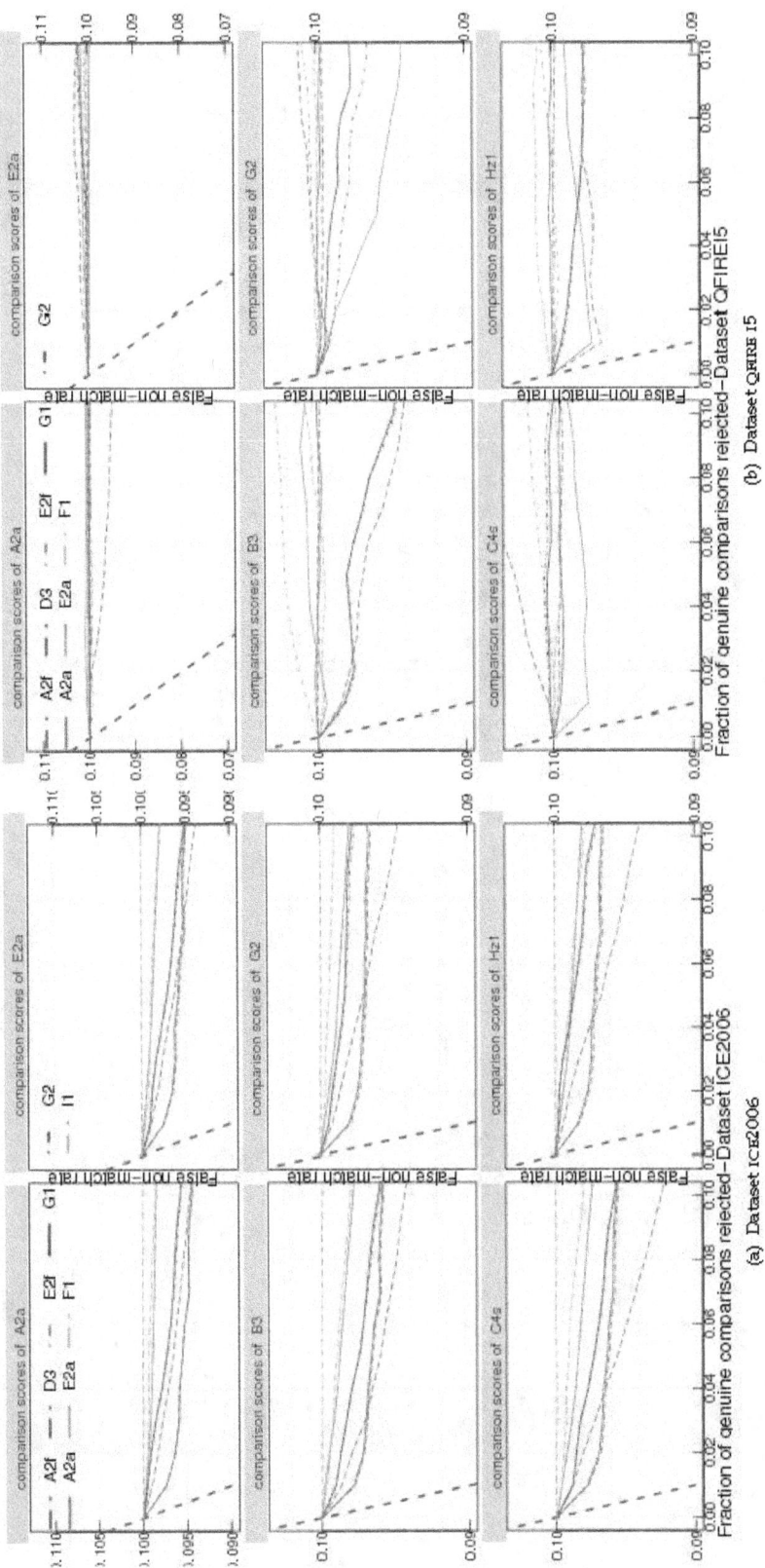

Figure 102: FNMR vs. reject curves for SIGNAL TO NOISE RATIO scores on datasets ICE 2006 and QFIRE 15. The threshold is set to give an initial FNMR = 0.1. The gray dotted line shows the ideal case where the rejection of the comparisons with the lowest ten percent quality results in zero FNMR. No IQAA shows a strong improvement in FNMR after rejecting images with its low IRIS SHAPE scores. No improvement in FNMR is observed after rejection of the images with the lowest SIGNAL TO NOISE RATIO scores.

| A2a=NEUROTECHNOLOGY-a | B3=CROSSMATCH | C4s=CAMBRIDGE-s | D3=AWARE | E2a=IRITECH-a | G1=IRISID-1 | I1=KYNEN | Hz1=L1-z1 |
| A2f=NEUROTECHNOLOGY-f | C4x=CAMBRIDGE-x | C4f=CAMBRIDGE-f | F1=MORPHO | E2f=IRITECH-f | G2=IRISID-2 | Hx=L1-x | Hz2=L1-z2 |

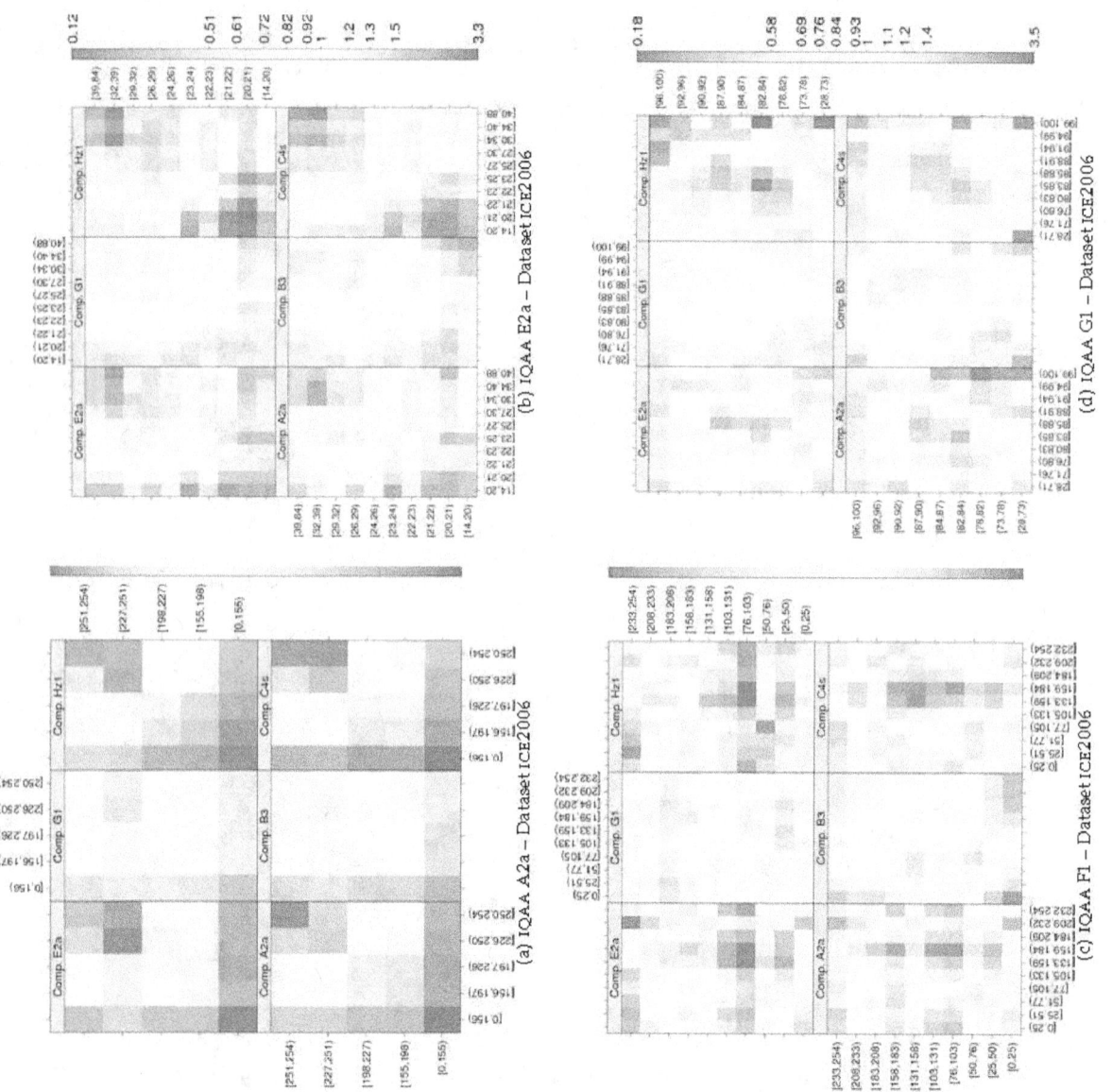

Figure 103: SIGNAL TO NOISE RATIO computed by primary IQAA submissions and FNMR for IQCE comparators for dataset ICE2006 . The y-axis represents enrollment samples' quality with verification samples' on the x-axis. The SIGNAL TO NOISE RATIO scores are quantized into 10 quantiles. The color scale plots $\frac{FNMR}{FNMR_0}$ for comparisons with verification and enrollment qualities $(q_{verification}, q_{enrollment})$. $FNMR_0$ is the nominal FNMR which is the false non-match rate computed over all the images at the same comparison score threshold, in this case at FMR = 0.001. Yellow/Green color represent an improvement in FNMR. Blue color represent a degradation of FNMR. White color means no change in FNMR.

196

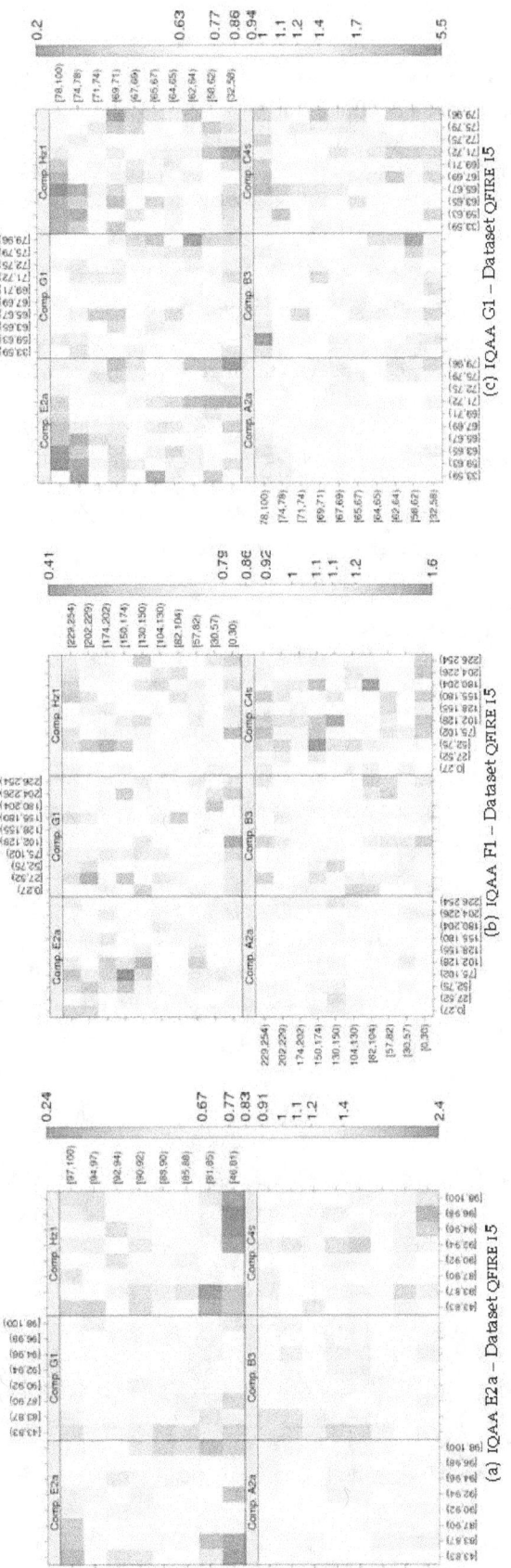

(a) IQAA E2a – Dataset QFIRE I5

(b) IQAA F1 – Dataset QFIRE I5

(c) IQAA G1 – Dataset QFIRE I5

Figure 104: SIGNAL TO NOISE RATIO computed by primary IQAA submissions and FNMR for IQCE comparators for dataset QFIRE I5 . (See caption of Figure 103 for more information.)

9.13   Gaze angle

One of the challenges and perhaps limitations of iris recognition algorithms has been reported to be off-axis images, where the subject's optical axis is not lined up with the camera's optical axis.

Several algorithms have been proposed to correct the projective deformation of the iris when it is imaged off-axis. Dorairaj et al. [22], assuming availability of a rough estimate of gaze, approximated the gaze direction that optimizes the value of the Daugman's integro-differential operator, which detects circular boundaries. Daugman [8] used Fourier-based trigonometry to estimated gaze, and corrected for off-axis imaging. Shuckers et al. [21] proposed the following two methodologies to account for the off-axis images: a) estimating the pitch and roll angles using the Daugmans integro-differential operator and incorporating a projective transformation; and b) training a planar model from the off-axis images, and then use the best fit of an unknown image to the model for transformation parameters.

Among IQCE datasets, ICE2006 and QFIRE I5 are more appropriate for evaluation of GAZE ANGLE . By design, QFIRE I5 contains images with varying gaze angle.

Eight IQCE submissions from five organizations (C4x, C4s, C4f, D3, E2a, E2f, Hx, and I1) generate GAZE ANGLE scores. The distribution of their GAZE ANGLE scores is shown in Figure 105. In order to make the boxplots more readable, quality scores in [0–254] range were linearly scaled back to [0–100].

Quantitative evaluation of these IQAAs follows.

RELATIONSHIP WITH THE DISTRIBUTION OF GENUINE SCORES

GAZE ANGLE vs. bins of genuine scores of IQCE primary comparators are shown in Figure 106. IQAA Hx shows the largest variation in the GAZE ANGLE across the bins of the genuine score. No change is observed for IQAAs D3 and I1's GAZE ANGLE scores.

QFIRE A5 images are given the lowest GAZE ANGLE scores by all IQAAS, however, only IQAA Hx's GAZE ANGLE score varies across the bins of the genuine scores. All IQAAs except E2a scored ICE2006 as the second lowest. The observations that GAZE ANGLE scores of IQAA E2a on QFIRE I5 and QFIRE A5 images are comparable suggests that either IQAA E2a's assessment of GAZE ANGLE is not accurate, or once the GAZE ANGLE is estimated and off-axis gaze is corrected, the matching result is not affected.

RELATIONSHIP WITH THE DISTRIBUTION OF IMPOSTOR SCORES

The relationship of GAZE ANGLE with impostors scores depends on the comparators. Comparators Hz1 and E2a's impostor scores are more sensitive to GAZE ANGLE scores than others, particularly on QFIRE A5 images. Images with low GAZE ANGLE scores have low impostor scores.

RANKED DET:: DO LOW-QUALITY IMAGES PRODUCE HIGH FNMR OR FMR?

The DET curves of Figure 108 shows that the GAZE ANGLE affects FNMR. Images with the lowest GAZE ANGLE scores result in up to an order of magnitude (IQAA C4x) higher FNMR than the images with the highest GAZE ANGLE scores.

GAZE ANGLE scores generated by IQAAs Hx, D3 and I1 do not predict performance, though they perform better on QFIRE

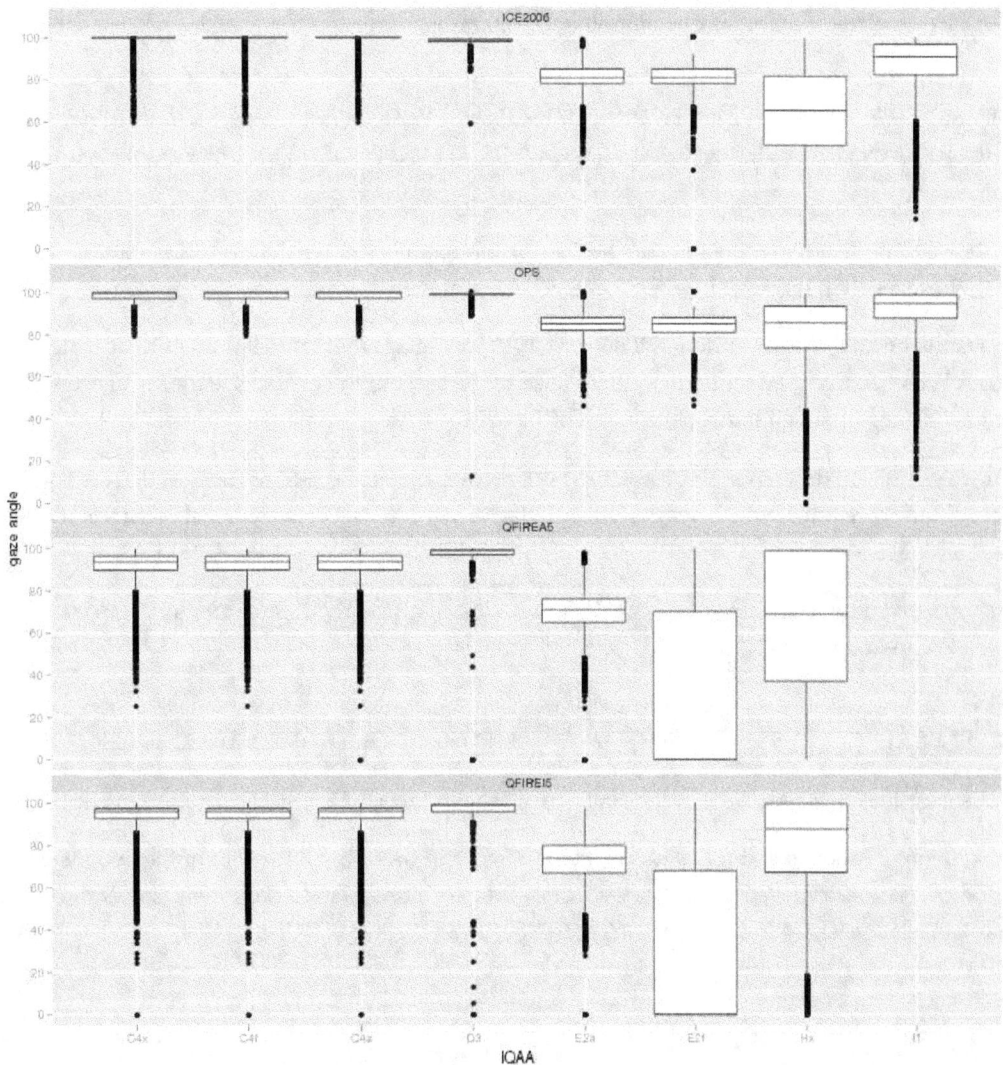

Figure 105: Box and whisker plots of the IQAAs that generate GAZE ANGLE scores.

A5 images than ICE 2006.

FMR is not as severely affected as FNMR.

EFFECT OF QUALITY ON FNMR : HOW QUICKLY FNMR IMPROVES WHEN POOR QUALITY SAMPLES ARE REJECTED?

Rejection of ICE 2006 images with the lowest GAZE ANGLE scores improves the FNMR of all comparators. IQAA E2a is the best performer, followed by C4x. E2a performance is close to the ideal case (gray dotted line). IQAAs D3, I1 GAZE ANGLE scores do not predict performance.

Performance of IQAA E2a drops on QFIRE A5 images. IQAA C4x is the best performer, with almost perfect performance for its mated comparator. Rejection of QFIRE A5 images with the lowest IQAA Hx GAZE ANGLE scores improves com-

| A2a=NEUROTECHNOLOGY-a | B3=CROSSMATCH | C4s=CAMBRIDGE-s | D3=AWARE | E2a=IRITECH-a | G1=IRISID-1 | I1=KYNEN | Hz1=L1-z1 |
| A2f=NEUROTECHNOLOGY-f | C4x=CAMBRIDGE-x | C4f=CAMBRIDGE-f | F1=MORPHO | E2f=IRITECH-f | G2=IRISID-2 | Hx=L1-x | Hz2=L1-z2 |

parator Hz1's FNMR, but it is not effective for other comparators.

TEST OF SIGNIFICANCE :: DO THE IMAGES INVOLVED IN SUCCESSFUL VERIFICATION ATTEMPTS HAVE SIGNIFICANTLY HIGHER QUALITY SCORES THAN THOSE INVOLVED IN FAILED VERIFICATION ATTEMPTS?

Table 31 shows that images involved in comparisons resulting in correct match have significantly higher GAZE ANGLE scores than those result in false reject, when GAZE ANGLE scores are generated by C4x or E2a.

Ignoring results on OPS images, the ICE2006 or QFIRE A5 images which result in correct match have significantly higher IQAA Hx's GAZE ANGLE scores than those falsely rejected, but lower GAZE ANGLE scores on QFIRE I5 images, as in evident by the negative sign in the 6th column of Table 31.

There is not a significant difference in IQAA E2f's GAZE ANGLE scores of QFIRE A5 images that are correctly matched and those that are falsely rejected, which suggest IQAA E2f's GAZE ANGLE scores are not an accurate measurement of GAZE ANGLE within the images.

Table 32 shows that only IQAA E2a's GAZE ANGLE scores are significantly different for all comparators (except C4s) and all datasets. Comparator C4s's FMR is not affected by off-axis gaze.

EFFECT OF VARIATION BETWEEN THE TWO SAMPLES:: DOES SAMENESS MATTER?

Figure 111 shows that GAZE ANGLE affects FNMR. Images with low GAZE ANGLE scores elevate FNMR.

An interesting observation is that for IQAA Hx, the difference in GAZE ANGLE scores of the two images being compared matters; lower FNMR is achieved if the GAZE ANGLE score are similar, and FNMR increases as the difference increases. This behavior is not observed for GAZE ANGLE scores of IQAA E2a or C4x.

OBSERVATIONS AND CONCLUSIONS

GAZE ANGLE significantly affects FNMR. Images with the worst GAZE ANGLE scores result in up to an order of magnitude (IQAA C4x) higher FNMR than the images with the best GAZE ANGLE scores. On QFIRE A5 images, IQAA C4x is the best performer with almost perfect performance for its mated comparator.

Rejection of QFIRE A5 images with the lowest IQAA Hx's GAZE ANGLE scores improves comparator Hz1's FNMR, but it is not effective for other comparators.

IQAA E2a is the best performer on ICE2006 images, but its performance drops on QFIRE A5 images. IQAA C4x performs reasonably good on ICE2006 and QFIRE A5 images.

GAZE ANGLE occurs when the subject does not look directly into the camera or if the subject is looking into the camera but his head is rotated or tilted.

A better user interface can correct GAZE ANGLE by guiding subjects through the process, e.g., visual or audio feedback on where to look.

| A2a=NEUROTECHNOLOGY-a | B3=CROSSMATCH | C4s=CAMBRIDGE-s | D3=AWARE | E2a=IRITECH-a | G1=IRISID-1 | I1=KYNEN | Hz1=L1-z1 |
| A2f=NEUROTECHNOLOGY-f | C4x=CAMBRIDGE-x | C4f=CAMBRIDGE-f | F1=MORPHO | E2f=IRITECH-f | G2=IRISID-2 | Hx=L1-x | Hz2=L1-z2 |

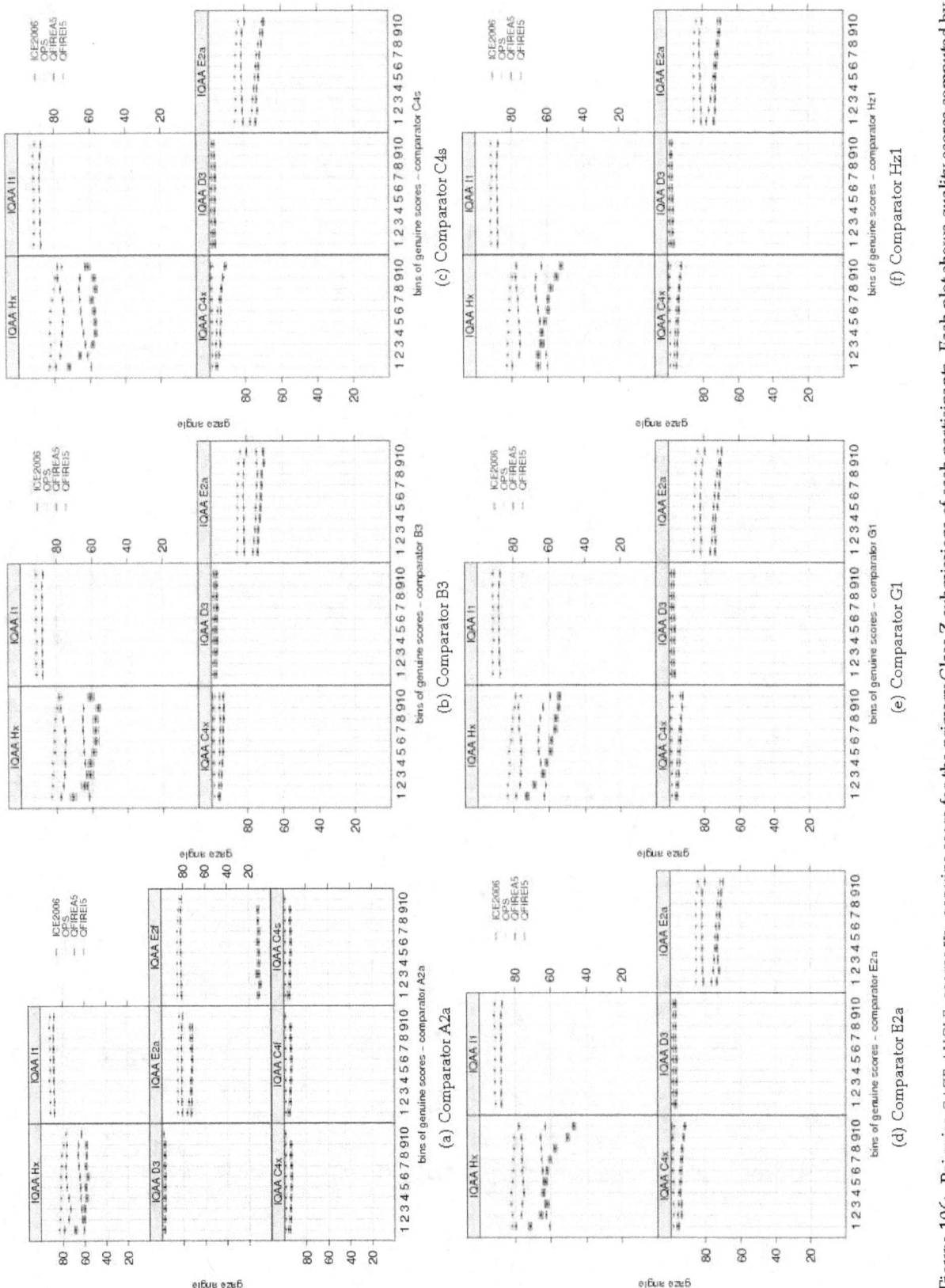

Figure 106: Pairwise GAZE ANGLE scores vs. genuine score for the primary Class Z submissions of each participants. Each plot shows quality scores computed by different IQAA. Genuine scores are divided equally into ten groups. Groups overlap by 5 percent. Bootstrapped pairwise quality for each group is shown in a box and whisker plot. Pairwise quality is computed as geometric mean of the quality of the two samples being compared.

| A2a=NEUROTECHNOLOGY-a | B3=CROSSMATCH | C4s=CAMBRIDGE-s | D3=AWARE | E2a=IRITECH-a | G1=IRISID-1 | I1=KYNEN | Hz1=L1-z1 |
| A2f=NEUROTECHNOLOGY-f | C4x=CAMBRIDGE-x | C4f=CAMBRIDGE-f | F1=MORPHO | E2f=IRITECH-f | G2=IRISID-2 | Hx=L1-x | Hz2=L1-z2 |

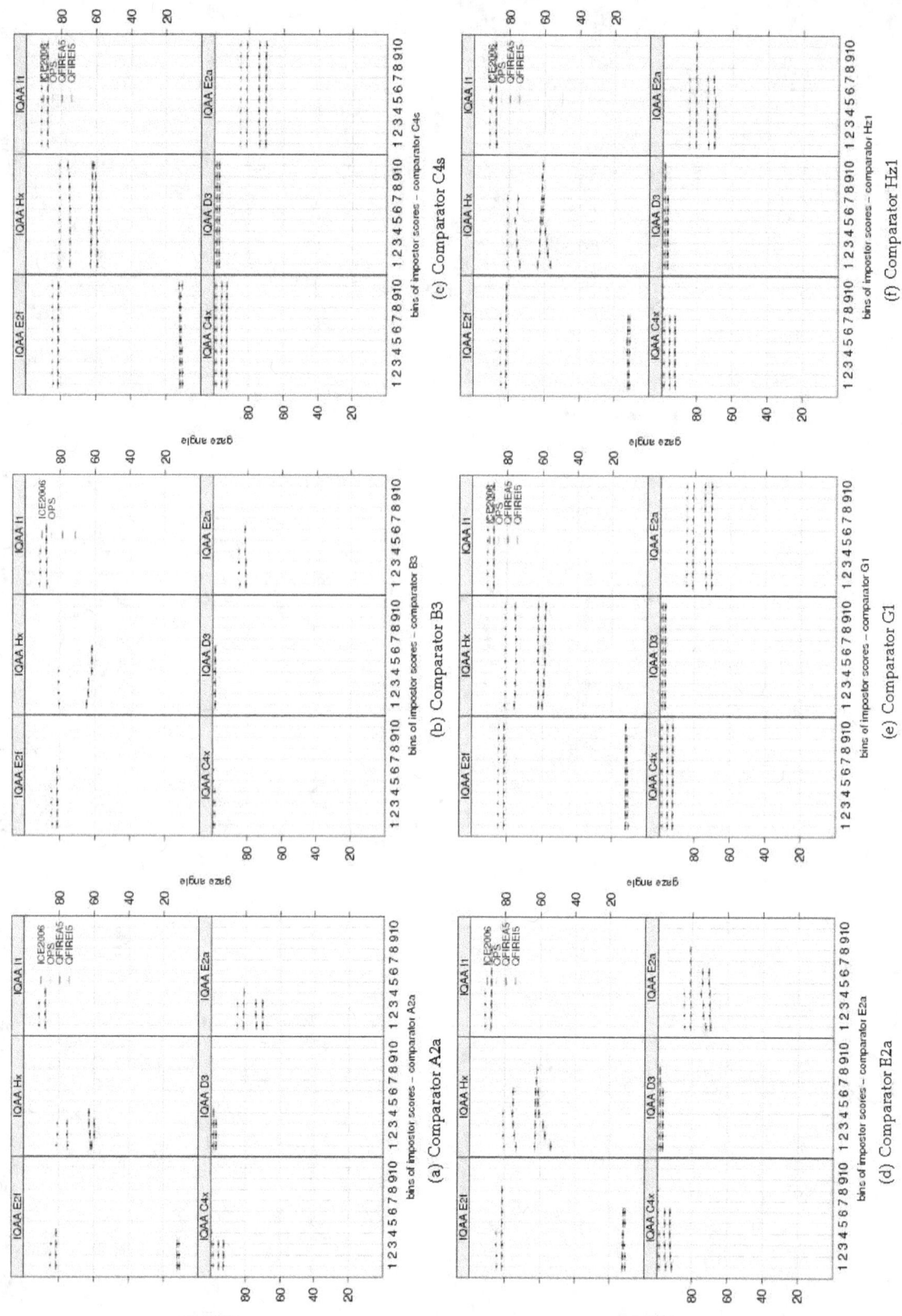

Figure 107: Pairwise GAZE ANGLE scores vs. impostor scores for the primary Class Z submissions of each participants. Each plot shows quality scores computed by different IQAA. Similar to plots of Figure 106, impostor scores are divided equally into ten groups. Groups overlap by 5 percent. Bootstrapped pairwise quality for each group is shown in a box and whisker plot. Pairwise quality is computed as geometric mean of the quality of the two samples being compared.

| A2a=NEUROTECHNOLOGY-a | B3=CROSSMATCH | C4s=CAMBRIDGE-s | D3=AWARE | E2a=IRITECH-a | G1=IRISID-1 | I1=KYNEN | Hz1=L1-z1 |
| A2f=NEUROTECHNOLOGY-f | C4x=CAMBRIDGE-x | C4f=CAMBRIDGE-f | F1=MORPHO | E2f=IRITECH-f | G2=IRISID-2 | Hx=L1-x | Hz2=L1-z2 |

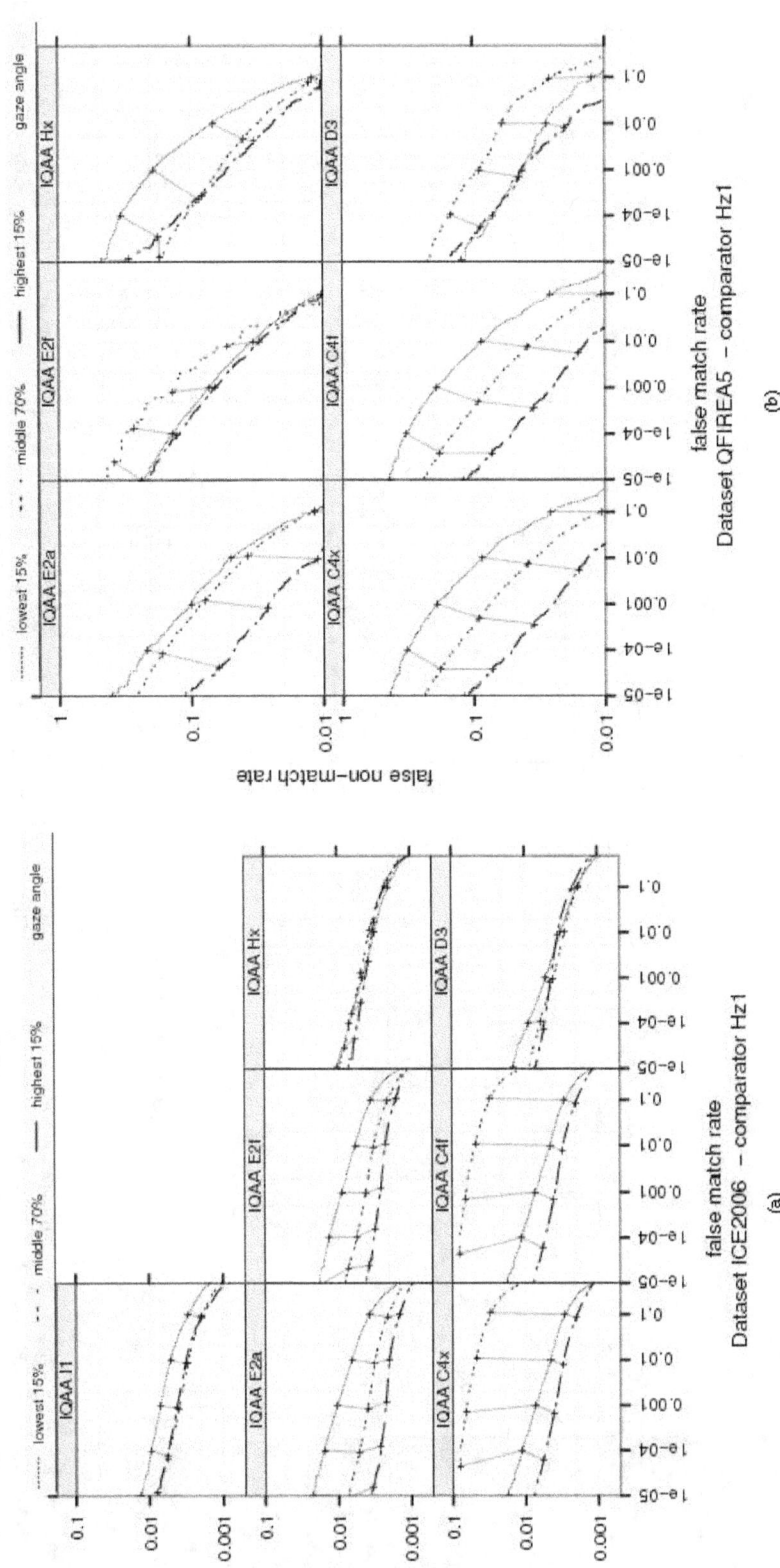

Figure 108: Ranked DET curves for comparator Hz1 and Datasets ICE2006 and QFIRE A5. The set of all comparisons were partitioned into three groups based on the pair-wise quality of the images being compared. The lowest quality set contains comparisons with pairwise quality in the lower 15 percentile. The highest quality set contains comparisons with pairwise quality in the upper 15 percentile. The rest of the comparisons, namely the middle 70%, made up the third set. The DETs are connected at the same score threshold values (brown lines). Lower FNMR and FMR rates are expected for better quality images.

| A2a=NEUROTECHNOLOGY-a | B3=CROSSMATCH | C4s=CAMBRIDGE-s | D3=AWARE | E2a=IRITECH-a | G1=IRISID-1 | I1=KYNEN | Hz1=L1-z1 |
| A2f=NEUROTECHNOLOGY-f | C4x=CAMBRIDGE-x | C4f=CAMBRIDGE-f | F1=MORPHO | E2f=IRITECH-f | G2=IRISID-2 | Hx=L1-x | Hz2=L1-z2 |

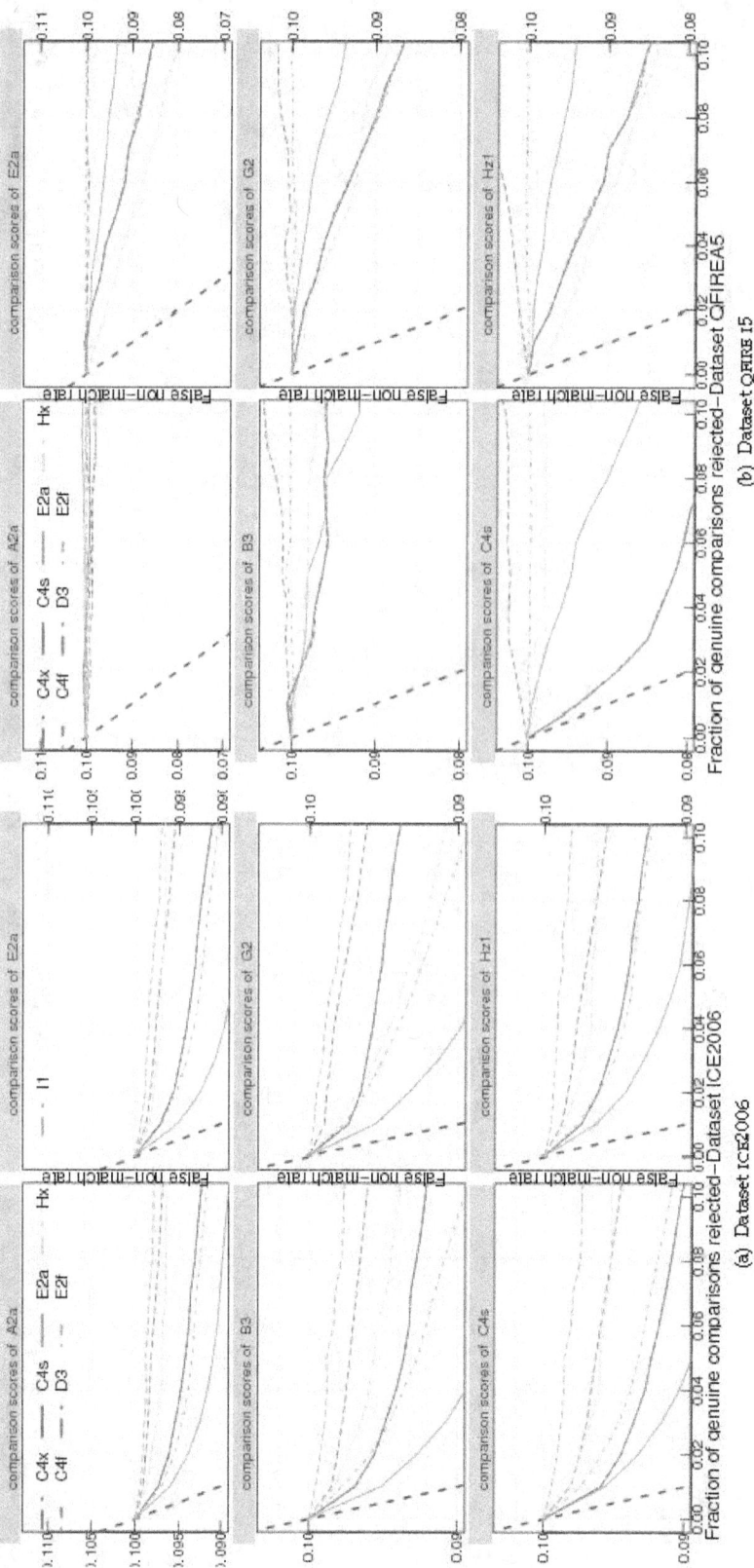

Figure 109: FNMR vs. reject curves for GAZE ANGLE scores on datasets ICE2006 and QFIRE15. The threshold is set to give an initial FNMR = 0.1. The gray dotted line shows the ideal case where the rejection of the comparisons with the lowest ten percent quality results in zero FNMR. No IQAA shows a strong improvement in FNMR after rejecting images with its low IRIS SHAPE scores.

| A2a=NEUROTECHNOLOGY-a | B3=CROSSMATCH | C4s=CAMBRIDGE-s | D3=AWARE | E2a=IRITECH-a | G1=IRISID-1 | I1=KYNEN | Hz1=L1-z1 |
| A2f=NEUROTECHNOLOGY-f | C4x=CAMBRIDGE-x | C4f=CAMBRIDGE-f | F1=MORPHO | E2f=IRITECH-f | G2=IRISID-2 | Hx=L1-x | Hz2=L1-z2 |

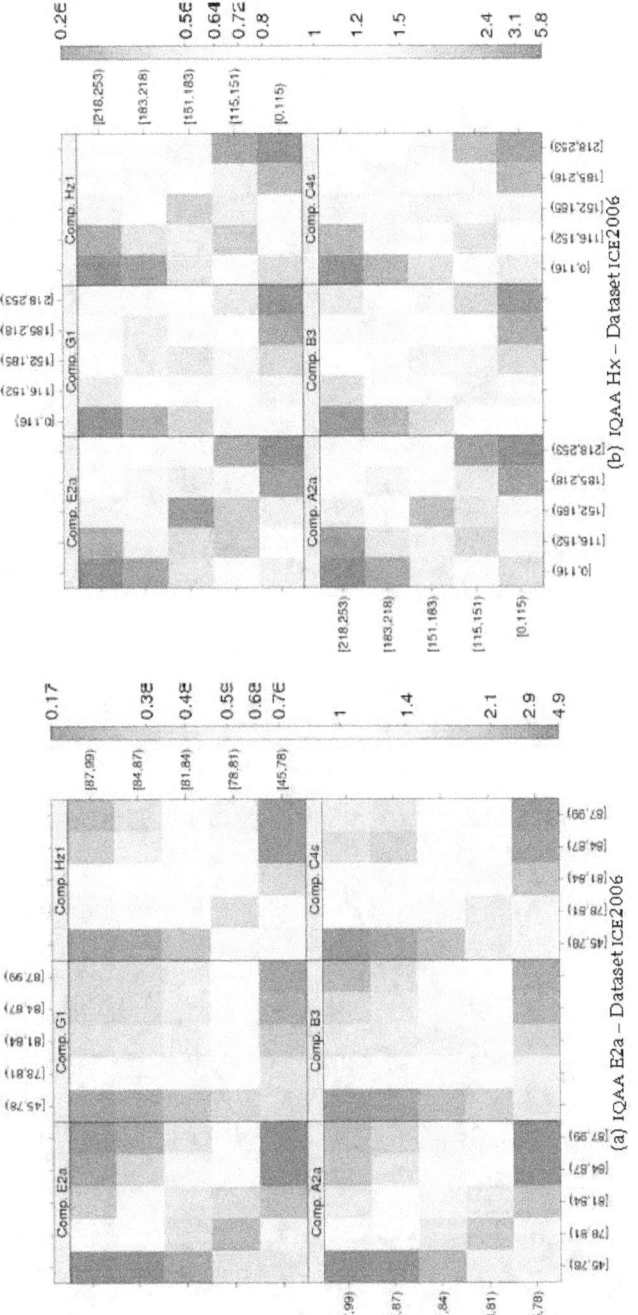

Figure 110: GAZE ANGLE computed by primary IQAA submissions and FNMR for IQCE comparators for dataset ICE2006 . The y-axis represents enrollment samples' quality with verification samples' on the x-axis. The GAZE ANGLE scores are quantized into 10 quantiles. The color scale plots $\frac{FNMR}{FNMR_0}$ for comparisons with verification and enrollment qualities ($q_{verification}, q_{enrollment}$). $FNMR_0$ is the nominal FNMR which is the false non-match rate computed over all the images at the same comparison score threshold, in this case at FMR = 0.001. Yellow/Green color represent an improvement in FNMR. Blue color represent a degradation of FNMR. White color means no change in FNMR.

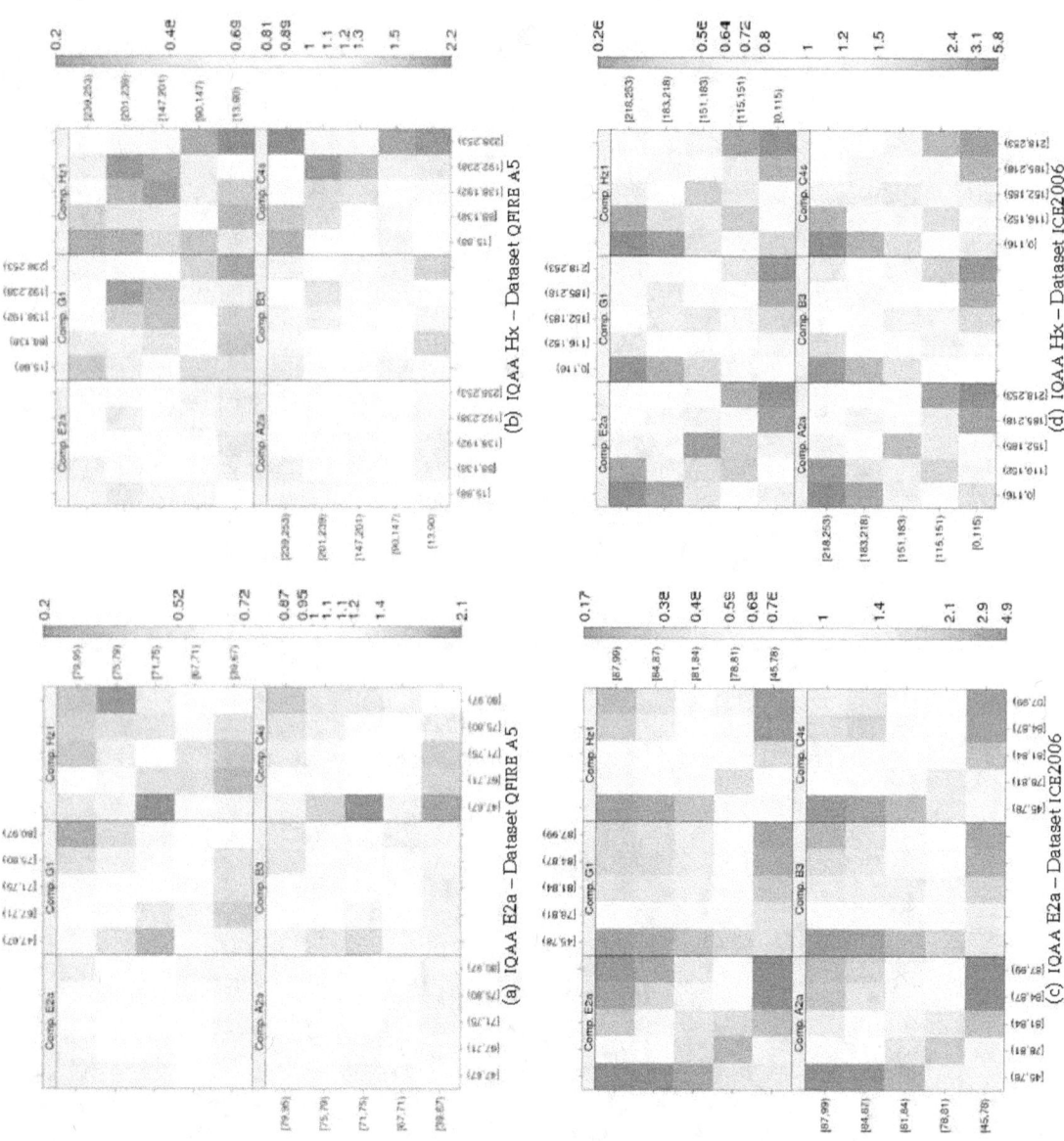

Figure 111: GAZE ANGLE computed by primary IQAA submissions and FNMR for IQCE comparators for dataset QFIRE A5 . The y-axis represents enrollment samples' quality with verification samples' on the x-axis. The GAZE ANGLE scores are quantized into 10 quantiles. The color scale plots $\frac{FNMR}{FNMR_0}$ for comparisons with verification and enrollment qualities ($q_{verification}, q_{enrollment}$). $FNMR_0$ is the nominal FNMR which is the false non-match rate computed over all the images at the same comparison score threshold, in this case at FMR = 0.001. Yellow/Green color represent a degradation of FNMR. Blue color represent an improvement in FNMR. White color means no change in FNMR.

206

Dataset	comparator	IQAA C4x	IQAA E2a	IQAA E2f	IQAA Hx
ICE2006	A2a	(0.92,0.95)	(4.28,4.39)	(3.13,3.25)	(1.78,2.23)
ICE2006	B3	(0.68,0.69)	(3.28,3.33)	(2.27,2.32)	(5.00,5.21)
ICE2006	C4s	(1.56,1.58)	(3.20,3.28)	(2.08,2.17)	(0.49,0.82)
ICE2006	E2a	(1.27,1.30)	(5.08,5.19)	(3.89,4.00)	(3.38,3.85)
ICE2006	G2	(0.64,0.65)	(3.83,3.89)	(2.38,2.44)	(6.28,6.51)
ICE2006	Hz1	(0.33,0.36)	(1.89,2.02)	(1.12,1.25)	(-0.59,-0.07)
OPS	A2a	(-0.25,0.84)	(0.72,3.03)	(0.56,3.22)	(-0.42,7.81)
OPS	B3	(-0.12,0.34)	(1.06,2.02)	(0.62,1.74)	(0.89,4.33)
OPS	C4s	(-0.56,0.32)	(2.02,3.89)	(1.15,3.30)	(0.25,6.87)
OPS	E2a	(-0.46,0.83)	(-0.37,2.35)	(-0.17,2.96)	(-3.09,6.59)
OPS	G2	(0.12,0.83)	(2.86,4.36)	(2.77,4.51)	(5.83,11.18)
OPS	Hz1	(-0.77,0.27)	(1.60,3.78)	(0.72,3.24)	(-1.41,6.36)
QFIREA5	A2a	(0.33,0.50)	(0.57,0.91)	(-1.06,0.45)	(1.99,3.24)
QFIREA5	B3	(0.94,1.18)	(1.66,2.15)	(-0.65,1.67)	(2.81,4.62)
QFIREA5	C4s	(2.31,2.53)	(2.87,3.32)	(-1.11,0.92)	(-1.25,0.43)
QFIREA5	E2a	(1.11,1.27)	(1.08,1.40)	(-0.47,0.94)	(8.30,9.44)
QFIREA5	G2	(1.70,1.86)	(2.26,2.59)	(-0.54,0.98)	(6.38,7.62)
QFIREA5	Hz1	(1.77,2.04)	(2.27,2.83)	(-0.39,2.14)	(8.23,10.30)
QFIREI5	A2a	(0.89,0.97)	(1.06,1.21)	(-1.46,-0.88)	(-1.56,-1.17)
QFIREI5	B3	(0.26,0.32)	(0.58,0.73)	(-0.96,-0.35)	(-2.51,-2.14)
QFIREI5	C4s	(4.99,5.08)	(4.14,4.32)	(-0.18,0.55)	(-1.95,-1.47)
QFIREI5	E2a	(2.68,2.78)	(2.67,2.87)	(-1.61,-0.83)	(-2.25,-1.74)
QFIREI5	G2	(1.86,1.95)	(2.03,2.19)	(-0.08,0.57)	(-1.23,-0.81)
QFIREI5	Hz1	(2.41,2.53)	(2.06,2.30)	(-2.69,-1.75)	(-0.56,0.05)

Table 31: Tukey HSD difference in mean of GAZE ANGLE scores. Each cell shows the 95% confidence level in difference in mean of pairwise quality for images verified correctly (i.e., the genuine score equal or less than threshold) and those rejected falsely (i.e., the genuine score larger than threshold). Quality scores were computed by the SDK identified by the column header and comparison scores were generated by the SDK identified by the row header. If the interval does not contain zero, the difference in mean is significant. Cells where difference in mean is not significant have pink background. For monotonically increasing quality components (all except DILATION, and depending on quality implementation GRAY SCALE SPREAD), the expected behavior is to have higher quality scores for the pair of enrollment and verification images that give genuine comparison scores less than threshold. The pairwise quality is computed as geometric mean of the quality of two samples being compared. Threshold is set to give false match rate of 0.001.

Dataset	comparator	IQAA C4x	IQAA E2a	IQAA E2f	IQAA Hx
ICE2006	A2a	(-0.12,-0.06)	(-0.25,-0.02)	(-0.14,0.10)	(2.01,2.96)
ICE2006	B3	(0.37,0.41)	(0.96,1.12)	(0.30,0.47)	(-5.79,-5.11)
ICE2006	C4s	(0.03,0.08)	(-0.06,0.12)	(-0.18,0.00)	(-1.36,-0.62)
ICE2006	E2a	(0.18,0.23)	(0.41,0.59)	(-0.04,0.15)	(-0.47,0.28)
ICE2006	G2	(-0.11,-0.06)	(-0.35,-0.16)	(-0.23,-0.04)	(0.55,1.31)
ICE2006	Hz1	(0.06,0.11)	(0.08,0.27)	(-0.11,0.10)	(-2.78,-1.96)
OPS	A2a	(-0.05,0.06)	(-0.26,-0.01)	(-0.17,0.11)	(-0.54,0.35)
OPS	B3	(-0.02,0.06)	(0.12,0.32)	(0.23,0.46)	(-0.08,0.65)
OPS	C4s	(-0.06,0.03)	(-0.05,0.15)	(-0.06,0.17)	(-0.27,0.47)
OPS	E2a	(0.05,0.14)	(0.08,0.28)	(0.13,0.36)	(0.42,1.16)
OPS	G2	(-0.10,-0.01)	(-0.28,-0.08)	(-0.32,-0.08)	(-0.93,-0.20)
OPS	Hz1	(0.03,0.12)	(0.02,0.21)	(0.02,0.26)	(-0.17,0.56)
QFIREA5	A2a	(-0.16,0.11)	(0.45,0.85)	(-1.10,0.70)	(-12.07,-10.45)
QFIREA5	C4s	(-0.03,0.21)	(-0.03,0.33)	(-0.62,1.02)	(-1.33,0.15)
QFIREA5	E2a	(3.82,4.06)	(1.50,1.86)	(0.55,2.17)	(38.25,39.72)
QFIREA5	G2	(-0.18,0.05)	(0.41,0.79)	(-1.38,0.32)	(-4.09,-2.58)
QFIREA5	Hz1	(1.19,1.43)	(0.50,0.86)	(0.01,1.65)	(12.17,13.64)
QFIREI5	A2a	(0.08,0.19)	(1.02,1.29)	(0.78,1.98)	(-1.91,-1.19)
QFIREI5	C4s	(0.85,0.94)	(1.72,1.95)	(-0.67,0.37)	(-1.45,-0.82)
QFIREI5	E2a	(2.07,2.16)	(3.63,3.86)	(-3.04,-2.00)	(-2.05,-1.43)
QFIREI5	G2	(0.15,0.85)	(0.61,2.36)	(-4.49,3.33)	(-6.20,-1.47)
QFIREI5	Hz1	(1.06,1.16)	(1.68,1.91)	(-2.97,-1.93)	(-0.27,0.36)

Table 32: Tukey HSD mean difference in GAZE ANGLE scores. Each cell shows the 95% confidence level in difference in mean of pairwise quality for images correctly rejected (i.e., the impostor score equal or greater than threshold) and those falsely matched (i.e., the impostor score less than threshold). Quality scores were computed by the SDK identified by the column header and comparison scores were generated by the SDK identified by the row header. If the interval does not contain zero, the difference in mean is significant. Cells where difference in mean is not significant are shaded in pink. For monotonic increasing quality components (all except DILATION, and depending on quality implementation GRAY SCALE SPREAD), the expected behavior is to have higher quality scores for the pair of (enrollment, verification) images that result in impostor comparison scores equal or greater than threshold. Pairwise quality is computed as geometric mean of the quality of two samples being compared. Threshold is set to give false match rate of 0.001.

9.14   Interlace

All contemporary iris acquisition devices use progressive scan rather than interlace, but interlace artifact remains an important issue for legacy data captured by older cameras.

Interlaced scan-based images use techniques developed for CRT (Cathode Ray Tube) TV monitor displays, made up of 576 visible horizontal lines across a standard TV screen. Interlacing divides these into odd and even lines and then alternately refreshes them at 30 frames per second. Interlace can reduce the effective vertical resolution by a factor of two.

Progressive scan differs from interlaced scan in that the image is displayed on a screen by scanning each line in a sequential order rather than an alternate order, as is done with interlaced scan.

ICE2006 images suffer from interlace impairment. The Dalsa camera used for collection the QFIRE images uses progressive scan technique.

The following nine submissions from five organizations generated INTERLACE scores: A2a, A2f, D3, C4f, C4s, C4x, E2a, E2f, and Hx. The distribution of their INTERLACE scores is shown in Figure 112. In order to make the boxplots more readable, quality scores in [0–254] range were linearly scaled back to [0–100].

Comparative analysis of these IQAAs follows.

RELATIONSHIP WITH THE DISTRIBUTION OF GENUINE SCORES

Figure 113 shows the dependence of IQCE primary comparators' genuine scores on INTERLACE scores.

IQAAs A2a and E2a give noticeably lower INTERLACE scores to ICE2006 images than the other datasets. ICE2006 images with high genuine comparison scores have low INTERLACE scores.

IQAA Hx gives its lowest INTERLACE scores to ICE2006 images, but its score does not change across the bins of the genuine scores. The biggest change is observed for QFIRE I5 images.

IQAA C4x's INTERLACE scores are 0, 2, 5, 7, or 10 for 79% of ICE2006 images and all the QFIRE I5 images.

IQAA D3 give comparable INTERLACE scores to the four IQCE datasets. No change in INTERLACE is observes across the genuine comparison scores.

RELATIONSHIP WITH THE DISTRIBUTION OF IMPOSTOR SCORES

Similar to Figure 113, the dependence of the impostor distribution on INTERLACE score is shown in Figure 114. The effect, if any, seems to be small.

The ICE2006 images with the lowest comparator Hz1's impostor scores have lower INTERLACE scores, particularly if generated by IQAA A2a or E2a.

RANKED DET:: DO LOW-QUALITY IMAGES PRODUCE HIGH FNMR OR FMR?

Figure 115 shows the DET curves of the lowest 15%, middle 70% and the highets 15 percentile of the ICE2006 images.

209

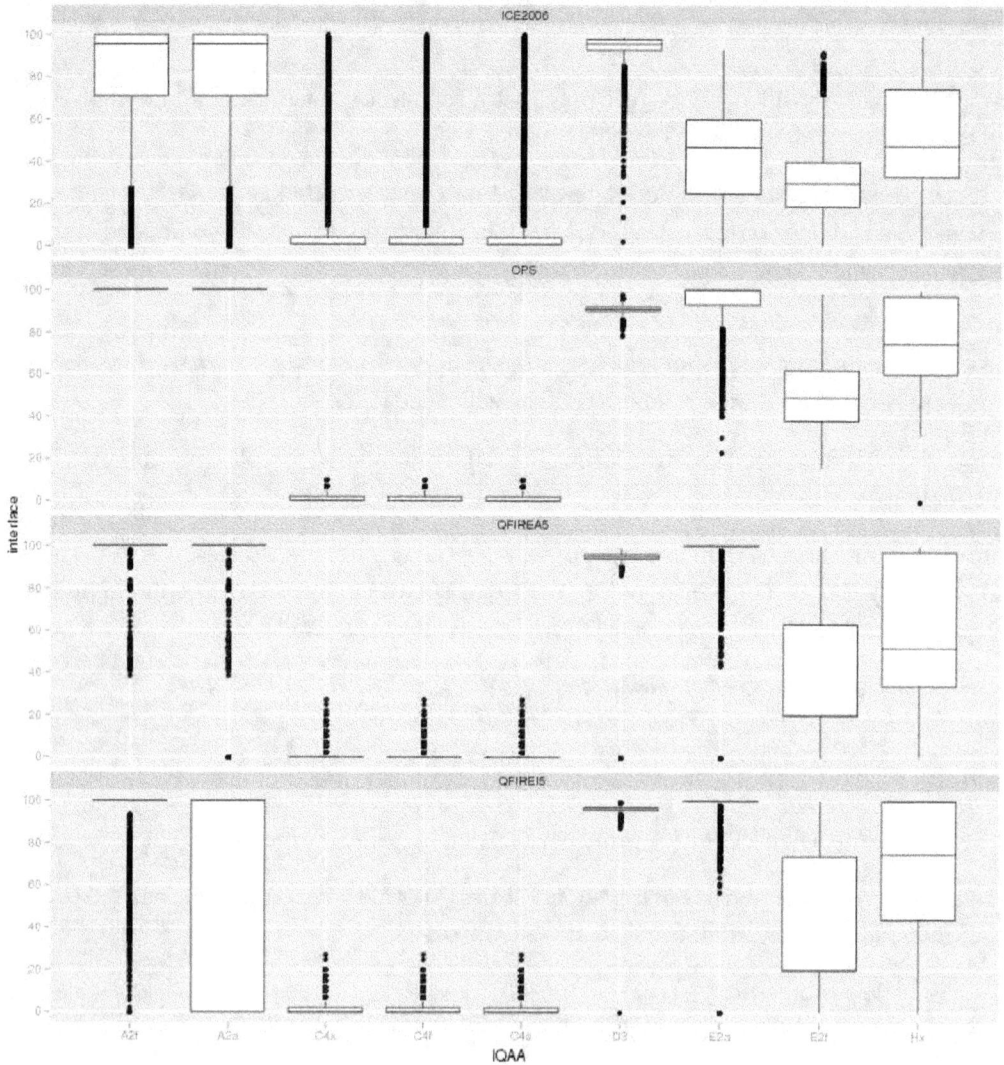

Figure 112: Box and whisker plots of the IQAAs that generate INTERLACE scores.

Only IQAAs E2a's and A2a's INTERLACE scores give a rank ordered of performance, though the change in FNMR is not large.

FMR seems to not be affected by INTERLACE scores.

EFFECT OF QUALITY ON FNMR : HOW QUICKLY FNMR IMPROVES WHEN POOR QUALITY SAMPLES ARE REJECTED?

Figure 116 shows that up to 10% rejection of comparisons involving images with the lowest INTERLACE score does not improve performance.

TEST OF SIGNIFICANCE :: DO THE IMAGES INVOLVED IN SUCCESSFUL VERIFICATION ATTEMPTS

| A2a=NEUROTECHNOLOGY-a | B3=CROSSMATCH | C4s=CAMBRIDGE-s | D3=AWARE | E2a=IRITECH-a | G1=IRISID-1 | I1=KYNEN | Hz1=L1-z1 |
| A2f=NEUROTECHNOLOGY-f | C4x=CAMBRIDGE-x | C4f=CAMBRIDGE-f | F1=MORPHO | E2f=IRITECH-f | G2=IRISID-2 | Hx=L1-x | Hz2=L1-z2 |

HAVE SIGNIFICANTLY HIGHER QUALITY SCORES THAN THOSE INVOLVED IN FAILED VERIFICATION ATTEMPTS?

Table 33 indicates that ICE2006 images involved in successful verification attempts have significantly different INTERLACE scores than the images which were falsely rejected.

INTERLACE scores of some IQAAS' are significantly different for images successfully verified and those falsely rejected.

The difference is not significant for the OPS and QFIRE A5 datasets

Table 34 shows that there is a significant but small difference in IQAA E2a's INTERLACE score of images falsely matched and images correctly rejected.

EFFECT OF VARIATION BETWEEN THE TWO SAMPLES:: DOES SAMENESS MATTER?

Figures 117-118 show that the difference between the INTERLACE scores of the two images being compared does not affect FNMR.

OBSERVATIONS AND CONCLUSIONS

The difference in mean pairwise INTERLACE score of ICE2006 images involved in successful verification attempt is significantly larger than the mean pairwise score of the images result in false reject. In other words, INTERLACE significantly affect genuine comparison scores. However its affect on FNMR is smaller than other and therefore FNMR. However the error vs reject curves of Figure 116 does not show negligible improvement in FNMR after rejection of 10% of comparisons of the lowest INTERLACE scores, suggesting the effect of interlace on FNMR is smaller than the effect of the other existing impairments in an images.

The difference between the INTERLACE scores of the two images being compared does not affect FNMR.

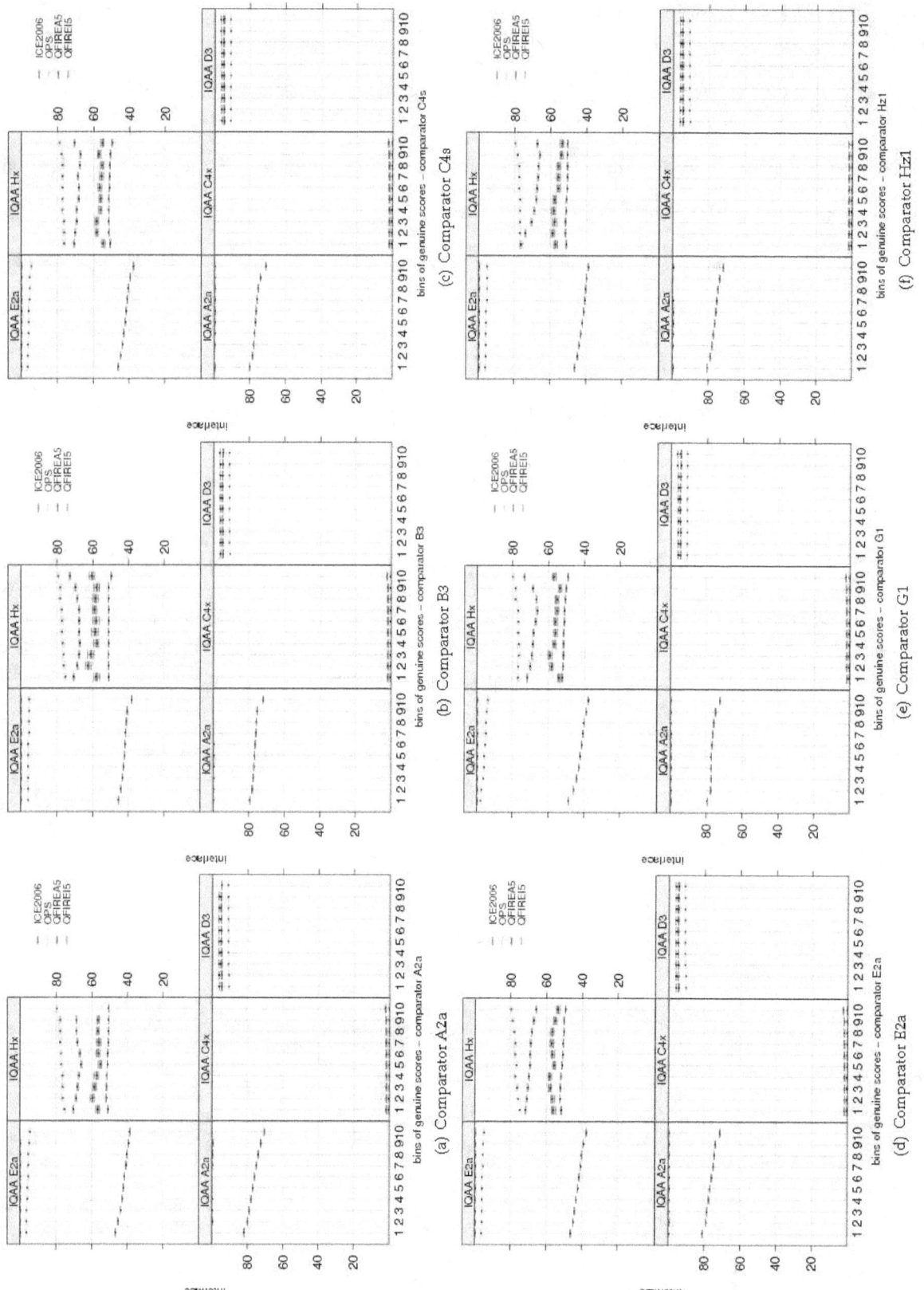

Figure 113: Pairwise INTERLACE scores vs. genuine score for the primary Class Z submissions of each participants. Each plot shows quality scores computed by different IQAA. Genuine scores are divided equally into ten groups. Groups overlap by 5 percent. Bootstrapped pairwise quality for each group is shown in a box and whisker plot. Pairwise quality is computed as geometric mean of the quality of the two samples being compared.

A2a=NEUROTECHNOLOGY-a | B3=CROSSMATCH | C4s=CAMBRIDGE-s | D3=AWARE | E2a=IRITECH-a | G1=IRISID-1 | I1=KYNEN | Hz1=L1-z1
A2f=NEUROTECHNOLOGY-f | C4x=CAMBRIDGE-x | C4f=CAMBRIDGE-f | F1=MORPHO | E2f=IRITECH-f | G2=IRISID-2 | Hx=L1-x | Hz2=L1-z2

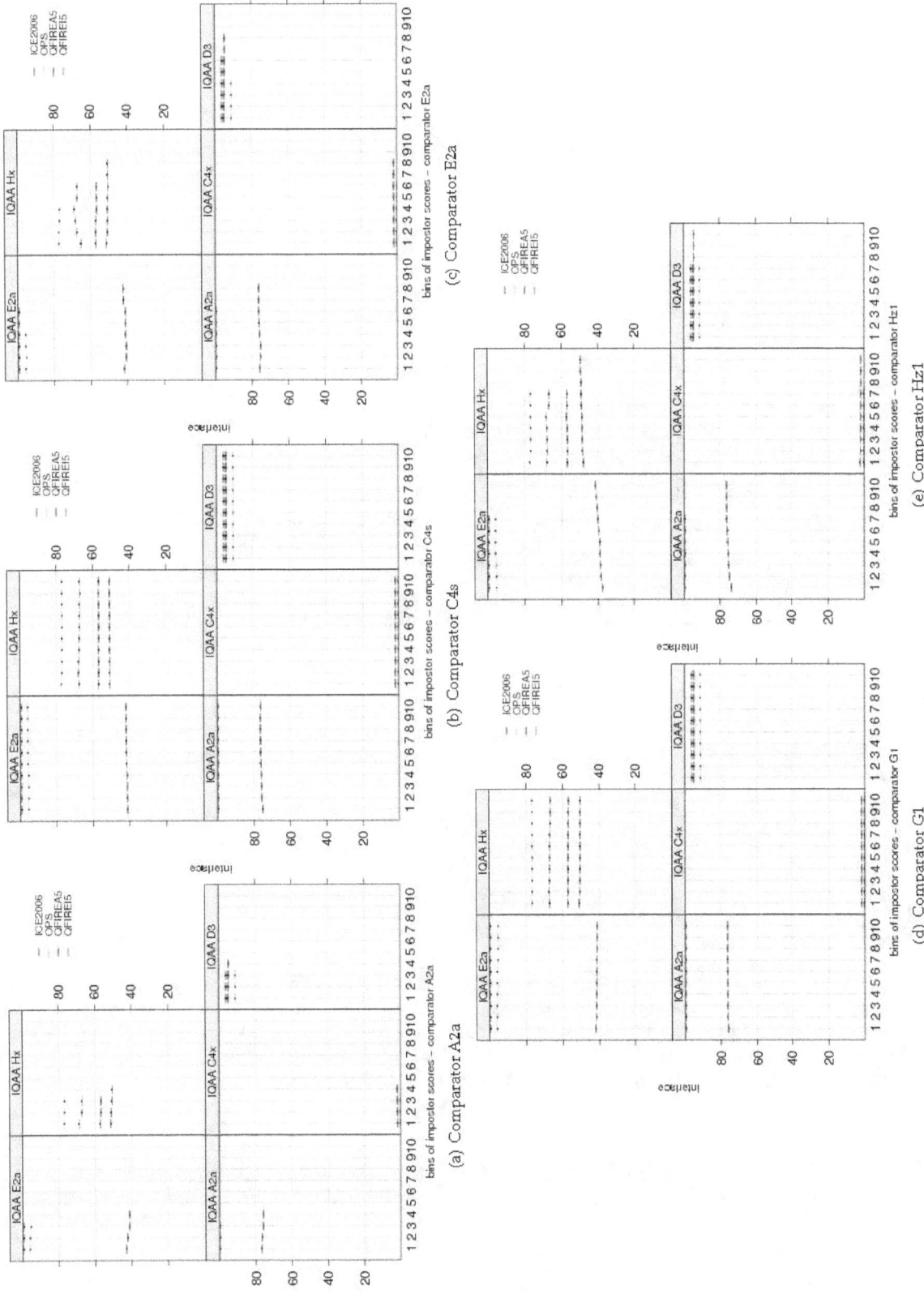

Figure 114: Pairwise INTERLACE scores *vs.* impostor scores for the primary Class Z submissions of each participants. Each plot shows quality scores computed by different IQAA. Similar to plots of Figure 113, impostor scores are divided equally into ten groups. Groups overlap by 5 percent. Bootstrapped pairwise quality for each group is shown in a box and whisker plot. Pairwise quality is computed as geometric mean of the quality of the two samples being compared.

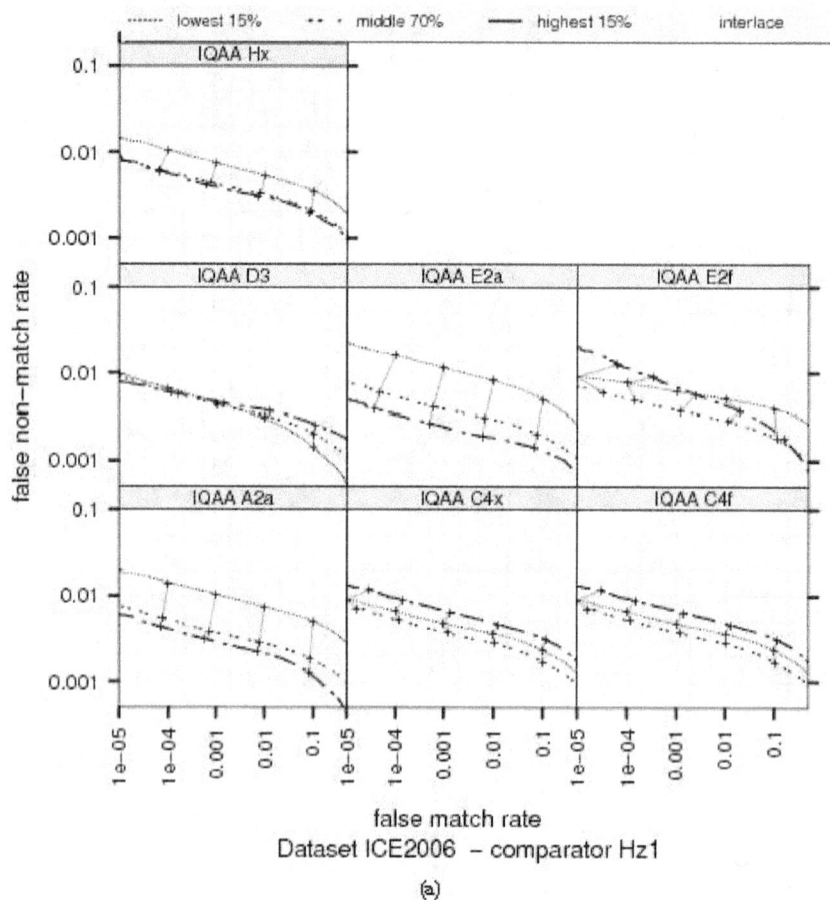

Dataset ICE2006 – comparator Hz1

(a)

Figure 115: Ranked DET curves for comparator Hz1 and Datasets ICE2006 and QFIRE I5 . The set of all comparisons were partitioned into three groups based on the pair-wise quality of the images being compared. The lowest quality set contains comparisons with pairwise quality in the lower 15 percentile. The highest quality set contains comparisons with pairwise quality in the upper 15 percentile. The rest of the comparisons, namely the middle 70%, made up the third set. The DETs are connected at the same score threshold values (brown lines). Lower FNMR and FMR rates are expected for better quality images.

| A2a=NEUROTECHNOLOGY-a | B3=CROSSMATCH | C4s=CAMBRIDGE-s | D3=AWARE | E2a=IRITECH-a | G1=IRISID-1 | I1=KYNEN | Hz1=L1-z1 |
| A2f=NEUROTECHNOLOGY-f | C4x=CAMBRIDGE-x | C4f=CAMBRIDGE-f | F1=MORPHO | E2f=IRITECH-f | G2=IRISID-2 | Hx=L1-x | Hz2=L1-z2 |

Dataset	comparator	IQAA A2f	IQAA C4x	IQAA E2a	IQAA E2f	IQAA Hx
ICE2006	A2a	(18.94,19.63)	(-2.22,-2.13)	(9.79,10.16)	(0.73,0.95)	(4.73,5.19)
ICE2006	B3	(9.82,10.14)	(-1.04,-1.00)	(6.75,6.92)	(-3.38,-3.27)	(3.63,3.85)
ICE2006	C4s	(20.28,20.79)	(-1.76,-1.70)	(8.31,8.58)	(-0.29,-0.12)	(4.62,4.96)
ICE2006	E2a	(19.18,19.88)	(-2.36,-2.28)	(11.35,11.73)	(-0.25,-0.01)	(5.78,6.25)
ICE2006	G2	(10.04,10.39)	(-1.28,-1.24)	(7.24,7.43)	(-2.70,-2.59)	(4.57,4.80)
ICE2006	Hz1	(10.33,11.21)	(-0.59,-0.48)	(5.07,5.54)	(-1.27,-0.99)	(0.87,1.45)
OPS	A2a	(-0.00,-0.00)	(-0.08,0.50)	(-2.94,0.55)	(-4.44,3.53)	(-6.08,2.51)
OPS	B3	(0.00,0.00)	(0.07,0.31)	(-1.25,0.21)	(-2.23,1.10)	(-4.79,-1.20)
OPS	C4s	(0.00,0.00)	(-0.18,0.29)	(-1.52,1.29)	(-1.77,4.64)	(-4.63,2.27)
OPS	E2a	(0.00,0.00)	(-0.18,0.50)	(-3.46,0.63)	(-5.31,4.04)	(-5.67,4.41)
OPS	G2	(0.00,0.00)	(0.05,0.43)	(0.09,2.35)	(-8.10,-2.92)	(-6.83,-1.26)
OPS	Hz1	(-0.00,-0.00)	(-0.03,0.51)	(-2.42,0.87)	(-3.19,4.33)	(-4.58,3.52)
QFIREA5	A2a	(0.21,0.38)	(-0.01,0.01)	(0.04,0.12)	(-0.74,0.24)	(0.10,1.34)
QFIREA5	B3	(-0.03,0.00)	(-0.06,-0.02)	(0.01,0.06)	(0.40,1.92)	(-0.57,1.30)
QFIREA5	C4s	(-0.43,-0.22)	(-0.03,0.00)	(-0.17,-0.07)	(0.05,1.37)	(0.37,2.04)
QFIREA5	E2a	(-0.05,0.10)	(0.00,0.03)	(-0.01,0.05)	(-0.12,0.79)	(0.33,1.49)
QFIREA5	G2	(-0.16,-0.01)	(-0.02,0.00)	(-0.07,0.00)	(0.72,1.70)	(0.27,1.51)
QFIREA5	Hz1	(-0.13,0.13)	(-0.03,0.01)	(-0.06,0.06)	(1.61,3.24)	(1.98,4.05)
QFIREI5	A2a	(-0.07,-0.02)	(0.07,0.08)	(-0.02,0.05)	(-1.07,-0.64)	(-0.06,0.43)
QFIREI5	B3	(-0.14,-0.09)	(0.02,0.03)	(-0.01,0.00)	(-0.64,-0.17)	(-3.24,-2.73)
QFIREI5	C4s	(0.02,0.08)	(0.22,0.24)	(0.17,0.19)	(0.37,0.92)	(-2.16,-1.54)
QFIREI5	E2a	(-0.04,0.03)	(0.21,0.23)	(0.24,0.27)	(-0.01,0.57)	(3.42,4.07)
QFIREI5	G2	(0.01,0.07)	(0.12,0.14)	(0.01,0.03)	(0.65,1.13)	(-3.77,-3.23)
QFIREI5	Hz1	(0.01,0.10)	(0.12,0.14)	(0.24,0.27)	(-1.30,-0.60)	(0.47,1.26)

Table 33: Tukey HSD difference in mean of INTERLACE scores. Each cell shows the 95% confidence level in difference in mean of pairwise quality for images verified correctly (i.e., the genuine score equal or less than threshold) and those rejected falsely (i.e., the genuine score larger than threshold). Quality scores were computed by the SDK identified by the column header and comparison scores were generated by the SDK identified by the row header. If the interval does not contain zero, the difference in mean is significant. Cells where difference in mean is not significant have pink background. For monotonically increasing quality components (all except DILATION , and depending on quality implementation GRAY SCALE SPREAD), the expected behavior is to have higher quality scores for the pair of enrollment and verification images that give genuine comparison scores less than threshold. The pairwise quality is computed as geometric mean of the quality of two samples being compared. Threshold is set to give false match rate of 0.001.

A2a=NEUROTECHNOLOGY-a | B3=CROSSMATCH | C4s=CAMBRIDGE-s | D3=AWARE | E2a=IRITECH-a | G1=IRISID-1 | I1=KYNEN | Hz1=L1-z1
A2f=NEUROTECHNOLOGY-f | C4x=CAMBRIDGE-x | C4f=CAMBRIDGE-f | F1=MORPHO | E2f=IRITECH-f | G2=IRISID-2 | Hx=L1-x | Hz2=L1-z2

Dataset	comparator	IQAA A2f	IQAA C4x	IQAA E2a	IQAA E2f	IQAA Hx
ICE2006	A2a	(0.23,0.43)	(-4.19,-3.29)	(0.15,0.69)	(-3.12,-2.01)	
ICE2006	B3	(-0.85,-0.71)	(2.63,3.27)	(-6.05,-5.66)	(2.30,3.11)	
ICE2006	C4s	(-0.15,0.00)	(0.19,0.89)	(-1.94,-1.53)	(-0.70,0.16)	
ICE2006	E2a	(0.03,0.19)	(-1.81,-1.10)	(-3.41,-2.99)	(-2.72,-1.85)	
ICE2006	G2	(0.19,0.35)	(-3.14,-2.42)	(0.53,0.96)	(-2.63,-1.73)	
ICE2006	Hz1	(-0.31,-0.14)	(1.07,1.83)	(-2.51,-2.05)	(0.34,1.29)	
OPS	A2a	(0.00,0.00)	(-0.04,0.02)	(-1.31,-0.90)	(1.39,2.28)	(-0.50,0.44)
OPS	B3	(-0.00,-0.00)	(0.03,0.08)	(0.00,0.34)	(-0.56,0.17)	(-1.77,-1.00)
OPS	C4s	(0.00,0.00)	(0.02,0.07)	(-0.14,0.20)	(-0.33,0.40)	(-1.13,-0.36)
OPS	E2a	(0.00,0.00)	(-0.01,0.04)	(-0.84,-0.50)	(0.59,1.33)	(-0.47,0.32)
OPS	G2	(0.00,0.00)	(-0.05,0.00)	(-1.01,-0.67)	(1.23,1.97)	(0.03,0.81)
OPS	Hz1	(0.00,0.00)	(0.03,0.08)	(0.23,0.57)	(-0.60,0.13)	(-1.42,-0.65)
QFIREA5	A2a	(-0.17,0.01)	(-0.35,-0.32)	(0.48,0.62)	(2.67,3.79)	(1.55,2.93)
QFIREA5	C4s	(0.00,0.17)	(-0.03,-0.00)	(0.03,0.16)	(0.18,1.19)	(-1.43,-0.17)
QFIREA5	E2a	(-0.04,0.12)	(0.04,0.07)	(-0.36,-0.24)	(2.80,3.81)	(-1.38,-0.12)
QFIREA5	G2	(0.13,0.31)	(0.00,0.03)	(0.15,0.27)	(-0.17,0.89)	(0.49,1.78)
QFIREA5	Hz1	(-0.19,-0.02)	(-0.02,0.00)	(0.09,0.22)	(2.03,3.04)	(1.13,2.39)
QFIREI5	A2a	(-0.06,0.09)	(-0.00,0.02)	(0.04,0.09)	(1.37,2.30)	(-1.43,-0.48)
QFIREI5	C4s	(-0.48,-0.35)	(0.06,0.08)	(-0.15,-0.10)	(0.41,1.21)	(1.11,1.93)
QFIREI5	E2a	(-0.45,-0.32)	(0.14,0.17)	(-0.09,-0.05)	(-3.22,-2.41)	(7.35,8.18)
QFIREI5	G2	(-0.57,0.42)	(-0.02,0.16)	(-0.14,0.20)	(-0.51,5.57)	(-1.35,4.90)
QFIREI5	Hz1	(-0.44,-0.31)	(-0.00,0.02)	(-0.12,-0.08)	(-2.63,-1.82)	(-2.06,-1.23)

Table 34: Tukey HSD mean difference in INTERLACE scores. Each cell shows the 95% confidence level in difference in mean of pairwise quality for images correctly rejected (i.e., the impostor score equal or greater than threshold) and those falsely matched (i.e., the impostor score less than threshold). Quality scores were computed by the SDK identified by the column header and comparison scores were generated by the SDK identified by the row header. If the interval does not contain zero, the difference in mean is significant. Cells where difference in mean is not significant are shaded in pink. For monotonic increasing quality components (all except DILATION, and depending on quality implementation GRAY SCALE SPREAD), the expected behavior is to have higher quality scores for the pair of (enrollment, verification) images that result in impostor comparison scores equal or greater than threshold. Pairwise quality is computed as geometric mean of the quality of two samples being compared. Threshold is set to give false match rate of 0.001.

216

A2a=NEUROTECHNOLOGY-a   B3=CROSSMATCH   C4s=CAMBRIDGE-s   D3=AWARE   E2a=IRITECH-a   G1=IRISID-1   I1=KYNEN   Hz1=L1-z1
A2f=NEUROTECHNOLOGY-f   C4x=CAMBRIDGE-x   C4f=CAMBRIDGE-f   F1=MORPHO   E2f=IRITECH-f   G2=IRISID-2   Hx=L1-x   Hz2=L1-z2

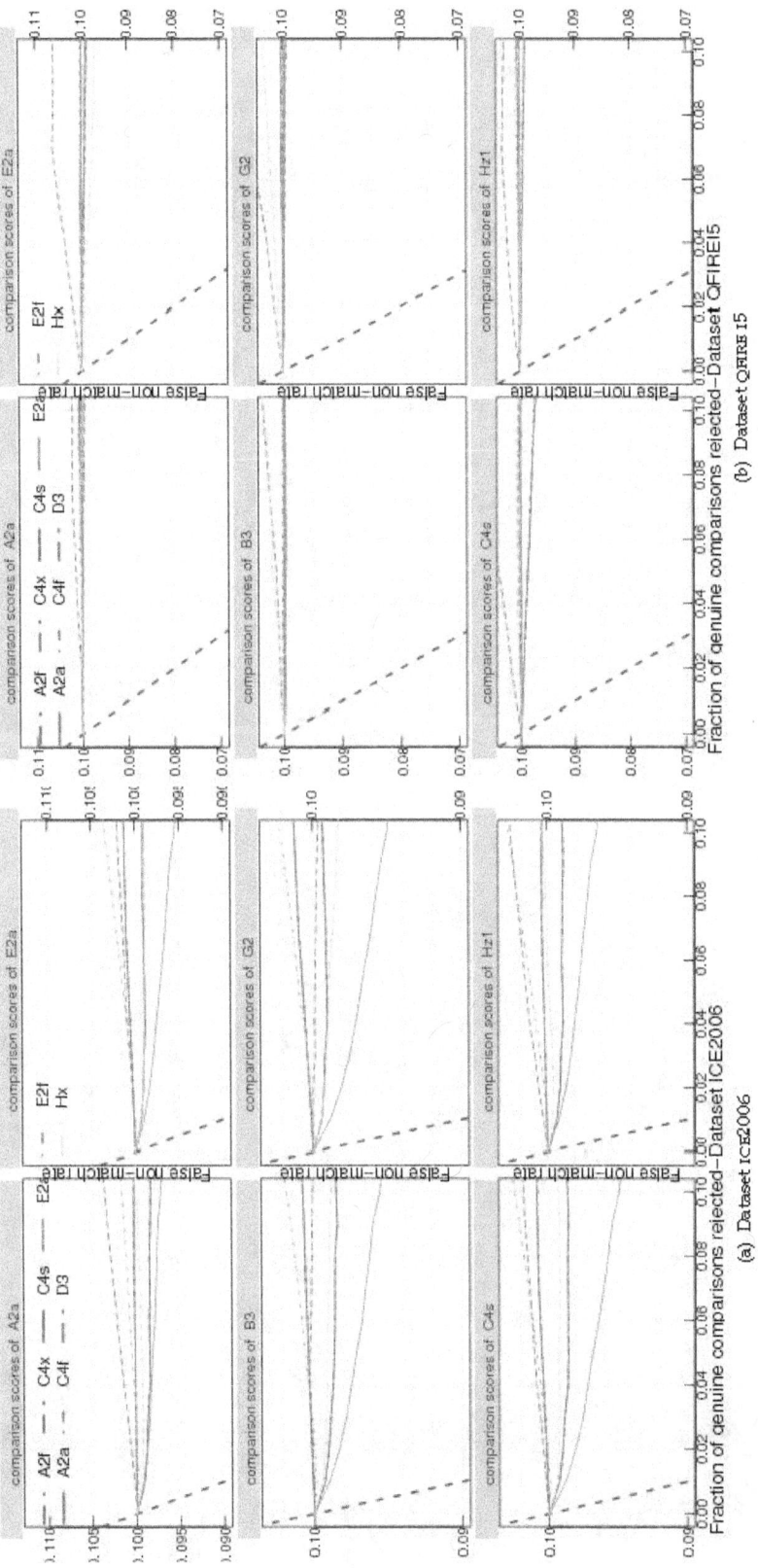

Figure 116: FNMR vs. reject curves for INTERLACE scores on datasets ICE2006 and QFIRE I5. The threshold is set to give an initial FNMR = 0.1. The gray dotted line shows the ideal case where the rejection of the comparisons with the lowest ten percent quality results in zero FNMR. No IQAA shows a strong improvement in FNMR after rejecting images with its low IRIS SHAPE scores.

| A2a=NEUROTECHNOLOGY-a | B3=CROSSMATCH | C4s=CAMBRIDGE-s | D3=AWARE | E2a=IRITECH-a | G1=IRISID-1 | I1=KYNEN | Hz1=L1-z1 |
| A2f=NEUROTECHNOLOGY-f | C4x=CAMBRIDGE-x | C4f=CAMBRIDGE-f | F1=MORPHO | E2f=IRITECH-f | G2=IRISID-2 | Hx=L1-x | Hz2=L1-z2 |

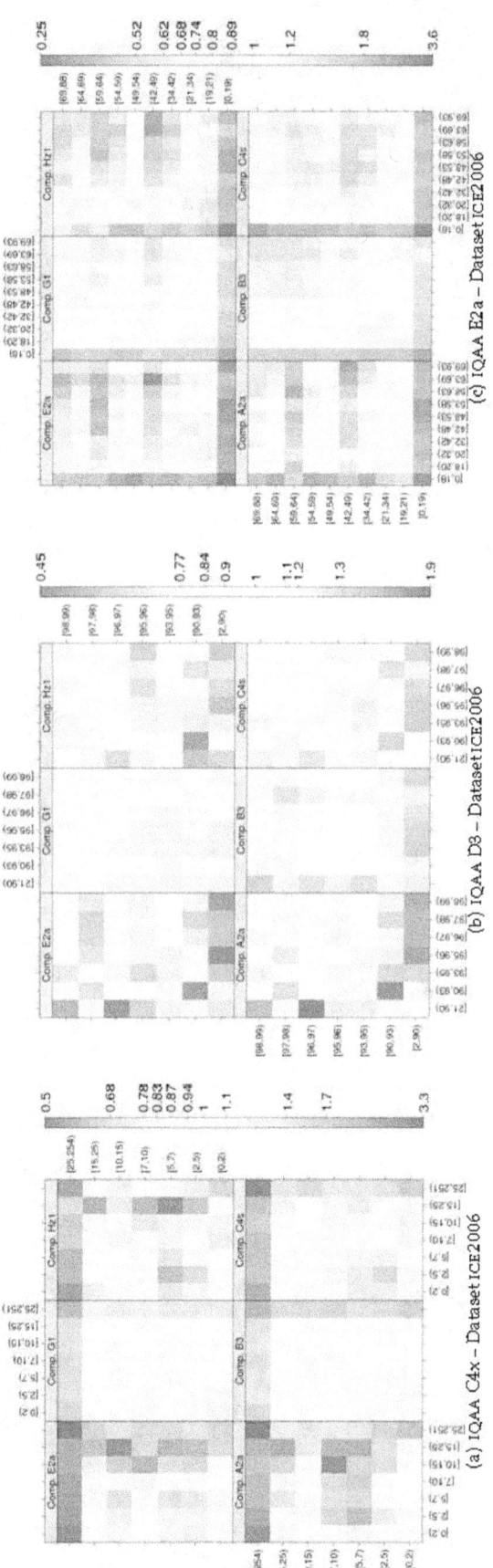

(a) IQAA C4x – Dataset ICE2006

(b) IQAA D3 – Dataset ICE2006

(c) IQAA E2a – Dataset ICE2006

Figure 117: INTERLACE computed by primary IQAA submissions and FNMR for IQCE comparators for dataset ICE2006 . The y-axis represents enrollment samples' quality with verification samples' on the x-axis. The color scale plots $\frac{\text{FNMR}}{\text{FNMR}_0}$ for comparisons with verification and enrollment qualities $(q_{verification}, q_{enrollment})$. FNMR is the nominal FNMR which is the false non-match rate computed over all the images at the same comparison score threshold, in this case at FMR = 0.001. FNMR$_0$ is the false non-match rate computed over all the images at the same comparison score threshold, in this case at FMR = 0.001. Yellow/Green color represent an improvement in FNMR. Blue color represent a degradation of FNMR. White color means no change in FNMR.

| A2a=NEUROTECHNOLOGY-a | B3=CROSSMATCH | C4s=CAMBRIDGE-s | D3=AWARE | E2a=IRITECH-a | G1=IRISID-1 | I1=KYNEN | Hz1=L1-z1 |
| A2f=NEUROTECHNOLOGY-f | C4x=CAMBRIDGE-x | C4f=CAMBRIDGE-f | F1=MORPHO | E2f=IRITECH-f | G2=IRISID-2 | Hx=L1-x | Hz2=L1-z2 |

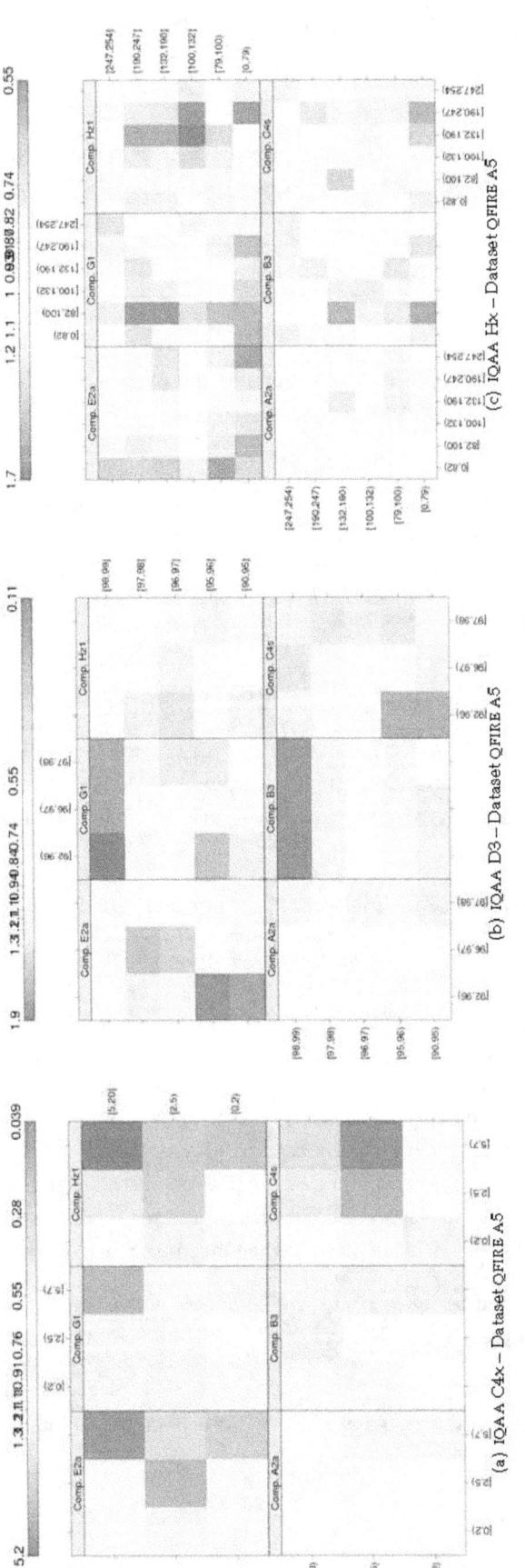

Figure 118: INTERLACE computed by primary IQAA submissions and FNMR for IQCE comparators for dataset QFIRE 15 . The y-axis represents enrollment samples' quality with verification samples' on the x-axis. The INTERLACE scores are quantized into 10 quantiles. The color scale plots $\frac{FNMR}{FNMR_0}$ for comparisons with verification and enrollment qualities ($q_{verification}, q_{enrollment}$). $FNMR_0$ is the nominal FNMR which is the false non-match rate computed over all the images at the same comparison score threshold, in this case at FMR = 0.001. Yellow/Green color represent an improvement in FNMR. Blue color represent a degradation of FNMR. White color means no change in FNMR.

(a) IQAA C4x – Dataset QFIRE A5

(b) IQAA D3 – Dataset QFIRE A5

(c) IQAA Hx – Dataset QFIRE 15

10 Spearman rank correlation of standard quality components and image error rates

An immediate question to ask is whether the 17 quality components defined in IQCE con-ops, or their measurement by the IQAAS, are actually 17 distinct measures of different aspects of iris image properties, or if some of them are highly correlated.

Another question is how each of these quality components correlates with recognition performance.

We employed Spearman rank statistics to answer the above questions.

Spearman rank statistic is a nonparametric (distribution-free) measure of the strength of the monotone associations between two variables. A perfect relationship yields a rank correlation of +1 (or -1 for a negative relationship) and no relationship yields a rank correlation of 0.

To measure the strength of association between quality components and recognition performance, as well as between any pair of quality components, we compute the Spearman rank correlation factor (ρ) between each IQAA's quality components and the log-transformed iFNMR (iFŇMR) of its mated comparator, or Hz1 in case of Class X IQAAS.

iFŇMR is our quantification of image-specific recognition performance. Specifically,

$$\mathrm{iF\check{N}MR} = log\left(\frac{\mathrm{iFNMR}}{1.0 - \mathrm{iFNMR}}\right) \tag{18}$$

Image-specific false non-match rates (iFNMRS) are computed according to Equation 11 in Section 5.4. iFNMR is the proportion of comparisons for which an image produces a false non-match (i.e., genuine comparisons above the operating threshold).

A pristine image *always* gives a very small dissimilarity score, therefore an iFNMR of zero, and iFŇMR $\to -\infty$.

A very poor quality image *always* gives a high dissimilarity score, therefore, an iFNMR close to one, and iFŇMR $\to \infty$.

As such, the quality component with the largest negative correlation factor, has the greatest influence on FNMR.

Results are illustrated in Figures 119-121.

Each plot shows a (symmetric) correlation matrix using ellipse-shaped glyphs for each entry. A line represents perfect correlation ($\rho = 1$), and a circle represents no correlation ($\rho = 0$). The numerical value of the correlation factor ρ in percent, is placed inside the ellipses. The ellipses are colored to emphasize the sign and magnitude of the corresponding correlation. Shades of blue are used to illustrate a positive correlation, and red for negative. In both cases a darker color means a stronger correlation, hence darker colors are present when the numerical value is high.

iFŇMR is labeled "log odds". The desired behavior is large negative correlation factors, i.e., highly non-circular shapes in dark red, in the row (or column) labeled "log odds", and small correlation, i.e., mostly circular white, pale blue or red shapes elsewhere.

Spearman rank correlations are computed for images where template generation and matching have been successful.

Notable observations are:

220

| A2a=NEUROTECHNOLOGY-a | B3=CROSSMATCH | C4s=CAMBRIDGE-s | D3=AWARE | E2a=IRITECH-a | G1=IRISID-1 | I1=KYNEN | Hz1=L1-z1 |
| A2f=NEUROTECHNOLOGY-f | C4x=CAMBRIDGE-x | C4f=CAMBRIDGE-f | F1=MORPHO | E2f=IRITECH-f | G2=IRISID-2 | Hx=L1-x | Hz2=L1-z2 |

▷ A somehow disappointing result is the lack of a strong correlation between iFNMR and quality components. The highest correlation is 0.37 for IQAA C4s's PUPIL SHAPE on QFIRE A5 image.

▷ There are some strong correlations between quality components of the IQAAS. For example, USABLE IRIS AREA and SCALAR QUALITY scores are highly correlated for IQAAs C4s, G1, F1, and Hx. Or IQAA E2a's GAZE ANGLE and PUPIL SHAPE are highly correlated. This strong correlation was expected due to the large number of quality factors defined in the CONOPS, with the intent of being comprehensive. Intuitively, some of the factors are strongly related, and high correlation values should be expected.

▷ The strength of correlation among the quality components varies greatly across different datasets. For example, on the ICE2006 images, IQAA C4s's two most correlated quality components are SCALAR QUALITY and USABLE IRIS AREA with a correlation factor of 0.76. On QFIRE I5 images, SCALAR QUALITY and SHARPNESS have the highest correlation factor (0.78) which is closely followed by 0.76 correlation with IRIS PUPIL CONTRAST .

▷ IQAA D3's quality scores on QFIRE images are highly correlated with each other, but not on ICE2006 images. The almost identical quality scores for all the quality components suggests that IQAA D3's measurement of the intended image properties are not accurate.

| A2a=NEUROTECHNOLOGY-a | B3=CROSSMATCH | C4s=CAMBRIDGE-s | D3=AWARE | E2a=IRITECH-a | G1=IRISID-1 | I1=KYNEN | Hz1=L1-z1 |
| A2f=NEUROTECHNOLOGY-f | C4x=CAMBRIDGE-x | C4f=CAMBRIDGE-f | F1=MORPHO | E2f=IRITECH-f | G2=IRISID-2 | Hx=L1-x | Hz2=L1-z2 |

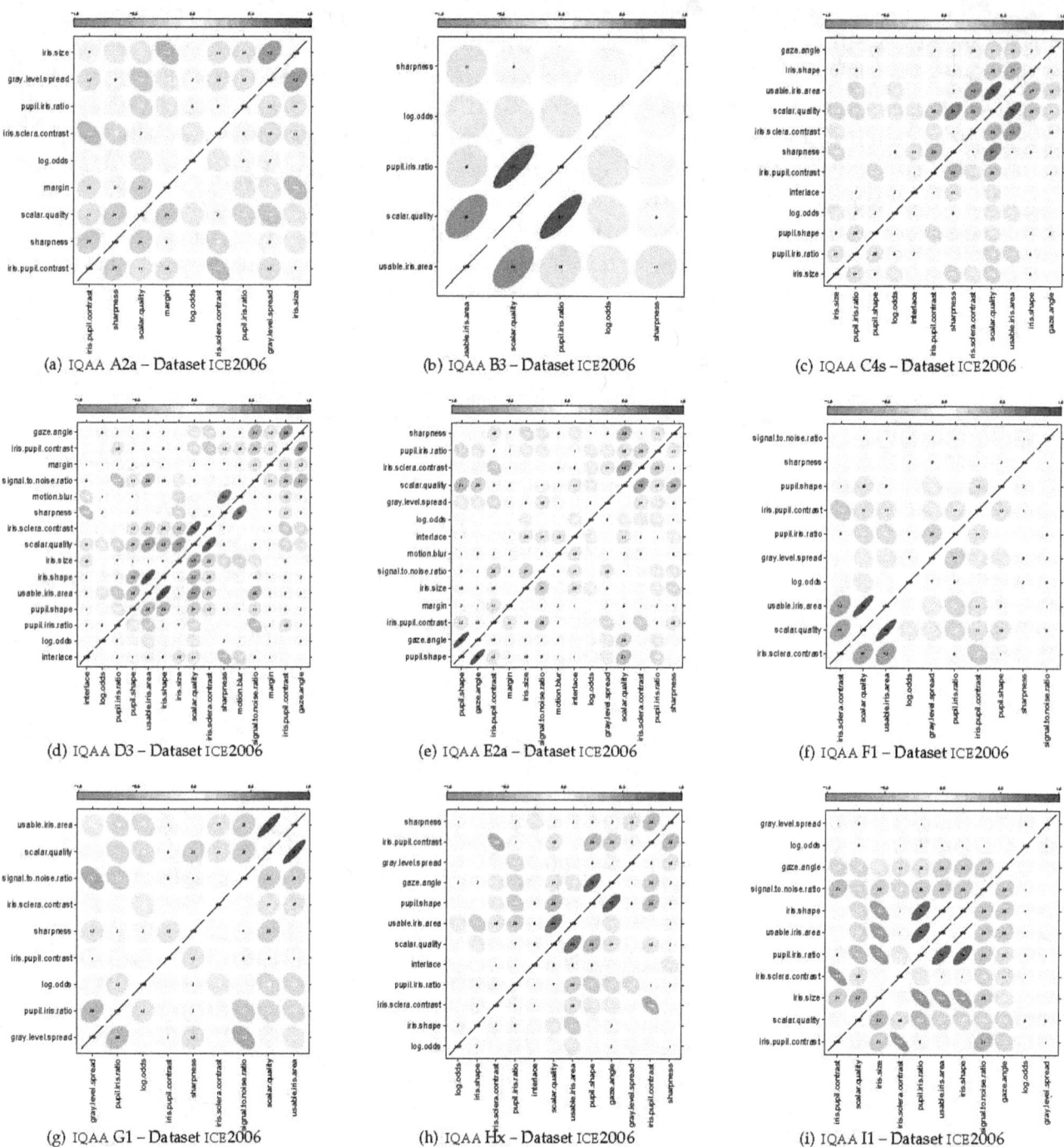

(a) IQAA A2a – Dataset ICE2006   (b) IQAA B3 – Dataset ICE2006   (c) IQAA C4s – Dataset ICE2006

(d) IQAA D3 – Dataset ICE2006   (e) IQAA E2a – Dataset ICE2006   (f) IQAA F1 – Dataset ICE2006

(g) IQAA G1 – Dataset ICE2006   (h) IQAA Hx – Dataset ICE2006   (i) IQAA I1 – Dataset ICE2006

Figure 119: Spearman rank correlation matrix, Dataset ICE2006. Each plot shows a (symmetric) correlation matrix using ellipse-shaped glyphs for each entry. The ellipses represent a level curve of the density of a bivariate normal with the corresponding correlation. A line represents perfect correlation ($\rho = 1$), and a circle represents no correlation ($\rho = 0$). The numerical value of the correlation factor ρ in percent, is placed inside the ellipses. The ellipses are colored to emphasize the sign and magnitude of the corresponding correlation. Shades of blue are used to illustrate a positive correlation, and red for negative. In both cases a darker color means a stronger correlation. Spearman rank correlation factors between iFNMR and quality components are shown in the row (and column) labeled as "log odds".

A2a=NEUROTECHNOLOGY-a	B3=CROSSMATCH	C4s=CAMBRIDGE-s	D3=AWARE	E2a=IRITECH-a	G1=IRISID-1	I1=KYNEN	Hz1=L1-z1
A2f=NEUROTECHNOLOGY-f	C4x=CAMBRIDGE-x	C4f=CAMBRIDGE-f	F1=MORPHO	E2f=IRITECH-f	G2=IRISID-2	Hx=L1-x	Hz2=L1-z2

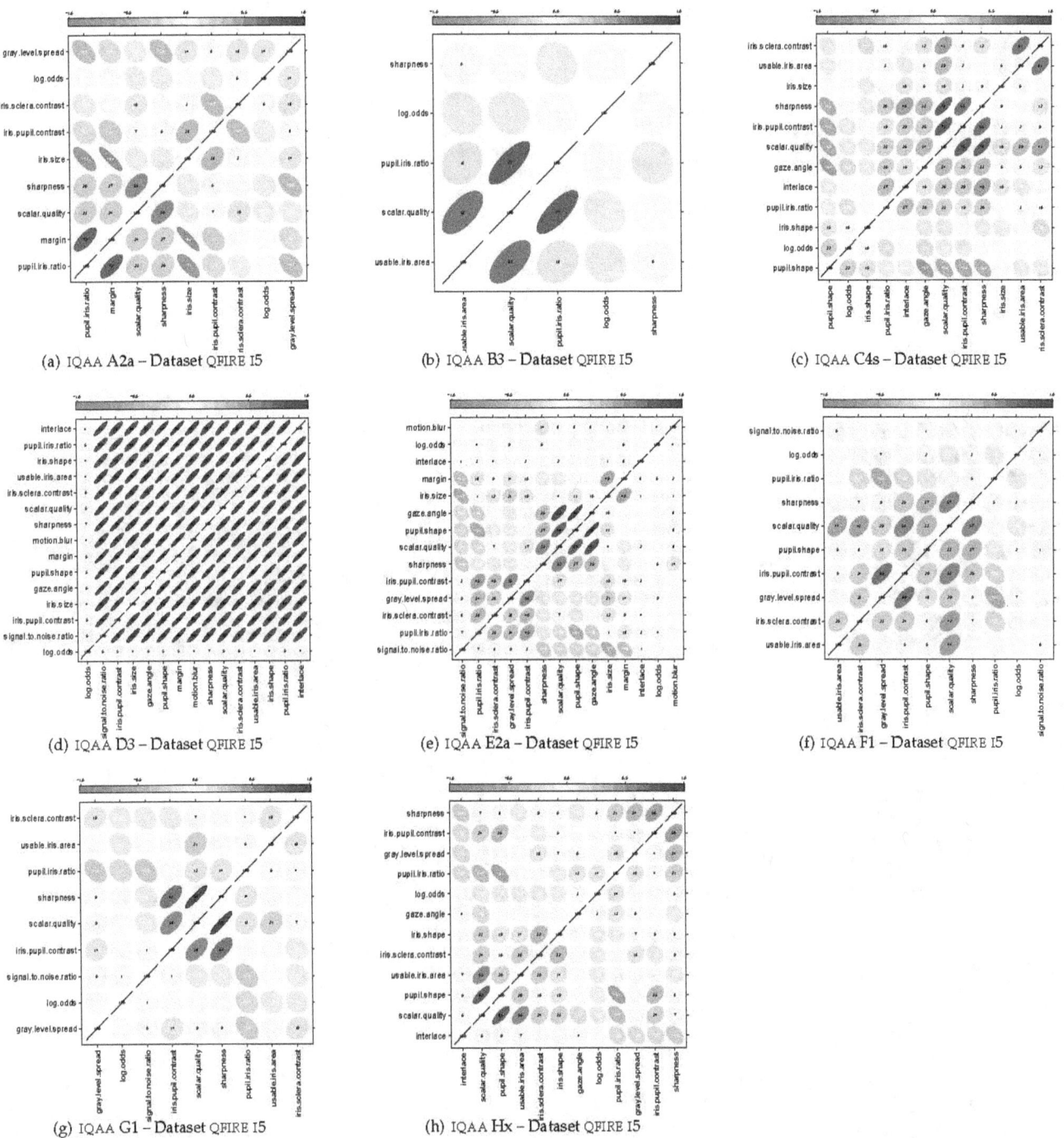

(a) IQAA A2a – Dataset QFIRE I5   (b) IQAA B3 – Dataset QFIRE I5   (c) IQAA C4s – Dataset QFIRE I5

(d) IQAA D3 – Dataset QFIRE I5   (e) IQAA E2a – Dataset QFIRE I5   (f) IQAA F1 – Dataset QFIRE I5

(g) IQAA G1 – Dataset QFIRE I5   (h) IQAA Hx – Dataset QFIRE I5

Figure 120: Spearman rank correlation matrix, Dataset QFIRE I5. Each plot shows a (symmetric) correlation matrix using ellipse-shaped glyphs for each entry. The ellipses represent a level curve of the density of a bivariate normal with the corresponding correlation. A line represents perfect correlation ($\rho = 1$), and a circle represents no correlation ($\rho = 0$). The numerical value of the correlation factor ρ in percent, is placed inside the ellipses. The ellipses are colored to emphasize the sign and magnitude of the corresponding correlation. Shades of blue are used to illustrate a positive correlation, and red for negative. In both cases a darker color means a stronger correlation. Spearman rank correlation factors between iFNMR and quality components are shown in the row (and column) labeled as "log odds".

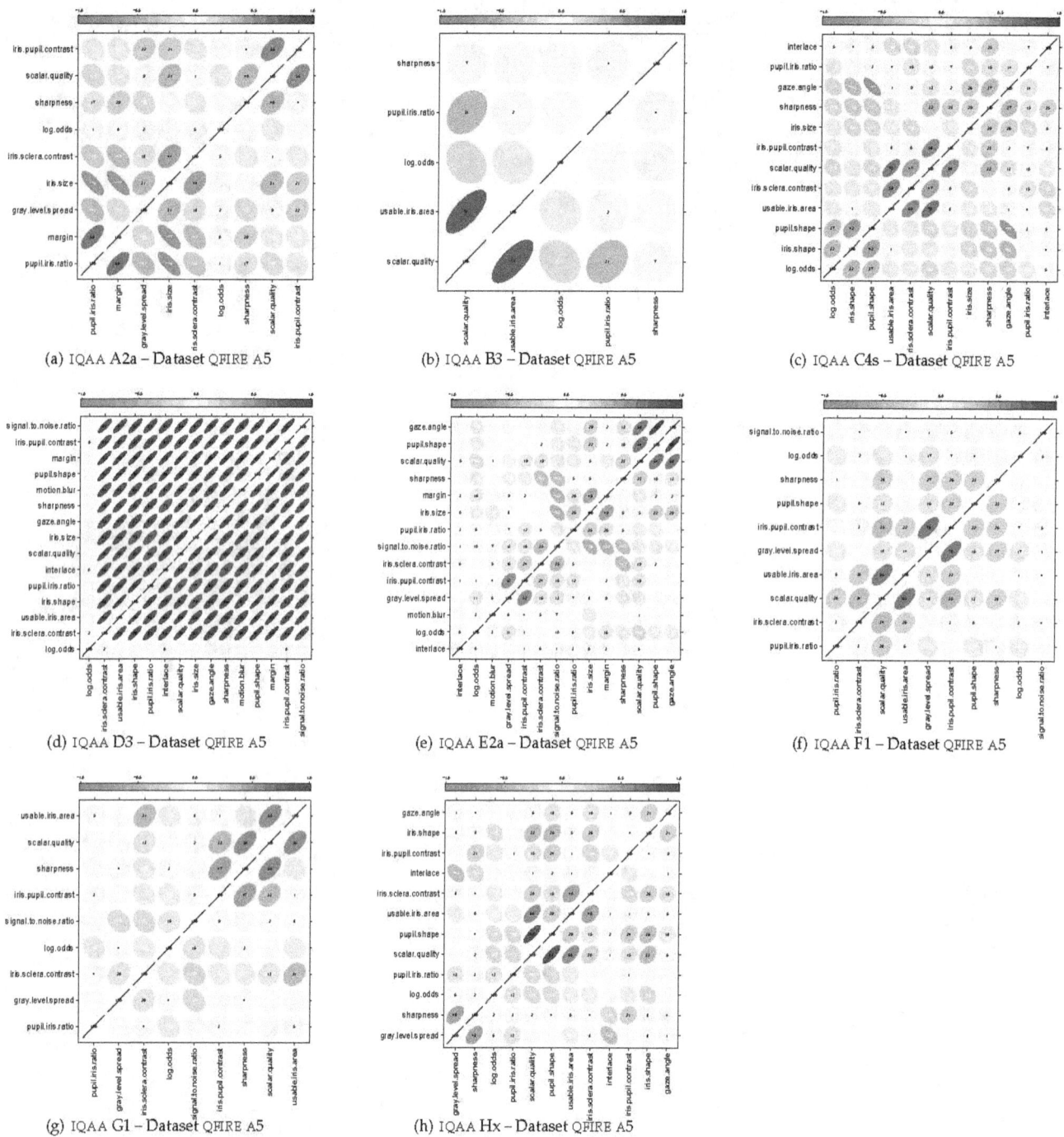

(a) IQAA A2a – Dataset QFIRE A5

(b) IQAA B3 – Dataset QFIRE A5

(c) IQAA C4s – Dataset QFIRE A5

(d) IQAA D3 – Dataset QFIRE A5

(e) IQAA E2a – Dataset QFIRE A5

(f) IQAA F1 – Dataset QFIRE A5

(g) IQAA G1 – Dataset QFIRE A5

(h) IQAA Hx – Dataset QFIRE A5

Figure 121: Spearman rank correlation matrix. Dataset QFIRE A5. Each plot shows a (symmetric) correlation matrix using ellipse-shaped glyphs for each entry. The ellipses represent a level curve of the density of a bivariate normal with the corresponding correlation. A line represents perfect correlation ($\rho = 1$), and a circle represents no correlation ($\rho = 0$). The numerical value of the correlation factor ρ in percent, is placed inside the ellipses. The ellipses are colored to emphasize the sign and magnitude of the corresponding correlation. Shades of blue are used to illustrate a positive correlation, and red for negative. In both cases a darker color means a stronger correlation. In both cases a darker color means a stronger correlation. Spearman rank correlation factors between iFNMR and quality components are shown in the row (and column) labeled as "log odds".

References

[1] Working Group 3. *ISO/IEC 19794-6 Information Technology - Biometric Data Interchnage Formats - Part 6: Iris image*. JTC1 :: SC37, international standard edition, 2011. http://isotc.iso.org/isotcportal.

[2] Working Group 3. *ISO/IEC 29794-6 Information Technology - Biometric Sample Quality - Part 6: Iris image*. JTC1 :: SC37, working draft 4 edition, 2011. http://isotc.iso.org/isotcportal.

[3] Working Group 5. *ISO/IEC 19795-1 Biometric Performance Testing and Reporting: Principles and Framework*. JTC1 :: SC37, international standard edition, August 2005. http://isotc.iso.org/isotcportal.

[4] G. Bradski. The OpenCV Library. *Dr. Dobb's Journal of Software Tools*, 2000.

[5] Andr Caroline. The effect of corneal diameter on soft lens fitting, part 1., 2002. Contact Lens Spectrum 2002;17(4)56.

[6] John Daugman. How iris recognition works. *IEEE Transactions on Circuits and Systems for Video Technology*, 14(1):21–30, January 2004.

[7] John Daugman. Probing the uniqueness and randomness of iriscodes: Results from 200 billion iris pair comparisons. *Proc. of the IEEE*, 94(11):1927–1935, November 2006.

[8] John Daugman. New methods in iris recognition. *IEEE Transactions on Systems, Man, and Cybernetics Part B:Cybernetics*, 37(5):1167–1175, 2007.

[9] P. J. Phillips et al. Overview of the multiple biometrics grand challenge. (NIST Interagency Report 7607), 2008.

[10] S. Schuckers et al. Qualityface and iris research ensemble (q-fire) dataset overview. Technical report, Dept. of Electrical and Computer Engineering, 2010.

[11] J. Fierrez-Aguilar, L.M. Muñoz-Serrano, F. Alonso-Fernandez, and J. Ortega-Garcia. On the effects of image quality degradation on minutiae and ridge-based automatic fingerprint recognition. In *IEEE International Carnahan Conference on Security Technology*, October 2005.

[12] P. Grother and E. Tabassi. In *Proceedings of the NIST Biometric Quality Workshop*, March 2006. http://www.itl.nist.gov/iad/894.03/quality/workshop/presentations.htm.

[13] Cambier J. Multi camera iris quality study. In *Proceedings of the NIST Biometric Quality Workshop*, March 2006. http://www.itl.nist.gov/iad/894.03/quality/workshop/presentations.htm.

[14] Pengfei Shi Jing Wan, Xiaofu He. An iris image quality assessment method based on laplacian of gaussian operation. *Conference on Machine Vision Applications*, pages 248 – 251, May 2007.

[15] N. D. Kalka. Image quality assessment for iris biometric. 2005.

[16] Teddy Ko and Rama Krishnan. Monitoring and reporting of fingerprint image quality and match accuracy for a large user application. In *Proceedings of the 33rd Applied Image Pattern Recognition Workshop*, pages 159–164. IEEE Computer Society, 2004.

[17] A. Martin, G. Doddington, T. Kamm, M. Ordowski, and M. Przybocki. The det curve in assessment of detection task performance. *In Proceedings of Eurospeech 97*, pages 1895–1898, 1997.

| A2a=NEUROTECHNOLOGY-a | B3=CROSSMATCH | C4s=CAMBRIDGE-s | D3=AWARE | E2a=IRITECH-a | G1=IRISID-1 | I1=KYNEN | Hz1=L1-z1 |
| A2f=NEUROTECHNOLOGY-f | C4x=CAMBRIDGE-x | C4f=CAMBRIDGE-f | F1=MORPHO | E2f=IRITECH-f | G2=IRISID-2 | Hx=L1-x | Hz2=L1-z2 |

[18] N.Kalka, J. Zuo, N. Schmid, and B. Cukic. Estimating and fusing quality factors for iris biometric images. *IEEE Transactions on Systems, Man, and Cybernetics Part A:Systems and Humans*, 40(3):509–524, 2010.

[19] P. Jonathon Phillips, Kevin W. Bowyer, and Patrick J. Flynn. Comments on the casia version 1.0 iris data set. *IEEE Transactions on Pattern Analysis and Machine Intelligence*, 29(10):1869–1870, 2007.

[20] Nadezhda Sazonova, Stephanie Schuckers, Peter Johnson, Paulo Lopez-Meyer, Edward Sazonov, and Lawrence Hornak. Impact of out-of-focus blur on iris recognition. *In Proceddings of SPIE*, 8029(doi:10.1117/12.887052), 2011.

[21] S.A.C. Schuckers, N.A. Schmid, A. Abhyankar, V. Dorairaj, C.K. Boyce, and L.A. Hornak. On techniques for angle compensation in nonideal iris recognition. *Systems, Man, and Cybernetics, Part B: Cybernetics, IEEE Transactions on*, 37(5):1176 –1190, October 2007.

[22] N. Schmid V. Dorairaj and G. Fahmy. Performance evaluation of non? ideal iris based recognition system implementing global ica encoding. In *IEEE International Conference on Image Processing ICIP-05*, pages 285–288, Genoa, Italy, September 2005.

[23] R.P. Wildes. Iris recognition: an emerging biometric technology. *Proceedings of the IEEE*, 85(9):1348 – 1363, 1997.

[24] R.P. Wildes, J.C. Asmuth, G.L. Green, S.C. Hsu, R.J. Kolczynski, J.R. Matey, and S.E. McBride. A system for automated iris recognition. pages 121–128, 1994.

[25] Y. Du Z. Zhou and C. Belcher. Transforming traditional iris recognition systems to work in nonideal situations. In *IEEE Transaction on Industrial Electronics*, volume 56, August 2009.

A2a=NEUROTECHNOLOGY-a	B3=CROSSMATCH	C4s=CAMBRIDGE-s	D3=AWARE	E2a=IRITECH-a	G1=IRISID-1	I1=KYNEN	Hz1=L1-z1
A2f=NEUROTECHNOLOGY-f	C4x=CAMBRIDGE-x	C4f=CAMBRIDGE-f	F1=MORPHO	E2f=IRITECH-f	G2=IRISID-2	Hx=L1-x	Hz2=L1-z2